The Epistles of Paul the Apostle
to
Timothy and Titus

The Epistles of Paul the Apostle to Timothy and Titus

by
Oliver B. Greene

The Gospel Hour, Inc., Oliver B. Greene, Director
P. O. Box 2024, Greenville, South Carolina

First printing, 1964 — 10,000 copies
Second printing, 1967 — 10,000 copies
Third printing, 1969 — 15,000 copies
Fourth printing, 1970 — 15,000 copies
Fifth printing, 1973 — 15,000 copies
Sixth printing, 1975 — 15,000 copies
Seventh printing, 1977 — 15,000 copies

Library of Congress Catalog Card Number: 64-20145

This volume is
affectionately dedicated
to my sister, Sadie Greene,
who untiringly prayed for my
conversion for more than ten years.
With unique faithfulness
she has contributed to my ministry,
as musician and as my private secretary,
since my call into the
ministry of evangelism.

The Author

THE FIRST EPISTLE OF PAUL THE APOSTLE
TO TIMOTHY

INTRODUCTION

The two epistles to Timothy and the epistle to Titus are known as the *Pastoral Epistles*, because they are addressed to servants of the Lord who had been put in charge of local churches. Timothy ministered in the church in Ephesus (I Tim. 1:3), while Titus ministered in the church in Crete (Titus 1:5). There is no doubt that Paul is the author of First and Second Timothy as well as the epistle to Titus.

Timothy is first mentioned in Acts 16:1. His mother's name was Eunice (II Tim. 1:5); she was a Jewess, but his father was a Gentile (Acts 16:1). Paul referred to Timothy as "my own son in the faith" (I Tim. 1:2). From this, Bible scholars agree that Timothy was undoubtedly converted through the preaching of the Apostle Paul. He had an excellent reputation among the believers in Lystra and Iconium.

Timothy's mother and his grandmother Lois were both devout believers (II Tim. 1:5). II Timothy 3:14,15 implies that even before the mother and grandmother of Timothy became believers, they were God-fearing Jewesses.

Because of the Jews, Paul had young Timothy circumcised, and he then became a fellow laborer with Paul in the Gospel (Acts 16:1–3). Undoubtedly Timothy accompanied Paul on his journey through Macedonia. Paul left him at Berea with Silas (Acts 17:14).

At Paul's request, Timothy visited the believers at Thessalonica and upon his return gave a report to Paul, and then remained with him in the city of Corinth. Timothy traveled with Paul from Corinth to Ephesus, from whence he was sent with Erastus to Macedonia and Corinth (Acts 19:22; I Cor. 4:17). Later we find that Timothy was with Paul the prisoner, in the city of Rome (Col. 1:1; Phil. 1:1; Philemon 1).

Scholars are in disagreement concerning the date of Paul's first epistle to Timothy; the date is questioned because Bible scholars do not agree as to whether Paul was imprisoned twice in Rome, or only once (Acts 28:30). If there were two imprisonments in Rome, then it is clear that I Timothy was written during the time between the first and second imprisonments; but if there was only one prison term there, as some think, then I Timothy was written shortly before Paul's last journey to Jerusalem.

Many scholars believe that Paul DID endure two imprisonments in Rome, and that between these two imprisonments, while he was a free man, he wrote First Timothy and the epistle to Titus. Personally, I accept the latter, and I believe the Scripture indicates that there were two imprisonments. Paul reached Rome as a prisoner in 61 A. D. He was there for two years (Acts 28:30), during which time he wrote his epistles to the Ephesians, Colossians, Philippians and Philemon. In each of these letters he speaks of himself as being in prison, but we note that in I Timothy he does not mention himself as a prisoner.

Writing to Titus, Paul speaks of spending the winter in Nicopolis (Titus 3:12). Here we have sufficient evidence that he was no longer a prisoner; his trust and confidence of being released had been realized (Phil. 1:25,26; 2:24; Philemon 22). Paul prayed—and in his letters he requested the churches to pray on his behalf—that he would be released, that the Word of God might have free course, and that he would be allowed to preach the grace of God again. Those prayers were answered.

For several years after his imprisonment, Paul was at liberty. It seems clear that there was an interval between his first and second imprisonments, and such an interval explains the statement in II Timothy 4:20: ". . . *Trophimus have I left at Miletum sick.*" When Paul was at Miletum before he came to Rome (Acts 20:17), he did not leave Trophimus there sick; Acts 21:29 tells us that Trophimus accompanied him to Jerusalem. Therefore, Paul undoubtedly visited Miletum and Ephesus again, and this must have been during the time between his first Roman imprisonment and that of a later date. If Paul wrote I Timothy before he was arrested in Jerusalem, then there is no explanation for his statement in I Timothy 1:3: "As I besought thee to abide still at Ephesus, when I went into Macedonia, that thou mightest charge some that they teach no other doctrine."

Paul here instructed Timothy to stay at Ephesus. In Acts we read the account of two visits by Paul to Ephesus. In Acts 18:19–22 we read of a brief visit to the city:

"And he came to Ephesus, and left them there: but he himself entered into the synagogue, and reasoned with the Jews. When they desired him to tarry longer time with them, he consented not; but bade them farewell, saying, I must by all means keep this feast that cometh in Jerusalem; but I will return again unto you, if God will. And he sailed from Ephesus. And when he had landed at Caesarea, and gone up, and saluted the church, he went down to Antioch."

This passage clearly states that even though the people pleaded with him to tarry longer, Paul *"consented not,"* thus indicating that he spent a very short time on this visit.

In Acts 19:1 through 20:31 we read that he spent no less than three years in the city of Ephesus teaching and preaching the Word of God:

"After these things were ended, Paul purposed in the spirit, when he had passed through Macedonia and Achaia, to go to Jerusalem, saying, After I have been there, I must also see Rome. So he sent into Macedonia two of them that ministered unto him, Timotheus and Erastus; but he himself stayed in Asia for a season" (Acts 19:21,22). At that time, Paul did not request Timothy to stay in Ephesus, but sent him into Macedonia.

In Paul's farewell address to the elders in the church at Ephesus, he predicted that much danger would come to the church:

"For I know this, that after my departing shall *grievous wolves* enter in among you, not sparing the flock. Also of your own selves shall men arise, speaking perverse things, to draw away disciples after them" (Acts 20:29,30). Paul knew that "grievous wolves" coming from outside the church and teachers of error from within would cause much persecution and many heartaches.

Later, Paul's prediction was truly fulfilled. Again he visited Ephesus, and this time he left Timothy to teach and preach against the heresies faced by the believers there. Shortly thereafter, Paul wrote to Timothy, beseeching him to abide in the city of Ephesus because his presence was sorely needed there to help keep the wolves from the flock. This Timothy did, for there was a deep love between him and Paul.

II Timothy was written from Rome, after Paul had been thrown into prison for the second time; and immediately after the writing of this second epistle to Timothy, Paul sealed his testimony with his blood:

"For I am now ready to be offered, and the time of my departure is at hand. I have fought a good fight, I have finished my course, I have kept the faith: Henceforth there is laid up for me a crown of righteousness, which the Lord, the righteous judge, shall give me at that day: and not to me only, but unto all them also that love His appearing. Do thy diligence to come shortly unto me" (II Tim. 4:6–9).

The purpose of I Timothy was Paul's communication, given to him by revelation from God, instructing Timothy concerning the church as the house of God. I Timothy 3:14,15 clearly states the purpose of the epistle:

"These things write I unto thee, hoping to come unto thee shortly: But if I tarry long, *that thou mayest know how thou oughtest to behave thyself in the house of God*, which is the church of the living God, the pillar and ground of the truth."

For this reason, I Timothy contains very important and practical instructions as to the order which should be maintained in the house of God—the local assembly where believers meet—and Timothy was to instruct the leaders in the church.

Paul set forth suitable conduct to be carried out in the house of God:

Pure doctrine—none save the doctrine of Jesus Christ.

Pure worship—worshipping none other than God's only begotten Son.

Faithful ministry—preaching nothing but the grace of God.

Pure doctrine, pure worship and pure Gospel are the leading thoughts in this pastoral letter to young Timothy; however, Paul also gives instructions concerning godly conduct on the part of *individuals* in the local church. According to the message given Paul by inspiration of God, and directed to Timothy for his specific instruction and the benefit of all, we know that there is failure on the part of both minister and congregation when men no longer endure sound doctrine, but heap to themselves teachers after their own choosing, who tickle their ears instead of preaching the pure Gospel. The minister of Jesus Christ preaches pure Gospel without fear, favor or apology, and the believer obeys that message *as from the Lord*, not as the words of man.

Therefore, if a minister fails to preach pure doctrine, or if the believer fails to *heed* pure doctrine, then the church is failing tragically. God has provided power whereby the believing individual can always *walk and live* in the truth. God's grace is sufficient to lead Christians and to maintain members of the body of Christ in the path divinely marked for true believers. (Yes, this can be true even in these perilous times in which we live—the times just before the coming of the Lord.)

In Paul's day, the local churches were rapidly increasing in number; and it was natural that questions of order, doctrine, faith and church discipline should arise. At first, the apostles themselves regulated these problems directly; but near the end of the Apostolic Period, the church had grown to such proportions that it became necessary for a clear revelation to be made for the guidance of all local assemblies. Such revelation is found in I Timothy and in Titus.

The key phrase in I Timothy is "THAT THOU MAYEST KNOW HOW THOU OUGHTEST TO BEHAVE THYSELF IN THE HOUSE OF GOD." Would to God that the churches had never added to nor taken from the divine blueprint God gave concerning order and discipline in the New Testament church, and concerning the faith once delivered to the saints. Certainly in this hour we need to return to the New Testament, which is the textbook for the New Testament church—and especially do we need to study the epistles God dictated to Paul. It was to this minister to the Gentiles that God revealed the mystery of the marvelous grace of God. Please read carefully Ephesians 3:1–12.

In the beginning of I Timothy, Paul speaks concerning unsound doctrine, and all that is connected with such error is rebuked and denounced. He puts strong emphasis on true doctrine and pure Gospel, without which there is no such thing as godliness and righteousness. True doctrine is the Gospel of the grace of God, concerning which Paul testifies, "According to the glorious Gospel of the blessed God, which was committed to my trust" (I Tim. 1:11). Paul was himself a true witness to the marvelous grace of God; for God revealed to him the truth concerning grace, through which the middle wall of partition is broken down, whereby *all men* are invited to drink of the water of life freely.

Prayer is the leading topic in the second chapter of I Timothy. *The house of God*—and true holiness, which *becomes* the house of God—comprise the theme for the third chapter. Here Paul sets forth the manner of persons God's overseers and deacons must be. In chapter four, he warns concerning those who will depart from the faith just before the Rapture—those who will give heed to seducing spirits and the doctrine of demons. These will speak lies in hypocrisy.

In chapters five and six Paul gives diversified instructions and exhortations, having to do with elderly women, young widows, and how elders and overseers should be supported. In these passages he also gives personal instructions to the young minister, Timothy.

The intimate friendship between Paul and Timothy, his son in the faith, is one of the most beautiful friendships in all history, secular or sacred. Paul is approximately thirty years the older of the two; but there is a deep, warm and intimate friendship between them—a close relationship and love such as is found between father and son.

Paul knew that Timothy was about to step into a position of great responsibility. This young minister was given the oversight of the church at Ephesus, a task great and weighty for a young man who was a bit timid and sensitive—and probably delicate. Paul was well aware of the perils and problems, the heartaches and heartbreaks, and the grave responsibility of the situation that existed in Ephesus. He wrote this first letter to Timothy to encourage and guide him in the divine way.

CONTENTS

I TIMOTHY

II TIMOTHY

TITUS

The First Epistle of Paul the Apostle
to Timothy

THE FIRST EPISTLE OF PAUL THE APOSTLE TO TIMOTHY

CHAPTER ONE

UNSOUND TEACHING REBUKED

1. Paul, an apostle of Jesus Christ by the commandment of God our Saviour, and Lord Jesus Christ, which is our hope;

2. Unto Timothy, my own son in the faith: Grace, mercy, and peace, from God our Father and Jesus Christ our Lord.

3. As I besought thee to abide still at Ephesus, when I went into Macedonia, that thou mightest charge some that they teach no other doctrine,

4. Neither give heed to fables and endless genealogies, which minister questions, rather than godly edifying which is in faith: so do.

5. Now the end of the commandment is charity out of a pure heart, and of a good conscience, and of faith unfeigned:

6. From which some having swerved have turned aside unto vain jangling;

7. Desiring to be teachers of the law; understanding neither what they say, nor whereof they affirm.

8. But we know that the law is good, if a man use it lawfully;

9. Knowing this, that the law is not made for a righteous man, but for the lawless and disobedient, for the ungodly and for sinners, for unholy and profane, for murderers of fathers and murderers of mothers, for manslayers,

10. For whoremongers, for them that defile themselves with mankind, for menstealers, for liars, for perjured persons, and if there be any other thing that is contrary to sound doctrine;

11. According to the glorious gospel of the blessed God, which was committed to my trust.

12. And I thank Christ Jesus our Lord, who hath enabled me, for that he counted me faithful, putting me into the ministry;

13. Who was before a blasphemer, and a persecutor, and injurious: but I obtained mercy, because I did it ignorantly in unbelief.

14. And the grace of our Lord was exceeding abundant with faith and love which is in Christ Jesus.

15. This is a faithful saying, and worthy of all acceptation, that Christ Jesus came into the world to save sinners; of whom

I am chief.

16. Howbeit for this cause I obtained mercy, that in me first Jesus Christ might shew forth all longsuffering, for a pattern to them which should hereafter believe on him to life everlasting.

17. Now unto the King eternal, immortal, invisible, the only wise God, be honour and glory for ever and ever. Amen.

18. This charge I commit unto thee, son Timothy, according to the prophecies which went before on thee, that thou by them mightest war a good warfare;

19. Holding faith, and a good conscience; which some having put away concerning faith have made shipwreck:

20. Of whom is Hymenaeus and Alexander; whom I have delivered unto Satan, that they may learn not to blaspheme.

The Salutation

Verses 1 and 2: "Paul, an apostle of Jesus Christ by the commandment of God our Saviour, and Lord Jesus Christ, which is our hope; unto Timothy, my own son in the faith: Grace, mercy, and peace, from God our Father and Jesus Christ our Lord."

In verse 1, Paul introduces himself by name. In his country it was customary to open a letter with one's name. This man Paul was first known as Saul of Tarsus, which was his Hebrew name. In Philippians 3:5 he describes himself as "an Hebrew of the Hebrews." He later dropped this description of himself; but I am sure he never completely lost the pride and affection of his national birthright, for he was a free-born Jew.

All through his life Paul maintained a deep love for his own people, Israel; and wherever he went, wherever he ministered, his first visit was always to the synagogue. However all-inclusive his message was, he said, "To the Jew first" (Rom. 1:16). In I Corinthians 9:22b he said, "I am made all things to all men, that I might by all means save some"; but his deep desire and the heavy burden of his heart was for Israel. In Romans 10:1 he proclaimed, "Brethren, my heart's desire and prayer to God for Israel is, that they might be saved!" So great was the burden he carried for his brethren in the flesh that he said, ". . . I have great heaviness and continual sorrow in my heart. For I could wish that myself were accursed from Christ for my brethren, my kinsmen according to the flesh!" (Rom. 9:2,3).

Read carefully the ninth chapter of Acts, and you will be exceedingly blessed by the soul-stirring account of the conversion of Saul of Tarsus, when *Saul*, the despoiler and destroyer of the church, became *Paul*, the church founder whom God used to establish many churches. Paul is the name given to him because he was a Roman citizen:

"And as they bound him with thongs, Paul said unto the centurion that stood by, Is it lawful for you to scourge a man that is a Roman, and uncondemned? When the centurion heard that, he went and told the chief captain, saying, Take heed what thou doest: for this man is a Roman. Then the chief captain came, and said unto him, Tell me, art thou a Roman? He said, Yea. And the chief captain answered, With a great sum obtained I this freedom. And Paul said, *But I was free born*" (Acts 22:25–28).

In Acts 13:9 we read, ". . . Saul, who also is called Paul." This man Paul had a specific and specialized ministry. The God who saved, ordained and commissioned him also sent him to the Gentiles as a special minister, and it was only natural that he should thenceforth use his Gentile name. From the day he was used of the Lord to establish churches in various cities, he was known as *Paul*.

In opening his letter to the young minister, Timothy, he was simply "Paul"; and in the next part of his introduction he was ". . . *an apostle of Jesus Christ*." In Romans 11:13 Paul said, "I *magnify* mine office";

and as he begins this epistle to Timothy he introduces himself—not only as the beloved Paul, but also as "an *apostle* of Jesus Christ." He was not one of the original twelve apostles, but he was none the less an apostle, as he claimed in his epistles.

The word *apostle* means "a sent one"; and Paul was "a sent one" to the Gentiles to make known to them the grace of God, salvation by grace, and the mystery of "Christ in you, the hope of glory" (Col. 1:27). In one sense, each believer is an apostle, for we should at all times be at God's disposal. We should be willing for Him to send us anywhere at any time. We are, in simple language, God's "errand boys"; and we should be willing to run an errand for Him at any and all times, regardless of how humble and insignificant the errand might be. We should be ready at all times to say, "Here am I! Send me!"

The angels stand in constant readiness to obey God's will: "I am Gabriel, that stand in the presence of God; and am sent to speak unto thee, and to shew thee these glad tidings." Thus Gabriel said to Mary (Luke 1:19). Believers, like the angels, should stand ready for Heaven's orders. We should be ready to speak, warn, exhort or comfort. We should be always in a spiritual position to hear the Holy Spirit when He speaks in a still, small voice to our heart, giving us directions.

Yes, all believers are apostles, though I am not suggesting that all of us are called and ordained for the ministry in the same measure that God called and ordained Paul, for Paul's apostleship was a peculiar one. John the Baptist was a special servant of God, as many others have been and will be until the Church is caught out to meet the Lord in the air.

To Timothy Paul said, "An apostle of Jesus Christ,

BY THE COMMANDMENT OF GOD OUR SAVIOUR."
Timothy was not for one moment to suppose that Paul
had made himself an apostle, that he had taken this great
responsibility upon himself apart from a commandment
from Almighty God. Paul assured Timothy that he was
not a self-appointed apostle. His apostleship had been
thrust upon him through commandment of the God who
spoke to him on the Damascus road—the One who said,
"(Paul) is a chosen vessel unto me" (Acts 9:15).

Since Paul was divinely appointed to the office of
apostleship, he speaks with divine authority; and what
he says is backed up by divine power. We should therefore give earnest heed to the things spoken by this man,
appointed by Almighty God as a minister and an apostle
to the Gentiles.

We notice in verse one that Paul says, "OUR Saviour," thus linking himself with Timothy in the Saviour.
He could have said, "MY Saviour," but he did not. By
revelation, God had made known unto Paul the fact that
we are all baptized into one body by one Spirit, and have
been made to drink into one Spirit (I Cor. 12:12,13). How
refreshing it is to sit together in heavenly places with
fellow believers and share the mutual joy and feelings
of belonging to the same body. Whether we be great or
small, rich or poor, bond or free, we all belong to the
Church of the living God, the Church of which Jesus is
the head and the foundation. Thus we are members of
His body, of His flesh and of His bones.

Note that Paul first points out, "GOD, our Saviour,"
and this is as it should be. Fundamentally, it is God
who must save us. It is God who must pardon our sins,
cleanse us, give us victory over sin and release us from
the bondage of sin. Then comes "our Lord"—for His
"Lordship" follows "Saviourhood." God has a right to
be Lord over that which He has purchased with His own

precious blood: "Forasmuch as ye know that ye were not redeemed with corruptible things, as silver and gold, from your vain conversation received by tradition from your fathers; but with the precious blood of Christ, as of a lamb without blemish and without spot" (I Peter 1:18,19).

Since God bought us with the blood of His Son, the Lord Jesus Christ, He has a complete right to every detail of our lives—our soul, spirit and body. Whether we eat or drink, or whatsoever we do, we are commanded to do all to the glory of God. Paul reminds Timothy that they share a common possession of a wonderful Saviour and mighty Lord—one who not only saves, but also takes complete control of heart and life when permitted by the believer to do so.

"... *God our Saviour, and Lord Jesus Christ, WHICH IS OUR HOPE.*" Christianity is the only religion that gives hope beyond the grave. No other religion on this earth plants in the bosom of man the hope that Christianity gives to the human heart.

The Lord Jesus not only *gives* us hope—He IS our hope! In Romans 8:24 Paul said, "... We are saved by hope." We love Him who is our Saviour; we dedicate our soul, spirit and body to Him in loyalty. He is our Lord, and He plants within our bosom the divine nature (II Pet. 1:4). He abides in us in the Person of the Holy Ghost (Rom. 8:9); He translates us into the kingdom of light (Col. 1:13); He is our Saviour; He is our light, our guide, our keeper and our hope. Paul is saying to Timothy, "God is OUR Saviour—yours and mine. He is OUR Lord—your Lord and mine. He is OUR hope—your hope and my hope."

In verse 2 Paul makes known the relationship between Timothy and himself: "... *my own son in the faith.*" When Paul made his first missionary journey, he

22

visited the city of Lystra. In that city lived a godly family. The head of the home was a Greek gentleman, his wife was a Jewess, and they had a son whose name was Timothy (Acts 16:1). From II Timothy 1:5 it seems that the grandmother also lived with them.

Timothy had been carefully trained in the home, being thoroughly taught in the Old Testament Scriptures (II Tim. 3:15). Now Paul, God's ordained minister of grace, showed this family how the Old Testament prophecies they loved and knew so well pointed to the coming of the Lord Jesus Christ, the Messiah for whom Israel had longed and prayed through so many years.

In Lystra Paul "preached the Gospel" (Acts 14:7). He had but one message—*Jesus*, crucified, buried, risen, ascended and coming again "according to the Scriptures" (I Cor. 15:1 ff). We do not know how many were converted in Lystra, but we do know that Paul had the joy of pointing young Timothy to Christ.

(Have YOU ever pointed someone to Jesus? Do YOU know the joy of winning a soul? Proverbs 11:30 tells us, ". . . He that winneth souls is wise," and Daniel 12:3 says, ". . . They that be wise shall shine as the brightness of the firmament." In the Paradise of God, soul-winners will shine like the stars in the heavens. I have found no Scripture for the song, "Will There Be Any Stars In My Crown?" but there IS Scripture that clearly teaches that soul-winners will shine "as the brightness of the firmament.")

Many times when a child comes forward to trust the Lord Jesus as Saviour, we put a question mark around him and wonder if he really knows what he is doing, and if his experience is genuine or if it will "wear off." In some instances, it may; but in many others, it does not—and such was true with Timothy. In Acts 16:2 we read of him, *"Which was well reported of by the brethren that were at Lystra and Iconium."*

Some years had passed since Paul first preached the Gospel in Lystra, at which time Timothy was converted; and now he returned to that city and inquired about his converts. He must have asked, "How is young Timothy doing in the church?" And the answer was given, "He is well reported of by the brethren." Timothy had a good testimony. He had grown in grace, his faith had increased, he was walking with the Lord. I know Paul's heart leaped for joy because of such report.

I have been an evangelist for many years. The first joy of my life is to see sinners born into the family of God; but the second joy of my heart is to return to a community where I preached five, ten or twenty years before, and meet people who were converted at that time and who are still going on with the Lord! John said, "I have no greater joy than to hear that my children walk in truth" (III John 4).

On the other hand, nothing saddens my heart quite so much as returning to a town or community where I previously held a meeting, and learning that someone who then made a profession of faith has now departed that faith, and perhaps is even worse than before. Such report always causes me to ask the heart-breaking question, "Was his experience genuine? Did the devil slip that person a counterfeit?" I know it is true that some Christians, though genuinely saved, do not grow in grace as they should—and it grieves me deeply to learn that some of my children in the faith are spiritual dwarfs, sadly undernourished; but we cannot overlook the fact that many who profess to be saved have never actually had a genuine born-again experience.

In Acts 16:3 Timothy joined with Paul and became a

24

fellow-minister with God's anointed messenger to the Gentiles. Although a very young man, Timothy knew that the ministry he had accepted would bring persecution, hardships, heartaches, suffering—and perhaps even death. He well knew what it had cost Paul to preach the Gospel that had brought HIM to a saving knowledge of the grace of God. It is altogether possible that Timothy had witnessed the stoning of Paul at Lystra—and if he had not actually witnessed the stoning, he certainly knew about it, because the entire community knew that Paul had been stoned and dragged outside the city for dead.

But in spite of his extreme youth and his evident timidity, he was willing to say, "Here am I! Send me!" I wonder how many of US have said, "I'll go where you want me to go, dear Lord/ Over mountain, or plain or sea/ I'll say what you want me to say, dear Lord/ I'll be what you want me to be." If you have not said that, God grant that you do it today.

Paul's party is complete once more. Silas has taken the place of Barnabas (Acts 15:40); and now this fine young Christian, Timothy, has taken the place vacated by John Mark (Acts 15:39). It would seem that Paul was a bit partial to young people in his evangelistic party. Perhaps he wanted to train his helpers in the things of the Lord, teaching them obedience to God so that they would not hinder the work because of stubbornness or a determined will of their own. Paul was a great strategist. He was well-educated; his head was filled with good common sense, and his heart was full of God-given, deep compassion for the unsaved.

Undoubtedly Timothy proved to be all that Paul desired in a young co-worker, because Paul ordained him to the ministry (II Tim. 1:6). In Philippians 2:22 Paul said of him, "But ye know the proof of him, that, *as a son with the father,* he hath served with me in the Gospel."

It could well be assumed that Paul was never disappointed in the life and conduct of Timothy, because near the end of Paul's journey he wrote to the young preacher and said, "Do thy diligence to come shortly unto me . . . Do thy diligence to come before winter" (II Tim. 4:9,21).

How refreshing it is to any minister to have a helper who is true—first to God and the Gospel, and then to his senior minister. Such a person is a help instead of a hindrance to the ministry. How we need young men today who are dedicated to God and to the pure Gospel of God's marvelous grace! All too many of our young preachers are more dedicated to a denominational machine than they are to the message of the Gospel.

Timothy accompanied Paul to Corinth, to Ephesus and to Athens. He was with him at Antioch, Philippi and Rome. His name is mentioned in six of Paul's epistles. This was no ordinary young man. Paul used him to go into delicate situations and to tackle hard problems, such as that mentioned in verse 3 of our present chapter.

In view of what Timothy was to face, the affairs in which he would be involved, it is not surprising that Paul prays for him a threefold intercessory prayer, that in the very midst of trouble, trials, heartaches, turmoil and peculiar situations he might have the inward assurance that God is able at all times to do exceeding abundantly above anything we ask or think, and in all circumstances keep the heart at peace:

"Unto Timothy, my own son in the faith: Grace, mercy, and peace, from God our Father and Jesus Christ our Lord."

First, Paul prays on Timothy's behalf for the needed grace—the grace of God. Paul was keenly aware of the all-sufficiency of God's grace (II Cor. 12:9), and in I Corinthians 15:10 he said, "But BY THE GRACE OF GOD

I AM WHAT I AM: and His grace which was bestowed upon me was not in vain; but I laboured more abundantly than they all: yet not I, but the grace of God which was with me."

In this great verse, Paul attributes his ALL to grace; and he knew that the same grace of God would prove adequate for Timothy, at all times, under all circumstances. God's grace would be at his disposal at all times—and not only at the disposal of young Timothy, but ours as well. Paul said, "I am what I am by the grace of God," and this same grace is bestowed upon believers today. Since God's grace is sufficient for every need, why should we ever fail in character, in Christian conduct, in service or in obedience? What excuse do we have? God pity us! His grace furnishes everything we need—salvation, service, victory and reward (Titus 2:11–15).

Paul prays for mercy on behalf of Timothy. He is praying here for his son in the faith, that the God of all grace will be merciful to him, and that He will never allow this young servant to be over-awed by the power of the enemy—the devil whom Paul knew so well and with whom he had so many bitter battles. He prayed that Timothy would never be over-driven by the pressure of circumstances around him under varied and sundry conditions; that he would never be over-strained by the problems of the task that faced him—that of leading the Ephesian believers; and that he would never be over-weighted by the perils of the way in which he would walk daily and hourly as God's overseer in the church at Ephesus.

Paul knew that the God of all grace is faithful, merciful, longsuffering and kind; and he was praying God's best upon his son in the faith. It was Paul who said, "There hath no temptation taken you but such as is common to men: but God is faithful, who will not suffer you to be tempted above that ye are able; but will with the temptation also make a way to escape, that ye may be able to bear it" (I Cor. 10:13).

You and I can also claim the promise of that Scripture, resting upon it with the assurance that the God of all grace will make merciful provision for us and give us divine protection if we are good soldiers in the army of the Lord. I personally believe that it is impossible for the devil to touch God's anointed without God's permission, and the Christian who lives right and serves God faithfully is absolutely indestructible. He cannot be destroyed by the devil and all the demons in hell, until God is finished with him . . . until his ministry is completed as Jesus completed His ministry when He said, "(Father) I have glorified thee on the earth: I have finished the work which thou gavest me to do" (John 17:4).

Paul prays for God's grace and mercy for Timothy, but that is not all: he also prays for PEACE! To His disciples, Jesus said, "Peace I leave with you, MY PEACE I give unto you: not as the world giveth, give I unto you. Let not your heart be troubled, neither let it be afraid" (John 14:27).

We are told that the ocean may be very rough and boisterous on the surface, while deep, deep down below, it can be as calm as a sleeping child. The surface may be stormy, but the depths are still and quiet.

Paul wanted Timothy to have "the peace of God, which passeth all understanding" (Phil. 4:7). God reserves the sole right to give peace to those who will trust in the shed blood and the finished work of Jesus Christ. Peace cannot be bought, it cannot be earned, it cannot be attained in any way save from the hand and heart of God. God gives peace through the *Prince of Peace*, the Lord Jesus Christ. The world cannot give the peace that surpasses understanding. Paul prays that Timothy will have God's grace, mercy, and the peace that only God can give. He wants Timothy's inner strength to be sustained by God's grace and peace, however trying and turbulent the conditions around him.

The Charge Concerning False Doctrine— Paul Indicates the Difficulties Ahead

Verses 3 and 4: "As I besought thee to abide still at Ephesus, when I went into Macedonia, that thou mightest charge some that they teach no other doctrine, neither give heed to fables and endless genealogies, which minister questions, rather than godly edifying which is in faith: so do."

When Paul wrote these lines, Timothy was at Ephesus. He was the overseer of that company of believers which came into being as a result of Paul's ministry in that city. No doubt the church had grown and been strengthened by the teaching of Apollos, Aquilla and Priscilla. Paul devoted a goodly portion of his time and care to the Ephesian church. He had a real love for the Ephesian believers, and he paid them a brief visit at the end of his second missionary tour: "And he came to Ephesus, and left them there: but he himself entered into the synagogue, and reasoned with the Jews" (Acts 18:19).

At the very outset of Paul's third missionary journey, he spent no less than three years with the Ephesians (Acts 19:1—20:31). On his last visit to the city of Jerusalem he stopped at Miletus, a seaside town about thirty miles from Ephesus: "And from Miletus he sent to Ephesus, and called the elders of the church" (Acts 20:17). Without a doubt Paul sent for these brethren for a farewell meeting, and from Acts 20:36—38 we learn that this meeting was certainly a touching occasion: *"And when he had thus spoken, he kneeled down, and prayed with them all. And they all wept sore, and fell on Paul's neck, and kissed him, sorrowing most of all for the words which he spake, that they should see his face no more. And they accompanied him unto the ship."*

The mother church in Ephesus and the daughter churches throughout the district seemed to have made good. They had grown in grace, they had made rapid progress in the spiritual life, and Paul had a very tender spot in his heart for these believers. It is true that there were some *individuals* in the churches who were by no means what they should be—they were babes in Christ and had not grown as they should have; but the church as a whole had advanced tremendously. It must have been a heartbreaking experience for Paul to know that he was fellowshipping with these dear brethren for the last time.

It certainly seems that the believers in the area of Ephesus had reached a high level of spiritual understanding, and their spiritual experience was a deep and stable one. Such was true in the Ephesian church in Paul's day; but how sad it is to read the record in Revelation 2:4: "Nevertheless I have somewhat against thee, because thou hast left thy first love."

The devil never stands idly by while the church grows in the depth of spiritual understanding and power; he does everything in his diabolical power to cool off the church that is ablaze for Jesus. What about YOUR church, dear reader? Is your church on fire for God? Is the desire of your church, "Lord, plant my feet on higher ground"? Or is it a *satisfied* church, more interested in reports at the convention than in the rejoicing in the presence of the angels over sinners coming home to God?

What about your individual life? Are YOU ablaze

spiritually for Jesus? John the Baptist was "a burning and a shining light." We have a lot of "shining" lights today, but the *burning* is absent. Many Christian workers take great pride in shining, but the heat is not present—they have the glow, minus the heat. John the Baptist burned for Jesus, and therefore he was a *burning* and *shining* light.

Our present verse teaches us that Paul left Timothy at Ephesus while he traveled into Macedonia, that Timothy might charge some "that they teach no other doctrine." There were those in the Ephesian church who were teaching doctrine that was not THE faith once delivered unto the saints; and since "other doctrine" was being preached, it was imperative that Timothy sound out *true doctrine*. In Acts 20:21 we have the account of Paul's doctrine, both to the Jews and the Gentiles, concerning man's part in salvation: "Testifying both to the Jews, and also to the Greeks, repentance toward God, and faith toward our Lord Jesus Christ." Paul's message was: First, *repentance toward God*; second, *faith toward our Lord Jesus Christ*. How often present day pastors and evangelists preach eagerly the necessity of faith in the finished work of Jesus Christ—and certainly that is true doctrine; however, we should never omit the *repentance* part of true doctrine. Jesus said, "Except ye repent, ye shall all likewise perish" (Luke 13:3,5).

True repentance is godly sorrow for sin, and turning face-about, turning to God from idols (I Thess. 1:9). Certainly without true repentance there can be no saving faith. True faith and true repentance are Bible Siamese twins.

The enemy (the devil) is always sowing tares among the wheat; it is therefore necessary that true ministers and true believers untiringly declare the glorious Gospel of the grace of God. Paul's admonition to Timothy—and to all preachers—is, "Preach the word; be instant in season, out of season; reprove, rebuke, exhort with all longsuffering and doctrine" (II Tim. 4:2).

Timothy was not to give heed to fables nor to endless genealogies, which only bring about questions and many times engender strife; but he was to devote his time to godly edifying, which is in faith; he was to preach sound doctrine always, under all circumstances. He was to preach the Word, never deviating from the truth of the glorious Gospel; he was not to permit anything contrary to sound doctrine (verses 10 and 11 in our present chapter).

I believe that the greatest need in the average church today is that God's ministers go to their pulpits and feed the believers with "sound doctrine." The only means of building up believers in the faith, the only food that will nourish a spiritual baby, is *the Word of God* (I Pet. 2:2). The only food that will strengthen spiritual adults is the meat of the Word—and sound doctrine is spiritual meat that strengthens, builds up and makes the believer strong.

I personally believe that the number one need in the pulpits today is for God's preacher to open God's Word and preach sound, scriptural, expository messages, instructing believers in the things of the Lord: Faith comes by hearing, and hearing by the Word of God. The Word of God is a lamp to our feet and a light to our pathway. The Word of God is bread to the hungry, water to the thirsty, strength to the weak—and the devil cares not how long, loud or fervently a minister preaches, just so long as his message is not saturated with the Word of God.

In Acts 6:4 we learn that deacons were appointed and ordained in order that ministers might give themselves continually to prayer *and to the ministry of the*

Word. I speak in love, and I am not attacking any individual or group—but ministers need to spend much more time behind closed doors studying the Word of God, than they need to spend knocking on doors and attempting to get people to church. (Yes, knocking on doors and inviting people to church is honorable and right—but the pastor should not have to do it. The deacons and the members should do that while the preacher prepares to feed the believers on Sunday morning.)

In verses 3 and 4 we have the two fundamental items in church business: Verse 3 — *To teach THE doctrine and no other*; verse 4 — *Godly edifying which is in faith.* The only way to educate a child of God in the things of God is to preach the Word; and the only message that will edify a spiritual life is the Word of God.

What were the dangers faced by the believers at Ephesus? There were perils "a-plenty" in the world around them, with all the evils that go along with the heathen atmosphere in which these new-born Christians had now to live. These believers at Ephesus did not live in a country where the Word of God had been preached for years, as it has in our country. We cannot fully appreciate the dangers faced by these babes in Christ, and the obstacles they had to overcome, because we have never known such. They were surrounded by pagan customs and habits—and Paul knew the extreme danger in being exposed to the evil power of paganism, because all heathenism is energized by the devil, who is the archenemy of the soul.

Ephesus was the center of the fanatical, frenzied worship of *"the great goddess Diana."* In Acts 19:27 we read, "So that not only this our craft is in danger to be set at nought; but also that the temple of the great goddess Diana should be despised, and her magnificence should be destroyed, whom all Asia and the world worshippeth." However, still more perilous were the dangers arising from false teaching within the circles of the church. In one way or another the devil had managed to get into the church through teachers of error. Wherever you find pure Gospel and true doctrine, it will not be long until the devil will sneak in by hook or crook, with some teacher of error or advocate of fanaticism.

Timothy was to keep an eye on the "other doctrine" crowd mentioned in verse 3, and forbid them to teach any doctrine other than that taught by the Apostle Paul—the doctrine of repentance toward God, the faith once delivered to the saints, and pure grace minus any mixture of law, tradition, or "whatsoever."

In the early days of the church when there was no written Gospel as we have it today, it was easy for heretics and teachers of error to introduce their doctrines by inventing *fables* regarding Jesus and Christianity. Some of the fantastic fables and stories of His childhood are still in existence and present anything but pure Gospel and divine truth.

Timothy was to warn the true believers to pay no attention to such fables, nor to the teachers and preachers who dealt in *"endless genealogies"*—that is, listing names of the Patriarchs of the Old Testament, adding to and taking from the list to suit their own fancy, thus bringing up varied and sundry questions concerning the prophecies of the Old Testament as having to do with the coming of the Messiah. These fables and endless genealogies accomplished only one thing: They put question marks around the true Gospel concerning the coming of Messiah—the Lamb of God, the Saviour of sinners—and Paul admonished Timothy to see to it that these fables and genealogies did not enter into the church at Ephesus over which he had charge. He was to keep out any who would deal in controversy rather than in the pure Word of God—the revelation God had given to Paul concerning the mystery of the grace of God not revealed in other ages, but now made known through divine revelation to this minister to the Gentiles.

Some dear church people, even in our day, do not know the Gospel when they hear it. When a minister comes to a church for revival services, if he is a master teller of sob-stories, causing people to weep or to clap their hands and shout, some think that they have had a great revival. Another minister may come, preaching only the pure Word of God, lifting up the blood-stained banner, delivering pure Gospel from the minute he steps into the pulpit until the last "Amen"—and these same church members never shed a tear when he proclaims the crucifixion of Jesus and pictures the horrible treatment He received at the hands of His enemies! They do not call this godly man a great preacher, but the one who can make people laugh or cry is an outstanding minister in their catalog.

Paul left Timothy at Ephesus to see to it that fables and endless genealogies did not take the place of sound doctrine and pure Gospel in that church. He knew that if false teachers and preachers took over the congregation, giving them fables and genealogies instead of the Word of God, it would kill the spirit and the power in the testimony of the believers in Ephesus.

The Law — Its Use;
The Law Contrasted With Grace

Verse 5: "Now the end of the commandment is charity out of a pure heart, and of a good conscience, and of faith unfeigned."

There were many teachers in Paul's day who were sticklers for the Law. They taught every minute detail of the Law and refused to hear Romans 10:4: *"For Christ is the end of the law for righteousness to every one that believeth.''* There are many today who refuse to believe the truth of this tremendous statement which was given to us through inspiration, penned down by the Apostle to the Gentiles.

In order that young Timothy might faithfully fulfill the design of his *appointment* as God's undershepherd, it was imperative that he have a correct view of the *design of the Law* given to Moses by God. The teachers to whom Paul refers were insisting that the Law was still in effect and that believers were obligated to *keep* that Law. Many taught grace (after a fashion), but insisted upon the importance of keeping the Law *after one had exercised faith in the grace of God.*

The minister who today preaches pure grace is accused of destroying the Law of God—and this, of course, is not true. God's Law is holy and righteous, and Paul is saying to Timothy that he is NOT making void the Law of God.

The Law is good when it is rightly understood and properly taught. God has not changed His mind about His Law; but in Jesus—the One who kept every jot and tittle of the Law—*He provided grace greater than all our sins.*

The teachers in Paul's day did not understand the nature and use of the Law in this Age of Grace; and since they were not teaching the Law of God in its proper relation to the Dispensation of Grace, it was of great importance that Timothy have a proper understanding and perspective as to the purpose for which the Law was given.

In Matthew 5:17 Jesus said, "Think not that I am come to destroy the law or the prophets: I am not come to destroy, *but to fulfil.''* (And He DID fulfil every jot and tittle of the whole Law of God.) The teaching of error concerning the Law had brought about contentions and bitterness among some of the people in that community, and this was not the purpose for which the Law was given. It was not given to place burdens upon believers, but to produce love—first to God, and then to one's fellowman.

A lawyer once asked Jesus which was the greatest commandment, and Jesus said, "Thou shalt love the Lord thy God with all thy heart, and with all thy soul, and with all thy mind. This is the first and great commandment. And the second is like unto it, Thou shalt love thy neighbour as thyself. *On these two commandments hang all the law and the prophets"* (Matt. 22:37—40). Therefore, the Law and the prophets can be summed up in one word: "LOVE!"

Thus Paul said, "Now the end of the commandment is charity"—that is, *all of God's Law is fulfilled in charity*—"out of a pure heart, and of a good conscience, and of faith unfeigned." True love can come *only* out of a "pure heart." Love which is genuine proceeds from a heart that is holy. The commandment was not designed by Almighty God to produce outward expressions of love, purity and holiness, but to produce *from the heart* love that is pure and unfeigned—love proceeding from a holy heart and a conscience free from all guilt.

There can be no pure and genuine love to God if the dictates of the believer's conscience are constantly violated . . . if he knows that he is continually doing that which is not pleasing in the eyes of the Lord. If a man desires the evidence of pure love to God, that man must keep a good, pure conscience—anything else is hypocrisy. Any man is a hypocrite if he knows that he is living in open sin while professing to love God with all of his heart!

Genuine Christian love, a holy heart, a good conscience and faith unfeigned are inseparable in the life of a true believer. *"Faith unfeigned"* means complete, unshakeable confidence in God. How can anyone publicly testify that he loves God *if he has no confidence IN God* . . . if his daily living does not demonstrate trust in God? Faith is as necessary under the LAW of God as it is under the GRACE of God: "Without faith it is impossible to please Him: for he that cometh to God must believe that He IS, and that He is a rewarder of them that diligently seek Him" (Heb. 11:6).

To sum up verse 5 of our present chapter, we might say that an unfeigned faith in Christ clears the conscience of all guilt and produces love that is pure, proceeding out of a holy heart.

Verse 6: "From which some having swerved have turned aside unto vain jangling."

Some had swerved from unfeigned faith—they had turned aside from the teaching of the grace of God unto vain conversation about Law, fables, genealogies and such. They gave heed to "Jewish fables and commandments of men" (Tit. 1:14). They refused the truth of the pure Gospel of grace and sought to be Law-teachers; they did not *understand* what they said nor what they so fervently declared to be truth. They were Judaizers rather than Gospel teachers. They insisted upon Law-keeping and ordinances; they perverted the Gospel and continually sought to injure Paul's ministry by announcing that he was a false teacher.

The meaning of "swerve" is to "miss the mark . . . to err." (Compare I Timothy 6:21 and II Timothy 2:18 with our present verse.) Paul does not mean that those who had erred had ever possessed that from which they had swerved. If a man misses a mark, the fact that he missed the mark does not suggest that he ever hit that which he is said to have missed. Those who swerved failed to put their faith and trust in the finished work of Jesus. Instead of trusting in His saving grace and shed blood, they had turned to vain talk. These people to whom Paul refers had never possessed a pure heart, a good conscience and "unfeigned faith."

The statement *"having turned aside unto vain jangling"* simply means that instead of listening to sound doctrine and pure Gospel truth, they turned to vain talk, empty declarations by man, and listened to discourses without sense or scriptural truth. Instead of obeying the teaching concerning the death, burial and resurrection of Jesus Christ, they turned to the traditions of men, the ceremonies of the Law and useless genealogies, making much of many names but never looking to the ONLY name given under heaven among men whereby we must be saved (Acts 4:12). No doubt, like some in Jesus' day, they boasted that they were disciples of the Law of Moses, and not of what they would term "heresy"— the doctrine of pure grace (minus works, minus Law) being sufficient within itself to satisfy every demand of a holy God.

Verse 7: "Desiring to be teachers of the Law; understanding neither what they say, nor whereof they affirm."

These people to whom Paul refers professed to be well versed in the Law of Moses and well qualified to teach and explain the Law to others. They claimed traditional honor among the Jews and advertised themselves as great teachers—but Paul here defines them as those who desire to teach, without understanding what they are trying to teach. Instead of being qualified teachers, they themselves desperately needed to be taught.

These would-be teachers of the Law did not understand the true nature and design of the Law which they were trying to explain to others. Many Jewish teachers in Paul's day were guilty of the gross sin of religious pride, and those in the church at Ephesus were attempting to place believers in the same position relating to Law as that which prevailed during the *Dispensation* of Law. Such teaching was in direct opposition to the teaching of Paul, who taught pure grace. He was extremely jealous for the grace of God and the finished work of Jesus according to the Scriptures.

Verse 8: "But we know that the Law is good, if a man use it lawfully."

Paul wanted it understood that he was not an enemy to the Law of God; he admitted that the Law is good. In Romans 7:12 he said, ". . . The law is holy, and the commandment holy, and just and good." And lest the charge be brought against him that he was attempting to destroy the Law of God, he said, *"We know that the law is good*—if a man use it lawfully."

Paul never for one moment suggested that the Law of God was not good; never did he call the Law into question. He only asked that it be rightly understood and properly explained. If one use the Law in the manner and purpose for which it was designed, then certainly the Law is good; but *grace cannot be supplemented by Law.* Law plus grace does not save nor keep saved. If it be Law, it is not grace; and if it be grace, then it is no more Law. Paul's teaching is crystal-clear on the fact that Law and grace will not mix. Study Gal. 2:16 and Gal. 5:1–4.

Verse 9: "Knowing this, that the law is not made for a righteous man, but for the lawless and disobedient, for the ungodly and for sinners, for unholy and profane, for murderers of fathers and murderers of mothers, for manslayers."

Notice the opening words of this verse: *"Knowing this . . . ."* If one knows and will admit the fact that the Law was never intended for a righteous man, he has the proper view of the design of the Law. What Paul is saying here is simply that the purpose of the Law of God was not to perplex the righteous man who desires to please God in every phase of life. It was not intended to produce a spirit of bondage and slavery, as the Jews interpreted the Law—and as some of the errorists were teaching at Ephesus. The whole trend of their teaching was to bring the soul of the believer into a state of bondage and make religion a condition of servitude on the part of the individual, after believing unto salvation. They demanded the *keeping of the Law* in order to keep *salvation* after the believer was born again by grace through faith. Paul did not believe nor teach such doctrine. His teaching was that Christianity produces freedom and liberty—not servitude, slavery and bondage. Thus the statement, "The law is not made for a righteous man."

But is not this the case with ALL law? A good man does not fear the laws of the land—it is the wicked man who breaks the law, who lives in fear. The person who obeys the law does not fear the approaching officer; the lawbreaker is the one who has fear and anxieties. Thus, in this sense, the law is instituted for the man who intentionally does wrong and *breaks* the law.

In Romans 3:20 Paul said, ". . . By the deeds of the law there shall no flesh be justified. . . ." Again, "Christ is the end of the law for righteousness to every one that believeth" (Rom. 10:4). The Law is not made for the man who has been made righteous through faith in the finished work of the Lord Jesus, but rather for the disobedient, the ungodly, the unholy, the profane, the murderers, and manslayers. Notice the different groups

41

pointed out here:

The lawless — those who are transgressors.

The disobedient — those who are insubordinate and lawless, under no subjection to authority, and who, like Judas, go their "own way."

The ungodly — those who profess no religion, who neither worship nor honor the true God. The true meaning here is that the Law of God is against all who do not worship and honor the God of all creation.

Sinners — (the Greek word used here is the word commonly used in the New Testament to denote those who commit all kinds of sins).

Unholy — (the Greek word used here means those who fail utterly in their duty toward God, and display no piety or respect whatsoever *for* God. They are against religion in any form).

Profane — (the Greek word here does not necessarily mean those who curse God or use His name in vain, but refers to those who are impious . . . scoffers, those who make fun and mock at religion. It refers to persons who treat religion with contempt and mockery).

Murderers of fathers — (the Greek word here literally means "smiter of a father." For a child to strike his father was strictly forbidden by the Law of Moses, and was considered a crime punishable by death—Exodus 21:15: "And he that smiteth his father, or his mother, shall be surely put to death").

Murderers of mothers — There have been those who have murdered their own mother; and some children, not realizing what they are doing, slowly murder their mother by their wayward living. There are many gray hairs in the heads of precious mothers, put there because of the sins of their children. There are mothers in graveyards today who would be living had their children lived godly lives. There are more ways of murdering a mother than to shed her blood with a knife or a gun! The Law of Moses strictly forbade a child to strike his mother (Exodus 21:15).

Manslayers — (The Greek word used here does not occur anywhere else in the New Testament, and means "homicide—a murderer.") The crime is strictly forbidden by the Law (Ex. 20:13). See also Genesis 9:6.

Verse 10: "For whoremongers, for them that defile themselves with mankind, for menstealers, for liars, for perjured persons, and if there be any other thing that is contrary to sound doctrine."

This verse is a continuation of verse 9:

Whoremongers — In Leviticus 19:29 and 20:5 we read the clear teaching of the Law concerning whoremongers: "Do not prostitute thy daughter, to cause her to be a whore; lest the land fall to whoredom, and the land become full of wickedness. . . . Then I will set my face against that man, and against his family, and will cut him off, and all that go a whoring after him, to commit whoredom . . . ."

Those who defile themselves with mankind — This is the sin of Sodomy, and such practice abounded in Paul's day and just before that time (Rom. 1:27). The Law of Moses strictly forbade the sin of Sodomy, and the punishment for such was death: Leviticus 20:13: "If a man also lie with mankind, as he lieth with a woman, both of them have committed an abomination: they shall surely be put to death; their blood shall be upon them."

Menstealers — The Greek word used here does not occur any other place in the New Testament. It means a man who steals another for the purpose of slavery— a kidnapper. There is much that could be said here, but time and space will not permit all that should be said.

There are men today who steal young women and make them slaves, to satisfy the lust of ungodly men. You may rest assured that the Law was made for such men. *Menstealing* was forbidden by the Law of God, and one who was found guilty of this crime was punished with death: Exodus 21:16; Deuteronomy 24:7 — "He that stealeth a man, and selleth him, or if he be found in his hand, he shall surely be put to death. . . . If a man be found stealing any of his brethren of the children of Israel, and maketh merchandise of him, or selleth him; then that thief shall die; and thou shalt put evil away from among you."

Liars — The law concerning liars is clearly stated in Leviticus 6:2–5 and 19:11: "If a soul sin, and commit a trespass against the Lord, and lie unto his neighbour in that which was delivered him to keep, or in fellowship, or in a thing taken away by violence, or hath deceived his neighbour; or have found that which was lost, and lieth concerning it, and sweareth falsely; in any of all these that a man doeth, sinning therein: Then it shall be, because he hath sinned, and is guilty, that he shall restore that which he took violently away, or the thing which he hath deceitfully gotten, or that which was delivered him to keep, or the lost thing which he found, or all that about which he hath sworn falsely; he shall even restore it in the principal, and shall add the fifth part more thereto, and give it unto him to whom it appertaineth, in the day of his trespass-offering. . . . Ye shall not steal, neither deal falsely, *neither lie one to another.*"

Perjured persons — those who swear falsely. The law concerning such persons is set forth in Leviticus 19:12 and Exodus 20:7: "And ye shall not swear by my name falsely, neither shalt thou profane the name of thy God: I am the Lord. . . . Thou shalt not take the name of the Lord thy God in vain; for the Lord will not hold

44

him guiltless that taketh His name in vain."

"And if there be any other thing that is contrary to sound doctrine . . . ." Thus Paul sums up all ungodly acts in this statement. The Greek for "sound doctrine," literally translated, reads, "the doctrine which is according to godliness."

The Law of God was given for those who practice or teach anything that is opposed to the instruction which the holy, righteous Law of God gives. The Law was not given for the man who wants to follow godly instruction, but for those who rebel against the authority of Jehovah God, the Creator of all things.

Verse 11: "According to the glorious gospel of the blessed God, which was committed to my trust."

The Gospel is God's truth, given through divine revelation. The heart of the Gospel is the glorious news that the Law of God has been perfectly satisfied in every minute detail—yea, every jot and every tittle—through the sacrificial death of the only begotten Son of God, the Lord Jesus Christ, on Calvary's cross. To the Corinthians Paul said, "I preached unto you the Gospel," and then he points out the death, burial and resurrection of Jesus, *"according to the Scriptures"* (I Cor. 15:1-4). The Gospel makes known the will of God. The Gospel clearly states what is the duty of man toward God. The Gospel is in perfect harmony with the Law of God and does not permit what the Law of God forbids. There is neither contradiction nor conflict between the Law of God and the glorious Gospel of our Lord and Saviour, Jesus Christ; they condemn the same things; they forbid the same things; and in regard to holiness, morals and true piety, *they agree.* God's ministers who preach the glorious Gospel are not against the Law of God. The true preacher of the Gospel recognizes and preaches the holiness of the Law of God, the purity of God's Law, and then declares *"according to the Scriptures"* that the only way any mortal can satisfy the Law of God is in Christ Jesus—He who fulfilled every jot and tittle of the prophets (Matt. 5:17), He who is the end of the Law for righteousness to all who believe in His finished work (Rom. 10:4). The true minister of the Gospel declares the holiness of God, the holiness of the Law of God, and then offers the righteousness of God in Christ Jesus to all who will believe on Him and surrender their life to Him in true faith.

What Paul is saying to the teachers of error—in his day and ours—is that if a man wishes to explain the Law, the best *explanation* of the Law of God is found *in the Gospel of the grace of God.* Paul was called, commissioned and ordained, to preach the Gospel that was revealed unto him—the Gospel to be preached in this dispensation of the grace of our God.

Romans 3:31: *"Do we then make void the law through faith? God forbid: yea, we establish the law."*

This glorious Gospel of which Paul speaks is the Gospel "of the blessed God"—that is, the Gospel revealed BY the blessed God, the same blessed God who was the author and the giver of the Law . . . the one true God, the God of all truth, law and grace . . . the God and Father of our Lord Jesus Christ, who purchased redemption for all who will believe. It is *God's* glorious Gospel; and Paul declares that God, the author of the Gospel, committed this glorious message to his trust.

Paul wanted Timothy (and all others) to know that what he declared, he had received directly from God by revelation. God had made known unto him the message of the glorious Gospel of the grace of God. He had entrusted to Paul this greatest message of salvation—God's gift to sinners who deserved hell instead of forgiveness for sins, and life eternal.

Exceeding and Abundant Grace

Verse 12: "And I thank Christ Jesus our Lord, who enabled me, for that He counted me faithful, putting me into the ministry."

Because of the truth declared in verse 11 (that the glorious Gospel of the grace of God was committed to Paul), he was led to give heartfelt thanks to the God who had called him to the ministry and to the preaching of this glorious Gospel.

From the standpoint of religious training and education, it is doubtful that any man was more qualified to preach the Gospel than Paul was. He could have boasted of his education and his ability—but he did not. He confessed with thanksgiving that the Lord Jesus Christ gave him the ability, strength and desire to preach the Gospel of God's marvelous grace, thus enabling him to carry out his great ministry. Paul gave God all the glory for what he was and for all that he ever accomplished; he took no credit for himself. He said, *"I am what I am by the grace of God!"*

In this verse we are told that *the Lord Jesus counted Paul faithful.* These are weighty words; they give to us the tremendous truth that God puts into His ministry men who are enabled by *His power*, men who are counted faithful to proclaim the whole Gospel—not as men-pleasers, but as servants of the most high God.

All true ministers of the Gospel are put into the ministry by the Lord God Almighty. The ministry is not a vocation, in the sense of other vocations; it is *a calling from Almighty God*—and preachers who do not know beyond the shadow of a doubt that GOD put them into the ministry should take up some other vocation through which they can earn a livelihood and be of service to mankind. Pity the man who attempts to preach the Gospel if he does not know beyond question that God put him into the ministry! The scourge of this hour is that there are so many pulpits filled by men who have "taken up" preaching as they would take up farming, carpentry, masonry or any other profession.

Paul was faithful. He was faithful first of all to the God who called him, ordained him and sent him into the field. Secondly, he was faithful to *the Word of God*—he preached pure grace, never deviating from the message God had given him by revelation; and in the third place, he was faithful *to those to whom he ministered*. Often he labored with his own hands to provide his livelihood while he preached. He lived before his charges as becomes a preacher; he daily practiced what he preached; he set the right example and instructed them to follow him, even as he followed Christ. God help us who claim to be ministers of the Gospel to follow the steps of Paul as he faithfully discharged the duties of a God-called, God-ordained minister.

No person should claim that he is called to the ministry unless he is faithful to God and to the pure Gospel of the *grace* of God. The office of the ministry is the most honorable, most responsible office in the realm of mankind. It is a grand and glorious privilege to preach the Gospel—but as grand and glorious as is the privilege, just so weighty and grave is the corresponding responsibility.

Verse 13: "Who was before a blasphemer, and a persecutor, and injurious: but I obtained mercy, because I did it ignorantly in unbelief."

Paul does not mean that he was an open blasphemer

in the sense that we think of blasphemy today. He does not mean that he was one who abused and mocked sacred things, nor one who took God's name in vain by use of profanity. Paul's testimony concerning his life before he met Jesus on the road to Damascus shows that he was exactly the opposite of all this.

Even before his conversion, Paul was a remarkable person in every respect. Concerning religion and things sacred, he lived after the strictest sect of the Pharisees (note Philippians 3:4—6). In this passage, Paul simply means that he reviled the precious name of the Lord Jesus Christ, opposed the *cause* of Christ and persecuted the *followers* of Christ. He did not believe Jesus to be the Messiah, and because of his unbelief and his persecution of those who followed the Christ, he felt himself to have been guilty of blasphemy. Salvation caused him to realize that he had treated the Messiah of God with contempt and ugly reproach, and he looked back upon his former life with deep regret and sorrow. Read Matthew 9:3 and Acts 26:9—11.

Paul's reference to himself as a blasphemer has to do with conduct—his attitude toward Christ and his behaviour toward the *followers* of Christ. At the time he persecuted the church and hated the name of Jesus, he thought he was doing his duty, and he did it with a clear conscience (Acts 23:1); but after his conversion he regarded his former conduct as blasphemous.

Many times, what men count harmless before they are saved becomes very sinful in the light of God's grace after they are born again. Even some believers who are not spiritually minded practice habits of life which to them seem harmless at the moment; but when they grow in grace and fully surrender soul, spirit and body to Jesus, they remember with deep regret and sorrow those things that previously seemed right in their eyes.

49

Paul not only calls himself a blasphemer, but also *"a persecutor."* This can be better understood by reading Acts 9:1 ff; Acts 22:4; 26:11; I Corinthians 15:9 and Galatians 1:13–23. Saul of Tarsus was a devout Pharisee. He was very zealous for the religion of his fathers, and he intended to stamp out Christianity and those who followed Jesus. He was sincere and conscientious in his persecution of the church, thinking he was doing God a favor. From Paul's experience we can see that it is possible for one to be strictly religious, conscientious with all of his heart—and yet be sadly lost. There are thousands today who are zealously religious, and *sincere* in their religion—but they are not saved because they have never put their trust in the finished work of the Lord Jesus Christ.

". . . And injurious." The Greek word used here is used only one other time in the New Testament; it is used in Romans 1:30, where it is translated "despiteful." "Injurious" here does not fully express what Paul is saying. He does not mean simply *doing injury*; his meaning goes deeper. It has to do with the *manner or spirit in which the thing is done.* The Greek word for "injurious" signifies a much deeper hurt than that used for "blasphemer" or "persecutor." The meaning is that the action was done with much pride and haughtiness and with an insolent spirit. There was wicked and malicious violence along with arrogance and the spirit of tyranny. Paul persecuted the followers of Jesus Christ with all possible fervor, and he was very proud of what he was doing. He therefore referred to himself as *injurious.* (Some Bible authorities translate the word as *"tyrant."*)

". . . But I obtained mercy because I did it ignorantly in unbelief." Paul is not saying here that he is excused because his actions were carried out in ignorance and unbelief. The fact that he was ignorant and an unbeliever

50

did not lessen his guilt, but it does show the longsuffering of Christ and His exceeding grace. Merciful and mighty was this grace that would save one who had previously displayed such hatred and unbelief. Paul's blessing is ours, too. None need despair; for if God could do this for such a persecuting, murderous person, then truly all can hope! But because Paul did this ignorantly, the moment he met the Lord Jesus and the light of the glorious Gospel of God's marvelous grace illumined his heart and spirit, he immediately turned his back on unbelief and became a follower of the Lord Jesus: *"And straightway he preached Christ in the synagogues, that He is the Son of God"* (Acts 9:20).

What Paul is saying here in verse 13 is in accord with the prayer of our Saviour on the cross as He looked down into the faces of those who had nailed Him there, and prayed to God, "Father, forgive them, *for they know not what they do!*"

It is my belief that persons who, in ignorance, live lives of wickedness and yet consider themselves to be *right* in what they are doing, are much more likely to be saved than are those who deliberately live wicked lives, knowing all the while that they are doing things they should NOT be doing. There is less hope for the person who is exposed to truth but rejects that truth, than there is for the person who is ignorant in the wickedness he commits.

Verse 14: "And the grace of our Lord was exceeding abundant with faith and love which is in Christ Jesus."

In verse 13 Paul said, *"I obtained mercy."* He was the object of the marvelous emancipating grace of God, and until God's grace saved and delivered him, he had been "a blasphemer, a persecutor, and injurious." The thought of his past life humbled him, and he felt that he was chiefest of sinners.

51

Paul had experienced saving grace . . . delivering grace—but he had also experienced *"employing grace."* When God delivered him from ignorance and error, He enlisted and used him. In his own words, *"He counted me faithful, putting me into the ministry."*

True salvation is always followed by true service to God. God saves to serve; He has never saved any sinner to sit idly by while the world madly rushes on to hell! God saves us that we might tell others. "And all things are of God, who hath reconciled us to Himself by Jesus Christ, and *hath given to us the ministry of reconciliation*; To wit, that God was in Christ, reconciling the world unto Himself, not imputing their trespasses unto them; and hath committed unto us the word of reconciliation" (II Cor. 5:18,19). Faith without works is dead. We are not SAVED by works, but salvation *produces* works: "For we are His workmanship, created in Christ Jesus *unto good works*, which God hath before ordained that we should walk in them" (Eph. 2:10).

Paul had experienced saving grace—grace that also *employed* him in the service of our Lord—and he also experienced *"enabling grace."* In verse 12 he testifies, "God hath enabled me." The believer need not be timid or hesitant; he need not hold back, for when God calls, God also *provides*. "Our sufficiency is of God" (II Cor. 3:5). God never bids us go on an errand for Him without supplying whatsoever we need for the journey; He never sends us to engage the enemy without providing the ammunition with which to win the victory. "Who goeth a warfare any time at his own charges?" (I Cor. 9:7). If you are a believer, take courage and comfort in this plain statement: *"If God command thee . . . thou shalt be able to!"* (Ex. 18:23).

In our present verse, Paul speaks concerning *exceeding* grace. He said, "The grace of our Lord was *exceeding abundant."* In other words, the grace of God is super, extraordinary, infinite. God's grace is unmerited, unearned, undeserved, all-sufficient and all-supplying. Paul could not find words to describe the grace that had changed him from a blasphemer, a persecutor and an injurious person to the valiant soldier of the cross and consecrated preacher that he was.

He cried out, "I am chief of sinners!"—and in that statement he did not exaggerate. He felt in his heart what he said with his lips. All sinners, when deeply convicted of sin and face to face with their own iniquity, will cry out in like manner. Isaiah proclaimed, "Woe is me, for I am undone!" (Isa. 6:5). In Luke 5:8 Peter cried, "Depart from me, for I am a sinful man!" The Publican standing in the temple would not so much as lift his eyes to heaven, but smote upon his breast, saying, "God be merciful to me a sinner!" (Luke 18:13).

Paul said, "For I am the least of the apostles, *that am not meet to be called an apostle"* (I Cor. 15:9). In Ephesians 3:8 he said, "I am less than the least of all saints." In spite of the fact that Paul did not feel worthy to be called an apostle and deep down in his heart felt that he was the least of all God's saints, God's exceeding grace made him what he was and enabled him to do the work of an evangelist, a true minister, a good soldier, and at last a faithful martyr for the glory of God. The grace bestowed upon him caused him to exclaim, ". . . by the grace of God, I am what I am! And His grace which was bestowed upon me was not in vain; but I laboured more abundantly than they all: yet not I, but the grace of God which was with me" (I Cor. 15:10).

Yes, merciful and mighty, exceeding and glorious was that grace, leading Paul on to *"faith and love,"* which he exhibited from that day forward in such abundant measure toward the Lord Jesus Christ whom he had so vigorously persecuted when he was a blasphemer, a persecutor and an injurious person. The grace of God changed hatred and unbelief to FAITH AND LOVE!

Verse 15: "This is a faithful saying, and worthy of all acceptation, that Christ Jesus came into the world to save sinners; of whom I am chief."

The literal Greek reads, *"faithful is the word."* Paul had just testified to the fact that he was a great sinner, that he had obtained great mercy through the exceeding grace of God, and his mind naturally turned to the singular purpose for which Christ came into the world—to save sinners, to give His life a ransom for many, to willingly lay His life down that He might take it again—to die, that we might live.

The Greek word here translated "saying" means *doctrine* or *declaration.* This is a faithful doctrine . . . a faithful announcement. The word "faithful" in the literal Greek means *"assuredly true"*; therefore this declaration, this doctrine, can be depended upon; and complete confidence can be placed in the declaration that Christ came to save sinners, that He came to lay His life down that we might have life. The doctrine of the death, burial and resurrection of Jesus "according to the Scriptures" is a doctrine or declaration that can be confidently accepted by all, because it is assuredly true.

"It is a faithful saying: For if we be dead with Him, we shall also live with Him" (II Tim. 2:11).

"This is a faithful saying, and these things I will that thou affirm constantly, that they which have believed in God might be careful to maintain good works. These things are good and profitable unto men" (Titus 3:8).

". . . *And worthy of all acceptation."* That is, the statement is worthy to be embraced, accepted and believed

54

by all, regardless of who they may be. This declaration is true because all are sinners: "For all have sinned, and come short of the glory of God" (Rom. 3:23); therefore, all need a Saviour—and all are welcome to hear the doctrine which declares that Jesus is seeking every sinner for the singular purpose of saving him. It is not God's will that any perish, but that all come to repentance. All we like sheep have gone astray, but Jehovah placed on Jesus, the Lamb, the iniquities of us all (Isa. 53:6).

This declaration is worthy of all acceptation, because *Christ died for all*. Jesus did not die for a select group. God so loved the WORLD, that *"whosoever believeth"* might be saved. He is the propitiation for our sins—and not for ours only, but for the sins of the whole world (John 3:16; I John 2:1,2). If Christ had died for only a part of the human race, if He could save only a part of mankind, it could not be said that this doctrine of salvation by grace is worthy of the acceptation of all. If Christ did not die for all, then how could all be interested in His death as having to do with salvation?

There are those who preach "limited atonement." They are those who are known as hyper-Calvinists, ultra-Predestinarians. They teach that if you are elected you *will be* saved, and if you are not elected, you *cannot* be saved. There is not a minister in existence who believes in election more strongly than I do; there is not a minister who believes in the sovereignty of God more strongly than I do, and no one believes in Bible predestination more firmly than I do—but I believe just as strongly that CHRIST DIED FOR EVERY SINGLE SOLITARY HUMAN BEING ON THE FACE OF THIS EARTH. If a minister does not believe that Jesus died for all sinners, he is teaching error! The Bible *does not* teach that some are elected to be damned (limited atonement—the doctrine held forth by hyper-Calvinists). Jesus Christ purchased redemption for each and every sinner!

To His own people Jesus said, "Search the Scriptures; for in them ye think ye have eternal life: and they are they which testify of me. And YE WILL NOT COME TO ME, that ye might have life" (John 5:39,40). Will you please note—"AND YE WILL NOT COME TO ME, THAT YE MIGHT HAVE LIFE!" According to the words of Jesus, some of His own people died and opened their eyes in hell—not because they were not elected or chosen, but because they refused to come to Him, accept Him as their Messiah and be saved! Never listen to any man who preaches limited atonement.

The declaration that Christ came to seek and to save that which was lost, to lay His life down that we might have life, is worthy of all acceptation because of the manner in which the provision for salvation has been made known through the Gospel. God's plan of redemption is so simple and so understandable that Jesus said, "Suffer little children to come unto me and forbid them not, for of such is the kingdom of heaven." To grown men He said, "Except ye be converted and become as little children, ye shall in no wise enter into the kingdom of God." This announcement is worthy of all acceptation because it is so simple, so understandable, so down to earth and so practical that even a child can understand the plan of salvation.

No mortal being could ever have conceived such a plan; no mortal could ever have supplied such a sacrifice. God commended His love toward us in that while we were yet sinners, Christ died for us! Christ died for the ungodly . . . He did not lay down His life for His friends, but for His enemies. He took the sinner's place; He bore our sins in His own body on the cross and tasted the bitter dregs of the cup, that you and I might drink freely of the water of life.

This declaration is worthy of all acceptation because of the provision made in the gift announced: *Salvation is free to all who will receive by faith the finished work and shed blood of Christ.* Salvation cannot be earned; it cannot be purchased; there is no way by which any man can merit salvation. The multimillionaire and the pauper must be saved identically. The college professor and the man who cannot read his own name must be saved the same way. Regardless of position, condition, color, creed, or whatsoever, there is only one name—the name of Jesus; one door—He is the Door; one way—He is the Way; one truth—He is Truth; one life—He is the Author of all life. We are all saved identically—by faith in the finished work of the Lamb of God on the cross—the Lamb who left the Father's bosom and in one gigantic step stepped from the bosom of the Father to the womb of the Virgin Mary—and from that moment until He said, "It is finished," everything He did, everything He said, every step He took, every miracle He performed, every detail of every moment of His life on earth was singular—*He was seeking and saving that which was lost!*

This declaration—"By grace are ye saved through faith; and that not of yourselves: it is the gift of God"— is worthy of all acceptation. Anyone, everyone, is invited to accept it, and all who WILL accept it shall be saved: "Verily, verily, I say unto you, He that heareth my word, and believeth on Him that sent me, hath everlasting life, and shall not come into condemnation; but is passed from death unto life" (John 5:24). "For by grace are ye saved through faith; and that not of yourselves: it is the gift of God" (Eph. 2:8). "So then faith cometh by hearing and hearing by the Word of God" (Rom. 10:17). "Being born again, not of corruptible seed, but of incorruptible, by the Word of God, which liveth and abideth for ever" (I Peter 1:23).

It is imperative that the sinner believe correctly about God, about Jesus, and about the Word if there is to be salvation for that sinner. We hear the Word, we believe the Word, we receive the Word—and in so doing, we believe *"in the beginning, GOD."* We believe *"God so loved the world that He gave His only begotten Son."* We believe *"Christ died for our sins, according to the Scriptures."* Also, *"He who knew no sin was made sin for us, that we in Him might be made the righteousness of God."* Believing thus, we confess that Christ, who came into the world to save sinners, existed *before* He came into the world—He existed with the Father in the beginning, and He came when He was under no obligation to do so. Because of His great love, He came to save man, created in the image of God. He came to save—not to destroy. He came to reveal mercy, not to destroy in judgment. He came to save sinners—poor, lost, wandering, condemned souls. He came to restore to God's favor those who had deliberately gone against God.

Dear reader, if you are not saved, all you need do to be saved is to first confess that you are a sinner, and then believe with the heart that Jesus came to save sinners; and if you will confess that you ARE a sinner, deserving only hell, and then put your trust in Jesus, He will make you fit for heaven—but He alone can do it, and before He will save you, you must confess that you are a sinner. Jesus said, "They that be whole need not a physician, but they that are sick" (Matt. 9:12). If you will confess that you are sin-sick, lost, and hell-deserving, and then turn your eyes toward heaven's mercy-seat where Jesus sits at the right hand of God the Father (Heb. 1:3; I Tim. 2:5), and in your own words call on God in the name of Jesus for mercy, mercy will be yours by faith in the finished work of the Lamb of God.

Verse 15 closes with this tremendous statement:

"... OF WHOM I AM CHIEF." I stated earlier in the message that Paul was not an ordinary person. He was extraordinary from every standpoint, and when he saw himself in the light of the Gospel, he confessed that he was chief of all sinners. (The word in the Greek denotes eminence, and it means that Paul occupied the first rank among sinners—he was a "general," not a "private.") He was not just an ordinary sinner—he was the chief . . . *an outstanding sinner.*

It is true that Paul was very religious—he was a Pharisee of the Pharisees, and he lived after the straitest sect of the religion of his fathers; but when he saw Jesus, he saw himself as chief of all those who were *against* the Christ. It is possible that when Paul referred to himself as chief of sinners, he was thinking of Stephen, God's first deacon, whose stoning Paul had witnessed and consented to. Perhaps he remembered the light of heaven on the face of Stephen as he prayed for his executioners, "Lord, lay not this sin to their charge!" Possibly these words of Stephen ran through Paul's mind as he saw himself chief of sinners. Saul of Tarsus, like Nicodemus, was moral—eminently so. Outwardly, his conduct was above reproach—until that day when he began to persecute the followers of Jesus Christ. Read Philippians 3:6; Acts 26:4,5.

Some people who enter the inquiry room in our meetings begin by saying, "I am not such a *bad* sinner; I have always been a clean moral person. I have never been in jail, and I have never been drunk." But Paul was not like that. After his conversion he never attempted to excuse himself, but at all times was ready to admit to the fullest the fact that he was a sinner—and more: *chiefest of sinners.*

A true believer is always ready to admit that his past life was a life of sin, regardless of how moral he might have been. When one is truly born again, he never tries to justify anything in his past life. The more fully consecrated we are and the more spiritually minded we become, the more we acknowledge our complete dependence upon the grace of God. The more dedicated we become, the more fully we recognize the weakness of the flesh and the total depravity of men; and we are prone to cry out with Paul, "I am what I am by the grace of God!"

Verse 16: "Howbeit for this cause I obtained mercy, that in me first Jesus Christ might shew forth all longsuffering, for a pattern to them which should hereafter believe on Him to life everlasting."

Here again, as in verse 13, we have the phrase, "*I obtained mercy.*" Paul was the happy, privileged recipient of God's grace and tender mercy, *in order that he might be a pattern* of the longsuffering and tender compassion of Jesus, that all might enjoy the same glorious salvation and obtain the same tender mercy obtained by Paul when he received the Lord Jesus Christ. Paul's entire life after his conversion was devoted to the proclamation of the message of Calvary—salvation by grace through faith in the finished work of Jesus, telling forth the good news that Christ is the propitiation for our sins, and not for ours only, but for the sins of the whole wide world (I John 2:2). Paul longed that ALL should hear this grand and glorious news. We today share in his blessing. God called Paul and sent him to the Gentiles; and we are still reaping the blessings made possible because of his total obedience to the call of God.

"*. . . In me first*" shows forth the Bible fact that if a poor, deceived, blasphemous persecutor like Paul could be gloriously saved and God's grace be abundantly shed upon *him*, then so could any man, however wicked or sinful he might be. Thus, the vital principle of Paul's philosophy of salvation. None is too wicked or sinful for redeeming grace, and Paul sets forth himself as a conspicuous specimen of that Bible truth. None need despair; if God's grace saved Paul and changed him from a blasphemer to a minister of the Gospel, then the grace of God is altogether sufficient to change ANY wicked sinner, regardless of how totally sinful that person may be.

The Greek word used here for "pattern" is used only one other time in the New Testament (II Tim. 1:13), where it is translated *"form."* The word means "a form, a sketch, or an example." The meaning here is simply that God chose to use Paul as an example for the specific purpose of encouraging sinners in all subsequent times. If God's grace could save and keep Paul, and make of him the great preacher and evangelist that he was, then none should doubt that God is able to save to the uttermost, regardless of circumstance. God saved "the chief of all sinners" and thus settled the question once and for all that the greatest of sinners can be saved and pardoned if they will only trust in the grace that saved the chief of sinners. Paul's example proves that there is no case beyond the pale of God's mercy and forgiveness.

From this verse we know that no sinner should despair of mercy. No one should ever say, "I am so great a sinner that God cannot save me!" If God saved Paul, then we know that sinners of all ranks and descriptions can be forgiven and saved. The drunkard, the blasphemer, the profane man, the adulterer, the murderer, the thief, the most ungodly reprobate upon the face of this earth can be pardoned if he will come to God by Jesus Christ, claiming forgiveness through His shed blood.

No wonder the Word of God tells us that Paul was a chosen vessel! God used Paul in many, many ways— and today we are still reaping the blessings of the ministry of this dedicated servant of God. I suppose no one who ever lived, saving the Lord Jesus Christ, was so totally and completely dedicated to God as was the Apostle Paul. No wonder that in his closing hours on earth he could testify, *"I have finished my course!"* I believe he preached every sermon God called upon him to preach. I believe he witnessed to every person God called upon him to witness to. I believe he traveled every mile God called upon him to travel. I believe he truly *finished his course!* I believe he bought up every opportunity to tell the good news of the marvelous Gospel of the grace of God. Yes, he is "a pattern to them which should hereafter believe on Him to life everlasting."

Verse 17: "Now unto the King eternal, immortal, invisible, the only wise God, be honour and glory for ever and ever. Amen."

In this verse Paul breaks forth into praises and thanksgiving to God—first the Person: "... *now unto the KING.*" In all of Paul's epistles he is very emphatic about the duty of believers to earthly rulers, even though among those rulers might be a Nero; yet he instructed the Thessalonians about "another King, one Jesus" (Acts 17:7). Therefore, when there is a clash of loyalties, it is always this "other King, Jesus" who is to be honored, cherished, and obeyed. The command of Jesus is always superior, and we are to honor earthly rulers insofar as that honor does not bring DISHONOR upon Jesus.

Jesus is the Monarch to whom Paul now directs his worship. This Monarch is *"eternal, immortal, invisible, the only wise God."* The words used here could be used to describe only one God—Jehovah, the great "I AM." God is eternal . . . the Greek word means "King of Ages." This King has *always been*, He *is*, He always *will be.* The Psalmist states it thus: ". . . from everlasting to everlasting, Thou art God" (Psalm 90:1,2). This King is immortal—He ever will be. This King is invisible; the King of ages is manifest only through the divine Son, the Lord Jesus (John 14:9). He abides incomparable. None can compare with Him. He alone is God.

The King of Ages is God alone—yet He is not aloof. Jesus said, "I and my Father are one." Jesus was God in flesh (II Cor. 5:19). In Romans 16:27 Paul said, "To God only wise, be glory through Jesus Christ forever. Amen."

I pause here to thank God (and I am sure you will thank Him with me) that His love always wants what is best for us—always and under all circumstances; His power does for us what is best at all times, under all circumstances; His wisdom knows what is best for us, at all times, under all circumstances; and He knows how to perform for us that which is for our good and His glory. *What a King*! Saviour, Keeper, Friend—*but is He really my King*? Is He King of my life? Ask yourself that solemn question.

The last part of verse 17 contains words of honor and praise. Paul wanted honor and glory to the King of Ages, forever and ever. All glory, honor, and praise is due the God of our salvation, for He is the *Provider* of salvation. It was God who so loved sinners that He surrendered His only begotten Son to die on the cross, that we through His shed blood might receive remission of sins. To God be all praise!

It is true that God uses human instrumentality to bring men to salvation. It pleases God, through the preaching of the Gospel, to save those who believe. In Romans 10:9–17 we have a beautiful picture of salvation. We are told that whosoever shall call upon the name of the Lord shall be saved—yet how shall they call upon Him in whom they have not believed? And how shall they believe in Him of whom they have not heard—yet how shall they hear without a preacher? And how shall they preach unless they be sent? In this dispensation God calls and sends ministers who preach the Word; the sinner hears the Word—quick and powerful, and sharper than any two-edged sword—and the Word brings faith. The Word is the incorruptible seed that brings the new birth. Faith comes by hearing, and hearing by the Word; therefore the Word is an instrument of God to bring men to Christ. But God saves us for Christ's sake (Eph. 4:32).

Timothy, to whom Paul was writing, was converted as a result of Paul's ministry—yet conversion is the result of a chain of events. Were there no others who had a part in Timothy's conversion? Lois—his grandmother, and Eunice—his mother, who had trained him in the Scriptures as a child . . . had they no part in it? We as individuals cannot say, "This person is MY convert," because we do not know how many others prayed or witnessed before we reaped the harvest. Some sow the seed, others water after the planting—but GOD gives the increase! Godly mothers pray for their children, Bible-loving Sunday school teachers faithfully teach the children, faithful pastors preach the Word from the pulpit. Then the evangelist may come into the community and reap a great harvest of souls—but the evangelist dare not take credit for winning those souls. He had a part in it, yes—but others also had a very definite part in every soul converted.

What a glorious privilege it is to be a link in the chain that brings men to Christ. But do not forget for one moment that the only actual soul-winner is God, through the drawing power of the Holy Spirit. God uses us, but it is God who does the saving. Therefore, all "HONOUR AND GLORY" belong to God.

II Thessalonians 1:10: ". . . He shall come to be glorified in His saints, and to be admired in all them that believe . . . in that day."

"I say unto you, that likewise joy shall be in heaven over one sinner that repenteth" (Luke 15:7). If there is joy in heaven over one sinner that repents, it seems sad that here on earth when people are saved, many times there is no expression of praise and joy to the God who saves them. I do not believe in indecency in the house of God, but I do believe that one of the sad sins of saints today is lack of praise to God, who saves to the uttermost even the chief of sinners. We should praise Him; we should honor Him; we should glorify His name. The church of the living God should be the most joyous place in any community. God help us to get back to old-fashioned salvation that produces joy unspeakable and full of glory (I Pet. 1:8).

Paul's Charge to Timothy; Warning Concerning the Danger of Shipwreck

Verse 18: "This charge I commit unto thee, son Timothy, according to the prophecies which went before on thee, that thou by them mightest war a good warfare."

I do not doubt that the "charge" (command or injunction) to which Paul specifically refers in this verse is stated in verse 8: *"We know that the Law is good, if a man use it lawfully."* In the name of Jesus, Paul charges young Timothy to be very, very careful to rightly divide the Word and preach the pure Gospel of the grace of God—without mixture.

". . . *According to the prophecies which went before on thee . . . ."* Paul was committing to Timothy an important trust, the discharge of which required such great wisdom and fidelity as only God can supply. In committing this trust to Timothy, Paul was acting in conformity with the hopes that had been cherished in

65

regard to this young minister—the hope that Timothy would follow in Paul's footsteps as Paul had followed in the steps of Jesus and without deviation had preached the Gospel as it was divinely revealed to him.

From childhood Timothy had been trained in the things of God, and the hope had been entertained by those close to him that he would be a man worthy of important trust: "And that from a child thou hast known the holy Scriptures, which are able to make thee wise unto salvation through faith which is in Christ Jesus" (II Tim. 3:15). It seems certain that at a very early age Timothy demonstrated seriousness, prudence, piety, and full surrender to the cause of Christ.

The prophecies referred to here were not necessarily inspired. In the early church there were many who had the gift of prophecy (Acts 11:27; I Cor. 14), and the prophecies concerning Timothy could have been spoken by some of the saints in the church who were very near to him. Whatever is meant by *the prophecies which went before on thee*," Paul was reminding Timothy and impressing upon his heart and mind the fact that there were those who were counting on him and who would be grievously hurt and sadly disappointed if he should deviate from the truth of the Gospel of grace.

A virtuous young man like Timothy will not knowingly disappoint the cherished hopes of his dedicated friends. Remembrance of their fond anticipation of his future success will likely make him more diligent. We who are ministers should always be faithful—first to God, and then to those who have prayed for us, supported us, and helped us in our ministry. If we do deviate from the truth, if we backslide or make shipwreck of our faith, we not only wound the heart of God, but we break faith with those who are near and dear to us.

". . . That thou by them mightest war a good warfare."
In other words, "May the remembrance of these prophecies
and the high hopes of mother, grandmother, and friends,
inspire you to lead a life of holiness, fidelity, and usefulness in the Church of the living God."

The Christian life is often compared to the life of
the soldier—a struggle for victory against a mighty enemy.
Read Ephesians 6:10–17 and II Corinthians 10:4. The
services of a believer—especially in the ministry of the
Gospel—are likened unto the services of a good soldier
(II Tim. 2:3,4; II Tim. 4:7). In the Christian life, he who
"wars a good warfare" is always alert, consistently engaged in the righteous cause of exalting Christ and rebuking the wicked. A good Christian soldier is one who
is faithful to his Commander-in-Chief, the Lord Jesus
Christ, and faithful to his company of fellow-believers
and fellow-saints. He is untiring; he does not slumber;
he at all times observes the movements of the enemy;
he is fearless, and with courage meets the enemy on his
own ground—but only in the name of the Lord Jesus Christ.
He who "wars a good warfare" never forsakes his convictions, his standards of holy living, and dedicated
service; but continues faithfully until the great Commander-
in-Chief sees fit to call the soldier home. Paul finished
his career by sealing his testimony with his life's blood.

Every believer should be a good soldier for Jesus
Christ, and this is especially true of ministers of the Gospel. Paul wanted Timothy to be the kind of soldier of which
Jesus would not be ashamed—that he would fight a good
fight and be a spiritual hero rather than a spiritual coward.

Verse 19: "Holding faith, and a good conscience; which
some having put away concerning faith have made shipwreck."

Paul points out two things that will be of help in

spiritual warfare: (1) *"Holding faith."* There must be unshakable, unmistakable trust in the Commander-in-Chief. (2) *"A good conscience."* One who would be a faithful and effective soldier of the cross must have no consciousness of having played fast and loose with the King's regulations. Spiritually speaking, we cannot tamper with the regulations of our Commander-in-Chief and hope to be a successful soldier in the army of the Lord. We must hold faith; we must trust Him completely; we must fulfill our duties and not be a slacker. We must not change the King's orders, but follow every detail of His command; and if we deviate from His orders, shipwreck of our faith will be the result.

Paul points out that there are some who, *"having put away concerning faith have made shipwreck"* . . . that is, they trampled on their conscience; they had their own way instead of following God's will—and because of following self-will and the desires of their own fleshly heart, they found themselves in the midst of spiritual shipwreck. They loved sin; they followed the leadings of the flesh, yielded to passion, indulged in carnal things— and by so doing, *eventually renounced the truth of the Gospel!* They were unfaithful to God; they rejected the true Gospel and substituted their own erroneous teaching. They therefore "concerning the faith have made shipwreck."

Verse 20: "Of whom is Hymenaeus and Alexander; whom I have delivered unto Satan, that they may learn not to blaspheme."

The two persons named in this verse made shipwreck of their faith. They trifled with their conscience, even to the extent of blaspheming. It is very significant that Paul points out here that false teaching—*particularly concerning the bodily resurrection of Jesus Christ*—is blasphemy. In II Timothy 2:17,18 we find that Hymenaeus

68

taught that the resurrection had already passed, and Paul calls such teaching blasphemy. Whether in his heart Hymenaeus ever knew the truth about the resurrection is not stated, and there is no point in speculating; but we are told that he was teaching in the church that the resurrection had already passed.

All believers should take warning. We need to be very careful how we treat the dictates of our conscience. Conscience is worthy of the utmost respect, and we should treat it with tender care lest we sear it, lest it become dead and dull—and eventually become silent! The conscience is very delicate. It is not the voice of God, but it is one of the means through which God guides His children. It has been said that man's conscience is *the umpire of the soul*, and that is a good definition.

The only believer who can trust his conscience is one who is fully dedicated to God, a student of God's holy Word, daily feeding the spirit (the inner man) on the bread, milk, and meat of the Word. The only helpful conscience is one that is spiritually well-fed. Church members who are not spiritually minded (referred to in I Corinthians 3:1-4 as "carnal") dare not trust their conscience; and if one trifles long enough with conscience, it will eventually become silent—and then that person can be expected to commit almost any act the devil suggests. Pitiful is the man who has seared his conscience until it has become silent!

Paul delivered Hymenaeus and Alexander unto Satan, *"that they may learn not to blaspheme."* It is quite evident in the epistles that in the early days of the church special gifts were given to men like Paul for the express purpose of promoting and preserving the purity of the infant church. He had the authority and power to turn these two false teachers over to the devil to be chastened. These gifts were given for edification of the church and also for the purification of its members—which special gifts and anointings were withdrawn as time went on, for the Word of God was fully completed, and the perfect law of liberty became ours. No one on earth today has either the power or the right to turn another over to the devil to be chastened or destroyed. It is true that God chastens, and chastisement does come to the children of God—but not through the power of man, whether he be minister, priest, or teacher. *God* permits the chastening. Many times He allows things to happen to us to bring us to our knees: *"Whom the Lord loveth He chasteneth, and scourgeth every son whom He receiveth"* (Heb. 12:6).

In I Corinthians 5 we have a clear outline of the subject we are discussing here. A young man had taken his father's wife and was living with her in open sin, and they were both members of the Corinthian church. Paul, hearing about this gross sin in the church, instructed the church officials to turn these two over to Satan "for the destruction of the flesh, that the spirit may be saved." Please notice: ". . . for the destruction of the FLESH"— not the destruction of the spirit, not the damnation of the soul—but "the destruction of the *flesh*, THAT THE SPIRIT MAY BE SAVED." We have something of the same sort in Acts 5:1–11, where we read of Ananias and Sapphira. It could be that they committed the "sin unto death" (I John 5:16). Paul speaks many times of his own physical weakness and disability, and in so doing he calls his physical disability "the messenger of Satan" (II Cor. 12:7).

I readily confess that I do not fully understand all about it, but it is in the Bible; God said it, and I must lay it before you. Whether Hymenaeus and Alexander opened their eyes in hell or not, I do not know. Whether Ananias and Sapphira burn in hell today or not, I cannot say. But concerning the young Corinthian who took his father's wife and was living with her, I do know that Paul instructed the leaders in the Corinthian church to turn these two people over to Satan, allowing him to destroy the flesh that the spirit might be saved. I repeat—I do not understand it; I cannot explain it, but it is in the Bible. *I believe it*, even though I cannot fully understand it.

The statement ". . . *whom I have delivered unto Satan, that they may learn not to blaspheme,*" simply means that Paul withdrew fellowship from Hymenaeus and Alexander and thereby placed them back in the world, from which they professed to have departed when they united with the church in Ephesus. We are commanded, *"Love not the world, neither the things that are in the world.* If any man love the world, the love of the Father is not in him. For all that is in the world, the lust of the flesh, and the lust of the eyes, and the pride of life, is not of the Father, but is of the world. And the world passeth away, and the lust thereof: but he that doeth the will of God abideth for ever"* (I John 2:15–17).

Paul simply means that he put these two outside the church, turning them over to Satan (no doubt to be afflicted with some physical ailment), to teach them not to blaspheme. It cannot be supposed that they were open blasphemers, as we think of cursing and blasphemy. They certainly would not have been allowed to remain in the church for so long a time had they been open blasphemers; but they taught doctrines which, according to Paul, amounted to blasphemy—doctrines which, in fact, brought reproach upon the divine doctrines of the Word of God, the faith once delivered to the saints.

In the spiritual sense a blasphemer is one who openly expresses views concerning divine doctrine and character which are a reproach to Almighty God and to the fundamentals of the Christian faith. As previously pointed out, the main error taught by Hymenaeus was "that the

71

resurrection is past already" (II Tim. 2:18). We do not know what Alexander was teaching, but it was probably the same false doctrine. The truth concerning the resurrection is imperative if we would become a true Christian, for it is impossible to be saved apart from the bodily resurrection of Jesus Christ "according to the Scriptures." Study carefully I Corinthians 15:1—5.

In Romans 10:9 we read, "That if thou shalt confess with thy mouth the Lord Jesus, and shalt BELIEVE IN THINE HEART THAT GOD HATH RAISED HIM FROM THE DEAD, thou shalt be saved." It is impossible to be born again apart from faith in the bodily resurrection of Jesus Christ; and if Jesus Christ be raised, then we who are His children will be raised in the first resurrection—Christ the firstfruits, then they that are His at His coming. The resurrection is NOT passed already; it is yet future. Study carefully I Corinthians 15:20 ff. It is gross, grave error to teach falsely concerning the resurrection of Jesus Christ or the resurrection of the saints.

Why did Hymenaeus and Alexander make shipwreck of their faith? Why did they fall from the profession they first announced? It seems that the answer is *prayerlessness*—first on the part of the two men, and secondly on the part of their fellow Christians. When the believers in the church first realized that Hymenaeus and Alexander were teaching error, perhaps they tackled the problem in the wrong way. Perhaps they argued with these men, or perhaps they merely shrugged their shoulders and treated them with coldness. I Timothy 2:1 certainly seems to imply that the spiritually minded believers in the church were not praying as they should: *"I exhort therefore, that, first of all, supplications, prayers, intercessions, and giving of thanks, be made for all men."* Could it be that the church had not prayed for Hymenaeus and Alexander as they should have? If Christians had brought these men to God in fervent, intercessory prayer, it is possible that they would not have fallen, or "made shipwreck" of their faith.

I do not know the eternal fate of Hymenaeus and Alexander, perhaps they were destroyed physically but saved in the end. But of this I am sure: *Many sad things could be nipped in the bud if the spiritually minded would spend more time in earnest prayer!*

EXHORTATIONS CONCERNING PRAYER AND WOMEN

1. I exhort therefore, that, first of all, supplications, prayers, intercessions, and giving of thanks, be made for all men;

2. For kings, and for all that are in authority; that we may lead a quiet and peaceable life in all godliness and honesty.

3. For this is good and acceptable in the sight of God our Saviour;

4. Who will have all men to be saved, and to come unto the knowledge of the truth.

5. For there is one God, and one mediator between God and men, the man Christ Jesus;

6. Who gave himself a ransom for all, to be testified in due time.

7. Whereunto I am ordained a preacher, and an apostle, (I speak the truth in Christ, and lie not;) a teacher of the Gentiles in faith and verity.

8. I will therefore that men pray every where, lifting up holy hands, without wrath and doubting.

9. In like manner also, that women adorn themselves in modest apparel, with shamefacedness and sobriety; not with broided hair, or gold, or pearls, or costly array;

10. But (which becometh women professing godliness) with good works.

11. Let the woman learn in silence with all subjection.

12. But I suffer not a woman to teach, nor to usurp authority over the man, but to be in silence.

13. For Adam was first formed, then Eve.

14. And Adam was not deceived, but the woman being deceived was in the transgression.

15. Notwithstanding she shall be saved in childbearing, if they continue in faith and charity and holiness with sobriety.

Concerning Prayer

Paul practiced what he preached: *"Pray without ceasing"* (I Thess. 5:17). Over and over again he touches on the subject of prayer. He delights to mention the sacrificial use of the ministry of prayer in the case of many of his helpers in the church. In Colossians 4:12

he mentions Epaphras: ". . . always labouring fervently (agonizing) for you in prayers." Paul frequently tells us of his own habit of intercessory prayer; and on occasion he includes in his letters some of the very petitions that he had offered on behalf of his friends, fellow laborers, and his children in the faith. We find some of his actual prayers recorded in Ephesians 1:15 ff and 3:14 ff. It will be a blessing to any believer to read these prayers over and over again.

There are some who excuse themselves from consistent praying in a specific place, at a specific time. They say, "I have a roommate . . . I live with those who do not believe in consistent prayer." Or, "I work with a group who would make fun of me should they see me praying." Let me remind you, fellow believer, *this man Paul was chained to a Roman soldier*—but that fact did not interfere with his prayer time. He prayed—regardless of where he was or who he was with.

At the beginning of chapter two, Paul wants Timothy to grasp the meaning of how great a part prayer plays in successful ministry. There will never be a great church unless there is a great leader in that church who can reach heaven in prayer. Revivals come without preaching—but never without prayer. Prayer is the key that unlocks God's great, eternal storehouse. Prayer brings power and victory. Regardless of how well-trained a minister may be, he will never be successful in the spiritual realm unless he can reach heaven in fervent, consistent, intercessory prayer. Verses 3 through 8 deal primarily with the business of a preacher and teacher.

Verse 1: "I exhort therefore, that, first of all, supplications, prayers, intercessions, and giving of thanks, be made for all men."

This second chapter opens with the words, "I exhort

therefore . . ." thus pointing back to the final verses of chapter one. Because of what he had said about the people he has mentioned, he proceeds at once to urge the necessity of prayer. In this verse, our responsibility in national life is clearly set forth. There is no doubt that through the mighty ministry of prayer, believers can strengthen and sweeten the life of the nation in which we live. I wonder how long it has been since devout Christians fell upon their knees in prayer closets and prayed fervently, agonizing to God in prayer, on behalf of our nation in this crucial time. We are to pray "for all men."

Verse 2: "For kings, and for all that are in authority; that we may lead a quiet and peaceable life in all godliness and honesty."

In this verse, two things are pointed out:

(1) We are to pray that the leaders of our nation may be led in the right path: pray *"for kings, and for all that are in authority."* I know there are many wicked men in places of authority, but there are also God-fearing men; and if we would pray as we should for the men who fear God, we could help them tremendously—and it is neither unscriptural nor un-Christian to pray for God to remove those who refuse to hear His voice and obey His directions.

Paul prayed, *"I would they were even cut off which trouble you"* (Gal. 5:12). I am aware of the fact that this pertains primarily to false teachers in religion; but if we have men in places of authority who are attempting to sell this country to the enemy, then it is perfectly in order for us to pray for God to save them—and *if they will not be saved* it is perfectly scriptural to pray for God to cut them off. God gave this great nation to us; and as believers with hearts filled with thanksgiving, we should pray for God to preserve our nation at any cost.

(2) We are to pray that our lives may be lived as

God would have us live daily: *". . . That we may lead a quiet and peaceable life in all godliness and honesty."* Paul is not necessarily speaking of the individual here, but of national well-being. Each individual should lead a quiet, peaceable, godly life, to be sure; but Paul is begging *all people* to lead such a life.

The Greek word for "quiet" here denotes tranquility from *without*—no disturbance from outward circumstances and conditions. Live in such a way that from the outside there will be a sense of quietness and tranquility—and how this nation needs those qualities today!

". . . Peaceable"—the Greek here denotes tranquility *within*. A believer automatically has peace with God (Rom. 5:1), and insofar as possible we should live peaceably with all men (Rom. 12:18). We should enjoy the peace of God—quietness that only Christianity can provide—and we should demonstrate that peace and quietness "in all godliness and honesty."

Verse 3: "For this is good and acceptable in the sight of God our Saviour."

God wants individual believers to so live that they daily give visible expression of a Christian frame of mind within. The behaviour of a believer should display righteousness and holiness. Such living is right in the sight of God—on the part of individual and nation. God does not count great victories in conquest, great industry, great discoveries, great wealth, great achievements in science and outer space as *first* in His program, although I believe He is interested in our advances in these things. *"No good thing will He withhold from them that walk uprightly"*; and if we seek first the kingdom of God and His righteousness, all these things shall be added. The lesson that our country so desperately needs to learn is that "RIGHTEOUSNESS EXALTETH

A NATION" (Prov. 14:34).

There has never been a time in the history of our country when we so needed to read, re-read, and *believe* this verse from God's holy Word. Many are bemoaning the increase in moral delinquency; crime is sweeping across our country, and sin is rampant. This great nation is fast becoming a Sodom with its lust, drunkenness, and open sin. God's true ministers are disturbed; and many political leaders are disturbed. The liberals are crying, "Peace, peace," when there is no peace. Those who are willing to face facts know that "whatsoever a man (or a nation) soweth, that shall he also reap" (Gal. 6:7). If we sow to the wind, we shall reap a whirlwind; and if we sow to the flesh, we shall reap corruption. Many men in places of authority face this, while others close their eyes and by their actions declare that things will work themselves out if we will just leave them alone—but this is not true.

Where is the limit for the religious dilemma we are in, with the prevailing racial unrest, the scholastic and educational turmoil? Have we gone too far? Can this nation be saved? The answer lies in great revival—old-time religion that will put the family altar back in the home and remove the cocktail shaker and the card table. We need to put the Word of God back in our churches and take out the book reports and current events; put God-fearing, Spirit-filled ministers back in the pulpits, instead of machine-made, denominationally-manufactured religious puppets who are motivated by denominational leaders. If we could have an old-fashioned revival brought down from heaven through intercessory prayer, and see revival fires burn through the preaching of the Word of God, much of the unrest, turmoil, strife, and moral decay in our nation would clear up overnight; but education and money will not do it.

We must remember that "righteousness exalteth a

nation." We must train up our children in the way they should go. We must seek God first—and until we as individuals and a nation *"find ourselves,"* things will get no better. Conditions will gradually worsen until the trumpet sounds and true believers are caught up in the clouds to meet the Lord in the air—and then all hell will break out here on earth!

Verse 4: "Who will have all men to be saved, and to come unto the knowledge of the truth."

I wish our hyper-Calvinist friends would use this text occasionally when they preach long and loud that there are those who cannot be saved because they are not elected or chosen. I believe in Bible election; I believe the Church *as a body* was chosen before the foundation of the world; I believe that every born again child of God is predestined to be conformed to the image of God's dear Son—but I do not believe that some are elected to be damned, while others are elected to be saved.

Verse 3 closed with the words, "God our Saviour," and verse 4 opens with "WHO . . ." referring back to God our Saviour. John 3:16 settles it: "God so loved the WORLD . . . ." If you are in the world, God loves you and Jesus died to save you. John, under inspiration, said, "Not for our sins only, but for the sins of the whole world" (I John 2:1,2). Therefore, it is not God's will that any perish, but that all come to repentance. In verses 3 and 4 we have the message of the Gospel—the Gospel of God our Saviour, who will have all men to be saved and come to the knowledge of the truth.

This, then, is the inspired proclamation to be sounded out by Timothy—and all of God's preachers. In these words we have the proclamation of the scope of the Gospel—the divine purpose of God, the divine plan and provision of God our Saviour. There has never been—nor ever will be—one person whom God does not love and want saved. If you who read these lines drop into hell at the end of life's journey, it will not be God's fault . . . it will be because of your own stubborn will and your rejection of Jesus Christ. God has done all He can do to keep you from going to hell. In the words of the parable in Isaiah 5:1–4, "What could have been done more . . . ?" He gave the best heaven had, and literally turned His head while Jesus died on the cross to pay the sin-debt. God smote Him, that we might be set free from the bondage of sin and death.

God's invitation today is the same as it was in Isaiah's day: *"Come now, and let us reason together, saith the Lord: though your sins be as scarlet, they shall be as white as snow; though they be red like crimson, they shall be as wool.* If ye be willing and obedient, ye shall eat the good of the land: but if ye refuse and rebel, ye shall be devoured with the sword: for the mouth of the Lord hath spoken it" (Isa. 1:18–20).

God's will is clearly stated here concerning all sinners. It is God's will to save every sinner; it is God's will that you spend eternity in heaven—but the will of man determines his own destiny. *God so loved* that He gave Jesus, His only begotten Son. *Jesus so loved* that He left the Father's bosom, came to earth's sorrows in flesh, and satisfied the holiness of God, in order that God could be just and yet justify the ungodly through the shed blood of Jesus. Friend, if you miss heaven it will be because of your refusal to believe on the Lord Jesus Christ. God created man in His own image—free to think and to will—and if God *forced* the will of man, then man would be a *machine*, not a man.

The only reason any soul has ever dropped into hell is stated in the words of Jesus: ". . . YE WILL NOT COME TO ME, THAT YE MIGHT HAVE LIFE" (John

5:40). Yes, in spite of God's love—in spite of all of His pleadings, in spite of His mercy, in spite of His longsuffering—the stubborn, sinful will of man persists in rejecting the love of God; persists in refusing to submit to God's will and surrender to Jesus; persists in rejecting the wonderful gift of God—eternal life through Jesus Christ our Lord. *"How shall we escape, if we neglect so great salvation?"* (Heb. 2:3). All one need do to miss heaven and burn in hell is reject the finished work of the Lord Jesus Christ.

Jesus sat looking out over Jerusalem, His beloved city, and cried, "O Jerusalem, Jerusalem, thou that killest the prophets, and stonest them which are sent unto thee, how often would I have gathered thy children together, even as a hen gathereth her chickens under her wings, *and ye would not!*" (Matt. 23:37). "AND YE WOULD NOT!" That settles it. That answers the question as to why men go to hell! God has done all He can do. The message of God's preacher—whether Timothy or the minister today—is that *God so loved the world* . . . all are included, not one is excluded. God our Saviour is not willing that any perish, but that all men be saved, that all men come unto the knowledge of the truth. Jesus said, "Ye shall know the truth, and the truth shall make you free" (John 8:32).

Verse 5: "For there is one God, and one mediator between God and men, the man Christ Jesus."

In this verse we have the method of God's dealing through the Gospel. "There is ONE GOD"—most religions agree on that part of the verse, but fail to agree on the remainder of it: ". . . One Mediator between God and men." In some religions there are many mediators—they do not depend upon the ONE Mediator. The last part of the verse names that Mediator: *"The Man, Christ Jesus."* Some religions mediate through a woman—but you may

81

rest assured that no man will ever stand before God and hear Him say, "Well done," unless that person comes to God by and through the Lord Jesus Christ—*the MAN*, Christ Jesus—not the woman, the virgin.

The reason Jesus is the one Mediator between the one God and man is that He "gave Himself a ransom for all, to be testified in due time." Jesus said, "Upon this rock I will build my church (the rock being Himself, not Peter); and the gates of hell shall not prevail against it" (Matt. 16:18).

Since its birth, the Church has faced false teachers and false teaching. In Timothy's day, false teachers were increasing in number; and of course today new religions, cults, and "isms" are springing up almost daily with varied and sundry teachings, doctrines, dogmas . . . men who profess to be God's representatives on earth, and even women who profess to be anointed of God in this hour. Gnosticism was the leading cult in Timothy's time, and it was growing rapidly. The Gnostics taught the necessity of many intermediaries and refused to accept Jesus as the ONE Mediator.

How grand an answer is verse 5 to Job's perplexity in Job 9:33: *"Neither is there any daysman betwixt us, that might lay his hand upon us both."* The figure set forth here is that of the man who, to reconcile an argument, stands between two men who have had a disagreement. The fact is that God has wonderfully provided for us a DIVINE DAYSMAN to stand between poor sinful man and the holy God. Jesus is our divine Daysman, and in His twofold nature (God in flesh) He is in a position to "lay His hand upon us both." He is the hand of *deity*—because He is God. He is the hand of *humanity* because He was "the man, Christ Jesus." And as Jesus lays His hands upon us—the hand of divinity and the hand of humanity—both hands bear the scars that were inflicted when He

82

paid the tremendous cost of our redemption. The scars in His hands are the seal of the mediation between sinful man and Jehovah God, perfected through the death of Jesus—the price of our ransom demanded by God's holiness, God's righteousness, *paid for* by God's love, *provided for all* and presented *on behalf* of all—WHETHER THEY TAKE ADVANTAGE OF IT OR NOT!

God was in Christ reconciling the world unto Himself (II Cor. 5:19). In the Garden, God gave Adam a command—that he might eat freely of all the fruit except that of the tree of the knowledge of good and evil. Adam sinned; communion between Adam and God was broken, and war was declared. God was offended; Adam was the offender—but Jesus (the second Adam) was God (the offended) in flesh, that offended Him. So in Jesus we have the offended and the offender in one. There is one God; there is one Mediator (and *only* one) between God and men. The only possible way any man can ever stand before God and hear Him say, "Well done," is to stand before God's holiness *in Christ Jesus*. In HIM we have salvation; in HIM we are holy and righteous, and apart from Him we are hopelessly lost.

God saved us "for Christ's sake" (Eph. 4:32), and it is *only* for Christ's sake that God forgives our sins. By way of sacrificial atonement, salvation is made possible for you and for me, although we deserve eternal hell. Sacrificial atonement is the only method announced by the Gospel concerning salvation, and *apart from sacrificial atonement there IS no salvation*. "Without shedding of blood is no remission" (Heb. 9:22). God pity us in this day of self-confidence, self-righteousness, self-reliance, religious practices, and good living—when men are seeking to save themselves by other methods than through the preaching and believing of THE Gospel. God help us to cry out against "another gospel, which is not another" (Gal. 1:6,7). God help us to warn people that the devil is the master deceiver, and he as joyfully sends people to hell from the church pew as from bars and from the street of forgotten men! God help all "Timothys" in this day to cry aloud the message that there is *"none other name under heaven given among men, WHEREBY WE MUST BE SAVED"* (Acts 4:12). Jesus said, "NO MAN COMETH UNTO THE FATHER, BUT BY ME" (John 14:6). "HE THAT ENTERETH NOT BY THE DOOR INTO THE SHEEPFOLD, BUT CLIMBETH UP SOME OTHER WAY, THE SAME IS A THIEF AND A ROBBER" (John 10:1). God help us that we may pray without ceasing and preach untiringly, that the multitude of religious people may "come unto the knowledge of the truth."

Before leaving these verses, let me again emphasize the Bible truth that there is ONE Mediator between God and men—*THE MAN, Christ Jesus*—not the pastor, not the evangelist, not the bishop, not the pope, not the priest, not the virgin. God Almighty *names* that one Mediator, in order that there be no mistake—*"the man, Christ Jesus"*— and if you ever stand before God to hear Him say, "Well done," it will be because Jesus is your Saviour, Mediator, and Confessor before God the Father (Matt. 10:32).

Verse 6: "Who gave Himself a ransom for all, to be testified in due time."

This verse clearly states that Christ Jesus *"gave Himself a ransom for ALL."* Paul points out to Timothy that the ransom has been paid for one and all; and thus it is not God's will that any perish, but that all come to repentance. Jesus willingly laid His life down (John 10:18). He came not to be ministered unto, but to minister and to give His life a ransom for many; therefore, *"Thou art inexcusable, O man"* (Rom. 2:1). The ransom has been paid; salvation is for all, and there is no excuse for any person dying without Christ and burning in

84

hell forever. Satan "kidnapped" the human race through the disobedience of the first Adam; but the second Adam, Jesus Christ, paid the ransom in full, willingly—that we who had been "kidnapped" by sin might go free by faith in His finished work.

In Genesis 3:15 God promised the seed of the woman, who would crush (or bruise) the head of the serpent—the devil. In Galatians 4:4,5 Paul tells us, ". . . When the fulness of the time was come, God sent forth His Son, made of a woman, made under the law, to redeem them that were under the law . . . ." Therefore, Jesus came into the world at the time appointed by Jehovah God. It was all settled before God made the universe or anything therein (I Pet. 1:18–23).

God has a program, a blueprint; and He has duly appointed times and seasons for all things pertaining to His economy, even unto the ages of ages. And according to God's duly appointed times, ". . . Christ died for the ungodly" (Rom. 5:6). The death, burial, and resurrection of Jesus "according to the Scriptures," the truth of the gift of God, the ransom paid, is *the Gospel of the grace of God* which is to be testified or proclaimed in due time, according to God's eternal program.

In Acts 1:4 Jesus told the disciples, *"But wait. . . ."* In Luke 24:49 He said, *"But tarry . . . ."* I am sure the disciples thought they were well equipped to carry out the preaching of the Gospel and herald forth the Gospel message. They had knowledge; they had zeal; they had great joy (Luke 24:52), and they must have been anxious to get into their ministry. Why then should the Master Teacher say, "But wait . . . but tarry"? The answer is clearly stated in the passages just mentioned: ". . . *Until ye be endued with power from on high.*" The disciples had not yet received the supreme, indispensable gift to empower them for the ministry that lay ahead—the infilling of the Holy Spirit. But "when the day of Pentecost was fully come"—the one particular day which God had fore-ordained and duly appointed in His calendar of divine events as having to do with the forming of the Church—then the wait was over: The Spirit came (Acts 2:1 ff). And when they were all filled with the Holy Ghost, they "began to speak as the Spirit gave them utterance." Peter preached a sermon which requires only about five minutes to read—and three thousand souls were saved! Peter had more converts from one sermon than most of us have in a lifetime.

Verse 7: "Whereunto I am ordained a preacher, and an apostle, (I speak the truth in Christ, and lie not;) a teacher of the Gentiles in faith and verity."

"To be testified in due time . . . whereunto I am ordained a preacher . . . ." Paul could say, "I KNOW." He was a positive Christian. He did not live on suppositions—he lived and grew on spiritual positives. In this verse he testifies that he was ordained "a preacher and an apostle," and assures us that the Holy Ghost knows he is telling the truth: *"I speak the truth in Christ, and lie not."* In the same verse he testifies that he is a teacher of the Gentiles "in faith and verity." Paul had a singular message: the cross, the finished work, the blood, and grace—inseparable. He preached Christ—crucified, buried, and risen "according to the Scriptures"; and he clearly commanded the Galatian believers, "If any come preaching any other Gospel . . . let him be accursed" (Gal. 1:8).

Verse 8: "I will therefore that men pray every where, lifting up holy hands, without wrath and doubting."

Notice again that in verse 1 Paul exhorts believers to pray for *all*—kings, rulers, those in authority—*everyone*; and now in verse 8 he admonishes men to *"pray everywhere."* The ministry of supplication is universal—we are to pray for all peoples—rulers, leaders, the mighty, the weak. We are to pray for Christians, and for unbelievers to be converted. We are to pray everywhere, under any and all circumstances.

Notice the words Paul uses in verse 1: ". . . Supplications . . . prayers . . . intercessions . . . and thanks." Paul was one of the best educated men of his day. He sat at the feet of the great Gamaliel; he was a Pharisee of the Pharisees—but he never used words loosely. He spoke under inspiration, and the words were not penned down just to fill up space. Paul could have said, "Prayers," and omitted "supplications, intercessions, and thanks." There must be a reason why he used all four terms. I wonder if we would be far wrong to say that *supplications* are prayers of particular import, while *prayers* are prayers of general import. *Intercession* is prayer of a much wider import, and *thanksgiving* is prayer that renders praise or grateful import. To the Thessalonians Paul said, *"In everything give thanks*; for this is the will of God in Christ Jesus concerning you" (I Thess. 5:18).

Paul points out the importance of prayer—not only prayer in general, but that we should pray specifically, with appointed times and places of prayer. We should pray always, everywhere, for all people. Notice that *in verse 1* we are to pray for "all men"; *in verse 4* we are to pray for "all men"; and *in verse 8* Paul points out that men—not just a select or peculiar group, but ALL men, saved men, should pray—*everywhere*. The Bible fact pointed out here is that in the Church it is not a few special men, but Christians in general who are to pray wherever they may be found geographically.

Jesus said, "Where two or three are gathered together in my name, there will I be in the midst of them." One individual can meet God in prayer anywhere, any

87

time of the day—and find God's ear attuned to the cry of His people.

I do not deny the fact that there are those who are "specialists" in prayer. The medical field has doctors who are specialists and those who are general practitioners. The same may be said of the Church: *there are those who have the gift of intercessory prayer*—but ALL men are invited to come to God and make their requests known through our Mediator, the Lord Jesus Christ.

The last part of verse 8 instructs us that we are to pray, *"lifting up holy hands, without wrath and doubting."* If we do not live holy lives in the Lord Jesus, we need not expect God to hear our prayers. If I regard iniquity in my heart, the Lord will not hear me when I pray. If I pray to consume it upon my own lust, God will not hear me. If I pray selfishly, God will not hear me; so my hands must be holy, my motive must be pure and to the glory of God. I must not regard or hold wrath in my heart—*and I must not doubt.*

James tells us, "If any of you lack wisdom, let him ask of God, that giveth to all men liberally, and upbraideth not; and it shall be given him. But let him ask in faith, nothing wavering. For he that wavereth is like a wave of the sea, driven with the wind and tossed" (James 1:5,6). The man who wavers or doubts need not expect to receive anything from the Lord.

In the Church, *all men* are invited to pray—*for* all men, under all circumstances, in all places—but with holy hands, a life free from wrath, and a heart free from unbelief. Jesus promised, "If ye abide in me, and my words abide in you, ye shall ask what ye will, and it shall be done unto you" (John 15:7). If we are consecrated, dedicated, Spirit-filled, we can make our requests known unto God, and He will give us the desires of our heart. No good thing will He withhold from them who walk uprightly.

It was a Jewish habit, when praying, to hold the palms of the hands upward, as if to receive an answer (compare I Kings 8:22). If we are truly born again, and if we are praying in the Spirit, we should hold our hands up by faith to God, *expecting* an answer; because if we are God's child in need, God is more anxious to supply that need than we are to have it supplied. Therefore, we should pray with full assurance that God will grant unto us our every need—to our good and to His glory.

We might use the following summary of conditions to be met in order that our prayers may be answered:

1. No sin
2. No quarrel
3. No doubt

The Divine Standard for Women

Verse 9: "In like manner also, that women adorn themselves in modest apparel, with shamefacedness and sobriety; not with broided hair, or gold, or pearls, or costly array."

Verse 9 begins, "In like manner also . . . *women*." Up to now, Paul has been dealing with the men; but at this point he turns his instruction toward the women. He instructs Christian ladies to adorn themselves in "modest apparel"—they are to dress in a way that is becoming to a Christian, not copying the gaudy and sinful styles of the world.

Christianity puts *the right kind of pride in a woman's heart* . . . a Christian woman should be neat, clean, and presentable—for Christ's sake. It is not a good testimony for a lady to dress shabbily or carelessly if she is financially able to dress better. She should dress her hair as becomes a Christian—she should not copy movie stars who have been married a half-dozen times; she should look nice but natural, and above all she should dress *as becomes a Christian*.

Christian ladies should not wear clothes which are suggestive and will stir the animal nature of men. When a woman wears garments for the specific purpose of attracting men, that woman is not adorning herself in "modest apparel," as becomes a Christian. It is a sin for women to dress in such a way as to create lust in the minds of the opposite sex. Christian ladies should be Christian in all that they do. The warning here is against immodesty and extravagance. It is a sin for a believing woman to be extravagant or extreme concerning her hair, her face, the jewelry she wears, or costly array—garments that cost beyond reason. It is a sin to spend hundreds of dollars for clothes in an attempt to stay ahead of some other woman in the church or community, when the money could be used to send the Gospel to those who have never heard. Ladies should look nice, be neat and clean . . . look as attractive for Jesus' sake as the world attempts to be suggestive for lust's sake. I repeat, be natural—do not try to make yourself look like what you are not.

The outline for Christian dress and outward appearance is threefold:

(1) Modest apparel:

It appears that this includes more than clothing or manner of dress—but also stands for deportment and demeanor as well.

(2) Shamefacedness:

Greek scholars tell us that this is a poor translation. One rendering of the word is *"shamefastness,"* meaning "made fast by an honorable shame." In other words, do not allow anything to happen because of you that would embarrass a proper sense of shame.

(3) Sobriety:

A believing woman should not have anything to do with strong or intoxicating drink—but the word here goes deeper than that, and points out that a believing woman is to be sober-minded. She is at all times to keep a well-balanced state of mind and think soberly about all things.

There are some exceptions, no doubt, but *most men* have more respect for a lady who is her natural self than for one who is made up to the extent that she is definitely artificial.   Natural beauty goes far beyond the beauty of cosmetics or man-made "gimmicks." If we would be ourselves as believers, God would bless us to a greater extent; and other Christians—as well as sinners—would respect us more.

Not only did *Paul* have trouble with the ladies in the church, but Peter had the same trouble, for in I Peter 3:3,4 we read: ". . . Whose adorning let it not be that outward adorning of plaiting the hair, and of wearing of gold, or of putting on of apparel; but let it be the hidden man of the heart, in that which is not corruptible, even the ornament of a meek and quiet spirit, which is in the sight of God of great price."

Verse 10:   "But (which becometh women professing godliness) with good works."

Such a spirit will manifest itself in "good works," which automatically follow a woman "professing godliness."   True profession of genuine conversion is not just idle words, but *words will be matched with works.* James tells us "Faith without works is dead"; and in Ephesians 2:10 Paul tells us, ". . . We are His workmanship, created in Christ Jesus unto good works." Faith does not become ours by works—but *good works testify that we have exercised saving faith.* Faith that produces no works is dead faith—and dead faith cannot save.

The attractiveness and drawing power of the charm demonstrated through good works and sane living on the part of the woman who professes godliness, is seen in I Peter 3:1: "Likewise, ye wives, be in subjection to your own husbands; that, if any obey not the Word (about the Saviour) they also may without the word (your testimony) be won by the conversation (life) of the wives." What this verse is saying is simply this: "Wife, it is not *what you say* to your husband that will win him to Christ—but *how you act.* It is not what you profess to be—but proof that you possess what you profess. Not just what you believe, but the way you behave—your good works and godly living—will cause your husband to come to Jesus."

I am sure that some of you who read these lines are believing wives who are concerned about your unbelieving husband. Perhaps he often conducts himself in such manner as to make it almost impossible for you to stay sweet and manifest godliness in your actions toward him; but let me assure you that if you love your husband and want him saved, you can win him to Jesus by displaying godliness, purity, chastity, and devotion to God and to your family and home in all that you do. Through good works you can prove what you profess to believe. You can behave in such a way that your husband cannot accuse you of "saying" but not "doing." And eventually, through your consecrated living, you can win him to Christ.

Verse 11: "Let the woman learn in silence with all subjection."

Verses 11 through 14 of this chapter are given over to women's relationship to the church. I have said many times—in pulpits of churches, in city auditoriums, and in our big Gospel tent—that if it were not for the godly ladies in some churches, those churches would be forced to close their doors. Were it not for godly mothers, thousands of children would never attend Sunday school, and thousands of husbands would spend Sunday morning lounging in bed.

I proffer my deep respect to Christian ladies—here and now! I have high regard for a Christian woman—and if it were not for godly women there would be no Gospel Hour, because it is primarily the ladies who write to us and contribute at least seventy-five percent of all contributions which keep the Gospel Hour broadcast on the radio from coast to coast. So ladies, please do not misunderstand me.

However—some ladies (like some of the men) have been a hindrance and nuisance to the church. In Philippi, for example, were two ladies (Euodias and Syntyche) who were at cross purposes with each other, causing much trouble in the church (Phil. 4:2). They threatened to disrupt the whole company of believers at Philippi and split the church. Paul begged them to settle their differences and "be of the same mind in the Lord."

On the other hand, in the same community was a very precious lady—a lovely soul—whose name was Lydia (Acts 16:14,15, and 40). We will never know the good that Lydia accomplished in her own quiet way. Paul wanted Timothy, who was to be God's undershepherd in Ephesus, to know how to handle the female side of the church.

Certainly church membership is one of the vital matters in the life of any believer. When we are born again we are not to forsake "the assembling of ourselves together" (Heb. 10:25). You can become a Christian without uniting with the local assembly; but you cannot be as *effective* a Christian, you cannot be what you should be and what God wants you to be, by isolating yourself from the fellowship of the visible assembly.

The Church of the living God is the body of Christ, made up of individual born again believers (I Cor. 12: 12,13); but we are to assemble in the *local* church and fellowship there, bearing one another's burdens and praying for one another. It is right to join the local assembly; and if you do not, you will not grow spiritually as you would if you united with a fundamental, Bible-preaching church.

Our present verses clearly outline the terms concerning women and the church. The principles of a woman believer's attitude are laid down, both in relation TO the local church, and worship IN the local assembly. I know there are those who will not agree with the next paragraph of this study; but before you condemn me, search the Scriptures, and ask yourself if we have a right to interpret this clear passage to fit the times in which we live—or *must we let God's settled Word be?* Does God change His mind to fit the times and seasons of this civilization? We know that He does not.

What about the woman and public worship service? What about her place in public assembly? Paul's admonition here has nothing to do with the woman in private worship nor in the privacy of her home; he is speaking of public worship in the local church: *"Let the woman learn in silence, with all subjection."* A born again believer—man or woman—should always be a student, desiring the sincere milk of the Word, that he may grow thereby (I Pet. 2:2); and then studying to be approved unto God, to become a workman that has no need to be ashamed (II Tim. 2:15). We obey the Lord's invitation: "Come unto me, all ye that labour and are heavy laden, and I will give you rest. . . . Him that cometh unto me, I

94

will in no wise cast out'' (Matt. 11:28,29; John 6:37). The moment we come unto Him, that same moment we should enter into God's great classroom and become a learner who may grow, become strong, and be fruitful. The woman is not to assume that she has every right the man has to speak or hold office in the local assembly or in public worship. The woman has no right to think that she can fill the office of discipleship, or become a bishop, deaconess or pastor. There is not one word in God's holy Bible to suggest that any woman has scriptural grounds for becoming a leader in public assembly.

No woman has a right to stand up in public assembly and argue with the pastor, the deacons, or those who are in the seat of authority. The believing woman is to place herself in subjection, listen in silence—and any remarks she may wish to make should be made in the privacy of the home after the service is over. She is to discuss these things with her husband—not stand in public assembly and argue with the pastor or the leaders of the church. According to the teaching of the Apostle to the Gentiles, the dear believing woman is to enter the school of silence and subjection, as having to do with public assembly in the house of God.

Verse 12: ''But I suffer not a woman to teach, nor to usurp authority over the man, but to be in silence.''

This verse is plain: For a woman to teach men in public assembly is definitely forbidden by God. Teaching in assembly is man's God-given position; it was never given to any woman. In I Corinthians 14:34,35 Paul says, ''Let your women keep silence in the churches: for it is not permitted unto them to speak; but they are commanded to be under obedience, as also saith the law. And if they will learn any thing, let them ask their husbands at home: for it is a shame for women to speak in the church.''

Some people suggest that the Greek word translated "speak" means "chatter," and that Paul is forbidding women to chatter in church, or continually fuss or speak in the assembly. But certainly we have no right to point out the women and make a special requirement of them, when the men are just as bad to chatter. It is a sin for either man or woman to stand up and chatter—or argue—in public assembly. But even though the Greek word can be translated "chatter," that is not the meaning here at all.

In I Peter 4:11 we have the same Greek word, and it is there translated "If any man *speak* . . ."—simply meaning to make an address or deliver a sermon. Therefore, the Greek word used by both Paul and Peter simply means that a woman is not to "speak"—or "teach"—in the public assembly where there are men.

Please read on: I will have some things to say at the close of this discussion which may change the minds of some precious believing ladies who do not agree with what I have said up to now! I cannot change the Word of Holy Writ: "But I (Paul) suffer not a woman to teach nor to usurp authority over the man, but to be in silence." That is God's Word, and I cannot do anything about it. It was dictated by the Holy Ghost, penned down by the Apostle Paul—and *we must believe it.*

Someone may ask, "WHY should the woman be silent and in subjection to the man in public assembly?" The answer is clearly set forth in the following verses:

Verses 13 and 14: "For Adam was first formed, then Eve. And Adam was not deceived, but the woman being deceived was in the transgression."

God created Adam from the dust of the ground, breathed into his nostrils the breath of life, and he became a living soul. Eve was created from a rib removed from Adam's side—she was taken out of man; man was not taken out

96

of woman. She was made for the second place; she is the weaker vessel. We have the clear, understandable statement, "And Adam was not deceived, but the woman, being deceived, was in the transgression." Adam was created first; Eve was created second—but Eve *sinned* first, and Adam sinned second, not being deceived directly through Satan, but led to commit sin indirectly through Eve. Satan did not approach Adam as he did Eve; he approached Adam *through* Eve; therefore, the temptation of Adam was indirect. Satan directed his words to Eve; she listened—*and transgressed*. The man was first in creation; the woman was first in transgression.

In public worship in the assembly of the local church, God's direction as dictated by the Holy Ghost to the Apostle Paul, is this: That MEN should lead in prayer and speak in the local assembly (verse 8), and that WOMEN should adorn the doctrine in silence (verse 9). Let me say some things that should encourage you ladies—and WILL encourage you if you have the right spirit: Believing women played a very important part in the early church. The record laid down in the New Testament concerning the infant church in Jerusalem and surrounding territory sets forth a beautiful picture of believing women and their stewardship.

To begin with, God placed upon woman the greatest honor He has placed upon any mortal: *the Virgin Mary was the mother of the only begotten Son of God*. Man had no part in His birth; God chose a virgin to bring His Son into the world. We read of Joanna and Susanna, who "ministered unto Him of their substance" (Luke 8:3). We read of Mary Magdalene with her love and devotion (John 20:11–16); and who could overlook Mary and Martha, the two dear sisters who were friends of Jesus. He loved to visit in their home (Luke 10:38,39; John 11:5). Consider Mary, the mother of John Mark, who permitted the apostles and believers to conduct prayer meeting in her house (Acts 12:12). We read of Philip's four daughters who prophesied—in private, not in the open assembly on Sunday, or in revival (Acts 21:9). And there was that noble soul, Lydia, Paul's first convert in Europe. Paul met with the ladies in their Sabbath Bible class out beside the river (Acts 16:13)—not downtown in the local assembly nor in the sanctuary, but on the riverbank. Paul "spake unto the women which resorted thither"; and his subject was the death, burial, and resurrection of Jesus, "according to the Scripture." As he preached Christ crucified, buried, and risen again, the Lord touched Lydia's heart; she was born again, was baptized, and then she opened her home to God's servants (Acts 16:14,15).

In Acts 9:36—43 we read of Tabitha ("which by interpretation is called Dorcas"), who was the founder of the Dorcas meetings. These dear ladies met and talked about the Lord Jesus and made garments. In Romans 16:1,2 we read of Phebe, servant of the church. We can bring this a little nearer home, for most of us can look back and thank God for a mother who prayed for us. My mother tenderly prayed for me—and wept bitter tears night after night until I was finally saved.

To the list of noble ladies I would like to add my sister—the one who came to my bedside and prayed. She said little in public, and she did not have much to say to *me* in public—but regardless of the hour of the night in which I might drag into my bedroom—sober or drunk— my sister (who was and still is unmarried) came to my bedside and prayed. She agonized in prayer that God would save her poor, lost brother, lest he drop into the pits of the damned. Many nights I would lie in bed, smoke cigarettes, and blow the smoke in her face as she prayed— but she did not stop praying. This noble sister—dedicated soul, spirit, and body to God—kept coming to my bedside;

and one night as she prayed, she claimed my soul for Jesus . . . she pleaded the blood and claimed me in agony and bitter tears. Finally God broke my heart through the Gospel, and I was saved.

I would be the last person on earth to abuse a godly woman—but a truly believing woman has no desire to usurp authority over godly men in God's church. You can mark it down and believe it—when a woman wants to dictate to and dominate the men in the church, that woman is not right with God. God made woman tender, sweet, kind, and loving. God help every man to face this solemn Bible fact.

God had created everything *except* woman—but Adam found none to be his helpmate. He was lonely. God saw the lonely heart of Adam, and created Eve to make his life complete and more beautiful. We should have the highest respect for womanhood. She is God's tender creation . . . He made her to make this world a sweeter place in which to live. A brawling, hateful, backbiting woman, a chattering woman in church, a woman who wants to dictate and usurp authority over men, is certainly not what God intended her to be; but a dedicated, consecrated, Spirit-filled, believing woman is the sweetest creation this side the Pearly Gates.

There is nothing in the Bible against a believing woman teaching in Sunday school or in private Bible classes in the home, even though debarred from the pulpit. But she is not to usurp authority over the men. It is in perfect harmony with the Scriptures for women to instruct in the privacy of the home or in the Sunday school room. For instance:

"And (Apollos) began to speak boldly in the synagogue: whom when Aquila and Priscilla had heard, they took him unto them, and expounded unto him the way of

God more perfectly" (Acts 18:26). This dear couple could have stood up in the assembly and rebuked the speaker—but they did not. They invited him to their home, and in private instructed this fiery preacher—who had more zeal than knowledge—in the deeper things of God. He was a good man, an eloquent man; he was well educated; he was mighty in the Scriptures, so far as he went in the Word of God. He had enthusiasm, diligence, and courage—and Aquilla and Priscilla saw in this man a potential that needed to be harnessed for God. Therefore, they instructed him—but not in the public assembly of the church.

As far as he knew and had been instructed, Apollos was a great preacher and a great leader; but Aquila and Priscilla knew that he was not preaching all of the revealed doctrine of the church . . . "knowing only the baptism of John." John the Baptist said, "I indeed baptize you with water unto repentance: but He (Jesus) . . . shall baptize you with the Holy Ghost, and with fire" (Matt. 3:11).

It was the latter thing in which the teaching of Apollos was deficient. You see that "certain disciples" of his told Paul that they had not so much as heard of the baptism of the Spirit on the Day of Pentecost. Paul challenged them concerning their baptism and their belief, and they said, "We have not so much as heard whether there be any Holy Ghost" (Acts 19:1,2). Apollos had taught them many things, but he had not taught them the doctrine of the Holy Spirit, nor the relationship of the Holy Spirit to the believer in this dispensation of the Church. He himself had not known it; therefore, he could not preach it. Aquila was too humble and dedicated to make this a public issue; but instead, Apollos was invited into the privacy of the home—and the Bible does not say "he" (Aquila) talked to Apollos, but *"they"* talked to this fiery preacher concerning the lack of power in his sermons. They instructed him more fully in the way of God.

The believing woman has a perfect right to witness and win souls, to teach Sunday school and Bible classes, and to teach anywhere that she does not usurp authority over the man. But when it comes to matters of business in the church, God appointed men to take care of the affairs of the church, to pastor, to serve as deacons and stewards in the church, and as elders, bishops, and teachers insofar as men are concerned.

Verse 15: "Notwithstanding she shall be saved in childbearing, if they continue in faith and charity and holiness with sobriety."

There are varied and sundry interpretations of this verse of Scripture. I admit readily that it is a bit difficult. One explanation given is that the woman shall find her own salvation by bringing up her children in faith, love, and admonition in the things of God—that she will be saved as she instructs her children in the things of the Lord and as she brings them up in the nurture and admonition of the Lord.

But this will not suffice, because this definitely adds works to salvation, and in Ephesians 2:8,9 Paul declares that salvation is by grace, through faith—minus works. What I believe, and what outstanding Bible scholars through the ages have agreed upon, is this: In the original language the verse reads, "Notwithstanding she shall be saved in (THE) childbearing." That is, the woman was in THE transgression; she was deceived, and it was through her that Adam was tempted, and sin moved upon the whole human race. Woman was in THE transgression (verse 14); therefore, she shall be saved through THE childbearing— "the seed of the woman" spoken of by Almighty God in Genesis 3:15.

As I stated earlier, God honored woman as he has

never honored any man: She (the virgin) was chosen of God to bring His Son into the world. You know as well as I know that God could have delivered Jesus to this earth in any form or fashion He chose; but He chose woman. Therefore, I personally believe that the Scripture in this difficult verse is simply saying that even though verses 11 through 14 seem to condemn woman to a sad fate, she shall be saved—just like the man—through the seed of the woman—the incorruptible seed, the Word of God. "In the beginning was the Word, and the Word was with God, and the Word was God. The same was in the beginning with God. . . . And the Word was made flesh, and dwelt among us . . ." (John 1:1,2 and 14). "(We are) born again, not of corruptible seed, but of incorruptible, by the Word of God . . ." (I Pet. 1:23).

Outstanding Bible scholars also suggest that what Paul is saying here is that even though the preceding verses seem to condemn women to the fate of uselessness and insignificance, the believing woman has her chance in the children whom she bears and trains in the home. She not only takes care of the children physically and in temporal things, she also ministers to their spiritual welfare. She is the one who trains them in the things of the Lord. Even though a woman may not *be* the mother of children (physically speaking), she CAN be the mother of *spiritual* children. Paul refers to Timothy as "my own son in the faith." Therefore, the woman who is dedicated to Christ can win souls—in Sunday school, through child evangelism, and in many other ways.

Timothy became a great preacher, a great pastor, an outstanding spiritual leader; but listen: ". . . I call to remembrance the unfeigned faith that is in thee, *which dwelt first in thy grandmother Lois, and thy mother Eunice*; and I am persuaded that is in thee also" (II Tim. 1:5). Yes, the ladies do have a chance to become great soul winners and spiritual heroines in the church, even though they are not privileged to pastor nor to be the leaders in the church, usurping authority over the man, whom God created in His own image. They can be queen of the home, teacher of the children, and instruments in causing little ones to become spiritual giants for Jesus.

I am sure most godly women will agree that a mother can do much more with her children in the privacy of the home than the pastor can ever do from the pulpit; so do not feel badly that you are denied public preaching and pastoring, because you have one of the greatest and most powerful of all ministries—the ministry conducted in the privacy of your own home as your children gather around your knee.

Certainly Timothy owed much to believing women—his grandmother and his mother. In the church at Ephesus he would have many women believers; and Paul wanted him to handle them wisely, in Christian love, teaching them their position in the church, their opportunities in the church and in the home, as well as in the community. Paul did not want Timothy to allow the women to run the church or usurp authority, but neither did he want him to offend or hurt the ladies who were believers and true servants of God.

Let me close this chapter by saying with all sincerity that there is no preacher on earth who appreciates Christian women more than I do. I repeat what I said earlier: I thank God for a Christian mother, a Christian sister who claimed me for Jesus, and I shall never cease to praise God for the Christian woman who is my wife, and who has been a helpmate indeed to me for the past 24 years. No man has ever owed more to godly women than does this preacher; and if it were not for the godly, believing, dedicated ladies who listen to the Gospel Hour and send in their gifts to keep the broadcast on our many radio stations across America, there would be no Gospel Hour.

Ladies, more power to you as you fill your honored position in the home, in the community, and in the church!

I TIMOTHY –– CHAPTER THREE

QUALIFICATIONS OF ELDERS AND DEACONS

1. This is a true saying, If a man desire the office of a bishop, he desireth a good work.

2. A bishop then must be blameless, the husband of one wife, vigilant, sober, of good behaviour, given to hospitality, apt to teach;

3. Not given to wine, no striker, not greedy of filthy lucre; but patient, not a brawler, not covetous;

4. One that ruleth well his own house, having his children in subjection with all gravity;

5. (For if a man know not how to rule his own house, how shall he take care of the church of God?)

6. Not a novice, lest being lifted up with pride he fall into the condemnation of the devil.

7. Moreover he must have a good report of them which are without; lest he fall into reproach and the snare of the devil.

8. Likewise must the deacons be grave, not doubletongued, not given to much wine, not greedy of filthy lucre;

9. Holding the mystery of the faith in a pure conscience.

10. And let these also first be proved; then let them use the office of a deacon, being found blameless.

11. Even so must their wives be grave, not slanderers, sober, faithful in all things.

12. Let the deacons be the husbands of one wife, ruling their children and their own houses well.

13. For they that have used the office of a deacon well purchase to themselves a good degree, and great boldness in the faith which is in Christ Jesus.

14. These things write I unto thee, hoping to come unto thee shortly:

15. But if I tarry long, that thou mayest know how thou oughtest to behave thyself in the house of God, which is the church of the living God, the pillar and ground of the truth.

16. And without controversy great is the mystery of godliness: God was manifest in the flesh, justified in the Spirit, seen of angels, preached unto the Gentiles, believed on in the world, received up into glory.

Verse 1: "This is a true saying, If a man desire the office of a bishop, he desireth a good work."

The office of bishop in Paul's day is not to be confused with the modern bishopric of our day. The word *bishop* means "to look upon, behold, to inspect, look after, see to, to take care of, the office of overseeing." The qualifications for a bishop are the same as those for a deacon, pastor, or any leader of the church, and as such will be fully dealt with in this chapter.

You may rest assured that Timothy did not wear a religious garb; neither did he display the spirit of dictatorship usually evident in the modern bishop. Yet in Timothy's time the position was one of great responsibility—and oftentimes of grave danger. The office of bishop is referred to as *"a good work,"* something *"to be desired."* The Greek word used here for "desire" has a much stronger meaning than does our English word. It indicates not merely a passive waiting for the office, but rather an eager, active *reaching out for it*. It borders on the strength of covetousness, as though one eagerly coveted such office.

In the early church, the office of a bishop was not an easy one to fill. It was a post of very real responsibility and ofttimes of much danger. The first believers did not seek after the easy tasks, but rather those of hardship and peril. Many of the early Christians actually longed to suffer even *severe* persecution—and some even craved martyrdom, while today the average Christian complains about the slightest persecution or discomfort. The early Christians were spiritual giants, compared with present day *pygmies* in the spiritual realm. May God forgive us for being so soft! You may rest assured that in the days of Paul, a bishop did not occupy a plush office with swivel chair and polished desk. He did not wear attractive religious garb nor draw a handsome salary with three or four assistants to do the work while he supervised. His position was far from that. The qualifications for such office are laid down one by one:

Verses 2-7: "A bishop then must be blameless, the husband of one wife, vigilant, sober, of good behaviour, given to hospitality, apt to teach; not given to wine, no striker, not greedy of filthy lucre; but patient, not a brawler, not covetous; one that ruleth well his own house, having his children in subjection with all gravity; (For if a man know not how to rule his own house, how shall he take care of the church of God?) Not a novice, lest being lifted up with pride he fall into the condemnation of the devil. Moreover he must have a good report of them which are without; lest he fall into reproach and the snare of the devil."

1. *A bishop must be blameless.*

A bishop must be without reproach, living in such a way that no one could point the finger of accusation at him or rebuke him for living a life unbecoming a leader in the spiritual life of the community. There are always critics who will abuse the best, most consecrated, sincerely dedicated of men; but if the accusation is false, then the blameless bishop has reason to rejoice and be exceedingly glad (Matt. 5:11,12).

One thing a bishop must be sure of is that any criticism of him is unjust, and not deserved because of some habit unbecoming a spiritual leader. Those of us who are leaders in our church can profit from this. When we are criticized we should not fly into a rage nor threaten to resign and leave the church. We should not answer back in haste. We should first check carefully to see if the accusation is true—and if an accusation is made against *us*, we *know* whether or not it is true. If it IS true, then

107

by the grace of God we should set about to correct it. If the accusation is against a fellow-believer, we will do well to check thoroughly before we judge; because there are those who criticize falsely and unjustly, who would tear down good men capable of being leaders in the church and in the community. And even if charges made against a fellow Christian are true, we should not condemn that believer until we have done all in our power, by the grace of God and on the terms of the Gospel, to help the one who has been overtaken in a fault, considering ourselves, lest we also be tempted and fall into the same snare. A bishop must be on guard at all times. He must be sure that the enemies of the cross have no grounds for criticism of him; he must be *blameless*.

2. *A bishop must be the husband of one wife.*

Paul, led by the Holy Spirit, clearly states that a bishop is to have *only one wife*—but I do not believe that is the entire purpose of this verse; for although the Jews practiced polygamy, that sinful practice was unknown among the Greeks and Romans. If any man in the church had had two wives at the same time, that would have been a scandal which would have completely discredited the church in the eyes of the Gentile unbelievers. I believe with all my heart that Paul is also saying here that a man appointed to the office of bishop should be a mature man, a *married man* (with one wife). (He warns against putting a novice in office.)

I believe verse 5 *proves* that a bishop or deacon should be married—the husband of a wife and head of a household: *"For if a man know not how to rule his own house, how shall he take care of the church of God?"* How could these words be applied to a single man, or to a young man still living in his father's house? It is my conviction that a man placed in the office of bishop, deacon—or in the capacity of leadership, regardless of the title of the office—should be a married man, a man who has only one living wife.

It is all right for a man to serve as bishop if his first wife is dead, and he has married again; but I do not believe a man who has two living wives should be a leader, nor serve on the deacon board of any church that calls itself a New Testament church. God will *save* a man with two living wives, and then what he does pertaining to continuing with the second wife or returning to the first must be settled between that man and God. Circumstances play a great part in what one will do who has been married, divorced, and remarried before he is born again. When a person with two living mates is converted, God will lead that person (if he wants to be led) by the Holy Spirit. God can and does save people who have been married several times; the grace of God is greater than *all* our sin—but for the sake of the testimony of our church, such a person must be careful. The pastor and leaders in the church must also be careful and guard against filling offices and places of public service in the local assembly with those who have more than one living mate.

3. A bishop must be vigilant.

Peter says, ". . . Be vigilant: because your adversary the devil, as a roaring lion, walketh about, seeking whom he may devour" (I Pet. 5:8). But the devil does not *always* walk about as a "roaring lion": ". . . We are not ignorant of his devices . . . for Satan himself is transformed into an angel of light" (II Cor. 2:11; 11:14). The devil can change his color to advance his cause; he can change his nature to trap his victim. He is astonishingly subtle when seeking to undermine and overthrow a believer.

DOUBT is one of the most effective tools of Satan— the art of putting a question mark around what God has said.   Read the sad story in Genesis 3, when the devil came into the Garden of Eden and asked Eve, "Yea, *hath God said* . . .?" (Gen. 3:1).   He KNEW what God had said, but he planted a question in the mind of Eve; and from that question he led her step by step until he caused her to sin: ". . . She took of the fruit thereof, and did eat, and gave also unto her husband with her; and he did eat" (Gen. 3:6).   By planting doubt in the mind of Eve, Satan caused her to sin; she in turn caused Adam to sin, thereby plunging the whole human race into sin and death.   The first Adam succumbed to Satan and his wiles; but thank God, the second Adam had all the answers.

In Matthew chapter 3, Jesus made His way to Jordan to be baptized by John the Baptist.   Immediately after He was baptized, the Spirit led Him into the wilderness to meet the devil.   A personal Jesus met a personal devil. (Never let anyone tell you that Satan is not a personality, but simply an "evil influence.")   The Man Christ Jesus met *the person—Satan*—on the mount of temptation; and in Matthew 4:1 and following, he hurled at Christ every temptation possible for him to throw in the path of mankind— the lust of the eye, the lust of the flesh, and the pride of life.   Read I John 2:15–17.

For each temptation, Jesus answered Satan with Scripture from Deuteronomy.   Satan suggested to Him that IF He were the Son of God, He could change the stones into bread.   Jesus replied, "It is written, Man shall not live by bread alone, but by every word that proceedeth out of the mouth of God" (Matt. 4:4).

Satan then took Him into the Holy City, "and setteth Him on a pinnacle of the temple, and saith unto Him, IF thou be the Son of God, cast thyself down: for it is written, He shall give His angels charge concerning thee: and in their hands they shall bear thee up, lest at any time thou dash thy foot against a stone." Jesus answered with Scripture: "It is written again, Thou shalt not tempt the Lord thy God" (Matt. 4:6,7). *Jesus was The Word—* and He did not need to quote the Old Testament; He could simply have spoken—and whatever He said would have been the Word of God; but He used the Word that was already written.

Satan does not give up easily, even when battling with the Son of God! He next took Jesus up "into an exceeding high mountain," showed Him all the kingdoms of the world, and said to Him, "All these things will I give thee, if thou wilt fall down and worship me." Again Jesus turned to the Word and said, ". . . It is written, Thou shalt worship the Lord thy God, and Him only shalt thou serve!" When Jesus had thus spoken, the devil departed from Him, "and behold, angels came and ministered unto Him" (Matt. 4:9–11).

The number one tool of the devil is to put a question mark around God's holy Word. If Satan could destroy the Word of God, he would damn every soul upon the face of this earth! We will never know this side of eternity the importance of God's Word. "In the beginning was the Word, and the Word was with God, and the Word was God. . . . And the Word was made flesh, and dwelt among us . . ." (John 1:1,14). We are born again—not of corruptible seed, but of incorruptible, by the Word of God. We are saved by God's grace, through faith. Saving faith comes by hearing, and hearing by the Word of God. NO WONDER THE DEVIL TRIES TO PUT A QUESTION MARK AROUND THE WORD!

False teachers and false preachers quote much Scripture to support their claims; but they mishandle and wrongly divide the Word; they are guilty of "wresting" the Scriptures (II Pet. 3:16). These ungodly men—who are ordained to damnation—are guilty of tearing text from context; they are guilty of wrongly dividing the Word of Truth, and believers must at all times be on guard against such false teachers and their damnable heresies.

A bishop must be vigilant, always alert, that he may detect any unscriptural teaching that may seep into the church. He must be on guard against all attacks of Satan—whether they be open or in secret. He must be careful that the wolves of hell do not scatter the lambs. ALL believers should be alert, but it is extremely important that a bishop be "on his toes" at all times—looking, listening, and guarding against false teachers and false doctrine.

4. *A bishop must be sober.*

We are not to think that this instruction has to do only with intoxicating drinks. Certainly a bishop is not to indulge in strong drink, but the Greek word used here means *"sober-minded"* . . . a man of calm, unimpassioned mind; one who is collected, composed, unexcitable. He must be humble, not easy to "fly off the handle" or become indignant. He is to be temperate and sober in all walks of life and behaviour; he is not to be drunk on pride, temper, nor in any other way.

5. *A bishop must be of good behaviour.*

A bishop must not only be able to talk well in public, able to teach and direct, but he must *walk* as he *talks*. He must live what he teaches. He must behave as becomes a Spirit-filled believer. He must not be guilty of inconsistency in any way. What he *says*, he must do; and what he *professes*, he must prove by the way he lives.

There are many things that leaders in the church could do—and not go to hell for doing them; but many things that seem harmless become harmful when practiced by church leaders. "No man liveth unto himself, and no man dieth unto himself" is especially true of those who are God's overseers and undershepherds. They must be of good behavior under all circumstances. When we cause a weak brother to stumble or a sinner to die in his unbelief, we must give an account for it at the judgment seat of Christ, where Christians will be rewarded for their stewardship.

6. *A bishop must be given to hospitality.*

In the early church special emphasis was placed upon this duty, because there was such a vast difference between the Christian and pagan manner of life that a traveling believer could not stay under a heathen roof. It therefore became necessary that the disciples open their homes to other Christians who might be traveling through the country. This was to be practiced among all believers, but especially by a bishop. It was part of his office that he be ready always to offer the hospitality of his home to other believers. After Lydia of Philippi was converted, she opened her house to Paul and Silas. The moment she opened her heart to the Lord, she opened her house and all that she had to the servants of God (Acts 16:15-40).

Today we should be far more given to hospitality than we are. We should be ready at all times to take God's men, God's servants, into our homes and care for them. You may rest assured that you will never lose by befriending and taking care of God's servants, whether it be minister, missionary, or whomsoever, if he is dedicated to the ministry of the Gospel and the winning of souls.

7. *A bishop must be apt to teach.*

This qualification points to maturity. As a general rule, a young unmarried man who has just been converted is not rooted, grounded, and seasoned in the deep things of God. A bishop must be alert and on guard, instructing believers with *truth*, on the positive side, and from the negative side warning them against false doctrine. Such are the two aspects of the teaching ministry, each so essential in our time, as in Timothy's day. There was much false teaching in Ephesus and throughout the area where the churches had been established—and certainly today we still must be *constantly on guard* concerning error, for there is much false doctrine abroad in our land today.

God does not want us to remain babes in Christ, tossed about with every wind of doctrine. He wants us to desire the sincere milk of the Word, that we may grow to be a strong Christian who is able to receive meat; and when we grow up spiritually, God wants us to be good soldiers of the cross, having a good testimony in all that we do. A bishop is to be an instructor—a capable one. He is to equip himself well, that he may be able to teach others; and if he is not equipped to teach others, then he is not qualified to be a bishop.

8. *A bishop is not to be given to wine.*

All believers should abstain from strong drink in any form, but especially should a bishop observe this admonition. Concerning wine, Paul's instruction to a bishop is very clear. He is not to participate in such practice. Greek scholars tell us that the word used here implies "sitting over wine," habitually drinking wine, as the people did in that day—even those who professed to be very religious. Not only for his own sake should a bishop abstain from the use of wine, but also for the sake of other believers.

9. *A bishop must be no striker.*

The word "striker" used here does not refer to a labor strike, a refusal to work, as we would think today;

but rather that a bishop is not to be a violent man. He is to be humble, kind, and gentle with hand and tongue. Many times the tongue is a deadly weapon, destroying even in a more cruel way than a sword or gun. (Read James 3:5–8.) The tongue can be set on fire of hell; it can become a violent beast or a deadly poison. All believers need to pray as the Psalmist did, *"Keep the door of my lips . . . let the words of my mouth be acceptable in thy sight."* This is especially true in the life of a bishop, for *he must not strike* with either weapon or tongue; he must be gentle and kind.

All believers must one day give an account to God for idle words. We will be judged for our deeds, our words, our thoughts. Therefore a bishop, a leader in the church, must not be of violent temper; he must not be violent in words nor violent in actions. The divinely appointed undershepherds who are in charge of the Word of the Great Shepherd must follow in His steps. The Lord Jesus was the most humble person who ever lived on earth; and a bishop must be humble, considerate, kind—certainly not "a striker."

10. A bishop must not be greedy of filthy lucre.

Money is a necessity, and it is not evil within itself. There are wealthy men today who are also godly men. In the Old Testament, Abraham was a very rich man—yet he was a righteous man, the friend of God. Joseph of Arimathaea was a rich man, and it was in his new tomb that the body of Jesus was laid (John 19:38–42). Money becomes the tool of evil only when LOVE of money eclipses duty to God. Paul said, "The LOVE of money is the root of all evil" (I Tim. 6:10); not money as such, but *loving* money, making it one's god. Ill-gotten money is evil; ill-spent money is evil. That is when money becomes "filthy lucre." Money can be a great blessing, but it can also be a curse. Money can be a Godsend—but it can also be the bait of the devil. Remember Judas, who "had the bag" (John 12:6), and took what he wanted from it.

Any minister who accepts money from God's people is accepting that money under false pretenses unless he preaches the pure Gospel—*ALL of the Gospel*. When a minister derives his livelihood from a church, mission, or ministry, and yet preaches to please people instead of preaching the pure Word of God, the money he gets from such ministry is *ill-gotten and is "filthy lucre."* Any preacher who refuses to preach the truth to those who pay his salary and provide his living, is a thief and a robber of the lowest order. There is no dirtier gang of thieves this side of hell than preachers who compromise the truth and preach a social or a liberal gospel. It is not a sin to be rich—if those riches come through honest labor or business; but *love* of money and money acquired by devious means is the bait of the devil to cause a person to stumble into hell.

It is noteworthy that riches and sorrow, riches and tears, riches and hell are closely associated throughout the New Testament. Jesus said, "Where your treasure is, there will your heart be also." May God help us never to love money. It is necessary; we must have it—but we can certainly have money and use it without *loving* it and making it our god. The bishop is not to be greedy of filthy lucre; he is not to serve for money, but because of his devotion to God and his love for those over which he has been appointed by the Holy Spirit.

11. A bishop must be patient.

The Greek word here means "forbearing." It denotes a God-given quality of mind and heart that makes definite allowances for the mistakes of others. In our eyes, another believer may be awkward, rude, unlovely;

but if we could know his heart, if we could see him through his own eyes and understand his intentions, we might undergo a definite change of mind. Just so, a bishop must be patient, kind, forbearing, understanding—and slow to judge those who do not act exactly as the bishop would have them act.

"Judge nothing before the time" is the plan laid down in the Bible. "Judge not, lest ye be judged"; and do not try to fit everyone else into your own mold. We are all saved alike—through the blood of Jesus Christ; but we do not all conduct ourselves in the same way after we are saved, because each of us has our individual temperament, emotions, etc. A bishop, therefore, must be *patient*.

12. A bishop must not be a brawler.

This naturally follows the previous qualification, for the point here is that the bishop is to be a peaceable person—one who loves peace, works to that end, and is unhappy when there is unrest in the assembly. A bishop *is not to compromise the Word of God* in order to keep peace in the church (the Holy Spirit would never make such a suggestion); but a bishop must be peaceable when at all possible. Paul said, "If it be possible, live peaceably with all men" (Rom. 12:18). To His disciples Jesus said, "Be ye wise as serpents and harmless as doves" (Matt. 10:16). In our present study, Paul is saying the same thing in different words. God's bishop is to "earnestly contend for the faith which was once delivered unto the saints" (Jude 3); but while contending for the faith he must not be contentious, stubborn, and argumentative. He must be on guard against stirring up strife and causing division in the church—either by word or by action. He must admonish the believers in the church to be at peace among themselves; and then, yielding to the Spirit, he must do all in his power to see to it that there IS peace in the local assembly.

13. A bishop must not be covetous.

God thundered out on Mount Sinai, "THOU SHALT NOT COVET!" (Exodus 20:17). Today He still proclaims to all believers—especially to the leaders in His Church— "Thou shalt not covet!" In my years of travel and my experience in evangelistic meetings, I have become convinced that covetousness is one of the outstanding sins of Christendom today. It is probable that more evil results from covetousness than from any other sin in the church. If the devil cannot lead believers into deliberate sin and open rebellion against the pastor and fellow believers, he plants covetousness in the believer's heart, if possible. Church members covet offices, positions, praise—and a score of other things that time and space will not permit me to mention here. Covetousness is an ugly sin. It is gross sin for a believer to covet anything— whether it be money, a possession, a position, or praise.

To my fellow believers I would say that the happiest day of your life, apart from the day you were saved, will be when you can say with Paul, ". . . I have learned, in whatsoever state I am, therewith to be content" (Phil. 4:11). Such condition is reached by few believers. Very few Christians really enjoy their spiritual birthright. If I am one of the least in the church, yet if I do my best, if I do what I do in the name of Jesus and to the glory of God, then my reward will be just as great as that of the one who, from outward appearance, is greatest in the church and who also does HIS best.

God does not judge according to the *size* of our stewardship, but the *sort* (I Cor. 3:11–15). Whether we sweep the church floor, dust the pulpit stand, teach the beginners' class or keep the nursery—*whatever we do*, if it is done to the glory of God, heartily and unto the Lord,

God keeps a record, and we will receive a full reward. May God help us not to covet anything that our brother, our neighbor, or our fellow church member may possess. May God help us to learn that whatever we are, wherever we are, whatever we are doing, if we are doing the best we can for the Lord, we will have the good graces of God in this life and a full reward in the life to come.

14. A bishop must be one who "ruleth well his own house."

God created Adam first, and made him head of the house. The man is head of the woman, and God appointed man as head of the local church and leader in it. A man who will be successful as God's bishop must be a success in the headship of his own home. If a man cannot govern his own home, he certainly is not fitted to govern the household of God.

A man who allows his wife to boss him, dominate him and dictate to him, a man who permits his children to talk to him in a saucy, impudent manner and refuse to obey him, is not qualified to be a bishop, deacon, or leader in the church; the Scripture is very clear on that subject. *A man who cannot rule his own house* cannot see after the affairs of the house of God.

I repeat what I said previously in this message: I believe a bishop or deacon should be a married man, the husband of one wife—and unless it is a physical impossibility there should be children in his home. A man whom God has called to the oversight of the local church should have a household, and he should be *head* of that household in every respect . . . not a bully, not brutal, not a dictator . . . but *a leader in his home.* He should be a husband and father who is respected and honored by his wife and children, because God placed him at the head of the home. A man who cannot stand at the head of his own household is not qualified to be a bishop or a deacon. What a bishop does for his own children is a good measuring stick for what he will be able to do for the "spiritual children" in the church.

15. A bishop must not be a novice.

The word "novice" means "a beginner or recent convert"—one who has just been saved. A bishop should be a man of experience, a man trained in the Scriptures and who can teach the truth of the Scriptures. He should be one who has proved his experience by his daily living, in the church and before the community. He should be respected by those who work with him, live around him, and know him best.

In my years of preaching the Gospel—and almost all of those years I have been on the road—I have learned many things for which I am thankful; but I have also learned some things that I wish I had not learned! I have seen wonderful assemblies severely crippled and torn asunder because some young, inexperienced person wanted to dictate and dominate in the church in matters that only the pastor should be allowed to settle.

I recall one church in particular which was split because of one young man who joined that church. This young man had money, social position, and a wonderful personality; and he was immediately placed on the deacon board, as well as being made head usher. I went to that church for a revival, having known this young man previously, knowing that he had been a sinner of the baser sort. He had been converted only six months when he was placed on the deacon board—for no reason at all except his position in the community and his money in the bank.

When I learned of this, I remarked to my wife that *the church would suffer* because of that move on the part of the pastor. Within eighteen months this young man did all within his power to run the pastor out of the community, and through his leadership more than four hundred members left that church to establish *another*; and to this day *neither church has recovered from the blow!*

The most unwise thing any pastor can do is to put a new convert into a place of authority. Most young converts have zeal without knowledge. They want to do great things for Christ; but as beginners, they do not always know how to do them. They have need to be led— not to lead others. It is not fair to the young convert to be placed so soon in position of authority, for eminence is very likely to engender within him the sin of pride. Paul forbids such placing of a novice.

Babies cannot be presidents of banks, governors of states nor leaders in the community. By like token, *spiritual babies* cannot carry on the work of the Lord in the local church. They must first feed on the milk, bread, and meat of the Word; they must learn; they must study; they must grow. There may be exceptions to the rule; but the overall Bible instruction is to let a new convert be a learner, rather than putting him in position of power in the local assembly.

16. A bishop must be a man of good report.

According to Paul, this report must come from "them which are without"—that is, from the unbelievers. I know there are some in any community who will criticize and condemn a man who lives a clean, consecrated, dedicated life; but from the general run of unbelievers there must be a good report concerning a man who is a bishop or leader in the local assembly. By that, Paul means that the bishop must not participate in things of the world; because if he does, he cannot have the confidence of unbelievers—and a bishop MUST live a life that will command the confidence and respect of those outside the church.

121

Face it, beloved—the general run of mankind is a pretty shrewd judge of real character. Unbelievers are always ready to point out insincerity and inconsistency in the life of church people—especially those who are in places of authority. The heart's desire of a bishop should not be to win admiration, praise and applause from the world, but to live a life that will earn—yea, *demand*—respect and confidence in his work in the local church. If a bishop has character, if his conduct is above reproach, if he lives a godly, separated life, the life of that bishop will cause unbelievers to come to Christ and be saved. What about it—deacons, elders, stewards, leaders? *Do YOU qualify?*

Verse 7 closes with the words, "*. . . Lest he fall into reproach and the snare of the devil.*" All believers must be very careful that their good not be evil spoken of. It is especially important that bishops and leaders in the church be very careful.

The Deacon

Verse 8: "Likewise must the deacons be grave, not doubletongued, not given to much wine, not greedy of filthy lucre."

Qualifications for deacons are very similar to those laid down for a bishop. In verse 13 of this chapter we learn that they who have used the office of a deacon well, "purchase to themselves a good degree, and great boldness in the faith which is in Christ Jesus." It is honorable to be a deacon.

We find the first mention of deacons in Acts 6:2,3: "Then the twelve called the multitude of the disciples unto them, and said, It is not reason that we should leave the word of God, and serve tables. Wherefore, brethren, look ye out among you *seven men* of honest report, full of the Holy Ghost and wisdom, whom we may appoint over this business."

Here we learn that the first deacons were appointed to deal with the business affairs in church life—to take care of the material side, watching after the orphans, the widows, the needy; handling the temporal activities of the church, in order that the apostles might give their time to prayer, study, and ministry of the Word. Even though they were appointed to deal with the business affairs of the church, a very high spiritual quality was demanded of them. The Bible specifies that a deacon be "full of the Holy Ghost and wisdom" (Acts 6:3). I should think that being "full of wisdom" would pertain to the business end of the church. God have mercy on some church leaders for the way in which they conduct the Lord's business. If the secular businesses tried to function in the half-hearted, slipshod way many churches do, the business world would shortly be bankrupt!

No qualifications are mentioned implying that deacons are to be preachers of the Gospel; but a deacon should be apt to teach, capable of taking over the pulpit in the absence of the pastor. Let it be remembered that the first body of deacons included such flaming evangelists as Stephen and Philip. Being a deacon is honorable; it is a position next to the pastor; and a deacon who is true to his office will receive a full and great reward.

A godly deacon can be a tremendous asset to the pastor; but a deacon who is not godly can be a great hindrance—to the pastor and to the cause of Christ. Woe be unto the deacon who hinders the church, instead of helping both church and pastor.

According to verse 8 of our present chapter:

1. *A deacon must be grave.*

This means that he must be of serious mind—not

flippant and light-hearted. That does not mean that he must wear a long face, a sad look, and never smile. Proper gravity is certainly not an enemy to a happy spirit. A deacon should be happy, but flippancy has no place in the life of one appointed by the Holy Spirit to run the business affairs and assist in the spiritual affairs of God's church. A deacon should not be a shallow person. He must be deep-thinking, serious-minded, approaching the things of God with a grave spirit.

2.   A deacon must not be doubletongued.

A deacon must not tell one person about a matter in one way, and then tell another person about the same matter in another way. He must not be guilty of saying one thing and meaning another. He must be a man of straightforward, honest dealing; a man of clear, decisive speech. He must be a man who means what he says, in whom the people have confidence. If he makes a promise, he keeps it; if he undertakes a matter to the glory of God and the church, he does not give up until it is completed. When God leads His deacon into a movement in the church or community, then God will give him grace to carry it through. He must not be a man who begins things—and then stops short of the goal.

A deacon must beware the snare of presenting something slightly aside from the truth just because such statement will be agreeable in the assembly. He must have a single tongue, sanctified and dedicated to the truth.

3.   A deacon must be "not given to much wine."

The Bible command concerning strong drink is simply, "Look not on the wine when it is red . . . ." Certainly a deacon must not be guilty of partaking of strong drink. The only way to be an overcomer concerning these lusts of the flesh is to abstain; and when Paul made the statement, "not given to much wine," he did not leave a loophole for deacons to drink, so long as they do not become drunken. They are not to yield to the temptation of strong drink.

4. *A deacon is to be "not greedy of filthy lucre."*

Since the first deacons were to collect and distribute food and clothing to the needy, this qualification was essential; and the same qualification is just as necessary today, because the deacons are entrusted with the business of the church, and a covetous man might be tempted to use his spiritual office for monetary advantages or for his own personal gain.

Verse 9: "Holding the mystery of the faith in a pure conscience."

5. *A deacon must have "a pure conscience."*

It is not enough that a deacon hold the mystery of the true faith in a strict, orthodox fashion, though that is very important; but a deacon must also be proved (or tested) in order to see whether or not his life is blameless and that his conscience is clear before God and as touching his fellowman in the church and the community in which he lives, serves, and represents the Lord in the office of deacon.

Verse 10: "And let these also first be proved; then let them use the office of a deacon, being found blameless."

6. *A deacon must prove himself blameless.*

Before any man is elected or appointed to the office of deacon, that man should prove himself. He should be blameless. Fundamental Christians talk much about the impossibility of sinless perfection—and I agree that Jesus is the only One who ever lived entirely apart from sin. No man has ever lived a sinless life—but we CAN live a life that is *blameless.* Paul said to the Thessalonians,

"And the very God of peace sanctify you wholly; and I pray God your whole spirit and soul and body be preserved BLAMELESS unto the coming of our Lord Jesus Christ" (I Thess. 5:23).

Paul believed in, preached, and practiced blameless living. I cannot over-emphasize that a novice (a learner, a beginner, a new convert) should never be appointed to a position of authority in the church. A minister who appoints a new convert to a place of power in the church is making a sad mistake. One must first *prove himself*—he must live a blameless life before them that are without, as well as before the brethren in the church, before that person is qualified to be appointed as a deacon.

Verse 11: "Even so must their wives be grave, not slanderers, sober, faithful in all things."

7. *A deacon must have a faithful, godly wife.*

Please notice: ". . . EVEN SO . . . THEIR WIVES . . . ." I would not offend anyone, but I must emphasize the fact that there is no place in the New Testament church for a deaconess—or a woman deacon. I know some of the leading denominations of our day have appointed women to the office of deacon, but such action is unscriptural; it is not right, and the woman who accepts such position may be truly born again, but she will lose her reward by being out of the will of God.

Deacons are to be men who have wives, and I do not believe anyone would suggest that a woman could fill that qualification. The Word of God clearly states, "Even so must *their wives* be grave, not slanderers, sober, faithful in all things" . . . in the home, among the neighbors, and in the church. After all is said and done, believers who are united in marriage are no longer two, but ONE; therefore the qualifications a man must meet to become a deacon, must also be met by his wife. I cannot picture a woman filling the office of a deacon—having husband and children at home, perhaps members of the same church, with mother and wife serving as deacon. There is no Bible authority for such.

The Bible is very clear here: A deacon whose wife does not measure up to the same spiritual qualities required of *him*, is not to be chosen as a deacon. A man whose wife is bossy, a backbiter and a tale-carrier, is not to be elected to the office of deacon. The wife of a deacon must be sober, grave, a person of temperance and faith. She must not be a woman of frivolity; she must not slander others; she must not be intemperate in anything, lest she bring reproach on the office of deacon and thereby bring reproach upon the church! A deacon's wife must strive with heart and soul to be "faithful in all things."

A deacon can be a better deacon if his wife qualifies. She can be a tremendous help by encouraging him, sharing his burdens and heartaches, praying for him, and in the fear of God helping to lighten the load he carries to the glory of God. What a joy it is when a deacon and his wife are thus in complete and happy accord in the service of the Lord. Truly, in that case "two are better than one"—and if they have a child (or children) who shares in this work, then the "threefold cord is not quickly broken" (Eccl. 4:9–12). Happy is the man who is God's deacon, who meets these qualifications, having a wife who is truly a helpmate and children who honor father and mother. That man will receive a great and full reward.

Verse 12: "Let the deacons be the husbands of one wife, ruling their children and their own houses well."

8. *A deacon must be the husband of one wife.*

There are two things in this verse of Scripture which

it will not require your spiritual "bifocals" to see:

(a) A deacon is to be a married man—not a single boy.

(b) He is to have only one wife—he is not to be a divorced man.

As God's co-worker a deacon is to be an example; he is to be able to rule his children and his household well. If he cannot command and receive obedience from his own children, how could such a man be expected to rule in the house of the living God? My dear friend, if you are serving as deacon and you are not qualified to hold such a position, then you should resign. It is better to be a layman, faithfully serving the Lord in that capacity, than to be a deacon who does not meet Bible qualifications.

The argument today is that times have changed, people have changed, and these matters are not as important as they were in the days of Paul. I agree that times and people have changed—*but God Almighty has not*, and neither has His Word nor His command. What God commanded in the first church in Jerusalem, He still requires today. I had rather be the janitor of my church and clean the building to the glory of God, than to be a deacon who does not qualify for the office. There are not many deacons today who *do* qualify. I am sorely afraid that there are more who do NOT measure up to Bible qualifications than there are who meet the requirements for a deacon as laid down in the New Testament.

Verse 13: "For they that have used the office of a deacon well purchase to themselves a good degree, and great boldness in the faith which is in Christ Jesus."

A deacon who meets these qualifications, lives up to them and discharges his duties with faithfulness, will win for himself "*a good degree*." The degree here referred to is not a Ph. D. or a D. D. or a B. A. The word really means "a good standing"—or as some render it, a "step up."

Let me point out something interesting here:

(a) The man who desires the office of a bishop desires a *good work* (verse 1).

(b) The man who desires this office that is a good work must be of *good behavior* (verse 2).

(c) The man who desires the office of bishop or deacon, thereby desiring a good work, and who must be of good behavior, must also have a *good report* (verse 7).

(d) The man who desires this good work, demonstrating good behavior, thereby receiving a good report, will automatically receive a *good degree* (verse 13).

Such a man will receive a good reward—a full reward—and we might say he will "graduate with honors."

Lest someone misunderstand, let me point out here that God does not have one standard of living for an ordinary believer and another standard for a minister, deacon, or Sunday school teacher. *All believers* should live blameless lives; we should be careful what we do, the company we keep, the things in which we participate. However, if an ordinary parishioner does fall by the wayside and commit sin, it does not bring upon the church so great a degree of reproach as would that same sin committed by a bishop, deacon, pastor, or evangelist. Paul is here pointing out the seriousness of holding a position in the local church. All eyes—within and without, believers and unbelievers—will be constantly on the church leaders from the standpoint of their position of authority; therefore a bishop, deacon, or minister must be doubly careful. We must never forget the solemn fact that however lofty the position to which we may be pro-

129

moted, however far we may advance in the spiritual aspect—in holiness and in service—we shall never reach the point spiritually where we can for one moment let down our guard against the enemy. We must be watchful, careful, sober, and alert; because our adversary the devil is walking about, seeking to destroy our testimony and our usefulness, thereby bringing reproach upon the church and upon the name of Jesus.

Church leaders must be extremely careful lest Satan use them to bring reproach on the name of Jesus our Saviour, who suffered the agonies of the cross that we might have redemption—and not only redemption, but victory over the world, the flesh, and the devil! If you have not already done so, memorize I Corinthians 10:12,13—and never forget those two verses.

The House of God; the Mystery of Godliness

Verse 14: "These things write I unto thee, hoping to come unto thee shortly."

In this verse Paul simply states that though he is writing a letter now, he hopes to see Timothy in person soon. Paul had a deep love for his children in the Lord, and he hoped to come to Ephesus and personally give instructions to the church.

Verse 15: "But if I tarry long, that thou mayest know how thou oughtest to behave thyself in the house of God, which is the church of the living God, the pillar and ground of the truth."

In this verse Paul is saying, "I hope to come to you soon; but in case that becomes impossible, I am writing this that you may know how to behave yourself in God's house. The church is the house of God, the church of the living God, the pillar and ground of the truth."

You and I will never grasp the full meaning of the church of the living God here on earth. What a tremendous honor to be God's co-laborers, His undershepherds, His deacons and workers in His church. Woe be unto the church, the pastor, or the deacon who fails to preach and live the whole truth and nothing but the truth. The world watches the church—the church is God's testimony on earth today. He works through the individual members of the church, and especially through those appointed to position of bishop or deacon.

Verse 16:   "And without controversy great is the mystery of godliness: God was manifest in the flesh, justified in the Spirit, seen of angels, preached unto the Gentiles, believed on in the world, received up into glory."

"Without controversy . . . ." The fact Paul is about to proclaim is undeniable, indisputable.

Christ Himself is *"the mystery of godliness."* He who before was hidden in God "was made manifest" (John 1:1,14; Rom. 16:25,26). *The mystery*—the divine plan of redemption embodied in Christ (Col. 1:27), once hidden from, but now revealed to believers:

1.   *"God was manifest in the flesh."*

Here is stated the amazing fact of the Incarnation of the Son of God. Do I understand that statement? I do not! I cannot understand how the eternal God took a body, and in that body stepped into our realm of life. He had no beginning. He is the eternal God who spoke, and the world was. He is the Creator of all things by Jesus Christ. God was not born; God cannot die. He is eternal: "From everlasting to everlasting, thou art God" (Psalm 90:1,2).

In Genesis 3:15, in the presence of Satan, Adam, and Eve, God promised that the seed of the woman would crush the serpent's head; and in the fulness of time *Jesus*

131

came—the seed of the woman (Gal. 4:4). One night, from the skies over Bethlehem, angels announced the birth of a Saviour. They proclaimed "Peace on earth! Good will toward men!" (We have never yet experienced that peace on earth, *but we will* when King Jesus sits on the throne of David in Jerusalem.)

He was seen of men—a babe in a manger, God in flesh. In order to pay the sin-debt and make it possible for sinners to be justified, God (who was offended in the Garden of Eden through the disobedience of Adam and Eve) wrapped Himself in the flesh of the offender: *God became man.* This was a divine imperative in order to fulfill the mission upon which He was predestined to embark.

In Hebrews 10:5 we read, ". . . A body hast thou prepared me." It was in that human body of flesh that God appeared among men here on earth. In I John 1:1,2 we read: "That which was from the beginning, which we have heard, which we have seen with our eyes, which we have looked upon, and our hands have handled, of the Word of life; (for the life was manifested, and we have seen it, and bear witness, and shew unto you that eternal life, which was with the Father, and was manifested unto us.)

In this day and age, man has achieved the unbelievable—and, for the ordinary person, the *indescribable.* But there is one thing man cannot put into a test tube nor carry into his laboratories, and *that is the divine, eternal, Jehovah God!* God cannot be broken down and analyzed; we accept Him by faith. We believe that *God IS,* because the Word tells us that *"in the beginning . . . GOD."* We do not ask, "How? Why? Where?" We believe it because God said it—and God cannot lie.

God took a body of flesh, and "what the law could

132

not do, in that it was weak through the flesh, God sending His own Son in the likeness of sinful flesh, and for sin, condemned sin in the flesh" (Rom. 8:3). Paul clearly states that "God was in Christ, reconciling the world unto Himself . . ." (II Cor. 5:19).

I am a Trinitarian. Any person who reads the Bible with an open mind and open heart cannot deny the Trinity. I believe in one God manifested in three Persons—Father, Son, and Holy Ghost. Those who read the Word for the purpose of learning what the Word teaches, rather than for the purpose of proving a religious argument, can clearly see the Trinity. What a tremendous and majestic statement—the Incarnation declared and proclaimed in so few words: *"God was manifest in the flesh"*!

2. *"Justified in the Spirit . . . ."*

The word "justified" is not used here in the same sense in which it applies to Christians. It means to "vindicate," in the sense that Christ was shown to be divine "in the Spirit." He was manifested in the flesh and at the same time justified in the Spirit: "Concerning His Son Jesus Christ our Lord, which was made of the seed of David according to the flesh; and declared to be the Son of God with power, according to the spirit of holiness, by the resurrection from the dead" (Rom. 1:3,4).

His manifestation "in the flesh" exposed Him to misapprehension, as though He were nothing more: "And they said, Is not this Jesus, the son of Joseph, whose father and mother we know? how is it then that He saith, I came down from heaven?" (John 6:42). His justification (or vindication) *in respect to His Spirit* was evidenced by: (1) *His words* (Matt. 7:29; John 7:46); (2) *His works* (John 2:11; 3:2); (3) *His Father's testimony*—at His baptism (Matt. 3:17); on the Mount of Transfiguration (Matt. 17:5); and again in John 12:28–30, after Christ

133

had made His triumphal entry into Jerusalem.

Jesus came into this world on a singular mission, for a singular purpose: *He came to pay the sin-debt, that we might be justified.* "But now the righteousness of God without the law is manifested, being witnessed by the law and the prophets; even the righteousness of God which is by faith of Jesus Christ unto all and upon all them that believe: for there is no difference: For all have sinned, and come short of the glory of God; being justified freely by grace through the redemption that is in Christ Jesus: Whom God hath set forth to be a propitiation through faith in His blood, to declare His righteousness for the remission of sins that are past, through the forbearance of God; to declare, I say, at this time His righteousness: that He might be just, and the justifier of him which believeth in Jesus. Where is boasting then? It is excluded. By what law? of works? Nay: but by the law of faith. Therefore we conclude that a man is justified by faith without the deeds of the law" (Rom. 3:21–28).

In these verses we clearly see that the righteousness of God (without the law) is manifested . . . the righteousness of God which is by faith in Jesus Christ, unto all and upon all who have faith in His shed blood and His finished work. All have sinned; all have come short of the glory of God; and all are condemned, doomed, without hope, because sin pays singular wages—DEATH! But we who believe and have faith in God are justified freely by His grace through the redemption that is in Christ Jesus—not redemption through our good works, our baptism, or our religion. *We are redeemed and justified in Jesus Christ.*

God set forth Jesus Christ to be the propitiation through faith in His blood. God could and did declare His righteousness for the remission of sins that are past

134

through the forbearance of God. And in Jesus Christ, God announced His righteousness and displayed His righteousness in the sinless Son of God, the Lord Jesus Christ, that God might be just and holy and pure, and yet justify the sinner who believes in the shed blood and finished work of the Lord Jesus, who was God in flesh (II Cor. 5:19).

Since Jesus took a body of flesh like unto our own, lived on this earth for thirty-three and one-half years, was tempted in all points as we are, yet was without sin, He overcame the world, the flesh, and the devil, death, hell, and the grave. He satisfied the heart of God, the holiness of God, and the purity of God; and God said, "This is my beloved Son, in whom I am well pleased." Now, God saves and justifies us for Christ's sake (Eph. 4:32). Where is boasting? There IS no boasting—but rather, we conclude that man is justified by faith, *without* the deeds of the Law. We are saved—"not by works of righteousness which we have done, but according to His mercy . . . by the washing of regeneration, and renewing of the Holy Ghost" (Tit. 3:5). The chief purpose of the manifestation of God in flesh was that *in flesh* God could (and did) conquer sin. God did in flesh what the Law could never have done because of the *weakness* of the flesh—not because the LAW was weak, but because the *flesh* was weak. God was manifested in flesh to take away sin, in order that He could be just, and yet justify the ungodly.

"All we like sheep have gone astray," but Jehovah placed on Jesus the iniquity of us all (Isa. 53:6). At the cross on Mount Calvary, Jesus "was delivered" because of our offences. Our sins nailed Him to the cross—but death could not hold him, because *God cannot die!* In the flesh, He laid His life down (John 10:18), but the same power that laid it down raised it up again. Jesus "was raised for our justification" (Rom. 4:25).

Through His death, burial, and resurrection Jesus

135

accomplished the means whereby poor, hell-deserving sinners can be justified. That is what He came into the world to do. In John 17:4 Jesus announced to the heavenly Father, ". . . I have finished the work which thou gavest me to do." God accepted the sacrifice of His only begotten Son; He justified the action of Jesus, who willingly offered Himself in our stead, and when He died, said, "Father, into thy hands I commend my spirit" (Luke 23:46).

God accepted the sacrifice of Jesus—and I personally believe the blood of Jesus Christ is in heaven now—literally. God raised Him from the dead, and in the resurrection declared Him to be "THE SON OF GOD WITH POWER, ACCORDING TO THE SPIRIT OF HOLINESS, BY THE RESURRECTION FROM THE DEAD" (Rom. 1:4). In the resurrection, God declared Jesus to be His only begotten, virgin-born Son—*very God!*

3.   "*. . . Seen of angels.*"

Doubtless the angels watched Jesus as He left the Father's house and came to earth. They were very near the night He was born in Bethlehem. As His mother and Joseph fled with Him into Egypt, I believe angels watched every move with eagerness and angelic concern. They watched Him as a lad and were with Him in the temple at the age of twelve. They watched as He was baptized—and when He was led of the Spirit into the wilderness, legions of angels must have hovered near! When He said to Satan, "Get thee hence," the devil left Him; and *angels came an' ministered unto Him.* Surely angels must have watched __very miracle He performed, though human eyes could not scern them in attendance. When Jesus prayed in the Garden of Gethsemane and the honored trio of disciples fell asleep, it was an angel who lifted Him up and strengthened Him when His agony became so great that He fell prostrate on the ground, His perspiration stained with blood.

When Jesus was arrested, I believe there were un-numbered hosts of angels in the sky above Him—and had God the Father said the word, they would have come to His rescue. But He had come into the world for that hour, and angels must not interfere. They watched—and the cherubim must have covered their eyes with their wings as He was whipped, crowned with thorns, and His beard plucked out by the roots while men spat in His face! Surely the angels recoiled in horror as He was nailed to the cross, His flesh tearing as the cross was lifted between heaven and earth, then dropped into its place with a heavy thud. Even though angels may not have understood, Jesus was fulfilling the will of God: *His death was a MUST, if sinners were to be justified.*

Angels hovered about Calvary until Jesus said, "It is finished!" Then Joseph and Nicodemus took His broken body from the cross, wrapped it in fine linen and spices, and laid it in the tomb—but death could not hold Him (Acts 2:24). He was the Eternal One, the Living One—the One who could not die! And angels were nearby. They witnessed the resurrection.

The resurrected Lord was seen of Mary and of the women, of Cephas, of the twelve, of five hundred—and, Paul said, "Last of all, by me" (I Cor. 15:5–8). But these did not see Him first. It was the angels of heaven who rolled the stone away and sat one at the head and one at the foot of the place where the body of Jesus had lain. Angels saw Him! And what glad news they must have taken back to those in heaven, after witnessing the resurrection.

4. "*. . . Preached unto the Gentiles.*"

The literal rendering of the Greek here should read, "Preached unto the *nations.*" This glorious message is not for the Jew only—nor for any specific peoples—but

137

for the whole wide world. The message is to "whosoever will." It is not God's will that any perish, but that all come to repentance (II Pet. 3:9). At Pentecost every man heard the message in his native tongue (Acts 2:8–11). (Study these verses carefully.) But what IS this message? It is the glorious truth that Jesus—God in flesh—has paid sin's tremendous debt and purchased redemption for "whosoever will." The message is *Christ*, a Person—not a religion, a dogma, a tradition—but *Jesus Christ, crucified, buried, and risen*—"according to the Scriptures."

"In the beginning was the Word, and the Word was with God, and the Word WAS God . . . and the Word was made flesh, and dwelt among us, (and we beheld His glory, the glory as of the only begotten of the Father,) full of grace and truth" (John 1:1,14). The Gospel is Christ. Christianity is Christ. The command of Almighty God to believers is still "Go ye—and teach all peoples, baptizing them in the name of the Father, and of the Son, and of the Holy Spirit." The commission to preach this Gospel is to you and to me, just as truly as it was to the early disciples. If we refuse to give out this good news and proclaim this glorious Gospel, we are criminally selfish; we are literally withholding water from souls dying of thirst . . . the water of life, the only thing that will quench the thirst of the soul! God help us not to hold back, but to press on and shout out the good news that Jesus saves "whosoever will"!

It is a grand and glorious privilege to be a child of God; it is a wonderful thing to be saved: but as grand and glorious as is the privilege of being a Christian, just so weighty and grave is the responsibility! We cannot let those around us die in their sins; we will be held accountable. If we do not warn them, we will suffer loss; and we will stand before God with bloody hands. God help us to be good stewards and herald forth the message that salvation has been purchased and is presented to "whosoever will"!

5. ". . . Believed on in the world."

Not all will believe, but many will hear this good news. Man is created incurably religious, and it is just as natural for him to worship as it is for the sun to rise in the east. When we present the truth to the masses, many will believe. Some will refuse, for various reasons— but thank God, "YE KNOW THAT YOUR LABOUR IS NOT IN VAIN IN THE LORD" (I Cor. 15:58). We know that "the Word of the Lord is not bound"; and we have His divine promise, "My Word . . . shall not return unto me void" (Isa. 55:11). Therefore, "He that goeth forth and weepeth, bearing precious seed (the Word of God), shall doubtless come again with rejoicing, bringing his sheaves with him" (Psalm 126:6).

The message of redemption is, "Believe on the Lord Jesus Christ, and thou shalt be saved." It is not enough to believe ABOUT Him; it is not enough to believe IN Him to the extent that we acknowledge that He is a divine power; but we must believe ON Him—we must rest our spirit, soul, and eternal future ON HIM. We must literally place ourselves on Him in the same manner as we rest on a chair, as we drive our automobile on a bridge, or as we get on a train or a plane. We prove our trust by getting on the chair, the train, the plane. When we believe ON the Lord Jesus Christ, He saves!

All through the pages of history we find recorded the accounts of great men—noble, outstanding men in every walk of life; men who acknowledged Jesus Christ as their personal Saviour. They believed on Him—and proved it, not only with testimony by mouth, but by daily living, through their deeds. Those of us who are nineteen hundred years this side of His birth are compassed about with a great cloud of witnesses. He has always been "believed on in the world"—not by *all* men, but by many. If you are so unfortunate as to burn in hell, it will not be because it is God's will or because you are not elected to be saved: it will be because of your own stubborn will, your own refusal to trust the Lord Jesus Christ. "Believe on the Lord Jesus Christ, and thou shalt be saved, and thy house" (Acts 16:31).

6. ". . . *Received up into glory*"!

At first glance, this statement seems to be out of order. On the surface it seems that the resurrection and the ascension should precede the preaching and the believing—but not so. The statement "received up into glory" is not out of order. The commission to preach was given immediately before Christ's ascension (Mark 16:15, 16, 19; Acts 1:8, 9). Jesus gave the commission and instructed the disciples to tarry in Jerusalem until they were endued with power; and "when He had spoken these things, while they beheld, He was taken up; and a cloud received Him out of their sight."

I think these two verses are very fitting here: "Wherefore seeing we also are compassed about with so great a cloud of witnesses, let us lay aside every weight, and the sin which doth so easily beset us, and let us run with patience the race that is set before us, looking unto Jesus the author and finisher of our faith; who for the joy that was set before Him endured the cross, despising the shame, and is set down at the right hand of the throne of God" (Heb. 12:1, 2).

Jesus despised the shame of the cross, but He endured it—and He now sits at the right hand of God the Father. Why did He endure the shameful cross? The answer is found in Hebrews 12:2: "Looking unto Jesus the author and finisher of our faith; WHO FOR THE JOY

THAT WAS SET BEFORE HIM endured the cross, despising the shame . . . ." Jesus saw the glory on the other side of the cross. He willingly suffered; He willingly bore the cross, because He saw the glory beyond—the day when He would ascend back to the Father and receive again His place in the Father's house. Today He sits at the right hand of God to make intercession for you and for me (I Tim. 2:5; Heb. 1:1–3).

Can you imagine the jubilee which must have occurred as Jesus re-entered glory? Can you share the joy with which the disciples bade Him farewell (Luke 24: 51,52) . . . joy originating in the understanding of the meaning of His ascension—the meaning to Himself and the meaning to those of us who believe on Him as Saviour. It was imperative that He go away so that the Comforter would come. Had Christ not risen and ascended, we would have no salvation, no Comforter, no Guide through this pilgrim journey. When Jesus departed, He sent the Holy Spirit on the Day of Pentecost.

Because Jesus died, rose again, and sits today at the right hand of God the Father, WE share this glory—for we are united with Him, identified with Him; we are hid with Christ in God, and we sit together with Him in heavenly places (Eph. 2:5,6). This is the message that every bishop, deacon, pastor, and evangelist should proclaim around the world: The Saviour who died and was buried, rose again, ascended—and is coming again "according to the Scriptures."

I TIMOTHY -- CHAPTER FOUR

THE WALK OF A GOOD MINISTER OF JESUS CHRIST

1. Now the Spirit speaketh expressly, that in the latter times some shall depart from the faith, giving heed to seducing spirits, and doctrines of devils;

2. Speaking lies in hypocrisy; having their conscience seared with a hot iron;

3. Forbidding to marry, and commanding to abstain from meats, which God hath created to be received with thanksgiving of them which believe and know the truth.

4. For every creature of God is good, and nothing to be refused, if it be received with thanksgiving:

5. For it is sanctified by the word of God and prayer.

6. If thou put the brethren in remembrance of these things, thou shalt be a good minister of Jesus Christ, nourished up in the words of faith and of good doctrine, whereunto thou hast attained.

7. But refuse profane and old wives' fables, and exercise thyself rather unto godliness.

8. For bodily exercise profiteth little: but godliness is profitable unto all things, having promise of the life that now is, and of that which is to come.

9. This is a faithful saying and worthy of all acceptation.

10. For therefore we both labour and suffer reproach, because we trust in the living God, who is the Saviour of all men, specially of those that believe.

11. These things command and teach.

12. Let no man despise thy youth; but be thou an example of the believers, in word, in conversation, in charity, in spirit, in faith, in purity.

13. Till I come, give attendance to reading, to exhortation, to doctrine.

14. Neglect not the gift that is in thee, which was given thee by prophecy, with the laying on of the hands of the presbytery.

15. Meditate upon these things; give thyself wholly to them; that thy profiting may appear to all.

16. Take heed unto thyself, and unto the doctrine; continue in them: for in doing this thou shalt both save thyself, and them that hear thee.

It has been said that the Bible is a book man *could not* write if he wanted to, and *would* not write if he *could.* The Bible tells all; God's Word does not hide anything. It records the good and does not attempt to hide the evil.

In the Bible we read of Abraham, Moses, Elijah, David, Gideon—and the great things these men accomplished for God; but the Bible also records the *ugly side* of their lives. When *man* writes the biography of a great man, the ugly details are usually omitted, and only the *praiseworthy* things are published; but not so with the Bible. Paul wanted Timothy to know that as God's undershepherd he would find much of good cheer and encouragement—but beware! He would also find things that were ugly and evil. Enemies of the Gospel would appear, and Satan would attack—even through those who were supposed to be preachers of the Gospel.

Verse 1: "Now the Spirit speaketh expressly, that in the latter times some shall depart from the faith, giving heed to seducing spirits, and doctrines of devils."

In the last verse of chapter 3, Paul gave Timothy the tremendous truth of the Incarnation: "*God*—manifested in the flesh, justified in the Spirit, seen of angels, preached unto the nations, believed on in the world, and received up into glory." Now he solemnly warns Timothy to be on guard because "*the Spirit speaketh expressly.*" That is, "What the Spirit is saying is for a specific purpose and is tremendously important; it is not spoken in symbols nor in figurative language, but in plain words. The *Holy Spirit* is speaking—not man, but GOD—dictating these words to Paul.

God does not put words in the Scriptures merely to fill up space or close a gap in the verse or chapter.

Every word in the Bible is important, regardless of how insignificant it may seem. For instance, here the word "expressly" denotes the tremendous importance of what is about to be said, and Timothy is to pay very close attention. He must be cautious and on guard against false teachers and preachers who will come.

Paul points out the time *when* these false teachers will come: ". . . *In the latter times.*" Someone may ask, "If these who depart from the faith were to come in the 'latter times,' why should Timothy be so concerned, since he has been dead for centuries—and seemingly we are NOW approaching these latter times . . . perhaps we are IN the last days of this dispensation?"

The Greek here should read *"later on"* or "in latter times . . . a little bit later." This is not the same Greek phrase used in II Timothy 3:1 and translated ". . . in the last days," where the Spirit is definitely referring to *the last days of this age of grace*—the time just before the Rapture of the Church. In our present verse the Greek term points to "days later on"—even in Timothy's lifetime—and we know that in Timothy's day these false teachers did appear. They were teachers who deviated from the faith once delivered unto the saints.

"Now the Spirit speaketh expressly, that in the latter times, SOME SHALL DEPART FROM THE FAITH." Paul is referring here to THE faith mentioned in Jude 3; for even in the days of Jude and Paul, evil men had crept in unawares and were preaching gross error, denying the Lord God who bought them through the blood of Jesus Christ.

There is only one true faith. Faith does not come in different brands or under different labels, as do products that we know. There is only one faith that will save, and that is faith exercised in the finished work

144

of the Lord Jesus Christ—His virgin birth, sinless life, death, burial, and resurrection according to the Scriptures. To exercise faith in His shed blood brings salvation; faith exercised in anyone else or any other religion is dead faith and will cause one to be eternally lost. It is not *what kind* of faith you have nor *how much* faith you have, but *"In WHOM do you have your faith?"* Paul said, *"I know WHOM I have believed*, and am persuaded that HE is able to keep that which I have committed unto Him against that day" (II Tim. 1:12).

The teachers of whom Paul warns will be men *"giving heed to seducing spirits and doctrines of devils."* The minister of Jesus Christ is to study with diligence, rightly handling the Word of Truth (II Tim. 2:15). He is to be led by the Spirit, for "the natural man receiveth not the things of the Spirit of God" (I Cor. 2:14). Natural man cannot know the things of the Spirit of God: *". . . The things of God knoweth no man, but the Spirit of God"* (I Cor. 2:11). The Holy Ghost is our teacher, and He will lead us into the deep things of God (I Cor. 2:10–12; I John 2:27).

Those who depart from the faith and give heed to seducing spirits depart from the body of truth—the fundamentals of Christianity. They preach a doctrine exactly opposite to the truth revealed to Paul concerning the mystery of godliness, as set forth in I Timothy 3:16. These false preachers and teachers deviate from that majestic truth.

The devil made his first attack upon man by simply placing a question mark around God's Word. He knew that God had instructed Adam what to do and what not to do; yet when he approached Eve in temptation he asked, *"Hath God said*, Ye shall not eat of every tree of the garden?"* (Gen. 3:1 ff). The devil asked Eve what appeared to be a harmless question, but which led to the passing of wholesale death upon the human race. The teachers of whom Paul warns Timothy will parade in religious garb and advertise themselves as ministers of the Gospel; but they will deviate from the whole body of truth, mixing truth with error in a subtle way, attempting to overthrow the faith of some and lead others into gross religious error. Paul warned against error in all the churches where he preached, and admonished them to be sure their experience was genuine: "EXAMINE YOURSELVES, WHETHER YE BE IN THE FAITH" (II Cor. 13:5). Every church member who reads these lines should ask himself these solemn questions: "Is my faith genuine? Is my experience authentic? Am I truly born again? Am I a Christian—or just a church member? Is my profession real—or counterfeit? Am I practicing genuine Christianity—or only making an outward show? Is my religion only a veneer—with the vessel clean outside but inwardly filled with hypocrisy?"

We read in the Sermon on the Mount that many will say in *that day*, "Lord, Lord, have we not prophesied in thy name? and in thy name have cast out devils? and in thy name done many wonderful works? And then will I profess unto them, I never knew you: depart from me, ye that work iniquity" (Matt. 7:22,23). This group of people served with their lips and with their hands—but never took time to check up to see if they were genuinely saved!

Beloved, *some people today are so busy with their religious activities that they have no time to get saved*! They are so taken up with church work, social work, clubs and community responsibilities that they do not have time to search the Scriptures and make their calling and election sure. The Bible clearly teaches that there were those who thought they were in the faith—and were counted so by their fellows—but they "departed from the faith."

They turned their backs on the truth and, according to II Peter 2:22, proved by turning away that they had never been changed—they were sinners all the time! They were parading in sheep's clothing, but inwardly they were ravening wolves—they had never been born again. There are many who claim to be backslidden who really have never been genuinely born again. To anyone willing to face Bible facts, it is clearly stated in the Scriptures: *"They went out from us, but they were not of us; for if they had been of us, they would no doubt have continued with us: but they went out, that they might be made manifest that they were not all of us"* (I John 2:19).

The Spirit "speaketh expressly" that those who are not genuine will eventually go out from the true believers. They may profess for a long time; they may put on an impressive religious show for a season; but eventually the pure Word of God will drive them out. One cannot be exposed to the truth and remain the same; he must either get IN the fold, or move on OUT. Those who profess to be genuine and then turn their backs on the fundamentals of the faith and go the way of the world, testify by such action that they were never IN the true Church—they professed, but did not possess. The fact that they went out from us "made manifest that they were not of us." A person who is not trying to prove a religious point can clearly see here that not all who *claim* to be backsliders *are* backsliders—some have never been saved. It is possible for a true believer to backslide, but I am persuaded that ninety-eight percent of those who *claim* to be backsliders have never been born again.

Paul clearly shows Timothy the source through which error will come: *"Seducing spirits, and doctrines of demons."* The word translated "devils" here in our King James version should be "demons." (There is only one devil, and the word should never be used in the plural.)

There is one devil, but there are multiplied millions of demons.

We must not suppose the devil will approach us in person, in the same manner as he did our wonderful Lord; he has his armies of demons and seducing spirits to do his work. The very air is filled with principalities and powers and spirits of wickedness. Some preachers are also filled with demons: "For such are false apostles, deceitful workers, transforming themselves into the apostles of Christ. And no marvel; for Satan himself is transformed into an angel of light. Therefore it is no great thing if his ministers also be transformed as the ministers of righteousness; whose end shall be according to their works" (II Cor. 11:13–15). The devil has a cheap counterfeit for everything God has that is good and genuine. Jesus called and ordained true apostles; the devil has *false* apostles. God called and ordained deacons, stewards, and elders to carry on the work of the Truth; the devil has workers of *deceit*. These false apostles and deceitful workers do not approach us in their true nature, but are "transformed" into the apostles of Christ— that is, they wear religious garb; they talk religious talk— but inwardly they are thieves and robbers. Paul tells us that we need not be astonished at this, since "Satan himself is transformed into an angel of light!" Satan can take any form that will work to his advantage in damning souls and leading Christians astray. He can manifest himself as a roaring lion—or as an angel of light. There— fore it is not surprising that his ministers appear, on the surface, to be ministers of righteousness—but *"their end will be according to their (evil) works."* There are men who don a scissor-tailed coat and a collar designed for the clergy, and on Sunday morning walk into a pulpit and in a religious monotone deliver a seminary-inspired message—but these are not necessarily God's men. Some of them are ordained by the devil, and their doctrine is deadly poison.

148

All demons are masters in the unholy art of seducing. They choose their victims, choose their time, set their trap—and through cunning precision they attempt to lead astray even the elect of God—if that were possible. But hallelujah! — ". . . It is also contained in the Scripture, Behold, I lay in Sion a chief corner stone, elect, precious: *and he that believeth on Him shall not be confounded (confused)*" (I Pet. 2:6).

Seducing spirits cause people to doubt. They come to those who have a troubled mind—when some heavy cloud of sorrow engulfs them, when disappointment in other Christians has overtaken them, or perhaps when they are sick and weak in body. Demons take advantage of a person in such an hour, and attempt to sow the seed that will ruin the soul and wreck the life, sometimes causing one to go so far as to commit suicide. You and I will never know the power of the devil until we reach our heavenly home and God reveals to us the full magnitude of Satan's corruptness and the massive kingdom of demons and evil spirits over which he has control. He is head of the underworld, spiritually speaking. He is the kingpin of all "spiritual rulers of wickedness in high places." He is the prince of the power of the air, the god of this age, and "the whole world lieth in the lap of the wicked one." Praise God, "We are more than conquerors through Him that loved us" (Rom. 8:31–39). No wonder Peter said, "Be sober, be vigilant, for your adversary the devil, as a roaring lion, walketh about, seeking whom he may devour" (I Pet. 5:8).

Verse 2: "Speaking lies in hypocrisy; having their conscience seared with a hot iron."

These statements refer to human instruments of demons. The evil (seducing) spirit is a counterfeit of the Holy Spirit, always "aping" the Holy Ghost and working through human agency. Dear believer, never

149

forget that even the best Christians, off guard, can become tools of the devil. When Peter was temporarily seduced into doing the devil's work, Jesus said to him, "Get thee behind me, Satan" (Matt. 16:23). You are no doubt familiar with that story. Peter had said to Jesus, "You will never go to Jerusalem and be nailed to a cross; that will never happen to you!" But that is the very thing Jesus came into this world to do; so it was not the *Holy Spirit* speaking through Peter, but the spirit of the devil—and Jesus recognized it as such.

These human instruments used by Satan have preached lies so long and so consistently that they have no conscience against lying! There was undoubtedly a time when it grieved the hearts of these men to preach a lie; but their conscience became seared, as a piece of meat on a red-hot iron—burned over, without feeling.

There are many men in the, pulpits of America today who deny the virgin birth—and brag about it! They deny the verbal inspiration of the Scriptures and the blood atonement—and brag about it. They deny the fundamentals of the Christian faith—and brag about it. They are tools of Satan; they are being used to seduce poor, ignorant people into error that will damn the soul—yet *they have no conscience*; they feel no remorse over what they are doing. To make it worse, one after another of our leading magazines and periodicals play them up as great spiritual leaders!

Verse 3: "Forbidding to marry, and commanding to abstain from meats, which God hath created to be received with thanksgiving of them which believe and know the truth."

In this verse we learn *what* is taught and preached by these false teachers. They *"forbid to marry"* . . . that is, they command certain people NOT to marry; and

150

without a doubt this is the beginning of the prominent teaching of the Roman Catholic church, that a clergyman should not be a married man. However, in chapter 3 of our present study we learned that a bishop or a deacon should be "the husband of one wife"—which leads me to say without hesitation that, according to the Word of God, it is far better for a minister to be a *married* man, with a wife who is in sympathy with his ministry. If a young man who is called into the ministry will pray and seek God's will, God will give that young preacher the right wife. I believe with all my heart that if men would pray more before they marry, and seek God's will for their lives, He would give them the right helpmate. The teaching of popes, priests, bishops, or ministers not marrying is contrary to the Word of God, strictly unscriptural. I do not hesitate to say that any minister needs a wife.

These false teachers will also command abstinence from meats. There are several religions today which command their members to abstain from meats. The doctrine of the Adventists teaches that it is a sin to eat pork—which teaching is strictly LAW. The Roman Catholics teach that no meat should be eaten on *Friday*—a teaching that is also definitely unscriptural. In the days of the Law there were commandments concerning certain foods; but in this verse from Timothy the Holy Spirit clearly tells us that meats are to be received with thanksgiving: ". . . *which God hath created to be received with thanksgiving of them which believe and know the truth.*" Born again believers who read their Bibles know that the Christian religion is not a religion of works. Christianity is "Christ in you." Christ IS Christianity—and if you are a Christian you possess Christ in your heart. Christianity is not abstaining from food or drink.

Even aside from Christianity, if certain foods are detrimental to your health, you should leave them alone.

151

Forgive my use of a personal illustration—but I do not eat hog meat because I have extremely high blood pressure, and pork definitely works against such condition. People who have physical ailments should abstain from any food that irritates those conditions, but such abstinence should be practiced for reasons of health—not because of Christianity. The body of a believer is the temple of the Holy Spirit, and a Christian who is led by the Spirit will not eat anything that tears down that body—but the doctrine of abstaining from hog meat or abstaining from all meats on certain days, is strictly man-made dogma; there is not one iota of Scripture to back it up. When we bow our heads and give thanks to God for the food on our table, Paul tells us that such food is sanctified with the Word of God and with prayer. Jesus said, "Ye shall know the truth, and the truth shall make you free" (John 8:32), and "If the Son therefore shall make you free, ye shall be free indeed" (John 8:36). Some preachers preach long, loud, and untiringly of "grace, grace, God's grace," and then put their members under Law.

The believer is a bondslave of Jesus Christ—not the servant of any man. A believer is to be led by the *Spirit*—not by a bishop, priest, pope, or pastor. A believer is free from all man-made dogma, tradition, and misconceived religious ideas. *Christianity is "CHRIST IN YOU, the hope of glory"* (Col. 1:27).

In this day there are thousands of ministers (so-called) teaching and preaching error—forbidding to marry, commanding to abstain from meats, commanding people to do this or not do the other, to give their money in one specific spot and no place else. They forbid their members to listen to certain ministers, whom they choose to call "false preachers." God's undershepherds are not to be lords over God's heritage. No minister has a right to dictate to his congregation. He is to *preach the Word*—

and let the *Holy Spirit dictate* to the heart of the believer.

Verse 4: "For every creature of God is good, and nothing to be refused, if it be received with thanksgiving."

This statement is clear. Every creature of God is good—nothing is to be refused—*IF it be received with thanksgiving*!

Verse 5: "For it is sanctified by the Word of God and prayer."

Any food or drink for which a believer can sincerely bow his head and thank God—praying for God to bless the food and give him strength, wisdom, a healthy body and a sound mind to God's glory—can be received with thanksgiving, because it is sanctified by the Word of God and prayer. Anyone who would misconstrue this verse of Scripture to justify getting drunk (or drinking drinks that will make him drunk) is a hypocrite and not a believer; the Word of God is very clear on these matters.

Matter is not evil or sinful within itself. Everything God created is good: "And God saw everything that He had made, and behold, it was very good" (Gen. 1:31). The good things of life are not to be refused, but are to be received with thanksgiving, as from the Lord.

I Samuel 9:13 offers the divine suggestion that grace should always be practiced before we enjoy the food on our table. In Matthew 14:19 the Lord Jesus blessed the loaves and fishes before He fed the five thousand; in Acts 27:35 the Apostle Paul gave thanks for food on the ship; and certainly we should always say grace and receive our food as from the Lord, with thanksgiving. Those who claim to be more spiritually minded and more consecrated because they abstain from certain foods or from normal forms of dress, are not advertising spirituality, but *Bible ignorance*.

Jesus prayed, "Sanctify them through thy truth: *thy*

word is truth" (John 17:17). In John 14:6 He said, "I am the Truth." In John 8:32 He said, "Ye shall know the truth, and the truth shall make you free." Those who know the truth are not led around by false teachers nor by those who try to mix law and grace. So you may rest assured that if your religion is based on what you eat or drink, what you wear or do not wear, where you go or do not go, then your religion is based on sinking sand; you are not building on the Rock of Ages, the Lord Jesus Christ. No minister or religious leader has any scriptural authority to put you under commands or demands. If you are set free by the grace of God, then you are "free indeed." *Enjoy* the liberty you have in Christ—but do not use that Christian liberty to your own advantage. Whether you eat or drink, or whatsoever you do, do it all to the glory of God. *". . . To him that knoweth to do good, and doeth it not, to him it is sin"* (James 4:17). *"The just shall live by faith"* (Rom. 1:17).

Remedies Against False Teaching

Verse 6: "If thou put the brethren in remembrance of these things, thou shalt be a good minister of Jesus Christ, nourished up in the words of faith and of good doctrine, whereunto thou hast attained."

". . . Put the brethren in remembrance" . . . that is, of the truths just stated—"nourished up in words of faith." The minister of Jesus Christ is to preach the Word, for the Word of God is the Rock of Gibralter, as having to do with Christianity. "In the beginning was the Word, and the Word was with God, and the Word was God. . . . And the Word was made flesh and dwelt among us, (and we beheld His glory, the glory as of the only begotten of the Father,) full of grace and truth" (John 1:1,14). We are set free by the truth; by the truth we go where Jesus is. He said, "I am the way, the truth, and the

154

life: *no man* cometh unto the Father, but by me" (John 14:6). We are *sanctified and kept* by the truth, the power of God. We will step inside the Pearly Gates through but one door, and that door is Jesus. Jesus is truth; truth is God; and God was in Christ reconciling the world unto Himself. Therefore, a good minister will lift up the Lord Jesus Christ and remind the brethren that there will be those who will preach a doctrine which is foreign to the Word of God (forbidding to marry, forbidding to eat certain foods, forbidding to wear certain garments, do certain things and go certain places.)

The secret of victorious Christian living is *Christ within*—not abstaining from things without:

"He leadeth me in the paths of righteousness (right living) for His name's sake" (Psalm 23:3).

". . . As many as are led by the Spirit of God, they are the (children) of God" (Rom. 8:14).

". . . Whatsoever is born of God overcometh the world: and this is the victory that overcometh the world, even our faith" (I John 5:4).

". . . Let him that thinketh he standeth take heed lest he fall. There hath no temptation taken you but such as is common to man: but God is faithful, who will not suffer you to be tempted above that ye are able, but will with the temptation make a way to escape, that ye may be able to bear it" (I Cor. 10:12,13).

". . . We are more than conquerors through Him that loved us" (Rom. 8:37).

A good minister preaches the Word—not tradition, dogma, nor man-made doctrine—but *The Word*.

". . . *Whereunto thou hast attained.*" The meaning seems to be that Timothy had followed out the doctrines

155

in which he had been trained, and his early training in the Scriptures had climaxed in his accepting the Lord Jesus as Saviour. He had faithfully followed up as a disciple, and now if he followed the directions of the Apostle Paul he would be a good minister and would live up to Paul's expectations of him.

Verse 7: "But refuse profane and old wives' fables, and exercise thyself rather unto godliness."

God's preacher is to refuse "profane and old wives' fables"—(irreverent legends; profane, impure, godless fiction; mere grandmothers' tales and silly myths). He should study the Word, feed on and assimilate the Word, and be godly in all of his activities, in order that he may feed the flock of God. He needs to be strong in the Lord and in the power of His might, in order to keep the wolves out of the flock.

Verse 8: "For bodily exercise profiteth little: but godliness is profitable unto all things, having promise of the life that now is, and of that which is to come."

". . . *Bodily exercise*" profits little. Paul was not against bodily exercise. The Greek here reads, "profiteth A LITTLE." Bodily exercise is good insofar as it goes, but godliness is the thing that is profitable in the Christian life. *Bodily exercise* here could refer to the mortification of the body by abstinence and penance, in an attempt to attain holiness and subdue the passions of the body. But there must be a deeper work in the soul than the mere mortification of the body. It is not what we eat, what we refrain from eating, nor what we put on or do not put on that brings holiness to the soul. God looks on the heart (the inner man), while man looks only on the outward appearance. It is from the heart that the issues of life proceed, and we are to keep the heart with diligence (Prov. 4:23). When the heart is kept "with diligence," the hands, feet, eyes and other members of the body are kept in subjection; because these members operate only on permission from the heart.

Bodily exercise builds up the physical part of man and contributes to his mental health; but godliness contributes to ALL phases of life—not only to life eternal, but to this life. A person who lives a godly life will have a stronger body, better health, stronger mentality, and will advance further in his or her particular field of endeavor.

Men who have attained the highest heights in God's economy have been men of character—godly men who obeyed the commandments of God insofar as it is humanly possible to keep them. Joseph was a successful and prosperous man. Why? Because ". . . the Lord was with Joseph" (Gen. 39:2). He was a godly man, and the Lord prospered everything with which he had to do. Jesus said, "Seek ye first the kingdom of God, and His righteousness; and all these things shall be added unto you" (Matt. 6:33). The Psalmist declares, ". . . No good thing will He withhold from them that walk uprightly" (Ps. 84:11).

Verse 9: "This is a faithful saying and worthy of all acceptation."

In this verse the Holy Spirit, through Paul, assures Timothy that what has been said in the preceding verses is faithful, worthy of all acceptation, and that any and all in the church can accept this doctrine without fear, because it is dictated by the Holy Spirit to a holy man appointed by God to pen down these truths which are to be preached by "a good minister of Jesus Christ."

The reason we have so many spiritual babies in our churches today is because they have never been fed the meat of the Word. Paul accused the Corinthians of being bottle-fed, when they should be eating strong meat. The only message that will bring a dead sinner to life in Christ is the Word of God. The only message that will feed the child of God is the Word. We are to desire the sincere milk of the Word (I Pet. 2:2)—but *we are not to remain on milk* throughout our Christian experience. We are to be partakers of *spiritual meat.*

In the Old Testament era, as well as in the New, God commanded His people to be strong. In Joshua 1:6, 7, 9 and 18 we read: "*. . . Be strong. . . . Only be thou strong. . . . Have not I commanded thee? Be strong . . . ONLY BE STRONG!*" In I Corinthians 16:13 Paul said: "*. . . BE STRONG!*" In Ephesians 6:10 he said: "*Finally, my brethren, be strong in the Lord!*" Again and again we are exhorted to be good soldiers, strong defenders of the faith, diligent workers, capable leaders— BE STRONG IN THE LORD. And God does not expect this only of His leaders; *He expects it of all Christians.*

There is no excuse for weak, anemic Christians. The God who saves us also provides food to make us strong; and if we are spiritual weaklings it is not God's fault—it is our own. We have too many ordinary Christians, too many jellyfish believers. We need more extraordinary, spiritual giants. We need more saints like Paul and Timothy—healthy, strong, spiritual leaders who are *nourished* by the Word of God, led by the *Spirit* of God, *obeying the command* of God.

There are two extremes today in the field of religion, and both groups are bad. One group of people do not believe anything, do not preach anything, and do not practice anything. They go to church as they go to a club meeting. Sunday is the accepted day to attend church, and this is strictly a form . . . a program. When the program is over they are through with church and with God until next meeting day.

On the other extreme, the minister plays on the emotions, the mind, and the flesh, instead of appealing to the spirit. A church built on emotion will not supply the need of man's hungry heart. Preaching which is directed to the mind and the emotions will not feed the heart and soul. A believer will never be a strong, healthy, full-grown Christian if he feeds on emotion instead of feeding on the pure milk, bread, and meat of the Word of God.

In verse 6 Paul referred to Timothy as having "already attained." He was a successful Christian, a healthy believer. From his childhood he had fed upon a well-balanced spiritual diet (II Tim. 3:15). I do not mean to sound sarcastic, but many Christians do not know a good sermon when they hear one. If a preacher can tell stories to make people cry, they think he is a great preacher; but Paul warns, *"Refuse profane and old wives' fables."*

Peter, giving his testimony concerning the Lord Jesus, said, *"We have not followed cunningly devised fables, when we made known unto you the power and coming of our Lord Jesus Christ"* (II Pet. 1:16). The message the church needs today is not one of fables or fancy stories to make parishioners laugh or weep; the church needs plain Bible facts—facts well established in the Word of Truth and upon which the believer can stand, knowing that when the floods come, the rains descend, and the hurricanes of hell move in, the house will not fall—because it is built upon a rock.

In Mark 4:24 we read, *"Take heed WHAT ye hear."* In Luke 8:18 we read, *"Take heed HOW ye hear."* We should be very careful *what* we listen to, *how* we listen, and *to whom* we listen.

Verse 10: "For therefore we both labour and suffer reproach, because we trust in the living God, who is the Saviour of all men, specially of those that believe."

Several times in his epistles, Paul testifies that his suffering and bonds came as a result of his ministry; yet he faithfully preached the Word of God, regardless of the suffering it brought upon him. As Christians we labor and we suffer reproach, "because we trust in the living God, who is the Saviour of all men"—*especially of those who believe.*

Anyone who dares teach that this verse suggests universal salvation would certainly be stretching a point and not comparing spiritual things with spiritual. God loved the world—*all men*; and He gave Jesus to die for all men—for the sin of the whole world (I John 2:1,2; John 3:16; II Pet. 3:9). But even though God is Saviour of all men, *not all men believe unto salvation.* Salvation has been purchased, paid for, and presented to all men; but not all men have accepted it. To His own people Jesus said, "And YE WILL NOT come to me, that ye might have life" (John 5:40). Many are called, but few are chosen. All are invited: *"Whosoever will,* let him drink." God is the Saviour of all men—*all who will come to Him by Christ Jesus.* If you die in sin and spend eternity in hell, it will not be God's will; *it will be your own stubborn will* that causes you to be eternally lost. It is not God's will that you perish, but that you repent.

Verse 11: "These things command and teach."

The minister of the Gospel need not apologize for preaching the Word. In verse 11 Paul tells Timothy to teach and command these things. When we deliver "Thus saith the Lord" from the pulpit, the parishioners may not like it and they may not obey it—but we have no reason to apologize for preaching it. The Gospel is to be declared without fear, favor, or apology.

In verses 9 through 11 we see the heart of Christian doctrine: "WE TRUST IN THE LIVING GOD." Trust

160

in God is the heart, soul, and essence of the Christian life. Faith in God is the initial act that brings eternal life. "Without faith it is impossible to please Him: for he that cometh to God must believe that He is, and that He is a rewarder of them that diligently seek Him" (Heb. 11:6).

My dear reader, ask yourself the solemn, eternal question: *"Do I trust in the living God? Have I put my faith in Him?"* Are you trusting in the Saviour, the shed blood, Christ's finished work? If you are, you are a Christian; if not, you are unsaved. To His disciples Jesus said, "Have faith in God" (Mark 11:22). The question today is, *"What think ye of Christ? Whose Son is He?"* The way you answer that question will determine your eternal destiny.

True faith produces labor; we labor because we trust. James declares, "Faith *without* works is dead" (James 2:20), and dead faith cannot save. We are not saved by works; but when we labor in the Lord we testify that we have exercised living, saving faith. There is so much to be done, and so little time to do it. The love of God constrains us to look upon the fields already white unto harvest. We should not say, "Four months—and then comes the harvest." We should labor and pray while it is yet day, for "the night cometh when no man can work" (John 9:4). I personally believe that what we do for Jesus must be done quickly. I believe He is at the door, the Rapture is at hand, and our days to labor for the Master are few.

We suffer . . . because we trust. A true, dedicated, laboring believer will suffer for the sake of the Gospel. "Yea, and all that will live godly in Christ Jesus shall suffer persecution" (II Tim. 3:12).

In II Corinthians 11:23–28 we read of Paul, "Are they ministers of Christ? (I speak as a fool) I am more; in

161

labours more abundant, in stripes above measure, in prisons more frequent, in deaths oft. Of the Jews five times received I forty stripes save one. Thrice was I beaten with rods, once was I stoned, thrice I suffered shipwreck, a night and a day I have been in the deep; in journeyings often, in perils of waters, in perils of robbers, in perils by mine own countrymen, in perils by the heathen, in perils in the city, in perils in the wilderness, in perils in the sea, in perils among false brethren; in weariness and painfulness, in watchings often, in hunger and thirst, in fastings often, in cold and nakedness. Beside those things that are without, that which cometh upon me daily, the care of all the churches."

When I read these verses, I feel so small and insignificant. Have I really ever suffered for the Gospel? When I read the account of the sufferings of Jesus, and hear Him say, "If you are not willing to take up the cross and follow me, you are not worthy to be my disciple," I ask myself if I know the real meaning of suffering! In Rome I stood in the dungeon where Paul was chained during his imprisonment, and the guide, with a little flashlight, showed me the big iron ring through which Paul's hands had been fastened. In the semi-darkness of that Roman prison, as I realized that centuries ago the Apostle Paul was chained on the very spot where I then stood, I keenly felt that I should remove my shoes because I was standing on holy ground. A hot tear ran down my cheek, and in my heart I prayed, "O, God! *Do I know the meaning* of suffering for the Gospel?" Most of us have been tried and tested on various occasions, but do we really know what it means *to suffer for Christ's sake?*

This Gospel that we preach cries out, "TRUST IN THE LIVING GOD." We are not to point men to a minister, pope, or priest—nor to a church, a religion, ceremony, dogma, or tradition. Gospel preachers are to point men to GOD—through the death, burial, and resurrection of Jesus Christ and the shed blood of His cross. He was dead and is alive forevermore. He is the Living One, the Saviour, who died to save all men—*all who will believe.* (He cannot save those who *refuse* to believe. He died for them; but unless they are willing to believe on Him and trust in the living God, He cannot save them. God is love—and love never drives nor forces. God is not a dictator—He is the Good Shepherd.)

The command is: "These things teach, preach, exhort, cry aloud—without fear, favor, or apology!" How thankful we preachers should be that we have the great commission, "Go ye . . . and preach the Word; and lo, I am with you all the way, even to the end!" *If God be for us, who can be against us?*

Verse 12: "Let no man despise thy youth; but be thou an example of the believers, in word, in conversation, in charity, in spirit, in faith, in purity."

Timothy was a young man—very young indeed for so important a position—while Paul was an old preacher (Philemon 9)—prematurely old because of his sufferings and the hardships through which he had come for the sake of the Gospel he so faithfully preached.

Though young in years, Timothy was not young in the Lord. He was a seasoned Christian, spiritually advanced in richness of character, soberness of mind, depth of soul and spirit. The believers at Ephesus soon forgot his youth by recognizing the depth of his spiritual experience. He was "an example of the believers." The original language here suggests that Timothy was a pattern of what every believer should be, and our present verses name the different points in which he excels spiritually:

1. *"In word."*

The speech of this young man—things he said and the way he said them—proved that he was a true believer. We are warned that we must give an account to God for every idle word. By our words we are justified, or by our words we are condemned: "But I say unto you, That every idle word that men shall speak, they shall give account thereof in the day of judgment. For by thy words thou shalt be justified, and by thy words thou shalt be condemned" (Matt. 12:36,37).

What comes out of the mouth is first manufactured in the heart: ". . . Out of the abundance of the heart the mouth speaketh" (Matt. 12:34). Our daily prayer should be the prayer of the Psalmist: "Let the words of my mouth, and the meditation of my heart, be acceptable in thy sight, O Lord, my strength, and my Redeemer" (Psa. 19:14).

2. *"In charity."*

All believers—especially those in a position of leadership—should be living examples of pure, fervent, Christian love. God is love (I John 4:8), and love is the strongest power in this world. The very essence of Christianity is love. Love provided our salvation; love brought that salvation down from God to man. Love is the sweetest element in all human experience.

In Romans 5:5 Paul said, *"The love of God is shed abroad in our hearts by the Holy Ghost which is given unto us."* As believers, if our hearts are not filled with love it is our own fault, because every believer possesses the Holy Spirit. "If any man have not the Spirit of Christ, he is none of His" (Rom. 8:9). Since the Spirit abides in our bosom and the love of God is shed abroad in our hearts by the Holy Spirit, if we are willing to yield our hearts to God to be filled to overflowing with His love, He will grant that request. That is our spiritual birthright as well as the solemn duty of every believer—but especially those in places of leadership. The visible church needs a baptism of God's love. We can win souls by loving them, but we cannot *drive* people into the kingdom of God.

3. *"In spirit."*

Bible authorities agree that "in spirit" as used here means that Timothy was an example to the believers in *enthusiasm.* Certainly enthusiasm is lacking in most Christians today. The average Christian becomes very enthusiastic at a football game or during an election campaign—but when he arrives at church his enthusiasm disappears; and he wants a nice, quiet, orderly service, where the dropping of a pin can be heard.

I do not believe in holding a barn dance in God's house, nor do I believe in a roll-in-the-floor service. I believe worship services should be conducted "decently and in order" (I Cor. 14:40); but one can be enthusiastic and still be orderly. For instance, we can sing from the bottom of our hearts with enthusiasm because we love Jesus and want the whole world to know it. We can witness for Him with convincing enthusiasm; we can smile; we can be always alert. Some Christians drag into God's house on Sunday morning as though their next step would be their last. Many arrive late, and there is no enthusiasm there; but those same people are wide awake and enthusiastic on Monday morning when they plunge into the days that lie ahead through the week.

Such enthusiasm and eagerness as is demonstrated by Jehovah's Witnesses, Roman Catholics—and even the Communists—puts most of us to open shame. Most Roman Catholics have already been to church at least once on Sunday, before the average Protestant is out of bed! If Jesus does for the soul what we claim He does, we should be the most enthusiastic people on earth! We should want everybody on earth to know about our salvation, to possess that salvation, and experience the "joy unspeakable and full of glory" that abides in the bosom of every true, blood-washed, born again believer.

In Hebrews 1:7 Paul declares that God's ministers are to be flames of fire. I wonder how many of us who claim to be pastors, evangelists, and missionaries are really flames of fire for Jesus. John the Baptist was "a burning and a shining light" (John 5:35). We have many "shining" ministers today—but how many of us are *burning*? We have hosts of church members who shine on Sunday morning—but how many are burning witnesses on Sunday night and at prayer meeting, or on revival nights and throughout the day on their secular jobs?

4. *"In faith."*

The Greek here suggests *faithfulness*. Timothy had exercised faith unto salvation many years before—but here he is a faithful example of that faith. During Timothy's lifetime the church encountered much opposition. There was danger—even bodily danger, danger of being killed. Enemies of the Gospel threatened the apostles. These men of God suffered much and endured many hardships. Temptations were great. It would have been very easy for Timothy to become discouraged and disappointed— but rather he proved a good example and a true pattern of born again believers. He was an example in faithful Christian living day by day.

5. *"In purity."*

We can sum up the meaning here by saying that Timothy practiced blameless, consecrated Christian living. He believed in and lived practical, Bible holiness— not the type advocated by some religionists today, but blameless, spotless, pure living as taught in the Scriptures.

Verse 13: "Till I come, give attendance to reading, to exhortation, to doctrine."

"*Till I come . . . .*" This definitely indicates that Paul planned to return to Ephesus to visit with and minister to the church there. He did not want Timothy to become discouraged, but to be faithful, alert, and enthusiastic in watching over the flock, feeding them and making sure that no wolves got in among them until his return. In Luke 19:13 Jesus instructs us to "occupy" until He comes.

Three things are pointed out for Timothy to do until such time as Paul can visit the church at Ephesus:

1. *"Give attendance to reading."*

In the early church, the minister read the Scriptures aloud to the congregation. The early Christians could not go to town and purchase a nice leather-bound Bible as we do today, and there were very few scrolls containing the books of the Old Testament. The letters Paul wrote to the churches were read from the original parchment on which he wrote them; and to Timothy he says, "Do not neglect systematic reading. Read the Scriptures to the people; keep them constantly under the sound of God's Word."

I believe Paul gave Timothy a twofold command here: He was not only to read the Scriptures to the people for their comfort, exhortation, edification—and rebuke, if necessary—but he was also to read systematically *to feed his own heart* and build up his own spiritual strength. One of the failures of ministers today is lack of reading the Word of God, studying, and equipping themselves to feed the flock.

Jesus gave attendance to reading: ". . . AS HIS CUSTOM WAS, (He) went into the synagogue on the

Sabbath day, and stood up for to read" (Luke 4:16). In the Old Testament days, Ezra read the Word from early morning until noon, and the people stood and listened to him (Neh. 8:3–5). What a grand and glorious privilege it is to read the Word of God to those to whom we preach— and yet some ministers do not even take the Bible into the pulpit on Sunday morning! God pity that poor preacher when he stands before God to give an account of his ministry.

The one message this world needs more than all other messages combined is that laid down in the Holy Scriptures, for no other message will bring sinners to Christ. The Word of God is the power of God unto salvation. The Word is a lamp unto our feet and a light unto our pathway. God's Word is milk to the babe in Christ, meat to those who need strong food, and the cleansing power for the believer: *"Now ye are clean through the Word which I have spoken unto you"* (John 15:3). "Sanctify them through thy truth: thy Word is truth" (John 17:17). We will never know this side of heaven the importance of God's Word. No wonder the devil has tried to destroy it, discredit it, and water it down through different translations of the Bible. How thankful I am that the Word of God is forever settled in heaven, and that it will not return unto Him void, but will accomplish that whereunto it is sent.

2. *"Give attendance . . . to exhortation."*

Timothy is to read the Word to the believers, but he is also to give them words that will challenge, instruct, comfort, guide, rebuke, and strengthen them in the inner man. There is not much real exhortation in the average Sunday morning "sermonette" today. A good minister of God exhorts the people *from the Word of God*— and this is drastically needed in these days of difficulty, perplexities and anxieties. How we preachers need to deliver a message that satisfies, strengthens, encourages, and pushes on! All too many times today the message from the pulpit is a message "which satisfieth not" (Isa. 55:2).

3. *"Give attendance . . . to doctrine."*

I pray that you see the significance of the fact that doctrine is mentioned last. In II Timothy 4:1,2 Paul says, "I charge thee therefore before God, and the Lord Jesus Christ, who shall judge the quick and the dead at His appearing and His kingdom; preach the Word; be instant in season, out of season; reprove, rebuke, exhort with all longsuffering and *doctrine.*"

Again "doctrine" is mentioned last. The Holy Spirit did not place doctrine last because it is of the least importance, but *there is no need to preach doctrine to people until they are born of the Spirit* and have become spiritually minded enough to practice the doctrine preached to them. Doctrine is important, and we must preach it; but there is no need to indoctrinate an unbeliever or a backslider. We need first to get the unbeliever converted and the backslider reclaimed. The sermon needed by sinners and backsliders is a sermon explaining the plan of salvation, that it is not God's will that any perish, that God is married to the backslider and it is His will that all repent. Today the average Sunday morning sermon is seasoned—not with the salt of the Word—but with the doctrine of the denomination. The people are commanded to be loyal to the program, instead of being exhorted to yield soul, spirit, and body unreservedly to Jesus.

There is a drastic need for a teaching ministry among the born again, because the average church is poorly instructed concerning Bible doctrine. Denominational beliefs . . . yes, they know those; they endure one study course after another on what this or that denomination

169

believes—but when it comes to pure, down-to-earth Bible doctrine, the average church member is woefully ignorant. The individual should read the Bible and study it, but the blame for Bible ignorance among church members can be placed primarily at the doorstep of the pastors. Ministers are called to study, rightly handle the Word of Truth, and feed the flock of God. We are not to be lords over God's heritage; we are to lead the flock where pastures are green and give instruction in the deep spiritual things of the Word of God which constitute true Bible doctrine.

Verse 14: "Neglect not the gift that is in thee, which was given thee by prophecy, with the laying on of the hands of the presbytery."

Neglect is sinful. Believers should not live lives of neglect. Paul warns Timothy, *"Neglect not the gift that is in thee."* As overseer of the believers in Ephesus, Timothy carried a grave responsibility concerning their personal spiritual needs—both doctrinally and morally; and to discharge his duty as God's undershepherd he must always be alert and ready to serve. Therefore God had given him a special anointing—a special gift.

Every believer possesses the Holy Spirit. There is no such thing as being a child of God *apart from* the Holy Spirit; but while every believer is *born* of the Spirit and *possesses* the Spirit, not every believer is *fully surrendered TO* the Spirit. God gives special anointings of the Spirit for special ministries, and no minister should ever enter the pulpit without first praying for God to fill him with the Spirit for that particular service and sermon. The Holy Spirit permanently abides in the heart of every believer; but the Bible clearly teaches that a specific anointing of the Spirit is scriptural, and Timothy possessed this gift. The Spirit furnished the power through which he discharged his duties as God's undershepherd

170

and leader of the flock. Paul therefore said, *"Neglect not the gift that is in thee."*

Many Christians are powerless and joyless because they have neglected the gift of God within. The Corinthians were carnal, worldly—and Paul rebuked them sternly by saying, "What? Know ye not that your body is the temple of the Holy Ghost which is in you, which ye have of God, and ye are not your own?" (I Cor. 6:19). The Corinthian believers were dishonoring the Lord by dishonoring their bodies and living in carnality. Paul admonished them to repent and recognize the solemn fact that the Holy Ghost abides within every believer. We are the temple of the Holy Ghost, and we should be very careful how we treat that temple.

The Corinthians possessed the power . . . they could have been strong, victorious believers, successful witnesses and outstanding examples of the believer; but they had quenched and dishonored the Spirit. They were not walking in the light; they were not permitting the Spirit to guide them into paths of right living and the warmth of God's love. They were following their own selfish desires—divided, arguing among themselves, drinking wine at the Lord's table. Paul declared that many of them were sick and some were dead because they had refused to judge themselves. They had refused to yield to the Spirit and dedicate their lives unreservedly to the Lord, allowing the Holy Spirit to possess and lead them in order that they might glorify God in all that they did.

This gift to which Paul refers was given "by prophecy." Prophecy has a twofold meaning: a prophet is one who *foretells*, but he is also one who *forthtells* what has already been foretold. The meaning here, applied to Timothy, is the telling forth of the Word of God. The "laying on of the hands of the presbytery" was an outward sign that this young man had been set apart by the

Holy Ghost to forthtell the message outlined in I Timothy 3:16—the mystery of godliness: God "manifested in the flesh, justified in the Spirit, seen of angels, preached unto the nations, believed on in the world, and received up into glory." Paul is saying here that Timothy was commissioned by the Holy Ghost to preach the Word, and the Presbytery laid hands on him as an outward symbol that God had chosen him.

In Acts 13:3 Barnabas and Saul were sent forth in the same manner. (In my own personal experience, I shall never forget the night the presbytery laid hands on me and set me apart—a minister of the Gospel. I have forgotten many things that have happened since that night; but I have never forgotten the moment when those men of God laid their hands on my head and prayed, dedicating me and setting me apart for God's work.)

Paul is here reminding Timothy to be very careful lest he neglect the gift that he possessed—a gift bestowed upon him to enable him to be the Lord's undershepherd, to preach the Word, to give out the good news that Jesus Christ was crucified, buried, and raised for our justification.

Verse 15: "Meditate upon these things; give thyself wholly to them; that thy profiting may appear to all."

There is no conflict of truth in the Scriptures; they agree from Genesis through Revelation. In the first Psalm we read, "Blessed is the man that walketh not in the counsel of the ungodly, nor standeth in the way of sinners, nor sitteth in the seat of the scornful. But his delight is in the law of the Lord; and in His law doth he meditate day and night. And he shall be like a tree planted by the rivers of water, that bringeth forth his fruit in his season; his leaf also shall not wither; and whatsoever he doeth shall prosper. The ungodly are not so: but are like the chaff which the wind driveth away. Therefore the ungodly shall not stand in the judgment, nor sinners in the congregation of the righteous. For the Lord knoweth the way of the righteous: but the way of the ungodly shall perish."

Please note: "IN HIS LAW (Word) DOTH HE MEDITATE DAY AND NIGHT." We are living in the age spoken of in Scripture as *"times of peril."* The average minister today has but little time to meditate. His time is taken up with committee meetings, oiling the denominational machinery and keeping the program going. In the early church, deacons were appointed in order that the pastor might give his time to prayer and study of the Word; but the majority of preachers today are entirely too busy to meditate, and as a result the church suffers.

Joshua was a spiritual giant of Old Testament days, and in his book we read, "This book of the law shall not depart out of thy mouth; but thou shalt meditate therein day and night, that thou mayest observe to do according to all that is written therein: for then thou shalt make thy way prosperous, and then thou shalt have good success. Have not I commanded thee? Be strong and of a good courage; be not afraid, neither be thou dismayed: for the Lord thy God is with thee whithersoever thou goest" (Joshua 1:8,9).

When Joshua received his command as a soldier of Almighty God, he was admonished not to let the Word of God depart out of his mouth, but to meditate therein day and night, to do according to all that is written in the Word; and by so doing he was promised blessings untold. His way would be prosperous, and he would have success in all that he did. God has never broken a promise, and He will keep His promises to you and to me. If we seek first His kingdom, if we will meditate in the Word day and night, we will be strong and of good courage.

We will not fear; we will not be dismayed. The Lord God will be with us whithersoever we go, and He will be with us "even unto the end."

Greek authorities tell us that the word used here for *"meditate"* is the same word that suggests an animal chewing the cud. We should experience what the Psalmist declared: "Thy word is sweeter than honey in the honeycomb." The more we feed upon the Word and the more we chew it, the sweeter it becomes. The more we feed upon the Word, the hungrier we become for the Word. Jesus lost a goodly number of would-be disciples when He said, "Except ye eat the flesh of the Son of man, and drink His blood, ye have no life in you. Whoso eateth my flesh, and drinketh my blood, hath eternal life; and I will raise him up at the last day" (John 6:53,54).

The Psalmist said, "How sweet are thy words unto my taste! yea, sweeter than honey to my mouth!" (Psalm 119:103). In Psalm 119:97 we read, "O how love I thy law! It is my meditation all the day." Paul tells Timothy to meditate upon these things—things that God had done and had prepared to do for and through Timothy. The more we meditate upon the things of God, the stronger we become spiritually and the more effectively we can serve the Lord.

Paul goes deeper: ". . . *Give thyself wholly to them.*" In other words, "Throw yourself completely into the ministry; throw yourself at the feet of Jesus. Give of your time, your physical strength, your talents Give everything, always. Put yourself entirely into the ministry of the Word."

I would not offend any innocent young preacher; it is perfectly honorable for a young minister to work at manual labor to supplement his livelihood during his school days or early ministry. (Paul made tents and thereby earned bread and other necessities for himself, in order to avoid placing the burden of dependence upon the young churches.) But "they that preach the Gospel should live of the Gospel" (I Cor. 9:14). Paul said, "My God shall supply all your need according to His riches in glory by Christ Jesus" (Phil. 4:19). And our present Scripture instructs, *"Give thyself wholly to them."*

It is a shame and disgrace to the ministry for the pastor of a large church to operate a business or work at a secular occupation to supplement the salary paid by the church, when in that church are business men and women, wealthy farmers, and people who could give liberally to the work of the Lord! Such a thing is uncalled for and brings shame upon the church. Any minister who pastors a church with even fifty families in it has as much to do as any one man *can possibly* do! A minister who is handling God's work as he should does not have time to work forty hours a week to earn bread for himself and his family. And any church large enough to provide a living wage for a minister should pay him enough to live on and furnish him with a decent place to live —otherwise, that church is not worthy of a pastor and should be padlocked and put out of business.

God pity people who claim to be born again, who claim to love Jesus—yet who will not give at least the tithe of their income to support a pastor who shepherds the flock of God. And God pity the preachers who use their ministry as a sideline. I say this in love, but today many ministers run a business, a farm, or some other secular job, and preach only on Sunday. Their ministry does not interfere with their business—but it should be the other way around. A preacher should never let anything—family, friends, or business—interfere with his ministry. It is a grave responsibility to be a minister of the Gospel.

A minister of the Gospel should be so completely

wrapped up in his ministry, so thoroughly permeated by the Gospel, that he would be continuously concentrating on the Gospel—given wholly to it, living in it. He should be so absorbed in things of the Spirit and the Word that he could not concentrate on things pertaining to the business world and making money.

One of the finest definitions to be found for a minister of the Gospel is found in Haggai 1:13: "Then spake Haggai, THE LORD'S MESSENGER, IN THE LORD'S MESSAGE UNTO THE PEOPLE, saying, I am with you, saith the Lord." That is what a true minister is—he is God's mouthpiece with God's message. He speaks as God orders, and he says what God tells him to say.

I am not suggesting that a minister should sit with a Bible in his hand twenty-four hours a day; that is not the idea at all. We must rest; we must have a time of recreation. Jesus said to His disciples, "Come ye apart and rest awhile." But we can rest and yet meditate upon the things of God. There are many clean sports in which a minister can participate, such as fishing, hunting, and others that I will not take the time to name here. The calm of a lake or the quiet of the deep forest gives a minister rest from the duties of his parish and community; and yet he can commune with God in a fuller, deeper way than he could in his study or in his home.

No, I am not suggesting that we drive ourselves until we drop from physical exhaustion; but we should meditate in the things of God and be ready to give forth the message of truth at all times—to rebuke, exhort, edify, comfort and strengthen by giving out the Word of God; and we cannot feed others until we have first fed ourselves.

The success of Daniel the prophet is summed up in Daniel 1:8: "But Daniel *purposed in his heart* that he would not defile himself with the portion of the king's meat, nor with the wine which he drank . . . ." Daniel made a vow to himself and to God—and he lived by it! Who would not want to be as successful as Daniel?

A church will climb to no higher heights nor reach deeper in spiritual things than the pastor leads the people; and the pastor cannot lead his people to heights of spiritual attainment that he himself has not experienced. Therefore, meditation, consecration, and dedication are imperative if a preacher would be the leader God intends his ministers to be.

Verse 15 closes with these words: ". . . *That thy profiting may appear to all."* The Greek word here translated "profiting" does not mean what we think of when we speak of profit in business; it means *growth and progress.* What Paul is saying to Timothy is that he must grow and advance—and the people must SEE that advancement, before they will follow him. A leader must first be led of God, moving onward, outward, upward, becoming ever stronger if he hopes for his people to follow in his steps.

Paul instructed those to whom he ministered that they should follow him—but only as he walked in the steps of Jesus. There is no such thing as spiritual stagnation— we either grow, or we diminish. We do not remain the same spiritually. We become stronger, or we become weaker.

Verse 16: "Take heed unto thyself, and unto the doctrine; continue in them: for in doing this thou shalt both save thyself, and them that hear thee."

What Paul is saying to Timothy is this: "Check yourself. Do not teach or preach anything unless you are sure you are preaching the doctrine that is right." A preacher must live what he preaches; he must measure up to the standards he sets for others. As ministers we should take heed unto ourselves—be sure our manner of life is right, be sure the doctrine we preach is right—and then we should command our people to follow us as we set the example in the footsteps of Jesus.

I am an evangelist. I have never been a pastor, and I do not know all of the heartaches and disappointments a pastor must endure. But I have worked with many pastors, and I do know some of the problems they face. Frankly, I think I should die of a broken heart if I were in the shoes of some pastors; for instance, if I were pastor of a church in which not one person was converted in the course of a year, with the same group attending services Sunday after Sunday, not bringing in new folks, going through the rituals, singing the same songs and leaving the service seemingly unconcerned. I could not bear being pastor of a church where people were not being converted, where the church did not move forward, where the membership did not increase.

I realize that in some localities the potential is not as great as in others, and some churches cannot grow as rapidly as others; but I do not believe there is a church in existence around which are not some people who need to be born again—and if the members of that church love the unsaved and go after them in a spirit of humility and love, *somebody WILL BE saved*! There may not be conversions in every service—perhaps not even every Sunday—but certainly people will be saved if God's representatives do their duty in the community.

Every minister should take stock of himself. He should ask himself what he has accomplished in the past month, six months, or year. What do his parishioners think of him? Do they respect him as God's representative? What is he really like in the eyes of those who sit in the pew? Each of us need to examine ourselves and our ministry. We need to cry out with the Psalmist, "Examine me, O Lord, and prove me; try my reins and my heart"

(Psalm 26:2). In II Corinthians 13:5 Paul said, "Examine yourselves, whether ye be in the faith; prove your own selves." When we see ourselves in the mirror of the Word, the reflection may be humiliating and painful; but if we will look with honesty—and then do something about what we see—it will pay great dividends in the results that follow.

Paul admonishes Timothy, ". . . *Continue in them.*" God's preacher does not change his doctrine to suit the times nor the parish where he preaches. Ministers of God are not driven about with every wind of doctrine; nor do they preach to please the people. They preach pure Bible doctrine—and they *continue* preaching Bible doctrine, even if it hurts to the extent that many members "walk with him no more," like the disciples in John 6:66. People change, and religions change their doctrines—but the Bible does not change, and *Bible doctrine* does not change.

We recently read in the papers about big religions bringing their doctrines up to date. The doctrine of the New Testament church does not NEED to be brought "up to date." It IS up to date—always has been and always will be. People who are driven about with every wind of doctrine, changing their doctrine every few months, need only one thing: *The New Birth!*

In Galatians 5:7 Paul said, "Ye did run well; who did hinder you that ye should not obey the truth?" But we read a refreshing statement in Acts 2:42: ". . . They continued stedfastly in the apostles' doctrine and fellowship, and in breaking of bread, and in prayers." These first Christians enjoyed their first love. They continued daily, stedfastly, in the same doctrine, and in fellowship, breaking of bread, and in prayer. The church needs more stedfast believers.

Three thousand souls were saved on the Day of

Pentecost, two thousand a bit later, many thousands still later—and if any of these first believers backslid or fell by the wayside, there is not one iota of Scripture to suggest it! They *continued*—and by continuing, *they grew*; and the more they grew, *the stronger they became*. The more they served the Lord, the more they wanted to serve Him. The Pentecost converts moved on; and if the church had continued to move on until this day as it did in the first days of Christianity, you may rest assured that things would be quite different here on earth today.

Our verse and chapter closes with these words: "... *For in doing this, thou shalt both save thyself, and them that hear thee.*" These words do not suggest that Timothy could redeem his soul nor save the souls of those to whom he ministered; but Paul is telling Timothy that if he will continue in the things of the Lord, meditate on the Word of God, continue in sound doctrine, not deviating from the truth, he will save his ministry, save his testimony, save his influence, and save his reward; and he will also save the influence, testimony, and rewards of those to whom he ministers in the church at Ephesus.

In I Corinthians 9:27 Paul said, "... I keep under my body, and bring it into subjection: lest that by any means, when I have preached to others, I myself should be a castaway."

This last phrase does not mean that Paul feared God would cast him out, or that he would lose his redemption after having been a minister preaching to others. Paul is saying here, "Lest I be laid on the shelf, no longer a vessel meet for the Master's use, and lose my influence." He did not believe, teach, nor suggest that he would lose his redemption; but he wanted to be sure he did not lose his reward. He did not want to bring reproach upon the Gospel and the people to whom he had faithfully preached. Jesus said, "HIM THAT COMETH TO ME, I WILL IN NO WISE CAST OUT" (John 6:37). The true meaning of the pure Greek used here is, "Him that cometh to me, I WILL NOT ON ANY ACCOUNT cast out." That does not mean that a person will come to Jesus, confess Christianity—and then live like the devil wants him to live, and in the end God will take him into the kingdom. It simply means that when one is born into God's family by exercising faith in the finished work of Jesus—when one is dead, hid with Christ in God (Col. 3:3)—that person will not be cut off nor cast out. He may become a castaway; he may lose his reward and his influence, and God may lay him on the shelf. He may suffer; he may be sick; *he may even commit the sin unto death*—but that does not mean that his redemption and eternal life are taken away.

There is a vast difference between salvation and rewards. Paul is here admonishing a born again, God-appointed minister to take heed unto himself and be careful; to know the truth and be sure he preaches true doctrine—the faith once delivered to the saints. By so doing he will save himself and save the people to whom he preaches. We know that NO MAN can save his soul; but he can save his influence . . . he can save his testimony, by being an upright, faithful Christian, daily practicing blameless living.

In Romans 11:1 Paul asks, "Hath God cast away His people?" Then he answers, "God forbid!" God does not cast away His people, nor cut them off. The vast misunderstanding on this subject among Christians today is due to the fact that many do not understand that not all who profess religion are redeemed and truly saved. They may join a church and be baptized, but that does not determine whether or not one is saved. Only God knows the heart—and He *judges the heart*, not the outward appearance.

181

Ministers need to give solemn warning that God does lay some on the shelf when they become so careless and unconcerned that He cannot use them any more. They become a castaway, laid aside because of negligence and a poor testimony. They become detrimental to the cause of Christ. They are no longer an asset to the church, and God lays them aside.

To all believers Paul says, "I beseech you therefore, brethren, by the mercies of God, that ye present your bodies a living sacrifice, holy, acceptable unto God, which is your reasonable service. And be not conformed to this world: but be ye transformed by the renewing of your mind, that ye may prove what is that good, and acceptable, and perfect, will of God" (Rom. 12:1,2).

May God help us to do as Paul says. If at this moment we do not have soul, spirit, and body on God's altar, may we yield unreservedly—parishioner and pastor, bishop and deacon, evangelist, missionary, and teacher. May we yield our all to Jesus and be a good example of the believer in all that we are and in all that we do.

I TIMOTHY — CHAPTER FIVE

THE WORK OF A GOOD MINISTER OF JESUS CHRIST

1. Rebuke not an elder, but intreat him as a father; and the younger men as brethren;

2. The elder women as mothers; the younger as sisters, with all purity.

3. Honour widows that are widows indeed.

4. But if any widow have children or nephews, let them learn first to shew piety at home, and to requite their parents: for that is good and acceptable before God.

5. Now she that is a widow indeed, and desolate, trusteth in God, and continueth in supplications and prayers night and day.

6. But she that liveth in pleasure is dead while she liveth.

7. And these things give in charge, that they may be blameless.

8. But if any provide not for his own, and specially for those of his own house, he hath denied the faith, and is worse than an infidel.

9. Let not a widow be taken into the number under threescore years old, having been the wife of one man,

10. Well reported of for good works; if she have brought up children, if she have lodged strangers, if she have washed the saints' feet, if she have relieved the afflicted, if she have diligently followed every good work.

11. But the younger widows refuse: for when they have begun to wax wanton against Christ, they will marry;

12. Having damnation, because they have cast off their first faith.

13. And withal they learn to be idle, wandering about from house to house; and not only idle, but tattlers also and busybodies, speaking things which they ought not.

14. I will therefore that the younger women marry, bear children, guide the house, give none occasion to the adversary to speak reproachfully.

15. For some are already turned aside after Satan.

16. If any man or woman that believeth have widows, let them relieve them, and let not the church be charged; that it may relieve them that are widows indeed.

17. Let the elders that rule well be counted worthy of double honour, especially they who labour in the word and doctrine.

18. For the scripture saith, Thou shalt not muzzle the ox that treadeth out the corn. And, The labourer is worthy of his reward.

19. Against an elder receive not an accusation, but before two or three witnesses.

20. Them that sin rebuke before all, that others also may fear.

21. I charge thee before God, and the Lord Jesus Christ, and the elect angels, that thou observe these things without preferring one before another, doing nothing by partiality.

22. Lay hands suddenly on no man, neither be partaker of other men's sins: keep thyself pure.

23. Drink no longer water, but use a little wine for thy stomach's sake and thine often infirmities.

24. Some men's sins are open beforehand, going before to judgment; and some men they follow after.

25. Likewise also the good works of some are manifest beforehand; and they that are otherwise cannot be hid.

Instructions Concerning Widows

The Christian religion is essentially personal. We are saved individually; but in the words of the Apostle Paul, "None of us liveth to himself, and no man dieth to himself" (Rom. 14:7). Even though Christianity is a personal thing, Christians cannot divorce themselves from family and fellowman. James tells us, "Pure religion and undefiled before God and the Father is this, To visit the fatherless and widows in their affliction, and to keep himself unspotted from the world" (James 1:27). The Christian is definitely obligated to others. It is a grand and glorious privilege to be a Christian, but such privilege carries great responsibility.

The first eleven chapters of Paul's letter to the Romans are primarily doctrinal. In chapter 12 he cries out for full surrender, begging believers in the church at Rome to present their bodies a living sacrifice—holy and acceptable unto God, which is the reasonable service of all Christians. From chapter 12 through the remaining chapters of Romans, Paul deals with practical daily Christian living. He deals with our attitude toward our fellow

Christians and toward mankind in general. For example, if eating meat offends a weaker brother, then we should be willing to forego the eating of meat for the sake of that brother. We cannot live as we please if we follow in the steps of Jesus. We must consider others.

Paul's letter to the church at Ephesus is deeply spiritual, and the theme of Ephesians is *"the heavenlies."* But in the last part of this great epistle he deals with the Christian and his duty to others here on earth, pointing out the relationship between husband and wife, parents and children, masters and servants.

In his letter to the believers at Corinth he points out that we are all members of one body, with Jesus as the Head—and when one member of that body suffers, the entire body suffers. It is very important that we consider our fellowman in all of our activities—in the church, in the community, in business—wherever we have to do with others. A good minister must instruct the people concerning these matters.

Verses 1 and 2: "Rebuke not an elder, but intreat him as a father; and the younger men as brethren; the elder women as mothers; the younger as sisters, with all purity."

These verses name the members of a family. Certainly the New Testament Church IS a family—ONE family, with Jesus as the Head. Members of the New Testament Church are named under many figures. We are soldiers in the army of the Lord, competitors in a race—not to receive a corruptible crown, but an incorruptible. We are members of the body of Christ; not all are the most important members, but even the least member is needed and cannot be ignored. We are servants in the household of God; we are branches connected to the Vine; we are singers in the heavenly choir; we are living stones in the building; we are born ones; we are a spiritual house; we are children of the Father, heirs of God, and joint heirs with Jesus Christ. *We are intimately related one to the other.* We are "blood kin" because we are all *under* the same blood, *washed* in the same blood, members of the same heavenly family.

In the church, *old men* are to be treated as fathers. The white-haired saints of God are not to be pushed around, abused, ignored; they are to be loved, honored, and revered as fathers. Paul instructs Timothy not to deal with these old saints as he would with the younger ones. He is not to rebuke them for some petty fault that they may have, but rather *intreat them* to do better. A child can be led, but it is wrong to take a stick and drive him. A twig can be bent and shaped, but it must be handled with tenderness; and when young men grow into old men, they possess for the second time many traits and habits of little children. Many times they are left out or pushed back and ignored, and thus are gravely injured and hurt. This should not be.

Young men in the assembly are to be treated as brothers. Those who are older in the Lord and better qualified to serve in the church are not to show superiority over the younger men; but rather, they are to treat them as brothers, loving them and sharing with them the joys of carrying on the Lord's work in the local assembly.

Old women in the church are to be treated as mothers— loved, honored, and esteemed. They are not to be ignored and left alone while the younger ladies carry out the duties of the women in the assembly. Real Christianity ignores neither the old folks nor the younger people. They may not all be fitted to do a task as efficiently as someone else might do it; but we must not ignore them, because they are members of the same body to which we belong.

Young women in the church are to be treated as sisters. They are to be loved, honored, guarded and protected against unholy lust and sin which could overtake them.

I John 2:12—14 gives a similar picture, referring to members of the church as *little children*—those who have been saved but a short while. John then refers to *young men*—those who have grown stronger in the faith; and then he refers to *fathers*—those who have been saved for many years, advanced in grace, knowledge, faith and strength—who have been used of the Lord to win others, thus begetting other sons through the preaching of the Gospel and the testimony they give.

The Church of the living God is definitely a family group. Paul refers to Timothy as "my own son . . . my dearly beloved son." Those of us who are spiritual, who have been saved for many years and have grown in grace and in the knowledge of our Lord and Saviour, Jesus Christ, should be extremely considerate of new converts. If we see them doing things or going places they should not, instead of rebuking them we should *intreat them* and do our best to lead them to a higher plane of spiritual living. We should treat the older people in the church in the same fashion. If we have advanced spiritually and are stronger than others, we should not look down on them but do all in our power to help them when they need help, because they are our brothers and sisters in the body of Christ.

Verse 3: "Honour widows that are widows indeed."

Please notice the statement *"widows indeed"*—not just ladies who have lost their husbands in death, but those who have lost *everything* and do not have a livelihood. If a husband passed away leaving sufficient funds to care for his widow, the church was not responsible for her; but in the early days of Christianity, a good percentage of believers were very poor—many of them slaves, earning the bare necessities of life. In that day it was not uncommon that a woman who lost her husband did not have any income from which to live, and it was more needful in that day than it is today that the church care for the widows who were "widows indeed."

Verse 4: "But if any widow have children or nephews, let them learn first to shew piety at home, and to requite their parents: for that is good and acceptable before God."

This verse points out that if a widow has children or close relatives who are able to care for her, she is not to be classified as a "widow indeed." It is a sad fact in our day that many of the aged parents in rest homes, and in county homes kept up by the state and charities, have children who are financially able to care for their parents. I say without apology that children who are financially able to give their aged parents a comfortable home are scripturally obligated to do so. Those of us who have living parents who are aged should realize that they cared for us when we could not care for ourselves. We owe our physical existence to their care and provision, and certainly we should appreciate what they have done for us enough to care for them in the declining years of their life. A little love goes a long, long way with a child, and the same is true of an aged person who has many of the *characteristics* of a child. There are so many lonely old people in this day of ours.

For children to place aged parents in a county home or turn them over to a welfare agency is not only ungracious and ungrateful, a very poor way to requite parents for what they have done for the children, but it is also no small matter in the eyes of God. In verse 8 of our present chapter Paul tells us, *"If any provide not for his own, and specially for those of his own house, he*

hath denied the faith, and is worse than an infidel."
We will discuss this further when we reach that verse.

From Mount Sinai God gave the command, "Honour thy father and thy mother." In Ephesians Paul reminds us that this is the first commandment *"with promise."* Children who dishonor their parents and lack respect for them can expect to die at an early age, because the Bible commands that children honor their parents. If we honor our parents, we are promised a long life; if we do not, our days will be cut short upon this earth. God provides a special blessing to the children who care for their aged parents and to those who show kindness, love and care toward the aged saints in the church and community.

Timothy is to instruct the believers in his parish, and see that his flock is keenly aware of the will of God in this matter of social obligation. The duty of believers toward the elderly saints is not to be overlooked, evaded, or neglected. It is a sad reflection on human nature when children permit their parents, who brought them into the world, to suffer physically when they could do something to alleviate that suffering; and it is a bad testimony for the church if aged members are permitted to suffer and lack the necessities of life when these dear saints could be provided for by the fat bank accounts which often are held in reserve by the local assemblies of this day!

Verse 5: "Now she that is a widow indeed, and desolate, trusteth in God, and continueth in supplications and prayers night and day."

The church has a responsibility toward widows who are "widows indeed." First, they are to be honored . . . verse 3 clearly declares this. A "widow indeed" is an honorable person and should be honored in the church. She may not dress as nicely as others; she may not have things of this life in such abundance as others do—but

189

she is not to be looked down upon. She is to be esteemed and honored by other ladies of the church.

Pride is one of the ugliest sins of which a Christian can be guilty. There is entirely too much pride in the lives of Christians today. The right kind of pride is good, but the wrong kind of pride is ugly and sinful.

A widow indeed *"trusteth in God, and continueth in supplications and prayers night and day."* When the husband of a dear, spiritually-minded woman dies, Jesus said He would be a husband to that widow; and we know that when a woman has a husband he naturally requires much of her time. Therefore, when she loses her husband in death, the love she bestowed upon him must be showered upon someone else—and the spiritually-minded widow will transfer that love to Jesus. She will pray more and trust God more fully. Before her husband passed away she put much of her trust in him concerning the needs of life. She shared her heartaches, heartbreaks, and disappointments with her husband—and after his death she has no one but God in whom to trust, to whom she can look for help, and upon whom she must depend for the necessities of life. Such widows indeed are jewels of great value, both to the local assembly and to the kingdom of God.

Verse 6: "But she that liveth in pleasure is dead while she liveth."

A widow (or any other woman) who lives in the pleasures of this world *"is dead while she lives"*! Any woman who lives only for the things of this life has more time for clubs, theatres, and parties than she has for prayer meeting, church, and Bible study. She lives for what the world calls "a good time," and such a woman is not a "widow indeed." She is not a living example of God's grace; *she is dead!*

It is not contrary to the Law of God to enjoy legitimate

pleasure. It is natural and right to enjoy the good things of this life; but it is sinful to live only for pleasure, as many people do. A believer should desire the things of the Spirit. We are admonished, "Set your affection on things above, not on things on the earth" (Col. 3:2). If a widow sets her affections on things of earth and lives for pleasure, the church is under no obligation to her—for she is dead, spiritually speaking.

I would like to pay my deepest respect to widows, and express my gratitude to them, for I am deeply conscious of the fact that my ministry is indebted to widows—and to precious mothers and wives who have supported me these many years in my evangelistic ministry—on the radio, through the printed page, in mammoth tents, in churches, and on foreign mission fields. Every penny I have invested in the Gospel has been given to me by God's people, and I do not believe I exaggerate when I say that ninety percent of the money contributed to my ministry has been contributed by God-fearing women! I do praise God for the business men who help me with liberal gifts; but it is the dollars, dimes, and quarters from precious widows, from the aged and the shut-ins—even from young wives and working girls—that make the Gospel Hour a nationwide ministry. I personally praise God for the widows who support my ministry; and if I have ever wronged an aged person, I did so in total ignorance. I have a very warm spot in my heart for widows; my own mother is a widow of many years.

Paul clearly states that responsibility for the livelihood of a "widow indeed" falls first upon her relatives; but if sons and daughters, nephews and other close relatives fail the widow, then *the responsibility rests upon the church*. (Note verse 16 in this chapter.)

Let me again point out that the Church is one body, with Jesus as the Head. We are members of that body—

bone of His bone, flesh of His flesh; and in I Corinthians 12:26 Paul tells us, "Whether one member suffer, all the members suffer with it; or one member be honoured, all the members rejoice with it." We are very definitely indebted one to the other, as believers and as members of the body of Christ.

Verse 7: "And these things give in charge, that they may be blameless."

In this verse Paul simply tells Timothy, "Preach the truth; charge widows and their relatives that they follow the Bible program of providing for the needy in the church, that they may be blameless." If we deny and disobey what God clearly lays down as our duty one toward another, we will be held accountable. It is sin to disobey the truth and refuse to walk in the light. Timothy is to preach this clearly and in a manner that can be understood, so that believing children can practice scriptural care for their widowed mothers and relatives.

Verse 8: "But if any provide not for his own, and specially for those of his own house, he hath denied the faith, and is worse than an infidel."

I referred to this verse earlier. Many times we think of an infidel as the vilest person on earth. He owes his very existence to God, because God is the Author of life; he breathes God's air, bathes in God's sunshine, walks with the strength God gives him, eats the food God permits to grow—and yet denies the very existence of God and blasphemes His name! Many atheists have even gone so far as to challenge God to kill them, and have made drastic statements concerning God; yet God has spared them and allowed them to live to a ripe old age.

There are no infidels in hell: They are believers NOW—but it is too late! The moment an atheist dies, he is converted from atheism. Three seconds after he drops into hell he knows by experience that there IS a God. Do not misunderstand me: I did not say the atheist was *converted to heaven.* He is converted FROM atheism; he becomes a believer—but he is still in hell. It takes only three seconds of hell fire to change the mind of an atheist, regardless of what he has said or written about hell, or how firmly he believed in its non-existence. There IS a hell, and those who do not believe that truth this side of the grave WILL believe three seconds after death.

Paul clearly states that a person who will not provide for his own household has denied the faith and is WORSE than an infidel. Husbands, are you providing for your household? Do you set the right example before your family and provide a livelihood for them? Do you labor untiringly that they may have the necessities of life? If not, then you should never testify in the assembly; you should not tell your neighbors that you are a child of God—for if you do not provide for your own family, the Word declares you to be worse than an infidel.

Verse 9: "Let not a widow be taken into the number under threescore years old, having been the wife of one man."

It seems that in the Ephesian church—possibly in all the assemblies in the early days of the church—there was a specific organization to which only widows belonged. Evidently they were recruited for a specialized service in the local assembly. Many times when a woman loses her husband she feels that she has lost everything, and in some instances confesses that she does not desire to live. The bottom drops out of her life, and she has no desire to continue alone in this world. But in the Ephesian church when extreme sorrow and grief began to subside, when such widows realized that there were other women in like circumstances, that they were still wanted and could be useful, this realization gave them a new lease on life.

There were rules and regulations concerning membership in this organization, and verse 9 tells us that no woman would be enrolled as a member unless she were at least sixty years old and had been the wife of only one husband. That means that, being a woman of sixty and having had only one husband, she was surely a woman of high Christian character and extremely helpful experience; and she could be a great blessing to the church and to others.

Verse 10: "Well reported of for good works; if she have brought up children, if she have lodged strangers, if she have washed the saints' feet, if she have relieved the afflicted, if she have diligently followed every good work."

A "widow indeed" must have a good report concerning her children . . . if she had successfully reared her little ones, had been a good mother with character above reproach; if she had used sound discipline and such love as only a mother can give in rearing her children, she was acceptable in this particular group. If she had failed in her own household, then it was concluded that she was not of suitable character for membership in that organization.

"If she have lodged strangers." In Paul's day it was extremely important that believers practice Christian hospitality. Hotels, motels, and such conveniences did not abound in abundant numbers as they do today; and many times a private home was the only place where a weary traveler could find a night's lodging and a warm meal. Before a widow could be admitted to the number of those over "threescore years" she must be one who had, in better days, cared for strangers and travelers.

". . . If she have washed the saints' feet." This was a courteous but practical service, and was practiced by

194

people in those days for various and sundry reasons. It was a lowly task, one that no ordinary person would willingly perform. Jesus set the example for such humility when He girded Himself with a towel and washed the disciples' feet, instructing them that though they did not at that moment understand what He was doing, they would understand in time to come (John 13:2–15). In that day, travelers wore sandals—and when they arrived at the home into which they were accepted, servants immediately bathed the dusty, tired feet of the visitors. These sixty-year-old ladies were to be humble; their humility was to be proved by their having washed the feet of the saints who came to visit in their homes. Such humble service would be practiced only by a deeply spiritual person—one who was willing to serve God with all of her heart.

"... If she have relieved the afflicted." She must be a lady with a tender, compassionate heart. There was no Salvation Army nor Red Cross in Paul's day; the saints in the church took care of the afflicted. In that day there was much suffering and very little sympathy. There was poverty and disease, and in many instances the slave-masters displayed scant sympathy toward their slaves. The "widows indeed" were to relieve the afflicted, care for the suffering and the distressed. (Read Luke 10:31–35.) Even though a widow might not have money or goods with which to help, she could relieve suffering insofar as she was able—and that is all God requires of any believer. Jesus said of Mary, "She hath done what she could." When Christians do what they CAN do for the Master, that is all God requires.

"... If she have diligently followed every good work." That sums up all else pertaining to good stewardship and righteous living. A living, healthy faith always produces good works. Paul said, "We are His workmanship, created in Christ Jesus unto good works, which God hath before ordained that we should walk in them" (Eph. 2:10). These ladies, to be eligible to join the organization of widows, must show their faith by their good works. We are not saved by works, but by good works we *prove that we ARE saved.*

In Titus 3:8 Paul said, ". . . That they which have believed in God . . . be careful to maintain good works." Requirements for widows above threescore years demanded qualities that prove both character and a high degree of spirituality.

Verse 11: "But the younger widows refuse; for when they have begun to wax wanton against Christ, they will marry."

In this and the following verses we find instruction concerning those who could not become members of the order of widows. Younger widows—women under sixty— were to be refused. Such widows in the early days of their grief might willingly dedicate their lives to the service of the church; but when the grief began to wear away and time began to heal the wounds, the young widow might become attracted to another man, desire to marry, and would neglect the work of the Lord and service she had pledged to render to the church. There would be an inclination for her to "wax wanton." In the original language, the word *wantonness* carries no idea of lasciviousness or lewdness. The idea of strength is the essential one; and the sense here is that the young widow would grow restless, and because of her less advanced age she would become impatient and desire the companionship and love of the opposite sex and would marry again.

Verse 12: "Having damnation, because they have cast off their first faith."

Greek authorities tell us that the wrong translation is given here. The Greek does not say, "having damnation," but "having *condemnation*." Certainly the Lord would not damn a born again widow for marrying again! Jesus clearly taught that if the husband be dead, the woman is free to remarry. What Paul is saying here is not that the women will lose their salvation, since they had pledged "their first faith" to the Lord's service, and now they wish to transfer it to a husband. He is teaching, rather, that they have broken their first pledge to God and to the church, and they will lose their *reward*. Therefore, the church should not admit younger women to this specific group—women who might marry again when their grief subsided. Paul taught that it is better for every man to have his own wife and every woman her own husband. These young widows should settle down and marry again. (See verse 14.)

Verse 13: "And withal they learn to be idle, wandering about from house to house; and not only idle, but tattlers also and busybodies, speaking things which they ought not."

The restlessness of these younger widows, if supported by the church, may lead to their spending their energies going from house to house (presumably on church business, but actually idling their time away) gossiping, slandering, being tattlers, busybodies, meddlers, inconsiderate and curious.

Verse 14: "I will therefore that the younger women marry, bear children, guide the house, give none occasion to the adversary to speak reproachfully."

If the husband dies in the younger years of a woman's life, it is perfectly legitimate and right that she marry again if she so desires. It is not a sin to remain single, however, if she does not live for pleasure; but if she cannot be a spiritually-minded servant of God, then it is much better for her to marry, bear children, guide the house, and give the devil no occasion to bring reproach upon her and upon the church, because human nature judges any organization by its least worthy member.

Verse 15: "For some are already turned aside after Satan."

In this verse Paul clearly states that some young widows have *already* turned aside and followed temptation. I repeat: *The Bible tells all.* God's Word does not cover up for anyone. Christians are to be wise as serpents and harmless as doves. We are not to mistreat widows—young or old—but we must use such wisdom as only God can provide in dealing with these ladies who have lost their husbands.

Verse 16: "If any man or woman that believeth have widows, let them relieve them, and let not the church be charged; that it may relieve them that are widows indeed."

If a believer in the church has widows in his family, *let him relieve them.* Each family is to take care of the needy in that family, and the church is not to be burdened or charged with that responsibility. The church then may have sufficient time and funds to take care of the dear widows who *have* no family, no income, and no means of support. It is Christian doctrine that believers should take care of needy persons in their own immediate families; they sin and bring reproach upon the church if they do not discharge this responsibility.

Concerning Elders

Verse 17: "Let the elders that rule well be counted worthy of double honour, especially they who labour in the word and doctrine."

The elders that rule well are to be esteemed and

198

honored—yea, counted worthy of *double honor*, especially those who labor in the Word of God and in doctrine. From this it is clear that while there were elders who labored "in the Word and in doctrine" (preaching), there were those who did not preach, but were appointed to rule in the church. There were some elders who were not capable of teaching and carrying on the ministry of the Word, instructing in doctrine; but there were others who were capable. Still others had good business ability and could help with the widows and the monetary business affairs of the church. The elder who gives out the Word in teaching and doctrine is worthy of "double honour." It is honorable to be God's deacon, elder, or bishop; and a person who is faithful in those offices will receive a full reward.

Verse 18: "For the Scripture saith, Thou shalt not muzzle the ox that treadeth out the corn. And, The labourer is worthy of his reward."

It was a law in the Old Testament (Deut. 25:4) that an ox could not be muzzled while he trod out the corn. The ox that labored and tramped on the corn to provide grain for the master was to be left free to eat as he worked and to enjoy the corn while providing food. If an ox is worthy of his hire, how much more the *laborer* is worthy of his reward! God does not overlook even a cup of cold water given in His name. A poor widow gave two mites, and Jesus commended her—declaring that she had given more than all the rest. He promises that if we are faithful over little, we shall be ruler over much. God pays well those who serve Him faithfully. The *most humble service* is not overlooked, and *the greatest service* will be fully rewarded.

It is right and honorable for the local assembly to pay a living wage to full time workers in the church. In verse 17 we learned that a faithful elder—one who rules well—is counted worthy of *double honor*. No congregation can *overpay* a faithful, diligent servant of God. No amount of money could equal his worth to the church and the community.

When Jesus fed the five thousand, there remained twelve baskets of fragments. Most people think that these fragments were scraps left by the people, but not so! The fragments gathered were pieces of good fish and bread—twelve baskets full—exactly one basket for each of the twelve apostles who had served the multitude (John 6:1–14).

The disciples were rewarded for their faithful distribution of food to the hungry five thousand. Paul also quotes from Luke 10:7: *". . . The labourer is worthy of his hire."* The minister should be well paid for his ministry; he should have no need to worry one moment about the secondary things of life. He should be free to give his entire time, thought, and energy to the ministry of the Gospel. People who love and appreciate their preacher as they should will not need to be begged to care for him; they will be happy to supply his needs. If you do not belong to a church where you can love and honor the pastor, or if you do not have a pastor whom you love to the extent that it gives you great joy to support him with money and gifts, then you should get into a church where there IS a preacher who preaches the Word and feeds your soul so that you will be happy to return unto him the necessities of life.

When a community fails to take care of its pastor and its full time Christian workers, it brings disgrace and sad reproach upon the Gospel. The pastor of a church should live in a home that is just as comfortable and nice as the homes of his members. He should drive a better automobile than the average member of his church, because when he is called upon to minister to the sick or dying he should not have to cope with a flat tire or a car that breaks down on the road. When he is called upon to preach the funeral of one of his parishioners he should have an automobile that will get him to his destination and back home again. The minister of a church should wear clothes as good as, if not better than, the members of his church—for after all, he is God's representative. I am not advocating that money should be wasted nor that a minister should be a squanderer; *but he should be taken care of*. . . comfortably housed, properly fed and clothed, his material needs supplied so that he can give all of his time and energy to the ministry of the Word. (I am, of course, speaking of *Bible preachers*. The "hirelings" have all this—and more.)

When laymen contribute money to the support of God's ministers, evangelists and missionaries, they are contributing to the salvation of souls. I could not preach on a hundred radio stations every day across America if God's people did not supply the money to pay the bills. It would be humanly impossible for me to make enough money to personally pay for the time on so large a number of radio stations. Each person who gives, regardless of how little or how much he contributes month by month, has a definite share in every soul saved and in every blessing received by our listeners through the preaching of the Word in the Gospel Hour ministry. I am only the mouthpiece; we are laborers together for Christ, and we would not accomplish much alone. We are brothers and sisters in God's family, members of the same body—and when one member of the body suffers, all the members suffer. We should see that God's ministers are well taken care of.

I have mentioned the material reward of a pastor as a duty of the church, but what about the spiritual recompense? How eternally rewarding a preacher's life can be, and those who share in providing his material necessities will also share in the eternal reward.

Verse 19: "Against an elder receive not an accusation, but before two or three witnesses."

It is possible for even a godly, separated, God-appointed elder to commit sin. Elders suffer human frailties—and, like preachers, they are simply sinners saved by the grace of God. It is possible even for those who live very near to the heart of God to be caught off guard and commit sin that will bring shame and disgrace upon the church. But we are not to accuse an elder unless there are two or more witnesses to testify that the accusation is an accomplished fact. We should never repeat anything we hear about a minister, deacon, steward, elder, Sunday school teacher or any leader in the church. If we hear reports of evil, we should investigate in the right way, through the right people—and certainly we should not discuss the situation with unbelievers. It is very clear in verse 19 that an elder must not be accused unless there are at least two or three witnesses who can prove the truth of the accusation.

Verse 20: "Them that sin rebuke before all, that others also may fear."

If an elder commits sin and there are witnesses to testify to the fact that sin HAS been committed, then he is to be brought before the church and exposed, ". . . that others may fear." If we had more church discipline today there would be less sin in the church. When an elder is brought before the church and judged, he is to be rebuked—and we are then to forgive him. We cannot consign him to hell, and we cannot judge him as will the Righteous Judge, Almighty God; but we can rebuke him, thus warning others in the church, lest they also sin and be brought before the assembly.

Sin should be brought out in the open—*when we are sure that the accused is guilty*; but we should never condemn another Christian on circumstantial evidence nor because of what some disgruntled church member may have said or suggested. The devil is a slanderer and a liar. He caused Jesus to be accused of every imaginable evil, everything that is ungodly and degrading—yet Jesus was the sinless Son of God. We should not falsely accuse any fellow believer, and we must be especially careful about bringing accusations against leaders in the church.

The early church grew by leaps and bounds. Acts 5:1—11 tells of Ananias and Sapphira, who sold a possession and brought part of the money to the church. They lied about the offering—and both of them dropped dead at the altar. They were buried without a song, without a prayer, without a verse of Scripture—and Acts 5:11 tells us that *"great fear came upon all the church."* The right kind of leader is a great asset to the church and an inspiring example to the flock; but an unworthy leader should be brought before the church, rebuked, and dealt with according to his behavior. We should not tolerate open sin in the church; but there should be two or three witnesses to testify in such cases—witnesses who actually saw the sin committed or who know for a fact that the accusation brought against the believer is absolutely true.

Verse 21: "I charge thee before God, and the Lord Jesus Christ, and the elect angels, that thou observe these things without preferring one before another, doing nothing by partiality."

The words translated *"preferring"* and *"partiality"* are very interesting. Both imply prejudice: "Preferring" implies prejudice against the accused, judging and condemning before hearing all the facts. "Partiality" is prejudice *in favor of* the accused. Paul here emphasizes that he is giving a charge to believers in the local assembly, and that this charge is given *before God, before Jesus Christ, and before the angels.* The charge is, *"Observe these things without preferring one before another, doing nothing by partiality."*

There must not be partiality in the church. We should not esteem one higher than the other, nor try to find some fault through which an accusation can be brought against an individual because of personal dislike. We should love all people alike. Such cases against leaders in the church are to be judged as in the sight of God and of Christ and of His holy angels. We are not to condemn them and pronounce them to hell; we must remember that the Righteous Judge will take care of all judgment at the appointed time, and we are to judge nothing before the time. The saints in the church are admonished to rejoice when sinners are saved. We are to lift up the fallen. If one is taken in a fault, we who claim to be spiritual are to "restore such a one in the spirit of meekness, considering ourselves lest we also be tempted." We are to weep when Christians sin; we are NOT to rejoice and take pleasure in condemning them and dragging them before the assembly to rebuke them. We are not to be either partial OR prejudiced toward the one accused. Give all that is due him—but no more. Judge him in every detail where he needs reproof—but no more. It is a grave and serious thing to wound and hurt a fellow Christian. We should always deal with our brothers and sisters in Christ as we would want to be dealt with if we were in their place.

Personal Instructions and Responsibility

Verse 22: "Lay hands suddenly on no man, neither be partaker of other men's sins: keep thyself pure."

Some Bible scholars say that Paul is referring here

to laying hands on the accused one and bringing him before the church; but, comparing spiritual things with spiritual (Acts 13:3), it seems that Paul is warning Timothy not to ordain deacons, elders, or young preachers suddenly, without due consideration. Let them first prove themselves. Do not hurriedly appoint them to an office in the assembly, and then possibly within a few months or a year find them falling back into sin and bringing reproach upon the church.

". . . *Keep thyself pure*" simply means that if Timothy appointed a person to a place of authority in the local church, and then that person brought reproach and disgrace upon the church in the name of Jesus, Timothy would be partially at fault for having put a novice in a place of authority and leadership. If he hurriedly put men in positions of authority and they did not measure up to the standards of spiritual living, it would bring reproach on Timothy as well as on the church—and Paul did not want that to happen to his dearly beloved son in the ministry.

Verse 23: "Drink no longer water, but use a little wine for thy stomach's sake and thine often infirmities."

I get great enjoyment from studying the words in a verse of Scripture. Notice carefully: "*DRINK no longer water.*" (The Greek here suggests, "Drink no longer water ONLY" or "Be no longer a drinker of water only.") Now notice: ". . . But *USE a little wine* for thy stomach's sake, and thine often infirmities."

Those who want to get drunk often use this Scripture to prove that it is perfectly all right to drink wine; but notice the wording—"drink *no longer*" water only, which definitely tells us that up to now Timothy was a total abstainer. Notice also the word "USE"—not *drink* (wine). Paul did not tell Timothy to drink wine in quantities, but to *use a little* for the stomach's sake. This suggests that Paul told Timothy to use, as we would say in this day, "a tablespoonful of wine" for his stomach's sake.

Dearly beloved, let us be reasonable. There were no drug stores and pharmacies in that day. Certainly Paul healed the sick and raised the dead—but he did not heal young Timothy. He said, "You are often sick; you have a bad stomach. Use a bit of wine for your health"— and that was not the kind of wine bought in wine shops today. It was pure juice made from the fruit of the vine— not chemicals and drugs that will give a man delirium tremens or cause him to murder his mother, his wife, and his own babies! I am not trying to dodge the issue; a born again child of God has no trouble with intoxicants— but certainly a tablespoonful of wine would not make one drunk. However, this wine was to be USED for *medicinal purposes*—not *consumed* for the purpose of getting drunk. Timothy was physically weak, had "often infirmities" (verse 23); and Paul, being deeply concerned, admonished him to take all possible care of his health.

Verses 24 and 25: "Some men's sins are open be-forehand, going before to judgment; and some men they follow after. Likewise also the good works of some are manifest beforehand; and they that are otherwise cannot be hid."

I do not profess to know fully what the Holy Spirit is saying here, for these are difficult verses; but this is what I believe is meant:

This declaration is to be taken in connection with choosing men for church offices (verse 22). Paul is giving Timothy a charge respecting the character of those who may be suggested as candidates for ordination as deacons, bishops, or other church leaders. He says that the characters of some men are manifest; there is no attempt at disguise; their daily lives testify to their un-fitness for leadership in the church. However, there are men whose character is not fully understood. They conceal their plans; they practice deception; but the character of such men will be developed and *their sins will follow after.* Even though such men are elected to church office, their hidden sins will come to light. In my years of traveling in evangelistic work I know this to be a fact.

In other words, Paul tells Timothy that there is no excuse for appointing some men to office in the church, because their lives in the community and their dealings with their fellowman plainly testify that they are unfit for such a position. On the other hand, a man may seem to be qualified—and yet after his appointment he may prove that all along he was unfit for a position of church leadership, but his unfitness was not evident to those who look upon the outward appearance.

"... *Likewise also the good works* ... *are manifest.*" The same is true of worthy candidates. Their good works are manifest beforehand. The idea here is that one's character may be so certain and above question that there should be no hesitation in setting him apart for church office. These people correspond, in respect to character, to those mentioned in verse 24, whose sins "are open beforehand." But there are those who are "otherwise." What they do in good deeds is hidden from the world—but not from God. Their good works may not be known to men now, but they will be recognized at the judgment by God Himself. However, Timothy can only be responsible for dealing with those whose sins are manifest, not those whose evil deeds are hidden and may only be brought out at the judgment . . . just as in good works, he can only be responsible for taking into account in his judgment those whose good deeds are evident to all—not those secret good works which only God can see.

The connection here seems to be this: Timothy was to be on guard in introducing men into church offices whose character for evil was not manifest; and he was to endeavor to search out the modest—those who, though now unknown, were good men—and bring them forth to a station of usefulness where their good works would be seen.

I TIMOTHY –– CHAPTER SIX

CONTINUED INSTRUCTION CONCERNING THE WORK OF A GOOD MINISTER OF JESUS CHRIST

1. Let as many servants as are under the yoke count their own masters worthy of all honour, that the name of God and his doctrine be not blasphemed.

2. And they that have believing masters, let them not despise them, because they are brethren; but rather do them service, because they are faithful and beloved, partakers of the benefit. These things teach and exhort.

3. If any man teach otherwise, and consent not to wholesome words, even the words of our Lord Jesus Christ, and to the doctrine which is according to godliness;

4. He is proud, knowing nothing, but doting about questions and strifes of words, whereof cometh envy, strife, railings, evil surmisings,

5. Perverse disputings of men of corrupt minds, and destitute of the truth, supposing that gain is godliness: from such withdraw thyself.

6. But godliness with contentment is great gain.

7. For we brought nothing into this world, and it is certain we can carry nothing out.

8. And having food and raiment let us be therewith content.

9. But they that will be rich fall into temptation and a snare, and into many foolish and hurtful lusts, which drown men in destruction and perdition.

10. For the love of money is the root of all evil: which while some coveted after, they have erred from the faith, and pierced themselves through with many sorrows.

11. But thou, O man of God, flee these things; and follow after righteousness, godliness, faith, love, patience, meekness.

12. Fight the good fight of faith, lay hold on eternal life, whereunto thou art also called, and hast professed a good profession before many witnesses.

13. I give thee charge in the sight of God, who quickeneth all things, and before Christ Jesus, who before Pontius Pilate witnessed a good confession;

14. That thou keep this commandment without spot, unrebukeable, until the appearing of our Lord Jesus Christ:

15. Which in his times he shall shew, who is the blessed

and only Potentate, the King of kings, and Lord of lords;

16. Who only hath immortality, dwelling in the light which no man can approach unto; whom no man hath seen, nor can see: to whom be honour and power everlasting. Amen.

17. Charge them that are rich in this world, that they be not high-minded, nor trust in uncertain riches, but in the living God, who giveth us richly all things to enjoy;

18. That they do good, that they be rich in good works, ready to distribute, willing to communicate;

19. Laying up in store for themselves a good foundation against the time to come, that they may lay hold on eternal life.

20. O Timothy, keep that which is committed to thy trust, avoiding profane and vain babblings, and oppositions of science falsely so called:

21. Which some professing have erred concerning the faith. Grace be with thee. Amen.

Concerning Servants

Verse 1: "Let as many servants as are under the yoke count their own masters worthy of all honour, that the name of God and His doctrine be not blasphemed."

The word "servant" in this verse is literally *slave.* In Paul's day, slavery was an age-old, established, familiar practice. The number of those who were under the rule of a slavemaster was very great. It is interesting to note that Jesus neither condoned nor condemned slavery and slaveholders at that time, but through the work of the Holy Spirit in the hearts of men He has done so since. Certainly slavery is wrong; no man has a right to own another human being nor to control another as he would an animal. All men are created free, insofar as dominating each other is concerned.

Down through the years, through the preaching of the Gospel, slavery has been almost abolished; and if the love of God abides in the heart, there is no desire to make slaves of one's fellowmen. Christianity solves problems that nothing else on earth could solve.

210

Paul instructs believing slaves that they are to *"count their own masters worthy of all honour."* The slave was to render to his master full obedience and dedicated service; and if he did not, then he brought reproach upon the name of Christ and the true doctrine of God. It is easy to see that if a slave were converted through the Gospel which declares that God is love and that by grace men are transformed into new creatures, and then that believing slave were to be lazy, hateful, and disrespectful to his master, the master in turn would naturally condemn God and the true faith because of the conduct of his Christian slave. Therefore, the Christian slave is to render to his master full obedience.

Perhaps someone is asking, "Did not the Lord Jesus plainly say, 'No man can serve two masters'?" Yes, in the Sermon on the Mount Jesus made that statement (Matt. 6:24). How then can Paul tell these Christian slaves to give full obedience to their masters? As Christians, should not they be slaves to God only? But in the sense that Paul is speaking here, a man CAN serve two masters. Let me illustrate:

Perhaps I employ a man to prune my shrubbery, cut my grass, and thoroughly clean my yard. While this man works for me, I am his master in the sense that I am paying him for services rendered; but when he finishes with my work he can go to my neighbor's house and render unto him the same service—and so my neighbor becomes his master. In this sense, he can serve two or three masters.

However, in Matthew the Greek word is a much stronger one, and the rendering should be, "No man can be a *slave* to two masters"—and that is true. A man may *serve* many earthly masters, but a slave cannot have more than one slavemaster. What Jesus said is simply that it is utterly impossible for any man to be a slave to two masters at the same time, for a slave is the exclusive property of his owner. From the spiritual standpoint, Jesus was teaching that one could not be a slave of the devil and of God at the same time.

Slaves were obtained in various ways. Some became slaves because of heavy debts which they were unable to pay; some were taken captive in war; still others were bought at auction and paid for, thus becoming the property of a slaveowner—the same as a donkey, a sheep, or any other personal property. He could not be the slave of two men, for he could not possibly serve two slavemasters.

Paul cautions Christian slaves to give their master faithful service in order that the name of their God and the Christian doctrine of grace be not blasphemed by the slavemaster. If the believing slave were careless, unconcerned, slack in his service, and insubordinate to his heathen master, his attitude and actions would be attributed to his religion.

I personally know dear men today who have been fired by their employer because they talked *too much* about Jesus while they were on the job; and I have also known professing Christians who did not give their employer a good day's work for salary received, and that is not right. It is not right for Christians to use company time to witness on the job. If one can witness without robbing his employer, that is fine; but a Christian's testimony will be hurt by his being seen talking when he should be working, even though he may be talking with an unsaved person about the grace of God and the saving power of Jesus. In Romans 14:16 Paul tells us, "Let not then your good be evil spoken of." Christians must be "wise as serpents and harmless as doves." Any Christian who has an employer must render to that employer a good day's work and proper respect, lest reproach be brought upon the Gospel.

Young man, young woman—if you are a Christian, do not be any less alert and on the job when the boss is absent than you are when he is looking at you. Your earthly master may not always be watching you, but the Heavenly Master sees and knows all that you do. So whether your job be that of superintendent in a huge plant or janitor in a small office, never forget that if you do not give your employer a good day's work in the right spirit, you are bringing reproach upon the name of Jesus.

Verse 2: "And they that have believing masters, let them not despise them, because they are brethren; but rather do them service, because they are faithful and beloved, partakers of the benefit. These things teach and exhort."

There were born again slaveowners as well as born again slaves. Christian slaves were not to despise their masters; they were brothers in Christ. They should not take advantage of a Christian master nor expect him to show partiality to believing slaves; but rather, they should render *even better service* because both slave and master belonged to the same family—the Church of the living God—and they were laborers together with Him. They were brothers in the body of Christ, even though they were not on the same level in the social realm.

It may be difficult to understand how a born again man would have slaves—but this was the transition period, and people cannot be abruptly changed from habits of life when those habits have to do with established customs and practices that have been trained into them since childhood. As Christianity spread and grew stronger, slaves were released.

In Romans 1:1 Paul proclaimed that he was God's

bondservant—or bondslave. He rejoiced in the fact that he was bound hand and foot to the Lord Jesus Christ, the Master of all believers. Paul was not decorated with religious emblems and golden crosses, but he rejoiced and counted it a great honor to bear in his body "the marks of the Lord Jesus" (Gal. 6:17). In his writings he enumerates his trials and persecutions, and tells us that he suffered these things because he was a minister of the Gospel—a bondslave of Jesus Christ.

As a slave, *he had no WILL of his own*, but adopted words used by Jesus when He said, "I come to do thy will, O God" (Heb. 10:9). Jesus was entirely yielded to God the Father, and He came into this world to do whatsoever the Father bade Him do. We, too, must lose our will in the will of God—and if we are not willing to be led by His Spirit and dominated by His power, we are not worthy to be called His disciples.

The bondslave of Jesus Christ has *no PROGRAM of his own*. He is to follow the bidding of the Holy Spirit in all his undertakings. He will have *no BELONGINGS of his own*, for all that God has is at his disposal and use. He will have *no CARES of his own*; Paul said, ". . . My God shall supply all your need according to His riches in glory by Christ Jesus" (Phil. 4:19). That is the Spirit's way of saying what Jesus said in His Sermon on the Mount: ". . . Seek ye first the kingdom of God, and His righteousness; and all these things shall be added unto you" (Matt. 6:33).

If we are truly God's bondslave, God is not only willing and ready, but *it is His responsibility* to furnish His bondslaves with the necessities of life . . . food, clothing, a place to live, and strength to labor in His harvest fields, already so white unto harvest. The bondslave of Jesus Christ need not take thought for tomorrow; he need not be anxious about his needs. He will have no supplies of his own. In I Corinthians 9:7 Paul asked, "Who goeth a warfare any time at his own charges?" In other words, the ammunition and strength with which to fight the battle, whatever the provisions or needs, all are met in Christ Jesus. "And God is able to make all grace abound toward you; that ye, *always having all sufficiency in all things*, may abound to every good work" (II Cor. 9:8). The supreme command to a bondslave of Jesus Christ is simply, "TRUST AND OBEY!"

I am asking myself these questions: Am I truly a bondslave of Jesus Christ? Have I truly yielded myself to Him—soul, spirit, and body? (I Thess. 5:23). Have I truly yielded my body a living sacrifice unto God, holy and acceptable unto Him, which is my reasonable service? (Rom. 12:1). Have I truly yielded my members unto God as instruments of righteousness? (Rom. 6:13). I have no right to keep back anything. It is my solemn duty to give God everything.

Will YOU have a heart-to-heart talk with yourself? If you are a person who employs workers, do you treat them as you would want to be treated if circumstances were reversed and *they* were *your employer*? Or if you are an employee, whether you work for saint or sinner, do you give of your best as unto the Lord, so that you will not bring reproach upon the name of Jesus? Are YOU a good bondslave of Jesus Christ? Think it over—and if something needs to be done about it, DO IT!

Concerning False Teachers

Verse 3: "If any man teach otherwise, and consent not to wholesome words, even the words of our Lord Jesus Christ, and to the doctrine which is according to godliness."

"If any *teach otherwise* (than I desire you to teach), and consent not to wholesome words (sound doctrine),

215

he is teaching false doctrine."

"... *The words of the Lord Jesus Christ.*" Paul's inspired words are not merely his own, but also Christ's words. Timothy is being warned to be very careful concerning the leaders in the church—for if a leader teach anything except the wholesome words of the Lord Jesus Christ and His doctrine according to godliness, then that man is not in the right spirit. He must teach true doctrine, and not his own views or suppositions.

Verse 4: "He is proud, knowing nothing, but doting about questions and strifes of words, whereof cometh envy, strife, railings, evil surmisings."

"*He is proud.*" That is, he is lifted up with his fancied superior knowledge. He is conceited, thinking he knows much about religion; but the fact is that he has no proper knowledge of the Gospel at all.

"... *But doting about questions and strifes of words ....*" The Greek dictionary says, "*Doting* means to be ill (sick); hence, to be taken with such a morbid interest in a thing as is tantamount to a disease." The meaning here, then, is that such persons had a *sickly* or *morbid* desire for debates of this kind. They had not a sound and healthy state of mind on religious matters.

"... *Whereof cometh envy ....*" The only fruit of such debates is the production of envy, strife, misunderstandings and "*evil surmisings.*" The church is not a place to argue; the Sunday school class is not a place to split hairs over personal or denominational differences. *The church is a spiritual cafeteria where people are fed and strengthened for the days that lie ahead.* When an unbeliever gets into the church and begins to take over the reins of leadership—perhaps becoming a leader in the young people's organization or in the Sunday school, perhaps serving on the deacon board, that person can

216

cause an unbelievable amount of unrest, disputing, and trouble in the local assembly.

Verse 5: "Perverse disputings of men of corrupt minds, and destitute of the truth, supposing that gain is godliness: from such withdraw thyself."

The apostle has already had something to say about financial affairs, but now in these next few verses he deals with the matter at greater length. In I Timothy 3:3 Paul warns bishops concerning covetousness; in 3:8 he warns the deacons not to be greedy of "filthy lucre." The solemn truth he is attempting to drive home to the hearts of believers is the fact that money can easily become an idol, and even believers can sometimes become entirely too involved in money matters.

We should be ever mindful that we are to put first things first. There are some who think that religion is a "paying proposition," and they accuse all preachers of being money mongers. In some remote instances I am sure there are men who choose the ministry merely as a vocation to receive a fabulous salary; but this certainly is not true of *God's* undershepherds. There are those who go to church for profit—everything they do is for gain, and the dollar-mark is the ruling passion of their lives. They are religious on Sunday because it contributes to their business; they attend church for no reason at all except to make a good impression on the community and build good will among other church members, thus promoting the sale of their own goods or services. I do not doubt that this is true in every church in the land, but it is more prevalent in some than in others.

Some people use religion only as a means to financial gain. I am sure you are aware that around election time all the politicians begin attending church, shaking hands, handing out their little cards, making a substantial bid for votes. If such people are not truly born again, they are heaping damnation upon their own souls. If any person attends church for any purpose except to worship God or hear the Gospel, he is committing a sin—and instead of the church helping him, when he stands before God his judgment would be lighter had he never seen the inside of a church building! We will be judged and rewarded for what we could have been but refused to be!

Jesus tells us of a man whose fields produced so abundantly that he had no room to store his goods; so he had a heart-to-heart talk with himself. (He did not invite God nor the Holy Spirit nor the community preacher.) He appointed himself chairman and sole member of a business committee, and he reached a decision: "And he said, *This will I do:* I will pull down my barns, and build greater; and there will I bestow all my fruits and my goods. And I will say to my soul, Soul, thou hast much goods laid up for many years; take thine ease, eat, drink, and be merry!" But God climaxed the story by saying, "THOU FOOL! This night thy soul shall be required of thee: then whose shall those things be, which thou hast provided? *So is he that layeth up treasure for himself, and is not rich toward God!*" (Luke 12:16–21).

Proverbs 1:7 tells us, "The fear of the Lord is the beginning of knowledge." A person who does not know God is a pitiful person. One who does not have God in his heart does not have good, sound, common sense in his head. "The fool hath said in his heart, There is no God" (Psalm 53:1). He who by his daily habits denies God, is living the life of a fool!

Someone may observe, "Surely God is with him; he lives in the best home in the community, drives the biggest automobile, wears the finest clothes—and look how he provides for his family! Surely God must be blessing

218

him, or he would not have so much of this world's goods."
My dearly beloved, money and earthly gain are not godliness. All through the New Testament, riches and sorrow, riches and tears, riches and ruin are very closely
connected.

When anyone in your local assembly begins to teach
anything except pure, wholesome, Christian doctrine from
the Word of the living God, you just bear in mind that the
person doing the teaching is proud in his own eyes.
Though he may be very wise in his own conceit, he is
an ignoramus in the eyes of God. He knows nothing.

Such people ask silly questions and partake of questionable discussions that cause strife in the church. Because of this endless strife, railings, and evil surmisings,
perverse disputings occur which will corrupt the minds
of the believers—and they cannot keep their minds on
God. The Word tells us, "Thou wilt keep him in perfect
peace, whose mind is stayed on (Jesus)" (Isa. 26:3).
The devil knows that if he can keep the believer's mind
on questionable things, that believer will not grow and
become strong in the Lord.

Paul says such people are *destitute* of the truth; they
do what they are doing to bring gain to themselves; and
Paul firmly commands, *"From such withdraw thyself."* We
are to have no personal contact or daily fellowship with
such a person in the name of Christianity. We should pray
for him and do all in our power to lead him into the light
of the Truth; but "Can two walk together, except they be
agreed?" (Amos 3:3). If we condone the spirit and attitude of such a one, permitting him to use the church for
monetary and personal gain, then we become partaker of
his evil deeds. We should pray for him, witness to him—
but never compromise with him.

Godliness with Contentment
Verse 6: "But godliness with contentment is great
gain."

This verse is certainly clear enough. To live a separated, godly life; to be dedicated, consecrated, yielded unreservedly to God; and to be content with whatsoever things He allows us to have, *is great gain.* Paul said, "I have learned, in whatsoever state I am, therewith to be content" (Phil. 4:11). To do the will of God at all times, knowing that all things work together for good to them who love God and are the called according to His purpose; knowing that nothing shall be able to separate us from the love of God which is in Christ Jesus our Lord; knowing that He who is able to save is able also to keep and to supply every need, is tremendous spiritual gain. The first interest and desire of all believers should be to serve God with their whole heart, in reverent fear and perfect truth.

Verse 7: "For we brought nothing into this world, and it is certain we can carry nothing out."

The truth set forth here is simple—but *overwhelming!* We have exactly nothing when we are born into this world; we are wholly dependent upon others; we must be fed and clothed by others. And *when we depart this life,* others will prepare us for burial. Someone will purchase our shroud and clothe us with it. The garments in which we are buried will have no pockets—we will take with us no checkbooks, fountain pens, nor news bulletins concerning the stockmarket. We come into this world penniless—and we leave it the same way. Therefore, *godliness with contentment is great gain.*

Verse 8: "And having food and raiment let us be therewith content."

After all is said and done, life's positive essentials are very few. According to this Scripture, the first essential is *food*; the second is *raiment.* If we have food and clothes, we are blessed of the Lord. He is the giver of every good and perfect gift, and He has promised to take care of His own. He clothes and feeds the sparrow; He dresses the lillies of the field—and "even Solomon in all his glory was not arrayed like one of these" (Matt. 6:29). We, His children, are of much more value than sparrows or the flowers and grass of the field.

Many times, those who are the richest enjoy the least contentment. They have money and all that money will buy—but they want more, *more*, and *MORE*. No man has ever had all the money he wanted. He keeps on investing and striving for that next million. I repeat: It is not sinful to be rich if one comes by riches honestly; it is not a sin to make money if we make it in honest, upright business and give God what belongs to Him. But the danger lies in *loving* money—using it to purchase luxuries and provide indulgences that may cause us to become unconcerned about the things of God and grow cold and indifferent, even to the extent of backsliding.

The Love of Money

Verse 9: "But they that will be rich fall into temptation and a snare, and into many foolish and hurtful lusts, which drown men in destruction and perdition."

I stated earlier in this study that throughout the New Testament, riches and sorrow, riches and tears, riches and damnation, are closely connected. Paul tells us here that there is grave danger that the rich will fall into temptation—they will be tempted to do many foolish and extravagant things; they will practice and participate in lusts made possible through much money. A person who has enough money can purchase just about anything on earth—*except salvation*! Money talks in this world, but not at the judgment bar of God.

The statement *"they that will be rich"* suggests

221

those who set heart and mind on making money. They strive with strength, energy, and talents just to acquire wealth. They are determined to get money and more money—honestly, if possible; *dishonestly*, if need be. Some men have declared that they will become millionaires at any price; they will do anything to make a million. There are men today who were honest, with character above reproach—until they made a little money and then set their hearts on MORE money. Little by little their consciences were seared; and now they are racketeers who will stop at nothing, however crooked it may be, to make another million.

Mark 10:17—27 gives the account of the rich young ruler—a young man who had acquired much money and had "much possessions." He ran to Jesus, fell down before Him, and asked, *"What shall I do that I may inherit eternal life?"* Jesus named six of the commandments, all having to do with one's fellowman. The young man declared that *he had kept these commandments* since he was a child. Then Jesus simply said to him, "One thing thou lackest: go thy way, sell whatsoever thou hast, and give to the poor, and thou shalt have treasure in heaven: and come, take up the cross, and follow me." The young man turned and went away grieved, *"for he had great possessions."* He had said he wanted eternal life—yet he was not willing to trust Jesus with his earthly possessions.

When the young man turned and walked away, Jesus said to His disciples, "How hardly shall they that have riches enter into the kingdom of God." The disciples could not understand. Jesus then explained, *"How hard is it for them that TRUST in riches* to enter into the kingdom of God!" The disciples were astonished beyond measure, and they said among themselves, *"Who then can be saved?"* And Jesus "looking upon them saith,

With men it is impossible, but not with God: for with God all things are possible." Jesus clearly taught that riches are not an asset to spiritual living.

Verse 10: "For the love of money is the root of all evil: which while some coveted after, they have erred from the faith, and pierced themselves through with many sorrows."

Many times we hear someone say, "Money is the root of all evil"; but that is not what the Bible says. As a matter of fact, money has been the root of much joy, much kindness, and much good. There are many things money can buy that will make life much happier. The Bible does not say that *money* is the root of all evil, but rather that *"the LOVE of money* is the root of all evil."

Bible scholars tell us that there is no definite article in the Greek before the word "root." It is not "THE root," but rather "A root" of evil. *"All"* signifies *all kinds* of evil, chief of which is that it causes men to "err from the faith" and forget God. They have erred (or been seduced) from the faith; that is, they have been so deceived that they turn their backs on the faith and all chances of being saved.

The Holy Spirit is saying here that if money occupies the place in your life that God should occupy, then *love of money* is the root of evil that will damn you. Many men make money an idol—and idolatry damns the soul. Money can bring many comforts; but it can also be the means to many sorrows, the greatest of which will come when misguided souls realize how foolish they have been to choose gold instead of God.

". . . Pierced themselves through with many sorrows." The word "pierced" cannot be well expressed in its translation. It means to pierce through from one end to

223

another, as a piece of meat on a spit, and conveys the idea of doing this all around, piercing everywhere. In this verse, it means the torturing of one's soul with many sorrows.

However, there are those who have money without loving it, while others who do not have it love and strive for it above all else. It is not a sin to have money if we do not allow money to become our god, a snare that causes us to err from the faith.

Final Exhortations

Verse 11: "But thou, O man of God, flee these things; and follow after righteousness, godliness, faith, love, patience, meekness."

". . . *O man of God*"—(man appointed by God to carry out His commission). This was said of Elijah (I Kings 17:24 and also of Elisha, successor to Elijah (II Kings 4:9).

". . . *FLEE THESE THINGS!*" Timothy was to flee from money and the lust that might be brought about by it. He was to flee covetousness; he was not to seek after and long for money and the things money could buy. He was God's undershepherd, and God would supply his every need. We are not to love the world; we are to resist the devil, flee from covetousness and the love of money, and run to the Lord in our hour of need, regardless of what that need may be. "*The name of the Lord is a strong tower: the righteous runneth into it, and is safe*" (Prov. 18:10).

When we are tempted, we are not to fight the tempter in our own strength; we are to run to the Lord Jesus. He who thinks himself able to overcome the devil should take heed *lest he be overcome BY the devil!* "There hath no temptation taken you but such as is common to man: *but God is faithful*, who will not suffer you to be tempted above that ye are able; but will with the temptation also make a way to escape, that ye may be able to bear it" (I Cor. 10:13). It is GOD who will not permit the devil to tempt us above what we are able to bear. Through Him we can overcome and be more than conquerors—*but ONLY through Him!* In the hour of temptation the name of Jesus is "a strong tower"—Satan trembles at the name of Jesus. He does not fear you or me; we are no match for him—but he knows that Jesus Christ is his conqueror.

All believers have the key to this "strong tower"; and if we do not use the key in the hour of temptation, it is our own fault when we falter and fail. God provides the tower—the "way to escape"; every believer has a key to that tower, and if we stroll along having conversation with Satan, it is our fault if we fall prey to temptation. When the tempter comes, we are to FLEE from him; we are to run to God.

"... *Follow after righteousness.*" This is positive instruction. We are to think on righteous things; we are to plan righteous living. We are not to make provision for the lust of the flesh, nor participate in things that are wrong. There is no middle ground ... it is either right or wrong, godly or ungodly. We are to seek after and follow that which is right. But what is the secret of righteous living?

"The Lord is my shepherd; I shall not want. ... *He leadeth me in the paths of righteousness FOR HIS NAME'S SAKE*" (Psalm 23:1,3). The Shepherd of the believer leads him into paths of right living—not that he might boast or be proud, but that he might not bring reproach upon the precious name of Jesus.

Not only are we to follow after righteousness (right living), but we are also to *"follow godliness."* We are

225

to be in the right relationship with God—and the only way to BE in the right relationship with Him is to study His Word, eat the meat and bread, drink the water and milk, of the Word. We should meditate upon His Word day and night; we are to hide the Word in our hearts that we might not sin against Him, whether we be at work, in the home, or at play. We are to be godly in all activities with which we have to do.

In II Corinthians 3:18 Paul said, ". . . We all, with open face beholding as in a glass the glory of the Lord, are changed into the same image from glory to glory, even as by the Spirit of the Lord." If we are in the right relationship to God, we will become more and more like Him day by day as we serve Him. We must set our affections on things above; we must love the Lord God with heart, soul, and strength.

The believer must also "follow . . . after *faith*." This is not THE faith that brings salvation; this refers to *faithfulness, fidelity*. We must live such a life that God and our fellowman can depend upon us and believe in us. We must live what we profess. We are not to say one thing and do another; we must do what we say we will do. "God moves in mysterious ways, His wonders to perform"; but he does not work in a haphazard, hit-or-miss manner. He has a plan and a program. To troubled Elijah God said, "Arise, get thee to Zarephath, which belongeth to Zidon, and dwell there: behold, *I have commanded a widow woman there to sustain thee!*" (I Kings 17:9).

This poor widow could have found many excuses for refusing hospitality to God's prophet. She had "but an handful of meal . . . and a little oil." Yet she did as God instructed—and He graciously and gloriously provided for her and her son. God would never have appointed this widow to feed Elijah if He had not known that He

226

could depend on her. When God commands, we need not ask for an explanation; we should faithfully do whatsoever He commands us to do, and leave the outcome with Him.

The believer must "follow after . . . *love.*" We are not only to love our friends and fellow-believers, but we are also to love the ungodly. In Romans 13:8 Paul said, "Owe no man any thing, but to love one another." In Matthew 22:36–40 a lawyer asked Jesus, "Master, which is the great commandment in the law? Jesus said unto him, *Thou shalt love the Lord thy God with all thy heart, and with all thy soul, and with all thy mind.* This is the first and great commandment. And the second is like unto it, *Thou shalt love thy neighbour as thyself.* On these two commandments hang all the law and the prophets."

If we love God with our whole heart, we will follow Him—in faith, in godliness, in righteousness; and if we love our neighbour as we love ourselves, we will not steal from him, lie about him, nor mistreat him. It is not difficult to love someone who always says nice things about us and does wonderful things for us; but Christianity loves the unlovely, the hated, the despised. Read the story of the good Samaritan in Luke 10:30 and following.

Believers are to "follow after . . . *patience.*" We who are God's children should not be quick to anger; we are not to "fly off the handle" and say harsh things; we are to be slow to oppose those who would fight us. In Hebrews 10:36 Paul said, ". . . Ye have need of patience, that, after ye have done the will of God, ye might receive the promise." Believers must be patient, regardless of what happens—because we have God's promise that "all things work together for good to them that love God, to them who are the called according to His purpose!"

Believers must "follow after . . . *meekness.*" Meekness is not weakness, however much alike these qualities

227

may sound. To exercise meekness does not mean that we are to be spineless, "jellyfish" Christians. Jesus said, "If any man will come after me, let him deny himself, take up his cross daily, and follow me" (Luke 9:23). If we would be disciples of Jesus Christ, *self must be crucified!* Paul said, "I am crucified with Christ: nevertheless I live; yet not I, but Christ liveth in me: and the life which I now live in the flesh I live by the faith of the Son of God, who loved me, and gave Himself for me" (Gal. 2:20).

We must not put confidence in self. We must not follow our own will nor seek praise and glory for ourselves. We are to deny self-importance . . . and God deliver us from self-pity! It is so easy for Satan to suggest to believers that they are mistreated, unappreciated, lacking the recognition that is due them. Self-pity is an ugly sin.

If we would be what God would have us be, He must have *pre-eminence in all things*. Next, we must love our fellowbelievers, and we are to love our neighbor as we love ourselves. After that, whatever is left we can bestow upon self! When we love God with our whole heart and love our neighbor as ourselves, there is but little time and energy left for selfishness. There is no place in a dedicated heart for the spirit of selfishness or self-interest. *Pride and spirituality do not abide in the same heart.*

Verse 12: "Fight the good fight of faith, lay hold on eternal life, whereunto thou art also called, and hast professed a good profession before many witnesses."

Paul often uses illustrations of a soldier to point out our duty to God. We are soldiers of the cross, soldiers in the army of the Lord; and we are not to be deserters, slackers, nor cowards. We are to *"fight the good fight of faith"* against Satan, the world and the flesh. The spiritual conflict will continue until we are safe in the arms of Jesus and He personally puts the devil, the beast, and the false prophet into the lake of fire. The knowledge of the Lord will then cover the earth as the waters now cover the sea, but until that day there will be a battle.

"For we wrestle not against flesh and blood, but against principalities, against powers, against the rulers of the darkness of this world, against spiritual wickedness in high places. Wherefore take unto you the whole armour of God, that ye may be able to withstand in the evil day, and having done all, to stand. Stand therefore, having your loins girt about with truth, and having on the breastplate of righteousness; and your feet shod with the preparation of the gospel of peace; above all, taking the shield of faith, wherewith ye shall be able to quench all the fiery darts of the wicked. And take the helmet of salvation, and the sword of the Spirit, which is the Word of God" (Eph. 6:12–17).

Please note: ". . . *We wrestle not against flesh and blood.*" We are fighting against principalities, powers, and the rulers of darkness of this world. We are fighting against spiritual wickedness in heavenly places. The devil is the prince of the power of the air; he is the god of this age; he is a mighty being—*but God is ALMIGHTY!* What a terrible host of wicked enemies we are battling! But praise God, when we are clad with the girdle of truth, the breastplate of righteousness, the shoes of the Gospel of peace, the shield of faith, the helmet of salvation, and the sword of the Spirit, we will completely win the victory in the end. We are more than conquerors—*but only through "the Captain of our salvation"* (Heb. 2:10).

In II Timothy 2:3 Paul told Timothy, "Thou therefore endure hardness, as a good soldier of Jesus Christ." In I Corinthians 15:57 he said, ". . . *Thanks be to God, which giveth us the victory through our Lord Jesus Christ!*"

If we are clad in the whole armor of God and if we keep our eyes on our Commander-in-Chief, we cannot lose; victory is assured!

". . . *Whereunto thou art also called* . . . ." (Timothy had received his induction papers. When he was converted in Lystra, he was called by Almighty God into the army of the Lord as a soldier to fight the fight of faith.) ". . . *And hast professed a good profession before many witnesses.*" Timothy had taken a stand and lived a life the effectiveness of which could not be denied. In the Greek language the expression is not "*a* good profession," but "THE good profession"—and this good profession is the fact that Timothy believed on the Lord Jesus Christ, confessed Him openly, was baptized into the local church in the name of the Father, Son, and Holy Spirit, and had proven true allegiance to Christ since that day. Timothy was called; he obediently took his place in the army of the Lord—unafraid, unashamed, a good servant and a worthy soldier of the cross.

Life eternal is what the future holds for such a soldier. The moment a person believes on the Lord Jesus Christ and places his trust in the shed blood, he receives eternal life; but the one who has received eternal life is to lay hold on that life with a firm grip day by day, feeding upon the Word, witnessing, nourishing the inner man, that he may be enlarged and strengthened for the fight of THE faith. Jesus said, "I am come that ye might have life, *and have it more abundantly.*" As long as a person has a spark of physical life, he is *alive*, though perhaps extremely weak; a born again person is alive spiritually . . . he may be weak—but he is *alive*, because he possesses life eternal. However, it is the spiritual birthright of every Christian to enjoy *abundant life*. We are to grow and become strong—good soldiers to fight the fight of faith. ". . . *And this is the victory that overcometh the world, even our faith"* (I John 5:4). A good soldier of Jesus Christ is commanded:

> *"Flee evil things . . .*
>
> *Follow after righteousness . . .*
>
> *Fight the good fight of faith!"*

Verse 13: "I give thee charge in the sight of God, who quickeneth all things, and before Christ Jesus, who before Pontius Pilate witnessed a good confession."

Paul here gives a charge to this young minister, and he gives that charge *in the sight of God.* The confession of the Lord Jesus Christ was His testimony that He was King, and that testimony is recorded in John 18:28 through 19:13. Pilate asked Jesus, "Art thou a king?" Jesus could have answered, "Yes, *I am a king!*" But instead He replied, *"Thou sayest* that I am a king. To this end was I born, and for this cause came I into the world, *that I should bear witness unto the TRUTH."* Jesus IS the Truth (John 14:6; 8:32; 17:17).

In His conversation with Pilate, Jesus was no doubt speaking of the truth of His being a King. Jesus was announced "King of the Jews" when He was born (Matt. 2:2). On one occasion, His followers attempted to take Him by force and MAKE Him a king (John 6:15). It was prophesied in Zechariah 9:9 that the people would cry, "Behold, thy King cometh unto thee" (fulfilled in Matthew 21:5); and at the close of His earthly ministry the crowds mocked Him by crowning Him with thorns, scoffing and crying out in mockery, "Hail, King of the Jews!" (Matt. 27:29). But in spite of the demonstration of cruel mockery, when Pilate prepared a title and set it up over the head of Jesus on the cross, he wrote, *"This is Jesus the King of the Jews"* (Matt. 27:37; John 19:19).

Israel missed her King because she did not understand

that the cross preceded the crown and suffering preceded glory; but one glorious day He will return—not as a babe in a manger, but as King of kings and Lord of lords. He will sit on the throne of David and will reign right here on this earth. Jesus "witnessed a good confession" before Pontius Pilate; He spoke the truth and did not turn aside from the fulfillment of the mission upon which He came into the world. It is worthwhile to make mention that we have here an interesting instance of the historical basis of our Christian religion, in the reference to Christ's appearance before Pontius Pilate.

The Christian religion is the only religion that can prove the fundamentals of its doctrine through history. In our present epistle we read, "And without controversy, great is the mystery of godliness; God was manifest in the flesh, justified in the Spirit, seen of angels, preached unto the Gentiles, believed on in the world, received up into glory" (I Tim. 3:16). Yes, the virgin birth is a great mystery; the crucifixion is a great mystery; the bodily resurrection is a great mystery; the ascension is a great mystery; and Pentecost is a great mystery. But all of these great mysteries are definitely recorded in history!

"The just shall live by faith." Saving grace becomes ours by faith. Victory is ours by faith. And "whatsoever is not of faith is sin"! Christianity is not a myth; it is a mystery . . . but *it is proved* by history and by the witness of the Holy Ghost in the heart of every believer.

Verse 14: "That thou keep this commandment without spot, unrebukeable, until the appearing of our Lord Jesus Christ."

The Greek reads, *"Keep THE commandment,"* but no specific commandment is named. In I Timothy 1:5 we read, "Now the end of the commandment . . ."—but again the commandment is not named. In II Peter 2:21 we read,

". . . The holy commandment," but the commandment is not named. In II Peter 3:2 we read, ". . . The commandment of us . . ."—but again we may ask, "WHICH commandment?" In I John 2:7,8 we read, "I write no new commandment unto you, but an old commandment which ye had from the beginning. . . . Again, a new commandment I write unto you . . . ." But what IS the new commandment?

The first believers knew which commandment Jesus meant, and those of us who study our Bibles by comparing spiritual things with spiritual should know.

When Jesus entered upon His public ministry, the scribes and Pharisees did their best to trap Him. They considered Him an impostor; they were sticklers for the Law, and to break the Law of Moses was the greatest sin one could commit in that day in the eyes of the religionists. On one occasion when they were trying to trap Jesus, a lawyer asked Him, "Master, which is the great commandment in the law? Jesus said unto him, THOU SHALT LOVE THE LORD THY GOD WITH ALL THY HEART, AND WITH ALL THY SOUL, AND WITH ALL THY MIND" (Matt. 22:36,37). This Scripture answers the question, *"What commandment?"* It is the commandment to love God with all of our being, and love our neighbor as ourselves. The commandment is LOVE!

But how are believers in the flesh going to "keep this commandment *without spot, unrebukeable until the appearing of our Lord Jesus Christ"?* The answer is found in Galatians 5:22: ". . . *The fruit of the Spirit* is love . . . ." Paul said, ". . . Now abideth faith, hope, charity, these three; but the greatest of these is charity (LOVE)" (I Cor. 13:13). The only way we can keep this commandment to love God above all, and love our neighbor as ourselves, is to be possessed, controlled, directed, filled, and kept by the Holy Ghost; and we are to keep this commandment *until the Lord Jesus comes for us*. When we see Him we will be like Him—we will be perfect in love, and we will have the mind of Christ. We will then automatically keep the commandment *because* we will be like Him (I John 3:2). God is love, and it is impossible for any person to know true love apart from knowing God. The very essence of God is love, and from God all love proceeds.

Notice that we are kept *"until the appearing of our Lord Jesus Christ."* In I Peter 1:3—5 we have tremendous truth clearly set forth: "Blessed be the God and Father of our Lord Jesus Christ, which according to His abundant mercy hath begotten us again unto a lively hope by the resurrection of Jesus Christ from the dead, to an inheritance incorruptible, and undefiled, and that fadeth not away, reserved in heaven for you, *who are kept by the power of God through faith unto salvation ready to be revealed in the last time."*

Believers are kept by the power of God. The *love of God* is the power that lifts us from the miry clay of sin, plants our feet on the solid rock, and *keeps us* until we are conformed to the image of His dear Son. The true Church will be displayed in the heavenlies throughout all eternity, that all God's new creation may witness the exceeding riches of His grace (Eph. 2:6,7; Rev. 21).

Verse 15: "Which in His times He shall shew, who is the blessed and only Potentate, the King of kings, and Lord of lords."

"Which in His times He shall shew . . . ." God is sovereign; He knows the end in the beginning. All things were created by Him and for Him. He has a program, and He works according to schedule. In Genesis 3:15 God promised the Saviour, and in the fulness of time Jesus came as promised (Gal. 4:4). In John 16:7 Jesus

234

told His disciples, ". . . It is expedient for you that I go away: for if I go not away, the Comforter will not come unto you; but if I depart, I will send Him unto you." Jesus ascended back to the Father, and at the appointed moment (Pentecost, exactly fifty days after the resurrection) the Holy Ghost came. Read Acts 1:1–26; 2:1–4.

God has appointed a day when the world will be judged (Acts 17:31) – "But of that day and hour knoweth no man, no, not the angels of heaven, but my Father only" (Matt. 24:36). We do not know the day nor the hour of His coming; but we do know that God works according to schedule, and everything prophesied in the Bible will be literally fulfilled to the letter IN GOD'S TIME.

". . . Who is the blessed and only Potentate, the King of kings, and Lord of lords." I cannot understand why some preachers will not preach the whole truth as laid down in the Word of God. The Gospel of Luke tells us that God sent Gabriel to the Virgin Mary, to announce to her that she would be the mother of God's Son. Mary was troubled when she saw the angel, and she asked him how these things could be. Gabriel told her that God would overshadow her, she would conceive and bear a Son, and "Thou shalt call His name Jesus. He shall be great, and shall be called the Son of the Highest: and the Lord God shall give unto Him the throne of His father David: and He shall reign over the house of Jacob forever; and of His kingdom there shall be no end" (Luke 1:26–33 in part).

Many ministers read and preach, "His name shall be called Jesus"; they continue, "He shall be great"—and they declare that He is the greatest teacher, healer, and worker of miracles who ever lived. They read, "He shall be called the Son of the Highest," and declare that He IS God's Son, virgin born. Up to that point they make everything literal: He was literally born; He is literally great; He is literally called the Son of God; but there they change their interpretation and *spiritualize* the truth laid down in the words, *"The Lord shall give unto Him the throne of His father David, and He shall reign over the house of Jacob forever, and of His kingdom there shall be no end."* They spiritualize the throne; they spiritualize the kingdom; they spiritualize the reign of Jesus. WE KNOW that David had a throne; we know that throne was in Jerusalem. Christ's occupation of that throne was prophesied seven centuries before He was born: "For unto us a child is born, unto us a son is given: and the government shall be upon His shoulder: and His name shall be called Wonderful, Counsellor, The mighty God, The everlasting Father, The Prince of Peace. Of the increase of His government and peace there shall be no end, upon the throne of David, and upon His kingdom, to order it, and to establish it with judgment and with justice from henceforth even for ever . . ." (Isa. 9:6,7).

Yes, Jesus was literally born. He was literally the Son of God. He was literally great . . . and HE WILL SIT ON A LITERAL THRONE IN JERUSALEM. He will be "the blessed and only Potentate, the King of kings and Lord of lords"; and we, the New Testament Church, will reign with Him for the glorious thousand years spoken of in the Word of God, commonly known as The Millennium!

Verse 16: "Who only hath immortality, dwelling in the light which no man can approach unto; whom no man hath seen, nor can see: to whom be honour and power everlasting. Amen."

The blessed and only Potentate, King of kings, Lord of lords . . . *"who only hath immortality"*! Immortality is in Him by essence—in *us* by *gift*. HE IS immortality. He was co-equal with the Father in the beginning; and to Philip He said, *"If you have seen me, you have seen the Father also."*

". . . Who only hath immortality, *dwelling in the light which no man can approach unto . . . ."* In II Timothy 1:10 Paul said, ". . . Who hath . . . brought life and immortality to light through the Gospel." We know that Jesus was the Gospel: "In the beginning was the Word, and the Word was with God, and the Word was God. . . . And the Word was made flesh . . . full of grace and full of truth" (John 1:1,14). Jesus said, "Except ye eat my flesh and drink my blood, you have no life." He was referring to assimilating and appropriating the Word into the very heart—the inner man.

The King of kings and Lord of lords dwells in light which no man can approach. According to astronomers and astrologers, the sun is more than 93,000,000 miles from us; and if we should approach it we would be burned to a crisp—*cremated*; but even though we cannot *approach* the sun, we can enjoy its warmth and light, and benefit from its health-giving rays. No man can approach God in the flesh—but we can enjoy His love, mercy, and peace. And "if we walk in the light, as He is in the light, we have fellowship one with another, and the blood of Jesus Christ His Son cleanseth us from all sin" (I John 1:7).

". . . *Whom no man hath seen, nor can see . . . .*" In Exodus 33:20 God said to Moses, "Thou canst not see my face: for there shall no man see me, and live!" John 1:18 tells us, "No man hath seen God at any time; the only begotten Son, which is in the bosom of the Father, He hath declared Him." I John 4:12 also declares, "No man hath seen God at any time!"

Philip said to Jesus, "Lord, shew us the Father, and it sufficeth us. Jesus saith unto him, Have I been so long time with you, and yet hast thou not known me, Philip? He that hath seen ME hath seen the Father; and how sayest thou then, Shew us the Father?" (John 14:8,9). God was in Christ, reconciling the world unto Himself (II Cor. 5:19). Jesus was God in flesh. Flesh offended God in the Garden of Eden. Jesus was the God who was offended, living in flesh that offended Him; and in flesh He conquered the offender and paid sin's debt, purchasing salvation through His blood. Jesus received His life from God; He laid His life down for the sin of the world and purchased the New Testament Church with God's own blood (Acts 20:28).

It is to "the blessed and only Potentate, King of kings and Lord of lords, who only hath immortality, dwelling in the light which no man can approach unto; whom no man hath seen, nor can see," that all honor, power and glory belong . . . *"that no flesh should glory in His presence.* But of Him are ye in Christ Jesus, who of God is made unto us wisdom, and righteousness, and sanctification, and redemption: That, according as it is written, *He that glorieth, let him glory in the Lord!"* (I Cor. 1:29–31).

The disciples said to Jesus, "Lord, teach us to pray," and He taught them in the following manner: "Our Father which art in heaven, Hallowed be thy name. Thy kingdom come. Thy will be done in earth, as it is in heaven. Give us this day our daily bread, and forgive us our debts, as we forgive our debtors. And lead us not into temptation, but deliver us from evil: For thine is the kingdom, and the power, and the glory, for ever. Amen" (Matt. 6:9–13).

". . . *Thine is the KINGDOM, and the POWER, and the GLORY — FOREVER!"* Yes, HE is the power, HE is the glory, and HE will sit on the throne in HIS kingdom. (The R. S. V. Bible leaves off "the kingdom, the power, and the glory," thus stripping the Lord Jesus of His kingdom and His power and His glory. Modernism denies all three!)

Verse 17: "Charge them that are rich in this world, that they be not high-minded, nor trust in uncertain riches, but in the living God, who giveth us richly all things to enjoy."

Those who are rich in this world's goods are cautioned to be not high-minded (proud and boastful), looking down upon others who have less wealth than they. They are warned to keep their faith centered in the living God, not in uncertain riches and things that money can buy. ("We are not redeemed with corruptible things, as silver and gold . . . but with the precious blood of Christ . . ."— I Pet. 1:18,19.) Timothy was to warn those that were rich not to rely upon their money to secure for them position and comfort, for riches are always undependable— here today and gone tomorrow . . . but rather let their trust be in the living God who *"giveth us richly all things."* Wealthy Christians should be reminded that God is not a pauper. His joy is to bless abundantly and give abundant life to those who will accept it and permit Him to grant it. God is the giver of every good and perfect gift.

Verse 18: "That they do good, that they be rich in good works, ready to distribute, willing to communicate."

The wealthy members of the church are to use their money to bring blessings to those who are less fortunate. They are to labor for the Lord, rendering humble service in the church and in the community, being *"rich in good works."* They must be ready to distribute their riches, communicating to the less fortunate anything that would help them and make life more complete. Wealth and an esteemed position in the community should not cause a Christian to expect special privileges from either the pastor or other members of the church. They should be willing to do any service that the Holy Spirit places upon them.

Verse 19: "Laying up in store for themselves a good foundation against the time to come, that they may lay hold on eternal life."

A person who professes to be saved, and yet allows riches to dominate his life, *has not laid hold on eternal life.* I John 3:17 says, "But whoso hath this world's good, and seeth his brother have need, and shutteth up his bowels of compassion from him, how dwelleth the love of God in him?" Paul wants Timothy to direct the wealthy members of his congregation into the right path and to warn them to build on the right foundation—that foundation is *Christ*—that their riches not rob them of their reward in the life to come. Paul tells us in I Corinthians 3:11, "For other foundation can no man lay than that is laid, which is *Jesus Christ.*" If any man build on this foundation he will have a reward. Ah, yes; money laid out for material help of the poor and for the spiritual advancement of God's work, is treasure laid up in heaven, according to Christ's own words: "Lay not up for yourselves treasures upon earth, where moth and rust doth corrupt, and where thieves break through and steal: But lay up for yourselves treasures in heaven, where neither moth nor rust doth corrupt, and where thieves do not break through nor steal: *For where your treasure is, there will your heart be also!*" (Matt. 6:19–21).

There is grave danger that rich believers will be tempted to use their money to try to *buy* their way through the Pearly Gates, or to try to buy a reward for the life to come. They should have their feet planted on the true foundation, in order that they may lay hold on that which is life indeed . . . that they may possess to the full all joys, powers, and blessings (whether here or hereafter) of that *Life* which is theirs through the shed blood of Jesus Christ.

Verse 20: "O Timothy, keep that which is committed to thy trust, avoiding profane and vain babblings, and oppositions of science falsely so called."

There is deep compassion and love for Timothy in this cry from Paul's heart. "O Timothy! *Keep that which is committed to thy trust!* Let nothing cause you to deviate from the Gospel message of the grace of God. Guard it with your life."

Greek authorities tell us that the figure here is that of a banker safely guarding the money or valuables that are placed in his trust. Timothy, then, is to guard his trust with vigilance and see to it that it is not broken by carelessness, nor by allowing false teachers to bring error into the church.

It should humble the heart of any preacher to realize that God Almighty has committed to our trust the message of redemption. What an honor—*but what a tremendous responsibility!* In I Timothy 1:12 Paul said, ". . . I thank Christ Jesus our Lord, who hath enabled me, for that *He counted me faithful*, putting me into the ministry." In I Thessalonians 2:4 he said, "But as we were allowed of God to be *put in trust with the Gospel*, even so we speak; not as pleasing men, but God . . . ." God calls faithful men, places the Gospel message in their hands, and those ministers (put in trust with the Gospel) are responsible for passing the good news on to those who are unbelievers. Sinners become Christians by being put in touch with the Gospel through the preaching of God's faithful minister.

Timothy is to avoid *"profane and vain babblings."* He is to see to it that there are no arguments and quarrels among believers in the church. It is unchristian to argue—even about the Scriptures and things spiritual. The facts of Christianity are by revelation—not by reason; and argument is largely a matter of clever, quick wit. One may be beaten in an argument and still be right. Only God Almighty, through the Word and the Holy Ghost, can convince a false teacher or false prophet that he is in error. There is no need to argue with a false preacher or the leader of a cult, for man's argument will never convince them that they are wrong. Their minds are closed; their consciences are seared; they are willingly ignorant, and it is a waste of precious time to argue with them. Jesus said, "Give not that which is holy unto dogs, neither cast ye your pearls before swine, lest they trample them under their feet, and turn again and rend you!" (Matt. 7:6). We are to avoid useless discussions which will lead to argument and "profane babblings" in the church. Paul wanted Timothy to preach the Word and make no apology for it . . . the grace of God, the blood of Jesus, the virgin birth, the crucified, risen Lord. No, do not argue; stick to your message. Instead of arguing about the seed—*sow it*.

Timothy was also to avoid *"oppositions of science falsely so called."* The Greek word here translated *science* just means *knowledge of any kind*—and not that particular department to which the name "science" is usually applied today. There were undoubtedly men of science in that day who denied the Lord and liked to boast of their knowledge; but God's Word tells us that "the FEAR OF THE LORD is the *beginning* of knowledge," and one who does not fear God is an ignoramus, regardless of the degrees of learning he may have!

Paul is not outlawing *the right kind* of discussion on Scripture or doctrine. (There is nothing wrong with reasoning together, comparing Scripture with Scripture and spiritual things with spiritual.) But Paul is warning Timothy not to allow teachers who boast of their wisdom and knowledge to come in and teach something that would bring about a disturbance in the assembly. A person who is right with God will never show off *"his"* knowledge and education from the pulpit. He will lift up Jesus Christ—not his own education and degrees of learning.

Verse 21: "Which some professing have erred concerning the faith. Grace be with thee. Amen."

Note that in this closing verse Paul states that some *"professing"* have erred from the faith. There are many people who have "head belief" in God, without "heart belief." Intellectually, they are religious—but with their hearts they deny the Lord; and that is the group whom these men of wisdom would lead astray—both in Paul's day and in this present time.

In I Corinthians 2:14 Paul said, ". . . The natural man receiveth not the things of the Spirit of God: for they are foolishness unto him: neither can he know them, because they are spiritually discerned."

One who is not born again cannot teach the Bible, because a person who has not been born of the Spirit *cannot understand* the things of the Spirit. The Spirit searches the deep things of God (I Cor. 2:10), and all believers have the Spirit, who teaches them (I John 2:27). The Holy Ghost will guide us into all truth, and those who are truly born again will not be confused or confounded by false teachers (I Pet. 2:6).

If you are genuinely converted, you need not worry about being led into error—because the Spirit of God will witness to your spirit if the things of the Spirit are being taught. When you listen to any minister, evangelist, missionary, Bible teacher—or whomsoever—if your spirit does not testify to you that this person is teaching truth, you had better withdraw from listening to such a teacher. It is a waste of time to expose your mind to error.

I am not against education, nor am I against educated preachers. I believe a call to the ministry constitutes a call to study and prepare. A young man or woman who is not willing to study and go to school if it is humanly possible, is not fit to preach nor be a full time Christian worker. God puts no stamp of approval on ignorance—but neither does He put a stamp of approval upon *wisdom apart from spirituality*! The foolishness of God is wiser than men; and when education magnifies the intellect instead of magnifying God, that is the wrong kind of education.

Timothy was instructed to guard the trust committed to him, to avoid profane and vain babblings—empty religious arguments in the church. He is to be on guard against men of learning and excessive knowledge who, professing to be wise, are not spiritually minded—and through their teaching of error would cause *professing* (not possessing) church members to be led astray.

Paul is now ready to close his message, and he closes with a beautiful statement: *"Grace be with thee. Amen."* He opened this message to Timothy with, "Paul, an apostle of Jesus Christ by the commandment of God our Saviour, and Lord Jesus Christ, which is our hope; unto Timothy, my own son in the faith: GRACE, mercy, and peace from God our Father and Jesus Christ our Lord."

"GRACE, mercy and peace . . . GRACE be with thee." This jewel (six diamond chapters of God's Holy Word directed to a young pastor) is bound with a covering of GRACE. What a beautiful cover for any book! And the intervening pages take their color from the cover. Through the inspired pen of Paul, the Holy Ghost speaks to us in this glorious epistle concerning God's feelings toward us, His attitude concerning us—*an attitude of grace*. Paul tells of God's assistance which He affords us—*an assistance of grace*. God is our all-sufficient assistant all the way, in every phase of life—but only by grace.

In this epistle, Paul tells us how we are to demonstrate the love of God so that others may see that love in us. We are to be living epistles, read of men; we are to be good soldiers; we are to be profitable servants; and we are to flee whatever would bring reproach upon the name of Jesus. We are to fight the good fight of faith, and in all that we do we are to cause men to take knowledge that we have been with Jesus.

The Christian life begins in grace; Christian victory is ours through grace; and when we stand before God to receive our eternal reward, it will be because of His grace! I know of no way in which Paul could have closed this letter that would have conveyed more meaning to a young preacher than to simply say, *"Grace be with thee. Amen!"*

The Second Epistle of Paul the Apostle to Timothy

THE SECOND EPISTLE OF PAUL THE APOSTLE
TO TIMOTHY

INTRODUCTION

Second Timothy is the last epistle dictated by the Holy Spirit to the grand old Apostle . . . called, commissioned, ordained of God . . . a minister and a teacher to the Gentiles. At the time of the writing, Paul was again in prison in Rome; and shortly thereafter he sealed his testimony with his blood—a martyr to the cause of Christ. Paul's movements and life between the first and second imprisonments in Rome (see my Introduction to First Timothy) may be traced as follows:

After writing his first epistle to Timothy, he returned to the city of Ephesus by way of Troas, as had been his intention. He left the books mentioned in II Timothy 4:13 with Carpus. From Ephesus he traveled to Crete, and after he left there he wrote the epistle to young Titus. Next he went by Miletus to the city of Corinth (II Tim. 4:20), from Corinth to Nicopolis (Titus 3:12), and from there he journeyed on to the city of Rome. Some Bible scholars think it likely that Paul visited Spain, but if he did so it was immediately after his release from his first imprisonment. Other scholars discount this claim and do not think it would have been possible for him to have visited Spain at that time.

Timothy evidently was still in the city of Ephesus, and undoubtedly it was in that city that he received the second letter from Paul. The names mentioned in the second epistle seem to substantiate this. It is evident from chapter 1:18 that Onesiphorus was an Ephesian; and as the direction is to salute his *"household,"* it seems certain that Timothy was then at Ephesus, the ordinary residence of Onesiphorus.

249

Priscilla and Aquilla lived in the city of Ephesus (Acts 18:26), and they are also saluted by the Apostle. In II Timothy 2:17 Hymenaeus is mentioned, pointed out as a teacher of gross error—and undoubtedly this is the same person mentioned in I Timothy 1:20. Alexander the coppersmith is mentioned as another false teacher in Ephesus. That city was a great center for false religions, and the church there was one of the great churches of Paul's day.

Within Paul's heart burned a deep desire to see his beloved son in the Lord just one more time. He knew that it could not be long until he would seal his testimony and his ministry with his blood; and in II Timothy 1:4 he evidences his feeling for Timothy by saying, "Greatly desiring to see thee, being mindful of thy tears, that I may be filled with joy." In II Timothy 4:9,21 he begs Timothy, "Do thy diligence to come before winter!" Evidently he was uncertain as to whether or not his martyrdom might come to pass before Timothy arrived.

In this second letter Paul warns, exhorts, and instructs Timothy concerning the ministry, knowing that it would be the last opportunity he would ever have to give such instruction. Some may ask, "Why *two* epistles? Why did not Paul write the entire message of instruction and exhortation in the first epistle?" There is a marked difference between First and Second Timothy. In the first epistle the house of God (the church) is seen in order (or free from discord, worldliness, and error); and Paul gives detailed instructions as to how this order, in all godliness and purity, is to be maintained and guarded. The house of God as such, is no longer mentioned in the second letter. In chapter 2:20 we read of *"a great house"*; and this great house is described as having vessels to honor and vessels to dishonor—and the believer is urged to purge himself from dishonor and be a vessel of honor, meet for the Master's use.

The professing church is foreshadowed as now becoming *a great house*; it will increase in number as the tiny mustard seed grows into a big tree that shelters fowls of the air in its branches. And this great house no longer manifests the order as laid down in the first Epistle. It has become dilapidated and is in disorder. As the house becomes greater and greater, disorder and division will be more noticeable than when Paul first wrote this Epistle. As we look back, we can see in the history of the church exactly what Paul meant when he referred to vessels of honor and of dishonor.

Jesus said, ". . . Upon this rock I will build my church; and the gates of hell shall not prevail against it" (Matt. 16:18). These words were not spoken of the local assembly nor of the local meeting house. The gates of hell certainly *have prevailed* against some of the local churches, to the extent that those churches have closed and padlocked their doors and have gone out of business. *But not so with The Church of the living God, the body of Christ!*

Above all the other apostles, Paul had labored in the local assemblies—and the pride and joy of his heart were those local churches God had used him to establish. Now, in the closing days of his life, he could see some of these assemblies departing from the faith, with corruption already setting in. Evil teachers, such as Hymenaeus, Philetus, and others, had brought in error. Paul knew that God had not failed, nor had God's power failed; but *man* had failed.

In this second epistle to Timothy, the failure and disorder of the professing church is anticipated. Not one word does Paul say concerning elders and deacons, nor is any promise made nor any instruction given about the church's recovery from conditions pointed out in this epistle. The decline and corruption of the local church will continue until the end of the age. Evil men and seducers will wax worse and worse, and there is no suggestion of international revival before the end of the Church Age and the consummation of the Day of Grace. There will be revivals in some areas, and some local assemblies will partially recover from their deadness and confusion; but generally speaking, there will not be either a national or international revival.

Ministers who preach that there will be a great revival before the Lord's return simply do not understand the Bible; they are preaching error. The professing, visible church will go from bad to worse, until such an hour as the Lord Jesus descends from heaven with a shout, and with the voice of the archangel and the trump of God. The true Church will then be taken out, caught up to meet the Lord Jesus in the air; and the lukewarm church—the rich, happy-go-lucky church—will be left behind. Read I Thessalonians 4:13—18 and Revelation 3:17—22.

In Revelation 3:10 we learn that the true Church will be taken out of the earth, and in Revelation 3:16 we read that the lukewarm church will be *spewed* out and left in the kingdom of Antichrist. At the close of the Church Age, Jesus is seen standing at the door—the *church door*, beloved, not the door of the human heart: "BEHOLD, I STAND AT THE DOOR, AND KNOCK: If any man hear my voice (one man, ANY man), and open the door, I will come in to him (singular—just ONE man), and will sup with him, and he with me" (Rev. 3:20).

God DOES knock at the door of the *individual heart*, and it is not wrong to use this verse of Scripture to illustrate that fact; but this passage speaks of the *church*, not the heart—and Jesus stands at the door, knocking. This is the *local church*, because we know Jesus is the head of *the true Church*, which is without spot or wrinkle

252

or any such thing . . . holy and without blemish (Eph. 5:27). This verse pictures a local assembly where not even ONE MAN will let Jesus in! When the Rapture takes place, beloved, there will be some churches where there is not one Christian to be found in the entire assembly!

When the true Church is taken out, the church of the Antichrist—"the great Babylonian house"—will be dealt with as revealed in Revelation chapters 17 and 18. The house will be completely abandoned by the Holy Spirit and turned over to the devil to become the habitation of "demons, foul spirits, and of every unclean and hateful bird." *What a picture!* And yet, we see this very thing shaping up today. This is indicated by the fact that outstanding religionists and great religious leaders are crying out for a world church. Protestants, Jews, and Catholics are coming together to iron out their differences and to write (or revise) a Bible which will fit all religions. Many outstanding men who a few years ago stood true to the faith are now compromising to such degree as to indicate that surely the stage is set and the hour is at hand when Jesus will call out His true Church and turn the great religious organizations over to the devil.

Bear in mind that Jesus Christ did not say to His disciples, *"Convert the world."* He did not put the Church here to convert the world, but to be a witness for Him, to tell forth the good news of the Gospel, and make disciples of all who would believe; and when the Church is complete, Jesus will take out His bride and turn this earth over to the devil. The Antichrist will run his evil course, and then Jesus will return to build again the tabernacle of David "which is fallen down," and He will set up the ruins thereof; and when Jesus sits on the throne of His father David we will have peace on earth, good will toward men—BUT NOT UNTIL THEN! Study

Acts 15:13–18 carefully. In that passage you will find a concise, understandable blueprint of God's dealings during this Gentile age and immediately following. Familiarize yourself with these verses, and you will have a good understanding of the outline of things that lie ahead.

I think the fact that Paul was in jail alone is a picture of what will happen to many faithful ministers and Christians in the end of the Church Age. Paul said, "All they which are in Asia be turned away from me" (II Tim. 1:15). Again, "Demas hath forsaken me, having loved this present world. . . . Only Luke is with me" (II Tim. 4:10,11). What a sad picture! This devout man of God who had been so greatly used of the Holy Spirit to organize many local assemblies, whose preaching had resulted in thousands of converts, now has only one friend by his side—his beloved physician, Dr. Luke. We need not be surprised when we stand alone—whether we be ministers or laymen. The masses have always followed the way of least resistance, and they always will.

This was a dark hour for Paul; but in spite of the fact that he stood alone except for Luke, he knew that his God stood with him—and his convictions did not weaken. Just before his execution he testified that *he had kept the faith!*

It was also a dark hour for Timothy. Knowing that his first duty was to God and the Gospel, he was facing the ministry and the labor for the Lord that had been appointed unto him, and during this ministry his days would be fraught with danger and filled with sorrow. His spiritual father, the man who had led him into the knowledge of Jesus Christ, was imprisoned and was soon to be martyred for the sake of the very Gospel Timothy was to preach!

The earliest mention of this young man is in Acts

16:1, where we read of his Gentile father and his Jewish mother. The last mention of him is in our present epistle. He is not mentioned again in the New Testament. Paul adopted Timothy as his helper in missionary work; Timothy proved faithful, and was later appointed pastor of the Ephesian church. He and Paul had been so close in fellowship, in spirit, and in their labors that they are referred to as father and son in the spiritual realm: "But ye know the proof of him, that, as a son with the father, he hath served with me in the Gospel" (Phil. 2:22).

The hearts of these two men beat in harmony, and their love welded them together. Paul was the strong-hearted spiritual father of this fine young man, dedicated soul, spirit, and body to the cause of the Lord Jesus; and Timothy was walking in his footsteps. I do not doubt that Timothy often leaned on Paul on occasions not recorded in the epistles.

Up to this point, he had Paul to confide in, to consult with and lean upon; but now he must face the solemn fact that in the future he may be standing alone so far as human instruments are concerned. In this last letter, Paul assures him that God is faithful and will stand by him, and admonishes Timothy to be faithful to the charge given him in the Gospel committed to his trust.

To such a burdened heart this letter came—this second epistle to Timothy, in which Paul poured out his mighty sympathies and begged Timothy to be strong and carry out the high calling of God. He exhorts him to be faithful to *God*, to the *Word*, and *to the saints to whom he would minister.*

The first chapter of II Timothy contains Paul's tender, loving greeting. It contains exhortations to faithfulness in all things—especially that Timothy hold fast to sound doctrine which he had heard from Paul. He was to stand firm in the truth. There are other exhortations to be strong, to endure hardness as a good soldier, to strive lawfully concerning all things, to be considerate at all times, and to remember former things he had enjoyed and the blessings that had been showered upon him since his conversion. Later on in the epistle, Paul describes the conflict that every true servant of God must face in the world and the battle in which every good soldier must engage with strength, alertness and diligence.

Paul then describes some who will depart from the faith, and concerning these he outlines the path that the believer must always follow. In the third chapter of II Timothy we read of the last days, which will be days of manifest evil. In the fourth chapter we find Paul's final testimony—his faithfulness to God and God's faithfulness to him.

THE SECOND EPISTLE OF PAUL THE APOSTLE TO TIMOTHY

CHAPTER ONE

PAUL'S PERSONAL MESSAGE TO TIMOTHY

1. Paul, an apostle of Jesus Christ by the will of God, according to the promise of life which is in Christ Jesus,

2. To Timothy, my dearly beloved son: Grace, mercy, and peace, from God the Father and Christ Jesus our Lord.

3. I thank God, whom I serve from my forefathers with pure conscience, that without ceasing I have remembrance of thee in my prayers night and day;

4. Greatly desiring to see thee, being mindful of thy tears, that I may be filled with joy;

5. When I call to remembrance the unfeigned faith that is in thee, which dwelt first in thy grandmother Lois, and thy mother Eunice; and I am persuaded that in thee also.

6. Wherefore I put thee in remembrance that thou stir up the gift of God, which is in thee by the putting on of my hands.

7. For God hath not given us the spirit of fear; but of power, and of love, and of a sound mind.

8. Be not thou therefore ashamed of the testimony of our Lord, nor of me his prisoner: but be thou partaker of the afflictions of the gospel according to the power of God;

9. Who hath saved us, and called us with an holy calling, not according to our works, but according to his own purpose and grace, which was given us in Christ Jesus before the world began,

10. But is now made manifest by the appearing of our Saviour Jesus Christ, who hath abolished death, and hath brought life and immortality to light through the gospel:

11. Whereunto I am appointed a preacher, and an apostle, and a teacher of the Gentiles.

12. For the which cause I also suffer these things: nevertheless I am not ashamed: for I know whom I have believed, and am persuaded that he is able to keep that which I have committed unto him against that day.

13. Hold fast the form of sound words, which thou hast heard of me, in faith and love which is in Christ Jesus.

14. That good thing which was committed unto thee keep

by the Holy Ghost which dwelleth in us.

15. This thou knowest, that all they which are in Asia be turned away from me; of whom are Phygellus and Hermogenes.

16. The Lord give mercy unto the house of Onesiphorus; for he oft refreshed me, and was not ashamed of my chain:

17. But, when he was in Rome, he sought me out very diligently, and found me.

18. The Lord grant unto him that he may find mercy of the Lord in that day: and in how many things he ministered unto me at Ephesus, thou knowest very well.

The Apostolic Greeting

Verse 1: "Paul, an apostle of Jesus Christ by the will of God, according to the promise of life which is in Christ Jesus."

These words mark the beginning of one of the most wonderful farewells ever given by one mortal to another. Today we close our letters with our signatures; but in Paul's day it was the custom to put the writer's name first, in salutation. It is generally believed that Paul was almost blind. It stands to reason, therefore, that he dictated this letter to Luke, his only companion as he sat in the semi-darkness of a Roman dungeon, and Luke penned down the words as the Holy Spirit spoke through the Apostle Paul.

When Timothy opened this letter, the first word he read was the name of his beloved friend, former companion, and father in the Lord—"*Paul.*" It has been nineteen hundred years since Paul walked this earth; yet down through the annals of history that name has been synonymous with dedication, bravery, zeal, suffering, and uncompromising faith; he had no double on this earth. With the exception of the Man Christ Jesus, I believe God honored Paul above all other men; to him He dictated more books of the New Testament than to any other writer.

Even before his conversion Paul was extraordinary.

He was outstanding in every respect—yet he was so human, so down-to-earth, so like many of us in so many ways. No other writer of the Word of God stands out in the Church of the living God as does Paul. He was one of the best-educated men of his day—yet in his deep humility he gloried only in the cross of Christ. He was not physically strong, but his strength in the Lord overshadowed the weakness of his body. In II Corinthians 12:9 he said, "And (God) said unto me, *My grace is sufficient for thee: for my strength is made perfect in weakness.* Most gladly therefore will I rather glory in my infirmities, that the power of Christ may rest upon me!" In Philippians 1:20 he said, "According to my earnest expectation and my hope, *that in nothing I shall be ashamed*, but that with all boldness, as always, so now also *Christ shall be magnified in my body, whether it be by life, or by death.*"

The Lord looked through the eyes of the Apostle Paul, and Jesus Christ spoke through his lips. He could cry out, "*I am crucified with Christ*: nevertheless I live; *yet not I, but Christ liveth in me*: and the life which I now live in the flesh I live by the faith of the Son of God, who loved me, and gave Himself for me" (Gal. 2:20). Paul's physical weakness is often mentioned—by himself and by others; but he did not allow his physical condition to hinder his ministry, and in some instances he even labored at his trade of tentmaking in order to earn funds to support himself while he preached. He was weak in body; but there was no place for weakness in his soul, no trace of weakness in his ministry.

Paul had an all-consuming love for God and a deep passion for the souls of men. He cried out, "I could wish that myself were accursed from Christ for my kinsmen according to the flesh" (Rom. 9:1–3). I wonder how many dear men of God have ever reached the place of dedication where they could say from a truthful heart and in the fear of God that they would be willing to be *lost* in order to see their loved ones and their people saved? Paul had such a passion for souls, such a burden for the ministry into which God had called him.

The deepest truths, the most glorious facts, the clearest exhortations to the believer for this day and hour are laid down in the books given to us by Almighty God through the Apostle Paul. God's message to the Church—the bride of Christ—is given in those writings. Paul was "an apostle of Jesus Christ," and in that capacity he was dedicated to *"the care of all the churches"* (II Cor. 11:28). This man was truly a bondslave of Jesus Christ; he was not his own, and he could truthfully say, "I live . . . yet not I." Christ lived in Paul to such extent that his every breath and every heartbeat were dedicated to the Christ who saved him and to the believers whom God had given him through the preaching of the Gospel.

Paul was not dedicated to a religion, a denomination, a group of religious dignitaries. He was "the apostle of Jesus Christ," and as such his dedication was to the ministry of the churches. His joy was to see the young churches grow and become strong; his heartbreak was to hear of division and strife among the members, or of error invading the local assembly. This apostle was truly "a vessel meet for the Master's use."

In the first two verses of this chapter, Paul refers to Christ Jesus three times. The reference appears again in the close of verse one, and also in verse two. *Christ Jesus* is our life; were it not for Him there would be no grace; were it not for Him there would be no eternal life; and were it not for Him Paul could not have been the man he was. He said, "By the grace of God, I am what I am" (I Cor. 15:10). In Christ Jesus "we live, and move,

260

and have our being" (Acts 17:28). He is the author and finisher of all things having to do with the believer. He is the lifeblood of Christianity. He is the one great secret of success in Christian living. He is the unsearchable riches of God's grace, God's power, and God's ability to supply our every need.

Paul said, "Unto me, who am less than the least of all saints, is this grace given, that I should preach among the Gentiles *the unsearchable riches of Christ*" (Eph. 3:8). Upon Christ Jesus rests the redemption, the peace, the security, the eternal life possessed by every believer. Christ Jesus came into the world to save sinners. He finished the work the Father sent Him to do, and ". . . when He had by Himself purged our sins, sat down on the right hand of the Majesty on high" (Heb. 1:3b). He sits at the right hand of God the Father as our Advocate, our Mediator, our Friend. He dwells in our hearts—"Christ in you, the hope of glory" (Col. 1:27). He is the cornerstone of all eternal truth and creation: "For by Him were all things created, that are in heaven, and that are in earth, visible and invisible, whether they be thrones, or dominions, or principalities, or powers: all things were created by Him, and for Him: And He is before all things, and *by Him all things consist*" (Col. 1:16,17).

One glorious day this same Christ Jesus will come in the clouds in the air to receive the true Church and resurrect the saints, and we will be caught up together to meet Him in the air (I Thess. 4:13–18; Acts 1:10,11; Heb. 9:28).

"Paul, an apostle of Jesus Christ by the will of God, according to the promise of life which is in Christ Jesus." What a tremendous verse! Apart from Christ there is no life, no hope, no peace, no rest, no redemption, no joy. Christ is all the believer needs, and His name is the only name given under heaven among men

261

whereby we must be saved. Timothy was to remember that Paul was an apostle of Jesus Christ, and that he held that office *"by the will of God,* according to the *promise of life which is in Christ Jesus."*

Christ Jesus did not come into the world just to bring eternal life—HE IS LIFE (Col. 3:4). Jesus said, "He that hath the Son hath life; and he that hath not the Son of God hath not life." To the sorrowing sisters, Mary and Martha, He said, "I am the resurrection, and the life: he that believeth in me, though he were dead, yet shall he live: and whosoever liveth and believeth in me shall never die" (John 11:25,26).

Dearly beloved, it matters not how many churches you may have joined nor how many times you have been dedicated, christened, confirmed, or baptized: *If you do not possess the Lord Jesus, you are dead, spiritually—for apart from Him there is no life!*

Verse 2: "To Timothy, my dearly beloved son: Grace, mercy, and peace, from God the Father and Christ Jesus our Lord."

Years ago Paul had preached the Gospel of the death, burial, and resurrection of Jesus "according to the Scriptures"; and through that Gospel, Timothy was saved. Paul had watched him develop and grow strong spiritually, to become the promising young minister in charge of the Ephesian assembly. No wonder Paul prayed for this young man, *"Grace, mercy, and peace,* from God the Father and Christ Jesus our Lord!"

It is interesting to note that in First and Second Timothy and Titus, Paul says, "Grace, *mercy,* and peace," while in all of his other epistles he simply says, "Grace and peace." Paul knew that it was through immeasurable mercy that he was afforded all spiritual blessings. As he neared the end of his earthly journey he recognized as never before that he was given life, joy, peace, and the opportunity to suffer for the Saviour who had suffered so much in his stead. To him was given the glorious opportunity to seal his testimony in martyrdom, thereby receiving the martyr's crown. Paul points out to Timothy and Titus that man is a recipient of God's grace and a joint heir with Jesus Christ—*because of God's unmerited and immeasurable mercy.* If we had justice, we would all burn in hell; but God's mercy has made possible grace and peace through the Lord Jesus Christ.

Verse 3: "I thank God, whom I serve from my forefathers with pure conscience, that without ceasing I have remembrance of thee in my prayers night and day."

"I thank God . . . ." This phrase does not seem particularly significant—until we consider where Paul was at the time of writing, what he was suffering—and would suffer in the near future. This man had sacrificed ALL for the Gospel, and now he was in prison awaiting execution for the preaching of that Gospel. But he could still *thank God!* Face it, dear reader: Some Christians today grumble and complain about the slightest inconvenience or hint of persecution for the sake of the Gospel.

"Whom I serve from my forefathers with pure conscience . . . ." It is true that Paul was in Judaism until he met Jesus on the road to Damascus; but he faithfully served Jehovah, the God of his fathers, from the time he was a lad until he met Jesus and became the minister, apostle, and teacher to the Gentiles. Paul consented to the death of Stephen—*with a clear conscience.* At the time of his conversion he was on the road to Damascus to persecute the Christians there—but his conscience was clear, because he was deceived by religion. He did not know the light of Christ whom he met on the Damascus road; and when he realized what he was doing he cried

out, "Lord, *what wilt thou have me to do*?" He obeyed God, became a preacher of the Gospel—and the first sermon he ever delivered was on the *deity of Christ*, declaring that He was God's virgin-born Son (Acts 9:20).

Therefore Paul could say, "I have lived in all good conscience before God until this day" (Acts 23:1). When Paul learned the truth, he became just as dedicated to the Gospel of grace as he had been to the ministry of Judaism. He was a Pharisee of the Pharisees, sincerely dedicated to the religion of his fathers—but he was sincerely wrong. There are many today who are lost, even though they are sincerely religious—yet they refuse to allow the Lord to instruct them.

Paul asked, *"Who art thou*?" and Jesus answered, "I am Jesus, whom thou persecutest." Paul then asked, "Lord, what wilt thou have me do?" Jesus told him to arise and go into the city, where he would receive instructions. Paul listened—and obeyed. He was saved, filled with the Holy Ghost, was baptized, and became the Gospel preacher most greatly used of God to minister to the churches—and through him we were given thirteen great letters known as the Pauline epistles.

In this verse Paul was thinking of his forefathers and of how, with a clear conscience, he had served the God of the Jews down through the years until he met the Christ. Now with tender affection toward his son in the ministry, longing to see Timothy face to face one more time this side of heaven, he remembers this young man night and day in his prayers.

Verse 4: "Greatly desiring to see thee, being mindful of thy tears, that I may be filled with joy."

This is a continuation of Paul's cry from a burdened heart. Remembering the tears of Timothy, probably shed at their parting, he yearns to see him once more. His mind no doubt retraced the journeys he and Timothy had made together as father and son, with hearts knit together in the love of God, spreading the good news that Jesus saves. Together they had seen pagans become believers; together they had seen new churches born. *"That I may be filled with joy . . .* by seeing you again." Paul is saying that the JOY would dispel the TEARS if he could just see Timothy again.

Verse 5: "When I call to remembrance the unfeigned faith that is in thee, which dwelt first in thy grandmother Lois, and thy mother Eunice; and I am persuaded that in thee also."

Paul called to remembrance Timothy's "unfeigned faith" . . . genuine faith, without hypocrisy. Paul tells us more about faith than any other writer of the New Testament. Through the inspired pen of this apostle we are told, "For by grace are ye saved *through faith*" (Eph. 2:8). "So then *faith* cometh by hearing, and hearing by the Word of God" (Rom. 10:17). Concerning the life of believers after we have exercised faith unto salvation, Paul tells us, ". . . Whatsoever is *not of faith* is sin" (Rom. 14:23). With Paul, it was by grace, *through faith*—not of works. But WHY? *"That no flesh should glory in His presence!"* (I Cor. 1:29). Paul's writings magnify FAITH—faith exercised in Jesus Christ, faith that receives and trusts Jesus. Christ is all, and we are nothing. In Titus 3:5 he said, "Not by works of righteousness which we have done, but according to His mercy He saved us, by the washing of regeneration, and renewing of the Holy Ghost." When we receive Jesus by simple faith, trusting Him with all of our heart, such a reception of Him gives to Him all the honor and glory, leaving absolutely nothing for the recipient of God's grace to boast about. Hebrews 11:6 tells us, *"Without faith* it is impossible to please God."

"Unfeigned faith . . . *which dwelt first in thy grand-mother Lois, and thy mother Eunice.*" Here Paul's mind travels back to the superstitious and violent town of Lystra where he had found this young man Timothy, the son of a Jewish mother and a Greek father (Acts 16:1 ff). Lois (his grandmother) and Eunice (his mother) were both believers; and even though Timothy did not attend the seminary in Jerusalem, these two women were very capable teachers and had instructed him in the Word of God from *early childhood.* Therefore, they must have been saved for a good many years, because when Paul called Timothy to be his missionary companion, he was a grown young man. It could very well be that they were converted at Pentecost or shortly thereafter. At any rate, they had proved that their faith was genuine; they had faithfully instructed Timothy in the Scriptures, and the example set forth here proves the importance of parents living a Christian life before their children and teaching them in the things of God. In God's Word we are told, "Train up a child in the way he should go: and when he is old, he will not depart from it" (Prov. 22:6).

If we bring up our children in the nurture and admonition of the Lord, they will not forget God when they grow into manhood and womanhood. The tragedy of this present hour is that children are neglected at home; many times pets and social activities get more attention than the children in the homes of supposedly Christian people. The molding of a child through the Word of God, prayer, and correct admonition from mother and father is the most important of all things in the tender years of childhood and youth. If we do not bring our children up in the nurture and admonition of the Lord, we will regret it and pay dearly for our failure—even in this life, as well as at the end of life's journey, when we stand before God to receive our reward.

When God permits a child to come into our home,

He entrusts to us a soul that will never die; and it is our grave responsibility and duty to train that child in the things of the Lord. Timothy had such training from his grandmother and his mother before him; and Paul said, "I am persuaded that you, Timothy, possess the same pure faith as your mother and grandmother possessed."

Words of Assurance

Verse 6: "Wherefore I put thee in remembrance that thou stir up the gift of God, which is in thee by the putting on of my hands."

Paul had told Timothy of his deep love for him, and of the tender memories of their days together. He had told him of his tears and of his yearning to see him just once more before he faced his executioner. But the greatest burden of his heart concerned Timothy's sacred duty to the divine call he had received. Paul felt that he should therefore put him "in remembrance" of that call.

Timothy's character was above reproach, and he was strong in the Lord; but he was not strong physically, and when one suffers in body, such suffering sometimes causes sensitivity and weakness that brings about compromise. Paul knew that Timothy was about to suffer a deep bereavement and would have to face a hostile world alone, while still carrying on his pastoral duties. The devil would tempt Timothy to yield to cowardice, and compromise with the enemies of the Gospel; and since the old apostle was soon to be martyred, he would no longer be there to strengthen the younger man during hours of trial.

What should Timothy do? Where should he turn in the hour of bewilderment for courage and power to labor on? Paul takes a practical approach; he points him to a concrete fact—the gift that God gave him and the sacred event of his ordination. Timothy had genuine saving faith, and Paul wanted him to remember how God had blessed him and given him victory down through the years. Paul urged him to *"stir up the gift"* . . . fan the flame of his zeal and keep the fires burning in his heart. I Timothy 4:14 says, "Neglect not the gift that is in thee, which was given thee by prophecy, with the laying on of the hands of the presbytery." Evidently these two passages refer to the same incident—the time when Timothy was ordained into the ministry by the laying on of the hands of the presbytery. Possibly he had been ordained at Lystra—and if not there, then in Ephesus. Paul and the leaders in the church had laid their hands upon the young man's head, setting him apart as pastor of the Ephesian church. It is possible that at that time Paul had reminded Timothy of what he should suffer for the sake of the Gospel; but he had also reminded him of the great victories he was to win in the strength of the Spirit. And now he wanted Timothy to remember that day of ordination, and by so doing, fan the flame in his heart and *stir up the gift* which he possessed by divine order. In Hebrews 1:7 Paul said, "(He) maketh His angels spirits, and His ministers a flame of fire."

Paul wanted Timothy to show forth the power of God in his life, the love of God in all that he did, and to practice discipline himself. Thus he would set an example for other believers in the church and be able to discipline them with a good conscience to the glory of God, that they might live lives of holiness and dedication.

Verse 7: "For God hath not given us the spirit of fear; but of power, and of love, and of a sound mind."

God has not given us the spirit of fear, but of *power*—which is the Holy Spirit . . . a power so utterly and so gloriously adequate for every demand laid upon us. God plants the Holy Spirit in the bosom of every believer (Rom. 8:9), and believers are led by the Spirit (Rom. 8:14).

All born again believers are kept by the power of God: "Blessed be the God and Father of our Lord Jesus Christ, which according to His abundant mercy hath begotten us again unto a lively hope by the resurrection of Jesus Christ from the dead, to an inheritance incorruptible, and undefiled, and that fadeth not away, reserved in heaven for you, who are *kept by the power of God* through faith unto salvation ready to be revealed in the last time" (I Peter 1:3—5).

We enter boldly into the holy of holies, into the very presence of God in the name of Jesus through the blood of His cross. God does not want us to be weaklings and spiritual cowards, but valiant soldiers of the cross, knowing that God has not given us the spirit of fear: *We are to fear no one save God.*

In Ecclesiastes 12:13 we read, "Let us hear the conclusion of the whole matter: *Fear God, and keep His commandments: for this is the whole duty of man.*" In Proverbs 1:7 we read, "The fear of the Lord is the beginning of knowledge." The Psalmist cries out, "The fear of the Lord is clean, enduring for ever" (Psalm 19:9). Jesus said, "Fear not them which kill the body, but are not able to kill the soul: but rather fear him which is able to destroy both soul and body in hell" (Matt. 10:28). The man of wisdom warns, "The fear of man bringeth a snare" (Prov. 29:25).

Fear produces physical weakness and emotional confusion. Fear will upset the nervous system. An outstanding physician in one of the great hospitals of America said, "Fear kills more people than does disease." *God is not the author of fear.* He gives us power to overcome the world, the flesh, and the devil, and to lift up the blood-stained banner without fear, favor, or apology.

He gives us love; He IS love—and love casteth out

269

fear: In I John 4:18 we read, "There is no fear in love; but perfect love casteth out fear: because FEAR HATH TORMENT. He that feareth is not made perfect in love."

". . . A sound mind" — self-control, self-restraint. Through the power of the Holy Spirit and the power of love God gives us a sound, healthy mind. Now according to our passage these gifts are not to be struggled for— but they are qualities which God has given us. They are His gifts to us. What forcefulness they bring to the obedient Christian. The fulness of God's grace, power, and love is the birthright of all believers.

Verse 8: "Be not thou therefore ashamed of the testimony of our Lord, nor of me His prisoner: but be thou partaker of the afflictions of the Gospel according to the power of God."

Paul was concerned lest, under fire, this young soldier of the cross might weaken, might become ashamed of Paul, in bonds for *preaching* that Gospel. But the warning given here is also to you and me: *We are not to be ashamed of the Gospel.* In Romans 1:16 Paul said, "For I am not ashamed of the Gospel of Christ: for it is the power of God unto salvation to every one that believeth . . . ." We should not be ashamed of fellow Christians when they are called upon to suffer persecution or hardship for the sake of Jesus Christ. We should lift our heads high and witness to the saving grace of God, the keeping power of God, and the glorious truth of the Gospel, regardless of what it may cost us personally.

". . . But be thou partaker of the afflictions of the Gospel according to the power of God." In II Timothy 3:12 Paul declares, "Yea, and all that will live godly in Christ Jesus shall suffer persecution." Whether minister or layman, the godly will suffer. I ask myself, "What has it cost ME to be a Christian? Have I ever been

270

afflicted or persecuted? What have I sacrificed to preach the Gospel? I do not mean in dollars and cents—but, have I lost any friends? Have I been criticized and lied about? Has the preaching of the Gospel brought reproach or afflictions on me?" Most of us do not know the meaning of suffering for the sake of Christ and the Gospel. If we suffer with Him, we will reign with Him; if we confess Him before men, He will confess us before the heavenly Father. But if we deny Him before men He will deny us before the heavenly Father.

Verse 9: "Who hath saved us, and called us with an holy calling, not according to our works, but according to His own purpose and grace, which was given us in Christ Jesus before the world began."

"*Who hath saved us* . . . ." Paul here reminds Timothy that salvation is by grace through faith plus nothing— "Not by works of righteousness which we have done, but according to HIS mercy, *HE hath saved us*" through His own death, burial, and resurrection. No man could take the life of Jesus. He willingly laid His life down that we might be saved. He willingly took our place and bore our sins in His own body on the cross. He who knew no sin was made sin for us, that we in Him might be made the righteousness of God.

In this last epistle to Timothy, Paul briefly points out the same tremendous truths explained in more detail to the believers in Rome, Galatia, Ephesus, and Colosse. He reminds Timothy that God not only saved him, but that He also *called* him "*with an holy calling, not according to our works, but according to His own purpose and grace, which was given us in Christ Jesus before the world began.*" Here Paul steps into the deep mysteries of God's sovereignty and points out that their call came not because of works of righteousness which they had done, but because *God had called and ordained them*

271

according to His own purpose, according to His own grace—grace given in Christ Jesus before ever the world was formed.

"Known unto God are all His works from the beginning of the world" (Acts 15:18). "Forasmuch as ye know that ye were not redeemed with corruptible things, as silver and gold, from your vain conversation received by tradition from your fathers; but with the precious blood of Christ, as of a lamb without blemish and without spot: who verily was foreordained before the foundation of the world, but was manifest in these last times for you. Who by Him do believe in God, that raised Him up from the dead, and gave Him glory; that your faith and hope might be in God. Seeing ye have purified your souls in obeying the truth through the Spirit unto unfeigned love of the brethren, see that ye love one another with a pure heart fervently: Being born again, not of corruptible seed, but of incorruptible, by the Word of God, which liveth and abideth for ever" (I Peter 1:18–23).

Paul always made it clear that God Almighty in His sovereign grace and eternal love saves sinners "FOR CHRIST'S SAKE" (Eph. 4:32). I believe in the sovereignty of God, although I confess I do not understand that sovereignty. God was in the beginning: "Before the mountains were brought forth, or ever thou hadst formed the earth and the world, even *from everlasting to everlasting*, thou art God" (Psalm 90:2). God knows the end from the beginning, and all that lies between. The Church as a body was elected and chosen before the foundation of the world; but *individuals who make up that body* choose the Lord Jesus *of their own free will*. The sovereignty of God does not clash with the free will of man. God put Adam in the Garden of Eden, gave him instructions, and Adam made his own choice—as has every other man who has entered heaven or plunged into hell

272

fire. What Paul is here saying to Timothy is, "We are saved and called—not according to our good works, but by God and for His own purpose, plan, and program. Salvation was given to us in Christ Jesus before God created the world."

Verse 10: "But is now made manifest by the appearing of our Saviour Jesus Christ, who hath abolished death, and hath brought life and immortality to light through the Gospel."

From the beginning, the grace of God was "safely deposited" (thus the meaning of the Greek) in the Lord Jesus. God does not work in a haphazard, hit-or-miss way. He has a program and a blueprint of all things, and in His appointed time He will work out His plan in detail *according to His blueprint.* In the fulness of time Jesus came (Gal. 4:4), and in the fulness of time this same Jesus will come again (Acts 1:11). The grace of God was deposited in Jesus—a place of safety and surety— until the appointed time, *"but is now made manifest by the appearing of our Saviour Jesus Christ."*

Jesus did not come into this world to set a good example, to be the founder of a new religion, nor to be the world's most unusual teacher, miracle-worker, and healer. Jesus brought God down to man in flesh where man could see Him, hear Him, and touch Him (I John 1:1,2). John bears witness of this that we may have fellowship and that our joy may be full. God was in Christ, reconciling the world unto Himself (II Cor. 5:19).

"What the law could not do, in that it was weak through the flesh, God sending His own Son in the likeness of sinful flesh, and for sin, condemned sin in the flesh: That the righteousness of the law might be fulfilled in us, who walk not after the flesh, but after the Spirit" (Rom. 8:3,4).

When Adam sinned, God was offended; and when Adam

attempted to cover the shame of his nakedness with the labor of his own hands, God was even more offended. He condemned the fig-leaf covering, condemned Adam's hiding place, and at the expense of the blood of innocent animals He provided a covering for Adam and Eve. He then promised the Lamb of God, who would bruise the serpent's head. Jesus was the fulfillment of that promise— GOD IN FLESH. JESUS WAS THE GOD-MAN . . . the God who was offended, in the flesh that offended Him. He was divine—yet human. He was very God; yet He was man—and in a body "like unto sinful flesh" He satisfied the offended One. Jesus fulfilled every jot and tittle of the Law (Matt. 5:17). He satisfied the heart of God (John 17:1 ff). He paid sin's debt; He purchased our redemption; He bore our sins in His own body. When He said, "It is finished" and gave up the ghost, God was satisfied. The price of redemption was paid, and death was abolished.

". . . *Who hath abolished death, and hath brought life and immortality to light through the Gospel.*" Jesus did not come to earth simply to bring a message. He did not come to bring a Gospel—He WAS the Gospel: "In the beginning was the Word, and the Word was with God, and the Word was God. The same was in the beginning with God. . . . And the Word was made flesh, and dwelt among us, (and we beheld His glory, the glory as of the only begotten of the Father,) full of grace and truth" (John 1:1, 2, 14).

In John 6:53,54 Jesus said, "Verily, verily, I say unto you, Except ye eat the flesh of the Son of man, and drink His blood, ye have no life in you. Whoso eateth my flesh, and drinketh my blood, hath eternal life; and I will raise him up at the last day." When Jesus made that statement, many of his disciples turned back "and walked no more with Him" (John 6:66).

274

Jesus abolished death: "I am He that liveth, and was dead; and, behold, I am alive for evermore, Amen; and have the keys of hell and of death" (Rev. 1:18). Jesus removed the sting of death. *He is our life*: "He that believeth on the Son hath everlasting life: and he that believeth not the Son shall not see life; but the wrath of God abideth on him" (John 3:36). Jesus is the Light of the world, and without Him we are in darkness. In John 3:19 we are told, ". . . This is the condemnation, that light is come into the world, and men loved darkness rather than light, because their deeds were evil." In I John 1:7 we read, ". . . If we walk in the light, as He is in the light, we have fellowship one with another, and the blood of Jesus Christ His Son cleanseth us from all sin."

Trials, tribulations, heartaches and tears will surely come: "For we know that the whole creation groaneth and travaileth in pain together until now. And not only they, but ourselves also, which have the firstfruits of the Spirit, even we ourselves groan within ourselves, waiting for the adoption, to wit, the redemption of our body" (Rom. 8:22,23).

Yet in spite of the heartaches, heartbreaks, trials and tribulations, even now those of us who have exercised faith in the finished work of Jesus and the shed blood of His cross, have been positionally placed with Christ in God in the heavenlies: "And hath raised us up together, and made us sit together in heavenly places in Christ Jesus" (Eph. 2:6). "If ye then be risen with Christ, seek those things which are above, where Christ sitteth on the right hand of God. Set your affection on things above, not on things on the earth. For ye are dead, and your life is hid with Christ in God. When Christ, who is our life, shall appear, then shall ye also appear with Him in glory" (Col. 3:1–4).

We who are saved are risen with Christ; we are dead to this world, and our life is hid with Christ in God. We are deposited in a safe place; and "when Christ who is our life shall appear, then shall (we) also appear with Him in glory." "For I reckon that the sufferings of this present time are not worthy to be compared with the glory which shall be revealed in us" (Rom. 8:18).

"Wherefore seeing we also are compassed about with so great a cloud of witnesses, let us lay aside every weight, and the sin which doth so easily beset us, and let us run with patience the race that is set before us, looking unto Jesus the author and finisher of our faith; who for the joy that was set before Him endured the cross, despising the shame, and is set down at the right hand of the throne of God" (Heb. 12:1,2). Jesus *endured the cross, despising the shame*"; He went willingly to the cross because of the joy that was set before Him. We, like our Lord, should look beyond this vale of tears to the joy that is set before us, and pray daily, "Even so, come, Lord Jesus!"

Verse 11: "Whereunto I am appointed a preacher, and an apostle, and a teacher of the Gentiles."

Paul did not make his own decision to enter the ministry. He did not choose to take up the ministry as a vocation—he was a *God-appointed* preacher. I shudder when I hear a statement like this: "That young man should enter the ministry; he has such a dynamic personality and such wonderful talent." It has not been many nights ago that a young man in a church where I was conducting revival services told me that many of the people in his church had suggested that he should enter the ministry because he had such an unusual voice and would make a dynamic speaker. He asked me, "What do *you* think I should do?" My answer was, "Never attempt to preach the Gospel unless you know God has called you to the ministry! Never let relatives, friends, or your church put you in the ministry." God-called preachers should be honored and revered as servants of the Lord, but pity the man who attempts to serve in the ministry without being appointed by God!

In I Timothy 1:12 Paul made it plain that it was God who enabled him, counted him faithful, and put him in the ministry. In his testimony before King Agrippa (recorded in the twenty-sixth chapter of Acts) Paul related word by word the details of his conversion and his call to the ministry. This man was a dignified, educated, traditional Jew, a member of the Sanhedrin; yet when Jesus called, ordained, and commissioned him to preach the Gospel to the Gentiles, he said, "For I speak to you Gentiles, inasmuch as I am the apostle of the Gentiles, I magnify mine office: If by any means I may provoke to emulation them which are my flesh, and might save some of them" (Rom. 11:13,14). The Gentiles were "dogs" in the eyes of the Jews in Paul's day—but when God appoints a preacher, whether that appointment be to a First Church in the city or to a mission on the street of forgotten men and women, that man will say in the words of Isaiah, "Here am I . . . Send me!" Paul obeyed the command of Jesus on the Damascus road; he believed, he was baptized, *"and straightway he preached Jesus in the synagogues, that He is the Son of God"*! (Acts 9:20). At the end of life's journey and the close of his ministry, Paul had not forgotten that day when God saved him and put him into the ministry.

Verse 12: "For the which cause I also suffer these things: nevertheless I am not ashamed: for I know whom I have believed, and am persuaded that He is able to keep that which I have committed unto Him against that day."

TREMENDOUS!!! *"For the which cause I also suffer these things."* Paul suffered abuse, slander, bodily pain, anguish, tears—and now imprisonment, the final result of the ministry to which God appointed him. Because he lifted up the Lamb of God (whom the world hates) and preached the grace of God (the message the devil despises), he was abandoned by man—but not by God. He said, "Only my trusted friend Luke is with me. All others have forsaken me. I am imprisoned, facing a martyr's death; I suffer in the dampness of this dungeon—hungry, cold, in bodily pain—but still I am not ashamed."

Paul is saying, "I am not disappointed, in spite of all that has come upon me and in spite of all that I am now facing; and if I had my life to live over, I would live it in exactly the same way—dedicated wholly and unreservedly to God and the Gospel. I am not ashamed; I am not disappointed. I am not going to deny the faith and say that I am sorry I met Jesus. Although I am in jail, convicted and condemned to die for preaching the Gospel, I am not ashamed because: *I know whom* (*HIM*); and I am persuaded that He (JESUS) *is able to keep that which I have committed unto Him.*"

Paul knew whom he had met on the Damascus road; and he knew that the same Jesus who saved him and called him, the same Jesus whom he magnified and lifted up throughout his ministry, *would keep THAT which had been entrusted to Him* "against that day"—the day when he would stand face to face with a holy God who judges in righteousness.

Peter puts it this way: "But sanctify the Lord God in your hearts: and be ready always to give an answer to every man that asketh you a reason of the hope that is in you with meekness and fear: having a good conscience; that, whereas they speak evil of you, as of evildoers, they may be ashamed that falsely accuse your good conversation in Christ. For it is better, if the will of God be so, that ye suffer for well doing, than for evil doing" (I Peter 3:15–17).

Three things experienced by Paul give a positive, sure cure for all doubt, worry, and anxiety; and these three things can be your experience and mine:

1. WHOM

There are many church members and religionists who can tell you *what* they believe—they have memorized a catechism, they have studied *what* their particular denomination believes, they have learned rules and regulations, and they can recite *what* they are—but when you ask them pointedly, "Are you born again? Do you KNOW that you are saved?" they cannot give a positive answer. They "hope so," they "think so," and they are trying to "do the best they know how." Paul knew *what* he believed—but he knew more than that: He said, *"I know WHOM I have believed."*

Christianity is not rules, regulations, covenants, dogmas, or doctrines of men. *Christianity is "Christ in you."* Paul met Christ on the road to Damascus—he saw the Light, he heard the Voice—and he asked, "Who art thou, Lord?" The Voice replied, "I am Jesus." Paul KNEW that he had had an experience with a Person—not a religion. Christ IS our salvation; there is none other name under heaven given among men whereby we must be saved. Christ is the Way, the Truth, the Life. No man can come to God but by Him. "Christ in you, the hope of glory"— and if Christ is not in you, you have no hope! If you know WHOM you have believed, you are ready for the second step in total victory over worry, doubt, and fear.

2. WHAT

Paul knew *what* he believed concerning *Whom* he believed. He said, "I am persuaded that He is able to keep *THAT which I have committed unto Him.*" Paul was persuaded in his heart that the Jesus who was able to save him in Damascus was also able to keep THAT which Paul had committed unto Him. If you have committed your spirit to the Lord for salvation, you are saved. If you have said from your heart, "Lord, I believe you died to save sinners. I am a sinner—save me!" you are saved.

But Paul pleaded in behalf of his converts that they would present soul, spirit, and body unto the Lord, sanctified completely (I Thess. 5:23). It is one thing to be redeemed, it is another thing to be wholly committed to Jesus and allow Him to have pre-eminence in all things. A mind committed to Jesus will not worry and doubt. If we have exercised saving faith in His shed blood, then surely, *if He is able to save us*, He is able to keep us; and if He is able to supply the need of the inner man, surely He is able to supply the needs of the flesh. It is a sin to doubt God!

Jesus said, "Seek ye first the kingdom of God, and His righteousness; and all these things shall be added unto you" (Matt. 6:33). If we put first things first, God is then duty bound to take care of us—and He will. He cares for the sparrow and the lily of the field; and we are of much more value than they. If you are a born again child of God and yet you are worried about your eternal welfare or your daily needs—physically, spiritually, mentally, or financially—you are sinning. The God who saved you is able to keep anything and all things committed unto Him. Your trouble may be that you have not committed your mind and your physical needs to the Lord. He is able; and if you will commit all things into His hands, then your part is to simply *trust*. He handles the rest of the transaction.

Paul knew HIM, and was persuaded that He is able to KEEP all that we are willing to commit unto Him. Do you believe God is able to do what He said He would do? Never doubt God; never let the devil place doubt in your mind. God cannot and will not fail you. Christians may fail God, but HE never fails His own. It was Paul who said, "We know that all things work together for good to them that love God, to them who are the called according to His purpose" (Rom. 8:28). In Romans 8:31 Paul said, "If God be for us, who can be against us?" Paul believed God, and in perfect trust committed everything to Him.

3. WHEN

Should we not be concerned about daily commitment? If we are saved, can we rest without worry that some time in the future we might backslide or be caught off guard and commit some horrible sin? The answer to that question lies in God's Word:

David did not have the New Testament, but he knew the GOD of the New Testament. David said, "The Lord is my Shepherd; I shall not want. He maketh me to lie down in green pastures: He leadeth me beside the still waters. He restoreth my soul!" *That is wonderful, is it not?* But that is not all: "HE LEADETH ME IN THE PATHS OF RIGHTEOUSNESS FOR HIS NAME'S SAKE!" (Psalm 23:1-3).

The Good Shepherd (Jesus) leads me into the paths of right living—not that I might brag and boast, advertising my own holiness, but "He leadeth me in the paths of right living *for His name's sake!*" I bear the name of Christian; I am God's son, and Jesus is a million times more concerned about my walking straight and making a success of my Christian life than I am concerned about myself! I am finite—but HE is *infinite.* He leads me and supplies my every need. He will go with me all the way, even unto the end—and then He will walk with me through the valley of the shadow of death. "Surely goodness and mercy shall follow me all the days of my life, *and I shall dwell in the house of the Lord forever!*"

It was Paul who asked the question, "Who shall lay anything to the charge of God's elect?" He answers that question: "It is God that justifieth!" He then asks, "Who is he that condemneth?" and answers, "It is Christ that died, yea rather, that is risen again, who is even at the right hand of God, who also maketh intercession for us." He then asks a third question:

"WHO SHALL SEPARATE US FROM THE LOVE OF CHRIST? Shall tribulation, or distress, or persecution, or famine, or nakedness, or peril, or sword? As it is written, For thy sake we are killed all the day long; we are accounted as sheep for the slaughter. Nay, in all these things we are more than conquerors through Him that loved us. For *I am persuaded*, that neither death, nor life, nor angels, nor principalities, nor powers, nor things present, nor things to come, nor height, nor depth, nor any other creature, shall be able to separate us from the love of God, which is in Christ Jesus our Lord" (Rom. 8:33–39).

"Who shall lay anything to the charge of God's elect?" Name everyone on earth or in heaven . . . none can be found who can lay anything to the charge of a blood-bought believer, because a believer who is covered by the blood is *justified*—and one who is justified is *just as just as Jesus is just*. It is true that "without holiness no man shall see God," but the only way any man can be holy is in Christ Jesus, covered by His blood. Therefore, when we are a member of God's elect by the new birth, then there is none in heaven or in earth who can charge us with sin that would damn us.

"Who is He that condemneth?" The answer is: Christ who died, Christ who is risen, Christ who sits at the

right hand of God. But Jesus will not condemn believers—because He loved us enough to die for us, we have trusted in Him, and He ever lives to intercede for us (I Tim. 2:5; I John 2:1,2). Jesus is the only one who *could* send me to hell—and He will not send me there because He is my Saviour, I am His son, I am covered by His blood; I am hid with Christ in God.

Paul asks, "Who, then, shall be able to separate us (tear us) from the love of God?" He then names various snares and pitfalls of the devil, and climaxes the entire passage by saying, "*Nor any other creature* shall be able to separate us from the love of God which is in Christ Jesus our Lord!" Whatsoever I have committed to Jesus, He is able to keep AGAINST THAT DAY. He will keep; and He will present every believer faultless before the Father.

Paul said, "I am not ashamed; I am not disappointed; I am not discouraged. My death is imminent; I have but few days left on earth. I am old, sick, and imprisoned. All friends except Luke have forsaken me; *but I know whom I have believed*, and I am persuaded that He is able to keep that which I have committed unto Him against that day. Timothy, *be faithful*, and preach the Word as I have preached it."

Exhortation to Faithfulness

Verse 13: "Hold fast the form of sound words, which thou hast heard of me, in faith and love which is in Christ Jesus."

Paul actually gave Timothy his personal testimony in verse 12. He did it to encourage and assure Timothy that he was not sorry for the life he had lived, the race he had run, the Gospel he had preached, and the end to which he had come. And by this testimony he was saying,

283

"If I had another life to live, I would live it for the Gospel. If I had another death to die, I would be willing to die for the Gospel."

"Hold fast the form of sound words, which thou hast heard of me." That simply means to hold to the simple, pure Gospel of God's marvelous grace—the true message concerning the Incarnation (I Tim. 3:16), the crucified, buried, risen Lord, according to the Scriptures. Paul wanted Timothy to be a good Gospel preacher; he wanted him to preach the whole Gospel. He did not want Timothy to allow the devil to run him down blind alleys, nor tempt him to ride a "spiritual hobby-horse."

There are some preachers who could never preach again if a dozen chapters were removed from the Bible, because they preach on the same subject every time they enter the pulpit. Some preach on baptism—according to their own formula. Others preach on storehouse tithing—and that is all they know. With others, it is some phase of prophecy. Thus the devil pushes them out on a limb or runs them down a blind alley. If Satan cannot cause a minister to become a liberal or a modernist, he will attempt to hinder his ministry in some other way. Paul wanted Timothy to preach ALL of the truth about God and about the Lord Jesus Christ; about man and his relationship to God; about God's relationship to man, about the forgiveness of sins, sanctification, holiness, heaven and hell, the second coming.

The Gospel is the milk, the meat, the bread, and the life that keeps a believer growing and becoming stronger and more useful. It was this Gospel to which Timothy was admonished to hold, being faithful first and foremost to God, then to the Word and to the people to whom he delivered his message.

Verse 14: "That good thing which was committed

unto thee keep by the Holy Ghost which dwelleth in us."

Timothy was to guard the full Gospel message with jealousy and ardent care. As I pointed out earlier in this study, the Lord Jesus Christ is the heart, soul, and the very *essence* of the Gospel; and Timothy was to preach the whole truth about the Person of the Christ— His glory, His love, the salvation He purchased with His own blood, and the coming glory that we will share with Him in His eternal kingdom. Timothy was able to do this *"through the Holy Ghost which dwelleth in us"*— and that is the only way ANY minister or teacher can give out the message of the Person of Jesus, as the Holy Ghost magnifies the Saviour.

"I have yet many things to say unto you, but ye cannot bear them now. Howbeit when He, the Spirit of truth, is come, He will guide you into all truth: for He shall not speak of Himself; but whatsoever He shall hear, that shall He speak: and He will shew you things to come. He shall glorify me: for He shall receive of mine, and shall shew it unto you. All things that the Father hath are mine: therefore said I, that He shall take of mine, and shall shew it unto you" (John 16:12–15).

Very few believers realize the importance of the Holy Spirit in this day of grace. No man can come to God for salvation except he be drawn by the Holy Spirit (John 6:44). We are BORN into the family of God by the Holy Spirit (John 3:5). We *possess* the Spirit (Rom. 8:9), and if any man *have not the Spirit* he is not a Christian. We are LED by the Spirit (Rom. 8:14). We have *assurance* through the Spirit (Rom. 8:16). We are *filled* with the Spirit (Eph. 5:18). We are *sealed* by the Spirit until the day of redemption (Eph. 4:30). And the Spirit will *quicken our mortal bodies* when Jesus comes in the Rapture.

As many as are led by the Spirit of God are the

285

children of God, and you may rest assured that the Spirit will lead us into the paths of right living. He will glorify Jesus in our lives when we submit and yield to Him.

The Unfaithful and the Faithful in Contrast

Verse 15: "This thou knowest, that all they which are in Asia be turned away from me; of whom are Phygellus and Hermogenes."

Who these two men were we do not know. They are not mentioned anywhere else in Paul's epistles nor in the Scriptures. We suppose that they were men who had been devout followers of Paul, and everyone knew about their devotion to him and to the Gospel. When they turned away from him it was particularly noticeable, and brought grief to Paul.

These were examples of a host of people in Asia who had deserted him in his hour of grief and suffering. *"All they that be in Asia"* would not refer to that country as we know it. Asia today is made up of an enormous portion of this earth, inhabited by millions of peoples. It is exceedingly difficult to determine the exact boundaries of Asia when Rome ruled, but we know that it was much smaller than it is today. The history of Asia consists almost entirely of the history of its important cities, which were Adramyttium, Assos, Cnidus, Ephesus, Laodicea, Miletus, Pergamos, Philadelphia, Sardis, Smyrna, Thyatira, and Troas. No doubt Paul was referring to the region where "the seven churches in Asia" were located, as mentioned in Revelation. The capital of that section was the big city of Ephesus, where Paul spent three entire years teaching and preaching (Acts 20:31). Throughout all Asia Paul preached the Gospel, and under his preaching hundreds were converted from idolatry to Christianity. By his enemies there, he was royally hated.

No doubt the time when "all they which are in Asia"

turned away from Paul refers to the time when he was arrested and shipped off to Rome to be imprisoned. Since he had had such success in his ministry in Asia, winning converts and establishing churches, it seems that a tremendous group of his followers would have come to his rescue; but not so. To them, Paul was a suspected victim of the state, a defeated leader of a hated, despised, and mysterious religion. His followers deserted him and left him to face imprisonment alone.

This reminds us of our Lord. As He broke the loaves and fishes, He had thousands at His feet; but when He fell beneath the weight of His cross, not one person volunteered to carry it for Him—and the Scripture tells us that Simon the Cyrenian was *compelled* to bear His cross (Mark 15:21). Many pastors know better than I that when a person needs a friend and stands condemned by those in authority, he will always learn who his real friends are. Many times a dear pastor believes that the majority of his church members stand with him—but when the enemies of the Gospel are ready to vote him out, he discovers that his friends are few and that the visible church embraces many spineless Christians. Paul had many converts and professing friends in Asia; but when the testing time came, like the disciples of Jesus they turned back and walked with him no more.

In his lonely, forsaken hours, Paul leaned heavily upon the Rock of Ages, and his weariness became strength. This heart-stricken apostle "knew Him whom he had trusted" and therefore was at rest about it all. He had followed Jesus and was sure of *Him*; therefore, he was enabled to count it joy to lay his life on the altar for the Gospel he loved and the Christ whom he met on the Damascus road.

Verse 16: "The Lord give mercy unto the house of Onesiphorus; for he oft refreshed me, and was not ashamed of my chain."

287

In this verse we find another person about whom little was known. No other epistle names him. He lived in Asia, had undoubtedly heard the Gospel preached by Paul, and he was the head of a family. Possibly Paul had spent some time in his home; and since he says, "Onesiphorus . . . oft refreshed me," we are led to believe that when he was arrested and sent to Rome, this man visited him, refreshing him in spirit as well as bringing him food and material needs, doing what he could to lighten the burden.

". . . And was not ashamed of my chain." Bible authorities believe that Paul was held in the security prison, a section where outstanding criminals were kept. On one occasion he dwelt for two years in his own hired house, chained to a Roman soldier (Acts 28:16, 23, 30); but the Scripture indicates that now he is locked in a dungeon—and according to history, the only way a visitor could see a prisoner under those circumstances was through a bribe. Onesiphorus was evidently a man of means, because he "often" visited Paul in prison. In this letter, therefore, he is remembered with grateful love and appreciation.

Verse 17: "But, when he was in Rome, he sought me out very diligently, and found me."

"He sought me out" would indicate that Onesiphorus had difficulty in learning which prison Paul was in. It may be that the enemies of the Gospel refused to tell him where his friend was; but he "sought . . . diligently" until he found Paul. Such friends are pearls of great price, and God always gives His preacher a few such friends upon which he can depend. The majority of friends (so-called) will forsake us in the darkest hour of need; but the friend who is to be treasured as a jewel is the man who stands with us when we need encouragement, when all others are against us, and seemingly we have lost the battle. No words could ever express the worth of such a friend!

Verse 18: "The Lord grant unto him that he may find mercy of the Lord in that day: and in how many things he ministered unto me at Ephesus, thou knowest very well."

In Paul's day, tremendous emphasis was placed upon the duty of the head of a house; and Paul prays God's mercy upon his dear friend in that day when he stands before the Lord to receive the reward for his faithful stewardship. He closes his prayer for Onesiphorus by saying, *"In how many things he ministered unto me at Ephesus thou knowest very well."*

The devoutness and sincerity of this man was no secret in the local assembly at Ephesus. He was a faithful servant of the Lord Jesus Christ and a dedicated friend to the Apostle Paul. He had rendered many services to him while he preached in Ephesus; and evidently, when this man surrendered his heart to Jesus, he surrendered his material means as well.

Jesus said that if we give even a cup of cold water in His name, we will not lose our reward for that service; and Paul prays that in the day when this dear Christian friend stands before God for HIS reward, he may hear, "Well done, thou good and faithful servant!"

II TIMOTHY — CHAPTER TWO

THE BELIEVER'S PATH IN THE TIME OF APOSTASY

1. Thou therefore, my son, be strong in the grace that is in Christ Jesus.

2. And the things that thou hast heard of me among many witnesses, the same commit thou to faithful men, who shall be able to tezch others also.

3. Thou therefore endure hardness, as a good soldier of Jesus Christ.

4. No man that warreth entangleth himself with the affairs of this life; that he may please him who hath chosen him to be a soldier.

5. And if a man also strive for masteries, yet is he not crowned, except he strive lawfully.

6. The husbandman that laboureth must be first partaker of the fruits.

7. Consider what I say; and the Lord give thee understanding in all things.

8. Remember that Jesus Christ of the seed of David was raised from the dead according to my gospel:

9. Wherein I suffer trouble, as an evil doer, even unto bonds; but the word of God is not bound.

10. Therefore I endure all things for the elect's sakes, that they may also obtain the salvation which is in Christ Jesus with eternal glory.

11. It is a faithful saying: For if we be dead with him, we shall also live with him:

12. If we suffer, we shall also reign with him: if we deny him, he also will deny us:

13. If we believe not, yet he abideth faithful: he cannot deny himself.

14. Of these things put them in remembrance, charging them before the Lord that they strive not about words to no profit, but to the subverting of the hearers.

15. Study to shew thyself approved unto God, a workman that needeth not to be ashamed, rightly dividing the word of truth.

16. But shun profane and vain babblings: for they will increase unto more ungodliness.

17. And their word will eat as doth a canker: of whom is Hymenaeus and Philetus;

18. Who concerning the truth have erred, saying that the resurrection is past already; and overthrow the faith of some.

19. Nevertheless the foundation of God standeth sure, having this seal, The Lord knoweth them that are his. And, Let every one that nameth the name of Christ depart from iniquity.

20. But in a great house there are not only vessels of gold and of silver, but also of wood and of earth; and some to honour, and some to dishonour.

21. If a man therefore purge himself from these, he shall be a vessel unto honour, sanctified, and meet for the master's use, and prepared unto every good work.

22. Flee also youthful lusts: but follow righteousness, faith, charity, peace, with them that call on the Lord out of a pure heart.

23. But foolish and unlearned questions avoid, knowing that they do gender strifes.

24. And the servant of the Lord must not strive; but be gentle unto all men, apt to teach, patient,

25. In meekness instructing those that oppose themselves; if God peradventure will give them repentance to the acknowledging of the truth;

26. And that they may recover themselves out of the snare of the devil, who are taken captive by him at his will.

Paul's Charge to Timothy

Verse 1: "Thou therefore, my son, be strong in the grace that is in Christ Jesus."

No one but a minister can fully appreciate the admonition Paul gives Timothy in this verse: ". . . *Be strong in the grace that is in Christ Jesus.*" It takes a double portion of grace to be God's undershepherd and love the sheep over which He appoints His preachers. Many times, those for whom we try to do the most will treat us most shamefully in our time of dire need, while those for whom we have done but little will come to our rescue and do more for us than those of whom we expect much.

Paul has just pointed out the disappointing fact that

"all they which are in Asia be turned away from me," and then he names two specific brethren who seemingly hurt him deeply. He reminded Timothy that only Luke stood by him, and then recounts the blessing of Onesiphorus visiting him in prison. All that he has said has led consistently up to the appeal before us here: "Be strong in grace." He is trying to point out to Timothy that he must be on guard every moment; that he must depend upon the grace of God, not leaning upon human help. He must be strong in grace, for he cannot hope to win the battle apart from God's grace and God's power.

This was precisely Timothy's need, for with the impending bereavement facing him, Paul knew that the devil would attack him with everything hell could throw against him. Knowing the fears that can befall a lonely individual when everything goes against him and all his friends let him down, Paul urged Timothy to be strong *in the grace that is in Christ Jesus*. He wanted Timothy to look *above*, not at circumstances around him; he should trust God for the victory and for grace to face whatever the coming days might bring.

Believers are kept by the power of God—and ONLY by the power of God. It is only through HIM that we can be more than conquerors. Christ dwelleth "in your hearts by faith" (Eph. 3:17), and we must always look within for victory. Paul had learned that God's grace is sufficient for any and all things (II Cor. 12:8–10); he knew that we are strongest when we think we are weak—and when we THINK we are strong, we are on dangerous ground!

Verse 2: "And the things that thou hast heard of me among many witnesses, the same commit thou to faithful men, who shall be able to teach others also."

God's grace is sufficient; the battle is the Lord's—and Timothy is to be a good soldier, enlisting others to

292

help in spreading the Gospel. Timothy should gather around him true soldiers of the cross to help him in his ministry, and the message he was to commit to these "faithful men" was *"the things that thou hast heard of me among many witnesses."* The reference to "many witnesses" evidently points back to the time of Timothy's ordination, his being set apart for God's work (I Tim. 4:14). It would seem as if, at that solemn service, there was included a public reading and a public conveyance of the Gospel he was to preach. In the presence of these "many witnesses" he was set aside to preach, and was given the message for his ministry. In Paul's own words, that message was to be:

"Moreover, brethren, I declare unto you the Gospel which I preached unto you, which also ye have received, and wherein ye stand; by which also ye are saved, if ye keep in memory what I preached unto you, unless ye have believed in vain. For I delivered unto you first of all that which I also received, how that *Christ died for our sins according to the Scriptures; and that He was buried, and that He rose again the third day according to the Scriptures:* And that He was seen of Cephas, then of the twelve: After that, He was seen of above five hundred brethren at once; of whom the greater part remain unto this present, but some are fallen asleep. After that, He was seen of James; then of all the apostles. And last of all He was seen of me also, as of one born out of due time. For I am the least of the apostles, that am not meet to be called an apostle, because I persecuted the church of God. But by the grace of God I am what I am: and His grace which was bestowed upon me was not in vain; but I laboured more abundantly than they all: yet not I, but the grace of God which was with me. Therefore whether it were I or they, so we preach, and so ye believed" (I Cor. 15:1–11).

Paul had a singular message: *The crucifixion*—accord-

293

ing to the Scriptures; *the burial*—according to the Scriptures; *the resurrection*—according to the Scriptures; and *the return of Jesus for His Church*—according to the Scriptures. Timothy was to commit this message to faithful men in the church. He was to be the director, they were to be his helpers, preaching the same Gospel Paul had preached—the Gospel of a crucified, buried, risen, ascended, and coming again Christ—the only Saviour, the only Mediator, the only hope of the believer and of the world. *See here the links in the chain*: The truth is given to Paul, then through him is given to Timothy, who gives it to "faithful men," and through them it is given to others. Every Christian then occupies a strategic position and is responsible for telling forth the Gospel.

Qualities Needed for Faithful Christian Living

The Christian life—and especially that of a minister— is a strenuous and serious business. A young man who enters the ministry thinking to have a soft life, a path strewn with roses, or a flowery bed of ease, should make a thorough check with the old, seasoned men of God before entering the ministry as a vocation. If a young man cannot say with Paul, "*Woe is me if I preach not the Gospel!*" that young man had better forget the ministry and enter some vocation. God puts preachers in the ministry, and they are empowered by Him. Any man who lives godly in Christ Jesus will suffer persecution, but especially is this true of a minister.

Paul gives three figures to illustrate the Christian life:

1. *The soldier* — Verses 3 and 4: "Thou therefore endure hardness, as a good soldier of Jesus Christ. No man that warreth entangleth himself with the affairs of this life; that he may please him who hath chosen him to be a soldier."

"Endure hardness as a good soldier." Greek scholars tell us that the verse should read, "Take thy share in suffering hardships as a true soldier of Jesus Christ." The thought seems to be that he is not merely "suffering hardship," but is suffering in company with others . . . meeting trials, toil, and perils—not alone, but side by side with other Christians. The beautiful suggestion of fellowship in suffering is introduced.

Paul cries out to his son in the Lord, "Timothy, take your share of suffering." If we read the context aright, the Apostle here means to call Timothy to suffer with the suffering messenger of the Gospel, to share the lot and the pain with his chief and friend.

Even so, the Captain of our salvation, Jesus Christ, cared that His disciples should share in His sufferings and, in some measure, in His sorrows. He said, "My soul is exceeding sorrowful, even unto death: tarry ye here, and watch with me" (Matt. 26:38). "Ye are they which have continued with me in my temptations" (Luke 22:28). "He that taketh not his cross, and followeth after me, is not worthy of me. He that findeth his life shall lose it: and he that loseth his life for my sake shall find it" (Matt. 10:38,39). In Luke 9:62 He said, "No man, having put his hand to the plough, and looking back, is fit for the kingdom of God."

The thought of sharing in suffering for every Christian in every age is clearly brought out in I Peter 5:7—11: "Casting all your care upon Him; for He careth for you. Be sober, be vigilant; because your adversary the devil, as a roaring lion, walketh about, seeking whom he may devour: Whom resist stedfast in the faith, *knowing that the same afflictions are accomplished in your brethren that are in the world.* But the God of all grace, who hath called us unto His eternal glory by Christ Jesus, after that ye have suffered a while, make you perfect, stablish, strengthen, settle you. To Him be glory and dominion for ever and ever. Amen."

If we suffer with Him, we shall be glorified with Him and reign with Him; but if we deny Him, He will deny us. Timothy knew well the sufferings through which Paul had gone and which he was presently enduring for the Gospel's sake; and Paul is here inviting—yea, *commanding*—Timothy to walk where HE had walked in the path of suffering.

I Kings 19 tells of Elijah's discouragement when he thought he was the only one left standing true to God; but the Lord said to him, "Yet I have left me *seven thousand* in Israel, all the knees which have not bowed unto Baal, and every mouth which hath not kissed him!" When we think we are standing alone, we can check up and find that there are others who are suffering as we are, if not even more severely. A good soldier has no time for self-pity. In his hour of disappointment and grief he must remember that others have suffered before him, and others will *follow him* in the path of hardship. Sorrows and sufferings should be stepping stones for the Christian, by which he reaches a higher plane of service for the Lord and becomes a better soldier of the cross. *"We are more than conquerors through Him that loved us"* when we exercise unshakable faith in HIS ability and not in our own strength and ability.

"No man that warreth entangleth himself with the affairs of this life . . . ." The soldier to whom Paul refers is not a man on furlough or working at a desk at headquarters; he is a soldier at war, a fighting man in the front lines. A soldier on active duty cannot allow other interests to interfere with his military responsibility to his country, his commander-in-chief, and his fellow soldiers. A soldier in the thick of battle has a full time job; he must be alert and active, both mentally and phys-

ically. That is the only way he can fulfill his duty, and a soldier who practices less than his duty would be counted as a deserter; he would grievously fail his commander, his fellow soldiers, and his country. A good soldier must be detached from all that would entangle him or draw his mind and attention away from the battle in which he is engaged, *"that he may please him who hath chosen him to be a soldier."*

The soldier of the cross must do all that he does to the glory of God. He must be completely surrendered to the Lord Jesus Christ—and especially is this true of the pastor whom God has appointed as His undershepherd to care for His flock.

2. *The athlete* – Verse 5:   "And if a man also strive for masteries, yet is he not crowned, except he strive lawfully."

Many times Paul uses terms that apply to the athlete in illustrating spiritual living. The runner who desires to win the race and receive the victor's crown must not run unlawfully. He must abide by the rules—and if he hopes to win, he must not participate in habits of life that will tear down his strength and curtail his ability to run. Paul speaks of "the prize of the high calling of God in Christ Jesus" (Phil. 3:14), toward which he labored; and he longed for Timothy to win that prize at the end of life's journey.

To be a good athlete, one must be dedicated to the particular sport in which he participates. He must be skillfully trained; he must practice self-control; he must not abuse his body; and he must play the game or run the race according to the rules, if he hopes to win. In the spiritual realm, if we would be successful in running the race set before us, we must first be born again; and then we must be wholly dedicated to God, presenting body, spirit and soul to Him, blameless. Like the physical athlete, we must keep our body under subjection. We must be trained; we must study; we must endure hardness; and if we hope to win the crowns for dedicated stewardship and separated Christian living, we must win them according to Bible rules. Whether in the physical or spiritual field of endeavor, he who strives to win must strive lawfully and according to the rules, if he would wear the victor's crown.

3. *The farmer* – Verse 6: "The husbandman that laboureth must be first partaker of the fruits."

Here Paul uses an illustration of the farmer, whose life is seen in drab contrast to that of the soldier or the athlete. A soldier is often decorated for service beyond the call of duty; he wins medals and decorations which are awarded with praise from his commander-in-chief. The athlete wins prizes and cups for his outstanding achievements in his field of competition; and as a rule, the crowds cheer and applaud the winner of such a prize.

The farmer leads a quiet life, primarily free from excitement, far removed from such glamor as attends the life of the soldier and athlete. His labors are carried on away from the perils of war or the applause of a stadium. Through the sweat of his brow he toils, and *patiently* waits for the rain and the warmth of the sun to bring the seed to life. He then must wait for the fruit; and after his patience, plowing, sowing, tending, and waiting, *finally he reaps*. But apart from his unsung labor, tending, and patience there can BE no reaping.

Many Christians think that all will share alike in the rewards on that day when the righteous Judge will reward His faithful servants; but these dear people have a tremendous surprise in store for them! Each believer will be rewarded *according to his faithful stewardship*:

"For we must all appear before the judgment seat of Christ; that every one may receive the things done in his body, according to that he hath done, whether it be good or bad" (II Cor. 5:10). In I Corinthians 3:11—15 Paul outlines exactly what he means: "For other foundation can no man lay than that is laid, which is Jesus Christ. Now if any man build upon this foundation gold, silver, precious stones, wood, hay, stubble; every man's work shall be made manifest: for the day shall declare it, because it shall be revealed by fire; and the fire shall try every man's work of what sort it is.   If any man's work abide which he hath built thereupon, he shall receive a reward.   If any man's work shall be burned, he shall suffer loss: but he himself shall be saved; yet so as by fire."

There is only one foundation: JESUS CHRIST . . . and that foundation is laid—*He is the chief cornerstone*; but we build upon that foundation two types of labors: *gold, silver, precious stones*, which will not burn—or *wood, hay, and stubble*, which WILL burn.   Every man's work shall be tried by fire, of what sort it is; and if our works abide, we will be rewarded; but if they are burned, we will lose our reward.   I am sure there will be many in heaven without a reward.

I must confess I do not know what it will mean to be in heaven without a reward, but I do know that there will be some believers who stand before God and see their works consumed.   Some will receive a full reward; others will receive only a partial reward, and some will receive no reward at all.   In II John 8 we are told, "Look to yourselves, that we lose not those things which we have wrought, but that we receive a full reward."

"But ye, beloved, building up yourselves on your most holy faith, praying in the Holy Ghost, keep yourselves in the love of God, looking for the mercy of our

Lord Jesus Christ unto eternal life. And of some have compassion, making a difference: And others save with fear, pulling them out of the fire; hating even the garment spotted by the flesh'' (Jude 20—23).

A soldier in combat cannot afford to relax and take his eyes off the enemy. An athlete who hopes to win the contest cannot be slack in his daily living nor break the rules in the stadium. The farmer who hopes to reap a harvest and partake of the fruit cannot sit under a shade tree; he must first labor. *The minister of Jesus Christ* who hopes to receive a reward must be faithful in the ministry. The first and foremost thing in his life must be his dedication to the calling God has so abundantly bestowed upon him. He cannot do the things that he might choose to do. He is God's undershepherd; he must therefore obey the voice of the Chief Shepherd and care for the sheep, feed the lambs, and keep out the wolves that would devour the flock.

Verse 7: ''Consider what I say; and the Lord give thee understanding in all things.''

Timothy is to study the scope of these illustrations of the soldier, athlete, and farmer that Paul has given him; he is to turn them over in his mind, pray, and think them through. Paul closes the verse with a prayer that the Lord will give Timothy a thorough understanding of these spiritual truths, and needed wisdom to fully appreciate what Paul is attempting to drive home to his heart in this, the last of his communications to the young preacher.

Suffering with Christ

Verse 8: ''Remember that Jesus Christ of the seed of David was raised from the dead according to my Gospel.''

In Paul's day, as in our day, there were many teachers

who denied the resurrection. In this verse Paul reaffirms the truth of the resurrection, which is *the heart of the Gospel*. In verses 7 and 8 he declares that the Lord Jesus (through the Holy Spirit) is the Interpreter of the truth, and will make the truth known to His servants. The only One who can interpret the Bible correctly is the Holy Spirit, through whom God dictated His message to holy men. Paul did not instruct Timothy to go to the church for Scripture interpretation, nor to the apostles, nor even to *him*; but rather, he pointed to the Lord Jesus, *who IS the truth*, and who makes known the truth to all who will listen to the voice of the Spirit.

When Paul met Jesus and was saved and ordained, he "conferred not with flesh and blood." He did not go into Jerusalem and seek the good graces of the religious leaders nor of the apostles. He preached the incarnation, the crucifixion, the resurrection, the ascension and the coming again of the Lord Jesus. He wanted Timothy to be that kind of minister. The best commentary on the Bible IS THE BIBLE! The only One who can reveal the deep things of God IS THE HOLY SPIRIT (I John 2:27; John 16:13; I Cor. 2:9–14).

It is wonderful to read books written by the great men of God; but when it comes to the final authority on a verse of Scripture, let *THE BOOK* be the final word; and if you cannot get the revelation in the Bible, then my friend, *you are not supposed to know the particular thing you are trying to understand*! God will give you all the truth you will obey, all the light in which you will walk; and when you walk in the light and obey the truth God has revealed, He will make known other things as you are able to partake of them.

"REMEMBER!" Paul wants Timothy to remember that the only message which will save, keep, strengthen, and make fit for the kingdom of God is the message of

301

the cross. In I Corinthians 2:1–8 he said, "And I, brethren, when I came to you, came not with excellency of speech or of wisdom, declaring unto you the testimony of God. For I determined not to know any thing among you, save Jesus Christ, and Him crucified. And I was with you in weakness, and in fear, and in much trembling. And my speech and my preaching was not with enticing words of man's wisdom, but in demonstration of the Spirit and of power: That your faith should not stand in the wisdom of men, but in the power of God. Howbeit we speak wisdom among them that are perfect: yet not the wisdom of this world, nor of the princes of this world, that come to nought: But we speak the wisdom of God in a mystery, even the hidden wisdom, which God ordained before the world unto our glory: Which none of the princes of this world knew: for had they known it, they *would not have crucified the Lord of glory*!"

Paul was educationally qualified to demonstrate his wisdom and knowledge, but he did not do that. He was determined to know nothing among those to whom he preached save Jesus Christ crucified. His preaching was not with enticing words of man's wisdom; the faith of his listeners was to stand in the power of God, not in the wisdom of men. Timothy was to remember that *the cross* is the message: the crucified, risen Lord who had revealed to Paul the mystery which had been hidden from the beginning and was now made known through him.

"For this cause I Paul, the prisoner of Jesus Christ for you Gentiles, if ye have heard of the dispensation of the grace of God which is given me to you-ward: How that by revelation He made known unto me the mystery; (as I wrote afore in few words, whereby, when ye read, ye may understand my knowledge in the mystery of Christ) which in other ages was not made known unto the sons of men, as it is now revealed unto His holy apostles and prophets by the Spirit; that the Gentiles should be fellow-heirs, and of the same body, and partakers of His promise in Christ by the Gospel: Whereof I was made a minister, according to the gift of the grace of God given unto me by the effectual working of His power. Unto me, who am less than the least of all saints, is this grace given, that I should preach among the Gentiles the unsearchable riches of Christ; And to make all men see what is the fellowship of the mystery, which from the beginning of the world hath been hid in God, who created all things by Jesus Christ: To the intent that now unto the principalities and powers in heavenly places might be known by the church the manifold wisdom of God, according to the eternal purpose which He purposed in Christ Jesus our Lord: In whom we have boldness and access with confidence by the faith of Him" (Eph. 3:1–12).

REMEMBER Jesus Christ: The Apostle seeks to reassure Timothy's heart for the dread days ahead by one last and highest argument. It is Jesus Christ—crucified and risen. Jesus Christ, the fulfillment of all the promises of the Old Testament, for He was born of "the seed of David." It is His humanity that is stressed at this point, for He could only die for the sins of man by taking a body of flesh. God cannot die; therefore He had to take a body in order that He could lay His life down for sinners.

"Wherefore seeing we also are compassed about with so great a cloud of witnesses, let us lay aside every weight, and the sin which doth so easily beset us, and let us run with patience the race that is set before us, looking unto *Jesus the author and finisher of our faith;* who for the joy that was set before Him endured the cross, despising the shame, and is set down at the right hand of the throne of God" (Heb. 12:1,2).

"*Remember . . . Jesus Christ . . . raised from the*

dead . . . ." Many outstanding religionists (*religionists*, not Christians) deny the resurrection of Jesus Christ, but Paul believed it and preached it. He reminded Timothy to remember that Jesus was raised bodily. The devil hates the doctrine of the resurrection. The greatest bomb-shell ever to explode in the face of a wicked, unbelieving world was the resurrection of Jesus Christ. The enemies of Jesus explained away everything about Him to their own satisfaction—except His missing body; they could not think of a lie that would stand up under common sense, reason, and Roman law. It is imperative to believe in the resurrection or burn in hell.

"Now if Christ be preached that He rose from the dead, how say some among you that there IS no resurrection of the dead? But if there be no resurrection of the dead, then is Christ not risen: and if Christ be not risen, then is our preaching vain, and your faith is also vain. Yea, and we are found false witnesses of God; because we have testified of God that He raised up Christ: whom He raised not up, if so be that the dead rise not. For if the dead rise not, then is not Christ raised: And if Christ be not raised, your faith is vain; ye are yet in your sins. Then they also which are fallen asleep in Christ are perished. If in this life only we have hope in Christ, we are of all men most miserable. But *now IS Christ risen from the dead*, and become the firstfruits of them that slept. For since by man came death, by man came also the resurrection of the dead. For as in Adam all die, even so in Christ shall all be made alive. But every man in his own order: Christ the firstfruits; afterward they that are Christ's at His coming" (I Cor. 15:12–23).

The verse that lifted me from the gutter and gave me the assurance of salvation reads thus: "That if thou shalt confess with thy mouth the Lord Jesus, and shalt believe in thine heart that God hath raised Him from the

304

dead, thou shalt be saved" (Rom. 10:9).

First: *"Confess with thy mouth the Lord Jesus."* That means to confess that He is God's Christ—virgin-born, sinless; that He died on the cross, was buried, raised, ascended, and is coming again. Confess that you believe everything the Bible says about Jesus Christ.

Second: *"Believe in thine heart that God hath raised Him from the dead."* Then, "THOU SHALT BE SAVED."

Any person who denies the bodily resurrection of Jesus Christ will burn in hell. No one who denies the bodily resurrection can go to heaven; and as we will see later in our study, there were some in the assembly at Ephesus who did not believe in the resurrection.

Verse 9: "Wherein I suffer trouble, as an evil doer, even unto bonds; but the Word of God is not bound."

Tremendous truth! Paul preached Jesus Christ, of the seed of David, born of a virgin, raised bodily from the dead—and because of this message he was in bonds, suffering as a criminal, an evildoer . . . but *"the Word of God is not bound."* Hallelujah! You can place God's *preacher* in the dungeon, but you cannot bind his message! The Word of God is quick and powerful, and sharper than any twoedged sword. The Word of God is a lamp unto the feet of all who will walk in its light. The Word of God is the incorruptible seed that "borns" us into God's family. Faith comes by hearing and hearing by the Word of God. No wonder the devil hates the Word! No wonder religionists are bringing the Bible "up to date," because the Bible and modern religions clash. They must therefore take the "king's penknife" and cut out the fundamentals of the faith. A minister cannot preach what Paul preached, and at the same time deny the bodily resurrection and other fundamentals of the faith that are being crucified today by liberals, modernists, and ministers of the devil.

During the years of my ministry I have seen the Word of God work many miracles. I have seen the power of the Word melt the hearts of hardened sinners. I have seen stony hearts rent asunder by the cutting power of the Word of God. I have seen darkened, blind souls made to see through the light of the Gospel. I have seen spiritually dead people raised to new life through the power of the Gospel. Hallelujah! *The Word of God is not bound*!

Verse 10: "Therefore I endure all things for the elect's sakes, that they may also obtain the salvation which is in Christ Jesus with eternal glory."

The "elect" here referred to is the Church, the body of Christ. Paul says, "Because I am God's anointed preacher of the Gospel, a defender of the faith, refusing to compromise or sell out to Judaism and the enemies of grace, I endure all things for the elect's sake."

Here, in a small degree, Paul demonstrates the spirit of Jesus who, when He was reviled, reviled not again. Jesus did not demand "an eye for an eye, a tooth for a tooth." Paul was willing to suffer these things for the sake of the Church, in order that the Church might move on and finally reap the end of salvation—a glorified body displayed in the Pearly White City, showing the exceeding riches of God's grace to all God's new creation. We are saved from the *penalty* of sin when we accept Jesus by faith; we are saved daily from the *power* of sin, as we trust Him to give us victory; and we will be saved from the very *presence* of sin when Jesus comes in the Rapture in the first resurrection.

Verse 11: "It is a faithful saying: For if we be dead with Him, we shall also live with Him."

"*For if we be dead with Him* . . . ." This is not in the future tense, but *past tense* . . . "If we DIED." When

306

did this happen? Potentially, when Jesus died; experimentally, when we accepted Christ by faith. At the time of our act of penitence and faith, our sin is laid on Him and His death is reckoned unto us (Rom. 6:11). Our personal faith has identified us with Him; and because He has fully borne the penalty, so also (in Him) have we.

Furthermore, ". . . *We shall also live with Him.*" Because He lives, we live. Galatians 2:20: "I am crucified with Christ: nevertheless I live; yet not I, but Christ liveth in me: and the life which I now live in the flesh I live by the faith of the Son of God, who loved me, and gave Himself for me."

II Corinthians 5:14,15: "For the love of Christ constraineth us; because we thus judge, that if one died for all, then were all dead: And that He died for all, that they which live should not henceforth live unto themselves, but unto Him which died for them, and rose again."

Verse 12: "If we suffer, we shall also reign with Him: if we deny Him, He also will deny us."

This verse is so plain there is not much that can be said. If we suffer with Jesus, we will reign with Him; if we share the cross, we will share the crown; if we share the reproach, we will share the glory. Therefore, if we hope to have crowns to cast at His feet when He is crowned King of kings and Lord of lords, then we must suffer with Him; we must endure hardness as a good soldier of the cross.

But if we deny Him, He will deny us. "Deny" is the opposite of "confess." In Matthew 10:32,33 Jesus said, "Whosoever therefore shall confess me before men, him will I confess also before my Father which is in heaven. But whosoever shall deny me before men, him will I also deny before my Father which is in heaven." If we continue to deny Him by not confessing Him as

307

Lord and Saviour, He must, because of His Word, deny us before the Father. He cannot break His Word. Continual denying of Him brings destruction.

Verse 13: "If we believe not, yet He abideth faithful: He cannot deny Himself."

"*If we believe not. . . .*" How many unbelieving believers there are—those who have believed on Him to the saving of the soul, but their belief stops there. How many really believe Him when He says, "Lo, I am with you alway, even unto the end"? Or, "Seek ye first the kingdom of God . . . and *all these things shall be added unto you*" (Matt. 6:33)? John 10:28,29 promises, "And I give unto them eternal life; and they shall never perish, neither shall any man pluck them out of my hand. My Father, which gave them me, is greater than all; and no man is able to pluck them out of my Father's hand." We should accept these promises and rest upon them, for the very fact that God is God means that He cannot break a promise.

"*. . . He abideth faithful: He cannot deny Himself.*" His program must be worked out—and it *will* be. God will keep His promise even though we, His children, may be doubtful and prove unfaithful. We may suffer loss of reward; we may not enjoy our full spiritual birthright; we may be saved as by fire, as a brand snatched from the burning—but God cannot deny Himself. We may let Him down, but He can never deny His blood-bought, blood-covered children!

"*This is a faithful saying*, and worthy of all acceptation, that Christ Jesus came into the world to save sinners; of whom I am chief" (I Tim. 1:15).

"*This is a true saying*, If a man desire the office of a bishop, he desireth a good work" (I Tim. 3:1).

"This is a faithful saying and worthy of all acceptation" (I Tim. 4:9).

"This is a faithful saying, and these things I will that thou affirm constantly, that they which have believed in God might be careful to maintain good works. These things are good and profitable unto men" (Titus 3:8).

These tremendous verses are all introduced by the phrase, "Faithful is the saying." The God known of Paul was a faithful God—a God who could not lie:

"In hope of eternal life, which *God, that cannot lie,* promised before the world began" (Titus 1:2).

"That by two immutable things, in which it was *impossible for God to lie,* we might have a strong consolation, who have fled for refuge to lay hold upon the hope set before us" (Heb. 6:18).

God cannot unsay what He has said. His Word cannot be revoked. Whether we believe it or not, it is true—and it abides faithful. Whether the Word be a precious promise or a warning of judgment, it cannot be changed; God will do what He says He will do, whether it brings blessing or judgment.

Words of Exhortation and Warning

Verse 14: "Of these things put them in remembrance, charging them before the Lord that they strive not about words to no profit, but to the subverting of the hearers."

There are many profitless words spoken today in the average church. Many preachers spend much time preaching in defense of their denomination and their beliefs—but when they come to the fundamentals of the faith (the Incarnation, the blood, the second coming), they spend little or no time on these things that would profit the hearers.

In Titus 2:11–13 Paul lays down these solemn facts: "For the grace of God *that bringeth salvation* hath appeared to all men, *teaching* us that, denying ungodliness and worldly lusts, we should live soberly, righteously, and godly, in this present world; *looking for that blessed hope, and the glorious appearing of the great God and our Saviour Jesus Christ.*"

No other subject on earth will cause Christians to live clean, consecrated, dedicated lives like the truth of the Lord's return: "Behold, what manner of love the Father hath bestowed upon us, that we should be called the sons of God: therefore the world knoweth us not, because it knew Him not. Beloved, now are we the sons of God, and it doth not yet appear what we shall be: but we know that, when He shall appear, we shall be like Him; for we shall see Him as He is. And *every man that hath this hope in him purifieth himself*, even as He is pure" (I John 3:1–3).

The devil is more shrewd than most people realize. He is a formidable enemy of the truth—and if he cannot lead a preacher into liberalism, he will persuade him to ride a spiritual hobby-horse every time he goes into the pulpit. He will lead a preacher to spend precious time on "word fighting" that will uphold his own opinions and his own pet theories. While he is bickering over "words," he is neglecting to preach salvation by grace through faith.

Man-made tradition is so full of loopholes that when compared to the Word of God it can be quickly *discovered* as man-made tradition and not divinely dictated truth. Paul wanted Timothy to keep the church free from religious arguments, avoiding words that divide the church, cause hard feelings, and tend to tear down the testimony of the assembly, thus *"subverting the hearers."* The word translated *subverting* is the word from which our word "catastrophe" comes. Much of this uncalled-for controversy over words tends to produce nothing less than catastrophe for those who are hearing it, causing them to be confused, bewildered, and disillusioned.

A dear lady came to me after one of my recent meetings and said, "Mr. Greene, you do not believe in sanctification." I answered the woman in this way: "I am glad that you can read the thoughts and intents of my heart—but judge not, lest ye be judged! I believe in *Bible sanctification* . . . I call it full surrender, complete dedication—while you call it a second work of grace, or sanctification. So why should we fight over words, if we both teach the experience that causes men and women to live dedicated, separated lives? If you and I both believe in the blood atonement and fully dedicated Christian living, why must we fight over words? Why can we not be united in Christ?" God pity people who live in such a small world, spiritually speaking!

The devil does not care how long, how fervently, nor how sincerely a man may preach, so long as that preaching is void of words that bring salvation. God spoke to Cornelius in a vision and said to him, "Send men to Joppa, and call for Simon, whose surname is Peter; who shall tell thee words, whereby thou and all thy house shall be saved" (Acts 11:13,14).

The devil does not fear the man who preaches man-made doctrine and dogma, rules and regulations, leaving out the words that tell the sinner God loves him, Jesus died for him and now stands ready to save, to forgive, to keep, to direct. As long as a preacher rides a religious hobby-horse, dividing Christians, tearing down the faith of believers, causing division in the local assembly, the devil does not care how often nor how long he preaches.

Verse 15: "Study to shew thyself approved unto God,

311

a workman that needeth not to be ashamed, rightly dividing the word of truth."

Timothy was to keep near to the Saviour and ever stand ready to do His will. He was to *present himself* for duty, ready for any orders from God. God approves of this attitude. May we then present ourselves each day: ". . . Present your bodies a living sacrifice, holy, acceptable unto God, which is your reasonable service" (Rom. 12:1).

". . . *Needeth not to be ashamed.*" A man who studies and presents himself to God for duty, has no need to stand ashamed. Many Christians will be ashamed in that day when their work is judged. They do their work badly; they do it selfishly, leaving off anything that would be a sacrifice to them, and they work spasmodically. If they feel like working, they work; if not, they leave the Lord's work undone. These people will have to hang their heads in shame when they meet the Lord face to face. "And now, little children, abide in Him; that, when He shall appear, we may have confidence, and not be ashamed before Him at His coming" (I John 2:28).

". . . *Rightly dividing the word of truth.*" "*Rightly dividing*" is one word in the Greek; and literally Timothy was to "*cut a straight line through the Word,*" as a man plows long furrows across a fertile field, each furrow as straight as an arrow. Paul is instructing Timothy to preach the whole counsel of God, *prefaced by much study and preparation.* There is to be no striving about words "to no profit," but he is to be faithful to the Word of truth and the revelation of Jesus Christ in its fullness and entirety.

"Which things also we speak, not in the words which man's wisdom teacheth, but which the Holy Ghost teacheth; comparing spiritual things with spiritual" (I Cor. 2:13).

The only way to rightly divide the Word is to compare spiritual things with spiritual, which thought takes us back to Paul's command to STUDY. Timothy was to preach the Word, turning neither to the right nor to the left, with his heart fixed on Jesus, his mind permeated by the Holy Spirit. In II Peter 1:20 we read, "Knowing this first, that no prophecy of the Scripture is of any private interpretation." To be approved unto God we must STUDY the word of truth. The Bible must have first place both in our personal life and in our spiritual life.

If we would feed the flock of God we must first feed ourselves. If we would instruct others, we must first be instructed. If we would preach the pure Gospel without compromise, we must seek the will of God in the WORD of God—not in some doctrinal treatise. A minister·who spends more time playing than studying, more time in fellowship with the brethren than in his study with an open Bible, is not fit to pastor the church over which he is appointed. Study is hard work; it is a weariness to the flesh. Paul previously commanded Timothy to give attendance to reading, and here he is instructed to STUDY. The Bible is a book that *must be studied* if we hope to understand the deep things of God. An ordinary book can be read, and to the alert mind, much of it can be absorbed at one reading; but the more we read and study the Bible, the more we recognize it as an extraordinary Book—*a living Book*. Only when we study diligently, rightly handling the Word of truth, will we be able to feed those over whom the Lord has appointed us a minister.

Verse 16: "But shun profane and vain babblings: for they will increase unto more ungodliness."

The devil is a very efficient devil . . . he is very alert; even in the first days of Christianity he began to sow tares among the wheat. In Paul's day, as today, there were "babblers" in the church—people whom the devil sent in to teach heresy and doctrines of men, tradition, or religion instead of the pure Word of God. The "mystery of iniquity" was already at work even in the early church—but where sin abounded, grace did much more abound; and where the spirit of the enemy was, the Spirit of God was also present. True believers are not confused or confounded by false doctrine (I Pet. 2:6).

Verses 17 and 18: "And their word will eat as doth a canker: of whom is Hymenaeus and Philetus; who concerning the truth have erred, saying that the resurrection is past already; and overthrow the faith of some."

We know practically nothing of these two men. Hymenaeus is mentioned in I Timothy 1:20, and undoubtedly he is the same man mentioned here. What the profane, unscriptural teaching of Hymenaeus and Philetus consisted of, we do not know for sure—except that it had to do with false teaching concerning the resurrection of Jesus. Their teaching was perhaps a type of Gnosticism, which later became very prevalent—a religion of *knowledge*, rather than *faith*. The leaders in this movement claimed to lead their disciples beyond the common believer and into a superior knowledge of the mysteries. To quote Dr. Gwatkin, in the International Standard Bible Encyclopedia, "Gnosticism is Christianity perverted by learning and speculation."

Gnosticism taught that simple faith and trust in the finished work of Jesus was not sufficient for salvation. This teaching claimed to lead its disciples far beyond those who depended upon faith alone. They claimed to lead their people to a superior and gifted plane, that they should know the mysteries of being, and by such knowledge should live completely delivered from the slavery of matter, enjoying liberty in the world of spirit. They taught that the soul is immaterial (not consisting of matter), and because it is not matter, it is therefore pure by knowledge—not knowledge of self, nor of sin, nor of God—but knowledge of a mystic secret in the spirit world, having been released from limitations having to do with matter. Some of the believers in Gnosticism practiced their religion by fiercely punishing the body, believing that the body was evil because it consisted of material (or matter). It is possible that this false doctrine was part of the teaching of Hymenaeus and Philetus, who also taught that the resurrection had already taken place.

On the opposite extreme were those who let the body run its free course, submitting to the desires of the flesh and yielding to sensual sin, believing that while the body enjoyed sensual sin the soul enjoyed transcendental liberty. These advanced thinkers (boasting extreme knowledge) advanced to more and more sensuality and impiety; therefore their "word" (the doctrine they preached) did eat as a canker (gangrene). Their end is destruction; their God is their belly, and their glory is in their shame! (Phil. 3:19).

The damnable doctrine of these ungodly teachers is still carried on. Today the cross is laughed at and considered foolishness. Men who preach a blood-bought salvation are called "slaughterhouse preachers." This is the age of higher learning; and ministers *increase* their knowledge through higher learning in atheistic institutions, where evolution and other false philosophies are taught—the same old pagan religions garbed in different costume. There are many religious "isms," "schisms," and "spasms" today.

Be careful what you listen to and what you read. I invite you to check this book against God's Word, and you should do the same with every other piece of literature you read. You should use God's Word as your yardstick to measure every sermon you hear on radio or from the pulpit. We are living in an age of false teachers, false prophets, and lying ministers of Satan, whose hearts are evil and whose consciences are seared with a hot iron. Their messages are poison, and we need to study God's Word as never before. We need to search the Scriptures and try the spirits to see if they be of God (I John 4:1,2).

". . . Who concerning the truth *have erred.*" Jesus said, "Ye shall know the truth, and the truth shall make you free. . . . If the Son therefore shall make you free, ye shall be free indeed" (John 8:32,36). In John 17:17 He prayed, "Sanctify them through thy truth: thy word is truth." These men preached error; and they overthrew the faith of some who were learners—not truly born again believers, but men and women who were on the verge of *becoming* believers. These teachers of damnable heresies shipwrecked the faith of these, and caused them to follow error unto damnation.

Vessels in the Great House

Verse 19: "Nevertheless the foundation of God standeth sure, having this seal, The Lord knoweth them that are His. And, Let every one that nameth the name of Christ depart from iniquity."

This is a tremendous verse: *"Nevertheless"* . . . in spite of the devil, demons, evil spirits, rulers of spiritual wickedness in high places; in spite of false teachers and false prophets, we have the promise of God that cannot be broken: "Wherefore also it is contained in the Scripture, Behold, I lay in Sion a chief corner stone (Jesus), elect, precious: and he that believeth on Him shall not be confounded (confused)" (I Pet. 2:6).

In spite of Hymenaeus and Philetus—and all the other teachers of "isms"—*the foundation of God will not be moved*, the chief cornerstone cannot be destroyed. Christians have the assurance that God's Word will never fail;

it is forever settled in heaven. We have nothing to fear; the Lord knows those who are His. If you are born again, *God knows it.* The Word tells us, ". . . He calleth His own sheep by name, and leadeth them out . . . and the sheep follow Him: for they know His voice. And a stranger will they not follow, but will flee from him: for they know not the voice of strangers" (John 10:3,4,5). In John 10:27,28 Jesus says, "My sheep hear my voice, and I know them, and they follow me: And I give unto them eternal life; and they shall never perish, neither shall any man pluck them out of my hand."

According to the words of Jesus, regardless of your denominational affiliation, *if you are a child of God you will hear His voice,* and a stranger you will not follow. Those who are driven about with every wind of doctrine, changing their religion every little while, need to be born again. True believers are not confused and led about in such a fashion. The foundation of God stands sure; the Lord knows those who are His; they hear His voice, and they will not follow the devil nor the devil's false teachers.

Believers know the voice of the Spirit, and they follow Him. When a false teacher speaks, the Holy Ghost witnesses this fact to the spirit of a Christian, and thus a born again person cannot be led into error. "Ye shall know the truth, and the truth shall make you free"—and you will STAY free if you are made free by the Word of the living God! *The foundation of God standeth sure; it shall not be moved; it is forever settled in heaven!*

"Let every one that nameth the name of Christ depart from iniquity." Believers are to abstain from the very appearance of evil . . . have no fellowship with the unfruitful works of darkness . . . come out from among them and be separate . . . touch not the unclean thing. "Set your affection on things above, not on things on the earth"—and if we are born again, God plants in our hearts

317

the desire to do what He commands. If we love the world, the love of God is not in us. Those of us who are born of the Spirit are LED by the Spirit—and He leads into paths of right living, not into paths of iniquity! If we name the name of Jesus, we should depart from iniquity because we are a new creation in Christ. Old things are passed away, all things are become new, and we live in newness of life.

Verse 20: "But in a great house there are not only vessels of gold and of silver, but also of wood and of earth; and some to honour, and some to dishonour."

In verse 19 the Apostle presented the true Church—the believing company—as the Lord sees it in its spiritual reality. Here Paul is giving us a picture of the church in the local sense—the external church—as he uses an illustration of *"a great house."* Jesus said to Peter, "Upon this rock I will build my church; and the gates of hell shall not prevail against it" (Matt. 16:18). Jesus is the Rock, the Chief Cornerstone; and He is not speaking of the local assembly. We know the "gates of hell" HAVE prevailed against some local assemblies; but the Church of the living God stands sure; the foundation will not be moved; the Church will not be overcome nor will the gates of hell prevail against it.

But Paul speaks of the local assembly, and illustrates by saying that in every great house there are vessels of gold and of silver, of wood and of earth—vessels of honor, and vessels of dishonor. In the local assembly the wheat and tares will grow together; there will be some Timothys, but there will be a Hymenaeus and a Philetus. There will be true disciples until Jesus comes for the Church, but there will also be an occasional Judas Iscariot! The local church is not perfect—it never has been, and it never will be; but the true Church of Jesus Christ IS perfect, without spot or wrinkle or any such thing (Eph. 5:25 ff).

318

There are certainly vessels of dishonor in the local church today, and every true pastor who will be honest will confess that there are some of those vessels in the assembly over which he has been appointed undershepherd.

Note the vessels named: *Golden vessels*—think of it! A vessel of pure gold; and *silver*—priceless vessels to be used only on very special occasions. *Vessels of wood* and *vessels of earth*—"vessels of dishonour" . . . the wooden vessels perhaps used as garbage containers, the earthen vessels (pitchers and similar items) used in the performance of menial tasks. The contrast between these two kinds of vessels is not a contrast of superiority on the one hand and an humble position on the other, but rather of the far different and essential distinction between the reputable and the degraded.

In the church there are vessels of honor—some believers may be golden lampstands, while others may be silver vessels. God calls and commissions Christians to different positions and ministries in the church; but rewards are for *faithfulness in stewardship*, not according to importance of position. We will be rewarded for our faithfulness in whatever capacity we serve, whether the place we occupy be outstanding or humble. However, in the same local church there will be vessels of dishonor—men like Judas, Demas, Ananias, Hymenaeus, and Philetus. There will be vessels of dishonor, as well as vessels of honor. The prayer of every individual should be, "Lord, regardless of how humble a vessel I may be, make me a vessel of honor meet for the Master's use."

Verse 21: "If a man therefore purge himself from these he shall be a vessel unto honour, sanctified, and meet for the master's use, and prepared unto every good work."

Certainly every believer should desire to be a vessel of honor, rather than a vessel that would bring reproach upon the church. If we purge ourselves from known sin, from things such as Paul discusses here, and if we are dedicated, surrendered and sanctified unto the Lord, we WILL be a vessel fit for His use. We should be willing to pray from honest hearts, "Lord, take me, break me, mold me into a vessel such as will be useful and honorable in the Church of the living God!"

The Path and Walk of the Believer

Verse 22: "Flee also youthful lusts: but follow righteousness, faith, charity, peace, with them that call on the Lord out of a pure heart."

Greek scholars tell us that *lust* had a much broader meaning than that in which it is applied today. When we think of "youthful lusts" we think of sensual sins; but in Paul's day the term was far more inclusive; it took in every sort of strong tendency. Timothy was a young man when he was appointed to the church at Ephesus. He was not a child, but neither was he a seasoned saint. For this reason Paul warns him concerning youthful tendencies—perhaps wanting to have his own way, becoming a strong-willed person, desiring preeminence in church affairs. Christ is to have preeminence in all things, and a minister must keep self out of the way. He must be able to deal firmly with problems that may arise, yet he must not be a dictator. He must not feel his own importance, even though he is guiding the local assembly.

In III John 9 we read of Diotrephes, "who loveth to have the preeminence" among those in the church; and it is possible that Paul feared that Timothy, little by little, might succumb to the wrong kind of pride, short temper, failure to recognize the rightful claims of others. He was therefore to run from these things—as the literal Greek puts it, he was to "FLY from them."

320

This verse is not all negative, however. In addition to resisting youthful lusts, Timothy was instructed to *"follow righteousness, faith, charity, peace, with them that call on the Lord out of a pure heart."* These are the graces opposite lust, and Timothy was to lay hold upon them and make them his own. In order to do that, he must surrender his will to the will of God. He must seek after the spirit of habitual fidelity and develop steady devotion to even the most insignificant duty that his ministry afforded. He must not only preach the Gospel, but *he must live it* in serving those over whom the Lord had appointed him as undershepherd.

Although Timothy had been placed in a position of authority and importance, he was not to exercise that authority to the extent that his *good* would be evil spoken of. He must bear in mind that he was a member of the same body as the believers over which he had oversight; and he should follow right living, right doing, and maintain the right spirit in faith, love, peace with God—and peace with his fellow Christians, *"them that call on the Lord out of a pure heart."* He must lead the believers in the local church through the exercising of faith and love.

Verse 23: "But foolish and unlearned questions avoid, knowing that they do gender strifes."

The closing verses in this chapter are not easy to understand; but the meaning in the original language is a bit clearer. The word "unlearned" means *"undisciplined or unchastened inquiries."* Thus Paul says, "But those foolish and unchastened inquiries decline, knowing that they beget fightings; and the Lord's bondservant must not be a fighter, but be gentle towards all men, explanatory, forbearing under wrong; in meekness correcting those contentiously disposed, in the hope that God may some time give them repentance, leading to a full knowledge of truth; and that they may wake up and escape out of the devil's trap, held willing captives henceforth by Him who sets them free to do His will—the will of God."

In verse 26 in the King James version, it could seem that these persons to whom Paul is referring as *"taken captive by him at his will"* refer to captives of the *devil*; but this is not true. They are literally *"taken alive"* out of the snare of the devil and set free to do God's will. The *"will"* here spoken of is the will of *God*, not the will of the devil. Timothy will need to exercise patience, love, longsuffering, peace, and gentleness; he will need to forget himself in an hour when he could easily be agitated by the silly, unchaste, undisciplined questions that are born in the hearts of those who are uneducated in the things of God. Those who ask foolish and unlearned questions are usually those who would attempt to dig into the secrets of God, secrets which can be known only through revelation, not by inquiry.

There are those who ask foolish questions today. I have been asked, "If God is almighty and all-powerful, why does He not kill the devil?" Or, "Why do we have a devil, anyway? Where did the devil come from?" I have also been asked, "Where did GOD come from?" and "Why did God allow evil to enter the Garden of Eden?" In verse 16 of this chapter Paul told Timothy to shun such babblings—and that is the best thing for any believer to do.

People who ask such foolish and unlearned questions belong to the group mentioned in II Peter 3:5 as being "willingly ignorant." There are those who have their minds made up; they are willingly ignorant—and God cannot help the person who is not willing to be helped! Those who exercise crude ignorance in asking foolish questions would deny the reality of sin and the holiness of God. Their questions originate in an unregenerated heart.

The man of God should inform himself; he should learn all possible spiritual truths in order to have answers for *sincere seekers* of truth; but he is to decline discussion of foolish questions. The Word of God is not to be debated; it is to be preached: "Preach the Word; be instant in season, out of season; reprove, rebuke, exhort with all longsuffering and doctrine" (II Tim. 4:2). In Titus 2:15 we read, "These things speak, and exhort, and rebuke with all authority. Let no man despise thee." We are not to apologize for preaching the Word of God. If God said it, then we are to preach it with authority and without apology. God's servant is not a philosopher; he is not a theorist, setting forth this theory and that theory, quoting this or that religionist. He is God's ambassador, and his message is God's message. He does not preach a "theory"—he preaches God's *truth*. He is an appointed vessel, ordained of God to bear a message that cannot be altered—a divine message dictated by very God!

Verse 24: "And the servant of the Lord must not strive; but be gentle unto all men, apt to teach, patient."

God's minister must not "strive"—he must not fight with the enemies of the Gospel. Paul is not suggesting compromise or coexistence. Amos 3:3 asks, "*Can two walk together, except they be agreed?*" We are not to cast the pearls of the Gospel before swine; we are not to give that which is holy unto dogs; and neither are we to argue, debate, and strive with those who ask foolish, ignorant questions. God's man must be gentle to all men, even to the enemies of the Gospel.

This is a hard saying, and one that is hard to obey. I frankly confess that I need the grace of gentleness. I need God's blessing to be gentle under fire from those who despise God's Word and deny the fundamentals of the faith. Yet God's Word tells us that as ministers we must be gentle to all men, ready to teach, not striving, not debating, but teaching in patience. Our own words will never convict a false teacher nor silence one who asks silly questions; but *the Word of God* can break a stony heart and enlighten a darkened mind.

Verse 25: "In meekness instructing those that oppose themselves; if God peradventure will give them repentance to the acknowledging of the truth."

God's undershepherd must not be an independent thinker; he must be led by the Spirit; he must depend upon the Holy Ghost to lead him into the truth of the deep things of God; he must let God give the answers; and he must declare *the Word of God*, which is absolute truth and authority. We need not back away from *"Thus saith the Lord."*

Those who oppose the Gospel actually *"oppose themselves."* The man of God should meet this opposition by explaining God's Word in love and patience, pointing out the reasonableness of the Word and the scriptural simplicity of salvation. A minister of Jesus Christ must not fight a mental duel with the devil's preacher just to satisfy the flesh or his own mental desire. God's man must not want to have his own way for his own sake, or in order to say, "I won an argument"—for in winning a religious argument we may lose the opportunity to help some errorist come to the knowledge of the truth. We are here as God's ambassadors to tell the good news of salvation and point men to the Saviour; we are not here to win denominational or religious arguments. Our commission is to preach the Word! And thereby we can combat the silly questions of non-believing errorists who set forth their theories instead of "Thus saith the Lord."

It was for this reason that Paul said earlier in this chapter, *"Study to show thyself approved . . . a workman* that needeth not to be ashamed." If we study the Word, memorize it and hide it in our hearts, we then have it always accessible; and we can use the sword of the Spirit and the "bullets of the Bible" in our duel with the errorists who ask foolish questions.

Verse 26: "And that they may recover themselves out of the snare of the devil, who are taken captive by Him at His will."

Paul is not suggesting that Timothy be soft and compromising, but that he saturate his soul with the Word of God and thus be able to answer any reasonable question with the Word. Paul knew that if a person were sincerely deceived and the young preacher argued with him roughly, he would lose the opportunity to help him; whereas, if Timothy instructed him with meekness and patience, using the Word of God, then *"God peradventure will give them repentance to the acknowledging of the truth."*

When the Word of God is given in all its power and purity there is a chance that the Word will soften hard hearts and cause those in error to accept the truth and repent; but if we fight and strive with them, we will lose the opportunity to help them. We may be forced to crucify our pride and our own will; we may even seem to others to be a compromiser; but if our heart condemn us not, and we lead errorists into the truth through love and humility, the joy will far exceed the cost insofar as mental or physical embarrassment on our part is concerned. The flesh will say, "Fight back! Put him in his place!" But we must remember that Jesus always answered His enemies with Scripture. Even in stern rebuke, He employed patience; and His words were often those taken from the Old Testament.

It is a wonderful experience to witness a conversion, whether it be a little child, an aged grandfather, a young man or young woman; but there is an unusual joy afforded the person who leads a misguided soul out of moral illusion and spiritual ignorance. To take one who has been taken captive by the devil and lead that one into the truth and the light of the Gospel and salvation, brings a strange joy that few Christians know.

The Word of God is not bound. It will not return unto Him void. The Word of God is sharp and powerful; Jeremiah describes it in these words: *"Is not my Word like as a fire? saith the Lord; and like a hammer that breaketh the rock in pieces?"* (Jer. 23:29).

II TIMOTHY -- CHAPTER THREE

THE APOSTASY THAT IS SURE TO COME

1. This know also, that in the last days perilous times shall come.

2. For men shall be lovers of their own selves, covetous, boasters, proud, blasphemers, disobedient to parents, unthankful, unholy,

3. Without natural affection, trucebreakers, false accusers, incontinent, fierce, despisers of those that are good,

4. Traitors, heady, highminded, lovers of pleasures more than lovers of God;

5. Having a form of godliness, but denying the power thereof: from such turn away.

6. For of this sort are they which creep into houses, and lead captive silly women laden with sins, led away with divers lusts,

7. Ever learning, and never able to come to the knowledge of the truth.

8. Now as Jannes and Jambres withstood Moses, so do these also resist the truth: men of corrupt minds, reprobate concerning the faith.

9. But they shall proceed no further: for their folly shall be manifest unto all men, as their's also was.

10. But thou hast fully known my doctrine, manner of life, purpose, faith, longsuffering, charity, patience,

11. Persecutions, afflictions, which came unto me at Antioch, at Iconium, at Lystra; what persecutions I endured: but out of them all the Lord delivered me.

12. Yea, and all that will live godly in Christ Jesus shall suffer persecution.

13. But evil men and seducers shall wax worse and worse, deceiving, and being deceived.

14. But continue thou in the things which thou hast learned and hast been assured of, knowing of whom thou hast learned them;

15. And that from a child thou hast known the holy scriptures, which are able to make thee wise unto salvation through faith which is in Christ Jesus.

16. All scripture is given by inspiration of God, and is profitable for doctrine, for reproof, for correction, for instruction in righteousness:

17. That the man of God may be perfect, throughly furnished unto all good works.

Characteristics of the Apostasy

Verse 1: "This know also, that in the last days perilous times shall come."

Paul changes his message to Timothy abruptly. He has been instructing him concerning error that will surely come, both in faith and in practice, warning him that some will depart from the faith and deny the truth, while others will introduce unscriptural and unchristian moral practices. Timothy is instructed to handle these problems with love and patience, always according to the Word of God.

In our present chapter, Paul speaks concerning things that will occur at the end of the dispensation of grace, just before the Rapture of the Church and the coming of the Lord.

"*THIS KNOW ALSO* . . . ." The Gospel is not a message of supposition, but of truth. It is not a book of question marks, but one of exclamation points! It makes no difference what our respective opinions may be, God said what He meant and meant what He said. As pointed out in chapter two, God cannot deny Himself; He cannot take back what He has said. If a minister steps into the pulpit and begins his sermon thus: "As it were . . . in a measure . . . in my humble opinion . . . by chance . . . the way I see it"—mark that man off your list; but if he steps behind the sacred desk, opens the Bible and reads, "Thus saith the Lord," *hear* him, *support* him, and *pray for him*! The Bible is a book of positives. Paul knew *whom* he believed; he knew *what* he believed; and without apology he preached a positive Gospel.

"Timothy, *this know*! It is a fact; you can depend upon it; it will come to pass. So preach it, stand by it, live by it, and die by it." But WHAT does Paul want Timothy to know?

". . . *That in the last days perilous times shall come.*" What is meant by *perilous times*? The Greek word suggests *dangerous* times, and I believe you will agree that these ARE dangerous times in which we live. There has never been a time in history when man was in so much danger as he is today. These are days of peril, days of anxiety and fear. Big men in every walk of life—politically and economically, religiously and educationally—admit that they do not know the answer; they do not know what lies ahead if things continue as they are. But those of us who read the Bible and who are spiritually minded know what lies ahead. We know that the stage is set, the day is at hand, and the next great world event will be the Rapture of the Church.

The following verses explain WHY the closing days of this age will be days of peril:

Verse 2: "For men shall be lovers of their own selves, covetous, boasters, proud, blasphemers, disobedient to parents, unthankful, unholy."

"*Men shall be lovers of their own selves.*" The world today stands on the edge of catastrophe because of selfish, powerful dictators. This is the age when men think only of self; and by the time they satisfy their own lust for power, fame, and fortune, they are so calloused by selfishness and so seared in conscience that they are past feeling. That is true of many world leaders today; they have no feeling for humanity, no conscience concerning bloodshed and the value of human life, and murder is the routine order of the day. They love themselves so much that they will stop at nothing to get what they want—and that leads to the next declaration:

"For men shall be . . . *covetous.*" The dictators of

earth *covet the world* for themselves. Dictators are co-operating to a degree—but any one of them would stab another in the back and laugh as his life blood ran out, if by doing so he could grab the possessions of the other. Men who are past feeling, in love with themselves, are covetous and will take anything from friend or foe if they can get away with it. This is an age of covetousness—not only in the political realm, but in the realm of religion. Even people who claim to be Christians are covetous. There is fussing, fighting, and bickering in the church because men and women covet positions held by others; and many times "crooked politics" is employed in the church to put some covetous, selfish person in office, instead of letting the Holy Spirit appoint the workers in the local assembly.

"For men shall be . . . *boasters.*" This is an age of boasting. The Communists boast that they will bury us, and we boast that we have the goods to bury them. Men boast in politics, in social life, in religion. We have a generation of braggarts today who are bypassing God, depending upon their own wisdom and their own ability, not knowing that achievement is "not by might nor by power, *but by my Spirit,* saith the Lord of hosts." Whether it be a nation, a home, or an individual, "Let him that thinketh he standeth take heed lest he fall." Jesus said, "Without me ye can do nothing." That settles it. All boasting is vain and empty. If God is on our side we cannot lose, and if God is against us we cannot win.

"For men shall be . . . *proud.*" God resisteth the proud, but giveth grace to the humble. Man breathes God's air, bathes in God's sunshine, enjoys the health and strength God bestows upon him; then he ignores God and serves the devil, proud to be what he is, boasting that he is no softie, saying, "Religion is all right for young folks, old folks, and sick folks; but *I* am a man with a backbone! I drink liquor, I dance, I gamble, I swear." If not in words, then in action men are proud. This is the age when religious leaders step behind the sacred desk—not to open the Word of God, but to open their little notebooks and demonstrate their degrees of learning! They are proud of their education and their ability.

The right kind of pride is right. It is not sinful to be proud of the right things in the right way; but it is sinful to exercise the flesh, depend upon and magnify the flesh and the wisdom of man instead of the wisdom and truth of God through the Spirit of God. I say this in love—but the church is cursed with too many dignified, educated, proud preachers. We need more men like Paul— men who magnify the cross, not their own wisdom. Paul could have spoken with great, swelling words, for he was a highly educated man; but he preached in the power and demonstration of the Holy Ghost (I Cor. 2:1 ff). There was a time when almost all churches sought a pastor who was dedicated, humble, and Spirit-filled; a man who preached the Word in all of its purity and power; a man who loved people and who gave himself in service for the people of his parish. But today the average church does not care too much about what a man believes nor how he lives, if he has the right degrees from the right university or seminary. This is the age of demonstrated pride, an out-standing sign of the end of this dispensation.

"For men shall be . . . *blasphemers*." This is the most blasphemous age that has ever been! Comedians curse on radio and television; newspapers and magazines quote curse words spoken by men who are supposed to be leaders in politics, education, and other phases of life. There are many places of business where a Christian is embarrassed by cursing patrons and proprietors; it happens in garages, barber shops, beauty shops, grocery stores,

331

and many other places. Those who are carrying on a conversation have no respect for a stranger who may walk in, whether he be minister, lady, or child.

Ungodly men and women curse and think nothing of it. They have no respect for the feelings and rights of their fellow citizens. Mothers curse, fathers curse, grandparents curse—even little children curse (after the fashion of what they hear at home). A mother or father who will curse before their children is not fit to rear a child; their offspring should be taken away from them and put in a Christian orphanage. God pity a father and mother who teach their little children to curse!

A student in a so-called Christian university recently told me that often the professor in one of his classes would curse the students, literally blaspheme before the assembled class, if a student did not give the correct answer or study as the professor thought he should! Can you imagine a teacher swearing before students in a school originally built with the money of God's saints? If you do not believe this is a cursing age, walk down the street or go in many places of business and listen: You will discover that this is an age of blasphemers!

But blasphemy goes deeper than cursing. To *hypocritically worship God* is blasphemy. A liberal who declares that he is a minister of God, a representative of Christianity on earth, and yet denies the virgin birth, the Incarnation, and the blood atonement of Jesus Christ, is the most despicable blasphemer this side of hell—and such practice of blasphemy will become worse and worse!

In the last days, children will be *"disobedient to parents."* I can well remember the discipline in our home when I was growing up. My father may have failed in many ways, but one thing he demanded was respect from his children toward himself and my mother. We did not talk back to our parents. When my father spoke, we obeyed; we respected what he said—and if we did not, we paid for it.

I am not an old man—but how times have changed! Today, children say to their parents, "I will not do it!" Or, "I will do it when I get ready," or "It is none of your business!"

We cannot classify little children as mean and ungodly—they are just hateful, stubborn, and naughty; but when you see such a child, do not feel badly toward *him*—the child is not to blame. Responsibility for a disobedient, badly behaved child lies at the doorstep of the parents. A child must be trained up in the way he should go if he is to be an honor to his father and mother in later years.

"Spare the rod and spoil the child" is not in the Bible; that is "grandma gospel"—but the man of wisdom said, *"He that spareth his rod hateth his son: but he that loveth him chasteneth him betimes"* (Prov. 13:24). The Bible says that if you spare the rod you do not love your child. Pity the little one who does not have parents who know how to use a switch or a paddle! A person who is not chastened and trained in childhood will never make a lasting mark for good upon civilization.

My mother knew how to use a switch. (My father knew how to use three at one time in the same hand!) And when either of my parents applied the rod, we did not forget it for a long time. I shall never cease to thank God for the discipline they gave me. I realize that I was very wicked, but I was correctly trained in my early years, and my early training has paid dividends since I met the Lord Jesus Christ.

This is the day of disobedient children, and born again parents should not permit their children to conform to that image. Born again boys and girls will respect their parents.

"For men shall be . . . *unthankful.*" Materially speaking, Americans have more today than any people who ever lived. Most Americans live after the fashion of the kings and queens of yesteryear. The average American family puts more food in the garbage can than many people have to eat in other lands. We have the finest homes, clothes, automobiles, comforts and conveniences—and most Americans have more money than any other people on the face of the earth. YET—*we are unthankful!*

I dare say there are more Americans who sit down to the food on their tables and eat it *without saying grace* than there are who *say grace* before eating the food which God so graciously provides. The Word tells us, "Every good gift and every perfect gift is from above, and cometh down from the Father of lights . . ." (James 1:17). God gives us the food we eat, the clothes we wear, the homes we live in, even the very air we breathe; and the *least* we could do is bow our heads and say, "Thank you, Father, for every good gift." We hear a lot of grumbling—but very little thanksgiving. We are a thankless people—and this is a sign of the end of the age.

"For men shall be . . . *unholy.*" The average professing Christian is half frightened to death lest someone accuse him of holiness! I do not believe in fanaticism nor in self-righteousness; I do not believe in a "holier-than-thou" spirit. Heaven knows the *best of us* are full of faults and shortcomings, and we fall far short of God's holiness. But a truly born again Christian *wants* to live a holy life; and the only way we CAN be holy is in Christ, covered by the blood.

But Paul is pointing out the situation that prevails today. The average church member does not desire to know how consecrated, surrendered, and holy a life he can live. The average professing Christian wants to know *how much he can get away with and still not go to hell!*

334

He wants to use God as a fire escape and salvation as a fire insurance policy. He wants to hold on to as much of the world as possible while he travels to the Pearly White City. The average church member wants to know just how close he can come to hell while he lives, and not go there when he dies.

This is an unholy age. People have lost respect for their bodies. Women (even church members, professing Christians) dress indecently and expose their nakedness. Men do the same. Men and women tear down the temple of the Holy Spirit: "What? know ye not that your body is the temple of the Holy Ghost which is in you, which ye have of God, and ye are not your own? For ye are bought with a price: therefore glorify God in your body, and in your spirit, which are God's" (I Cor. 6:19,20). A person who tears down and destroys his body through drink, tobacco, foods, and habits is unholy in his living.

This is an age when people have lost respect and reverence for a holy God, the holy Bible, and holy living. If you are "a good mixer," if you can play cards, dance, drink, dress indecently, laugh at a filthy joke, you are a wonderful fellow, a number one citizen; and you can teach a Sunday school class, pray in public, sing in the choir, and hold any number of responsible positions in the church. But the church member who refuses to drink cocktails, use tobacco, attend dances and parties, and who believes in old-time Christianity is called a fanatic or a "religious square."

Verse 3: "Without natural affection, trucebreakers, false accusers, incontinent, fierce, despisers of those that are good."

". . . In the last days . . . men shall be . . . *without natural affection.*" Men will love the unnatural. God created man in His own image, breathed into his nostrils

335

the breath of life, and man became a living soul. God created man as a trinity—soul, spirit, and body. He created him in such a way that God can fellowship with man, and man can fellowship with God; they can commune with each other. That is the way God wants it; that is the way He intended it to be, and *no man* will ever have peace and complete satisfaction until he is in the right relationship to his Creator.

If a man is normal mentally, physically, and spiritually, it is natural for him to love God, to love the Bible, to love church, righteous living, honesty, decency, purity, home, and family; but today these things are not loved by a large percentage of people. For millions, "home" has become a place to change clothes and get ready for the next meeting or the next party. Mother works—simply to be able to buy better clothes, drive a better car, have better things at home and be able to keep up with the neighbors. She works on one shift, the man of the household works on another shift, the children go to school or to a nursery—and the family scarcely ever gets together as a whole.

Many young couples marry, set up housekeeping, and since both of them work they agree that there will be no children. Often, they buy a pet and bestow upon it the love a baby should be getting. Woman was created to make man's life fuller, sweeter, brighter, more complete— and in the words of Paul, to be "keepers at home." It is born in the heart of woman to love and want a family, but many modern marriages agree that there *will be no family* because babies would interfere with social and business life. This is an age when mankind loves the unnatural.

When I was a boy, almost everyone attended church. Not everybody was saved, but it was natural for people to attend church on Sunday. Sunday was the Lord's day, and in our community it was natural for people to rest on the Lord's day; but today it is different. The *"holy day"* has become a *"holiday."* The rest day has become the busiest day of all for millions—playing, boating, traveling, fishing, golfing, going to the races, the fairs, and even shopping. Men are loving the unnatural.

"This know . . . that in the last days men shall be . . . *trucebreakers."* There was a day when a man's word was his bond, and with some this is still true; but today a truce does not mean what it once did. A man's word is no longer his bond; men make promises only to break them, and will enter into a truce knowing all the time that they have no intention of being honest and upright about it.

"In the last days men shall be . . . *false accusers."* There was a time when you could believe what people said—and of course there are still some who are truthful and who would not knowingly lie or falsely accuse others. But on the other hand, there are thousands who will lie and who will make up false accusations against their fellowman simply for the pleasure of it. A good policy to follow today is not to believe anything you hear unless you have seen it yourself or have *indisputable evidence* that it is true. Do not let anyone wreck your confidence in friends, family, or neighbors through false accusation or idle gossip. The devil tries to wreck the character of every Bible preacher and every true deacon. He makes trouble for every born again Sunday school teacher who teaches the pure Gospel. He does his utmost to wreck the testimony and tear down the usefulness of Christians through false accusation. This is the age of false accusers.

"In the last days men shall be . . . *incontinent."* Webster's unabridged dictionary defines this word as follows: "Intemperate; free and uncontrolled indulgence of the passions or appetites, particularly the sexual appetite;

indulging lust without restraint; unchaste; lewd." This has to do with a terrible sin—men and women in a state where they cannot control their passions from the standpoint of lust, sex, and immorality. They are like a ship with a broken rudder, driven by winds of passion in the things that are unbelievable among civilized people.

Jesus said, "As it was in the days of Noah, as it was in the days of Lot, so shall also the coming of the Son of man be" (Matt. 24:37; Luke 17:28). In the days of Noah, the sons of God were going in unto the daughters of men; lust and immorality were rampant, and when God saw the wickedness of man "it repented the Lord that He had made man on the earth, and it grieved Him at His heart" (Gen. 6:6). God destroyed the entire human race with the exception of Noah and his family. In Lot's day the outstanding sin was Sodomy, a practice too vile to discuss here. We know these sins are being practiced today all around us. Womanhood no longer demands respect; home is no longer sacred, and marriage vows are made only to be dissolved in divorce courts. This is the day of incontinence.

"In the last days men shall be . . . *fierce.*" Today, crimes of the vilest sort are being committed—not only in big cities, but in hamlets and rural areas as well. Some of the most brutal murders, assaults and sadist crimes ever to be recorded in history are being committed today— crimes that make the pagans and barbarians look like Sunday school pupils! Human life is cheaper today than it has ever been. Men are *fierce.*

"In the last days men shall be . . . *despisers of those that are good.*" Those who wish to discuss the Bible, righteousness, godliness, holiness, purity and decency are not invited to the average social gathering and are not wanted in the average conversation. In most groups of men and women, the one who brings up the discussion

338

of Christianity and godliness is ignored and not invited to the next gathering. I repeat: If you are a good mixer, if you can pray a little or curse a little, preach a little or drink a little, you are a "regular fellow"; but if you believe in the Christianity purchased by Jesus at the price of His own blood, you are a "square," a crackpot, you are "off the deep end" of religion, and you will be excluded from most community and civic affairs. Teenagers in school become "wallflowers" if they refuse to dance and join sex clubs, and many of them are persecuted by other young people.

Verse 4: "Traitors, heady, highminded, lovers of pleasures more than lovers of God."

". . . Men shall be . . . *traitors*." Today, one wonders how many people there are who can really be trusted, without fear of that trust being broken. Heads of governments, leaders in politics, religion, and business have proved to be traitors to their fellowman.

". . . Men shall be . . . *heady, highminded*." Today more emphasis is placed on brains and education than on the soul and spiritual matters. Men are headstrong and proud. Humility is a rare grace—and humble, dedicated Christians are few and far between. Politically, educationally, socially, and religiously, men are highminded.

". . . Men shall be . . . *lovers of pleasures more than lovers of God*." It seems a waste of time and space to discuss this statement. The average church member today does not allow the church service to come between him and his pleasure. Prayer meeting, revival or church duties no longer interfere with social activities. Almost any minister in this country would agree with this, for it is the simple truth that the average church member does not let church interfere with his social life nor with anything he or she wants to do in the line of pleasure.

If we are not today in the midst of the Laodicean age, we are certainly on the verge of it. The Philadelphian church is with us, to be sure—true believers who have kept the Word of God and who will be kept from the great Tribulation (Rev. 3:10); but we also have a host of lukewarm church members—neither hot nor cold, happy-go-lucky, participating in "religion" and in the world simultaneously. These Laodiceans will be *spewed* out as the *true Church* is caught out. Beyond question this is the age when men love pleasure more than they love God.

Verse 5: "Having a form of godliness, but denying the power thereof: from such turn away."

In the last days, men will have *"a form of godliness, but deny the power thereof."* Formalism, program, ritual: These are the order of the day. The devil knows in advance exactly what will happen in the average Sunday morning service. There are exceptions, of course, but the program of the average denominational church is drawn up, blueprinted, mapped, and mailed out from headquarters. Ninety-nine percent of everything that is done is written down and read by the pastor—a denominational puppet who dares not refuse to cooperate, lest he become an insignificant little preacher kept back in the sticks or out on the far side of the swamp! Today, if a preacher wants to advance in organized religion, he "plays ball" with the "big boys"; and if he does not play their way, he remains a little preacher and pastors little out-of-the-way churches.

I am not against organization. I believe in praising, honoring, and worshipping God in decency and in order. (The Bible abounds in praises; the book of Psalms is a book of praises to God; and in Revelation 19 John tells us that when the final victory is declared over Antichrist and the forces of evil are put down, there will be hallelu-

340

jahs "*as the sound of many waters!*") Yes, I believe in organization. Jesus organized the 5,000. He had them sit down in companies of fifty, and the disciples passed out the loaves and fishes in an orderly, efficient manner. But I believe that IN organization, Jesus should be chairman of the Board, the Holy Spirit should be the director, and whatever is done should be done to the glory of God— not according to denominational headquarters!

When Jesus was upon this earth, He rode into the Holy City on a little donkey; and as He passed, people threw their coats in His path, strewed the street with palm branches, and shouted praises to God. The Pharisees said to Jesus, "Make these hold their peace!" He replied, "If these should hold their peace, the stones would cry out!" (Luke 19:40). Please read Luke 19:28–40. *Jesus Christ will be praised*, even if the stones must praise Him; but in the average church today, if you say, "Amen," "Hallelujah," or "Praise God!" as the old-time Christians did, you will be asked to keep quiet or leave the sanctuary.

This is the age of "form"—*organized religion*. We have a local council of churches, the National Council of Churches, the World Council of Churches; and now one gigantic attempt is being made to get all churches together and cooperate to bring world peace. This sets the stage for the appearing of the false Messiah, Antichrist; and the only thing that hinders his revelation is the fact that the Church is still here. When the true Church is taken out (and it WILL be before the false Messiah is revealed), the lukewarm, liberal, and pagan religions will unite, the Antichrist will take over the reins of religion here on this earth and will set himself up as God, *to be worshipped as God*! The stage is set; the curtain is about to be drawn.

God give us more ministers who know that the cause of Christ is not advanced by organization or program, but through the demonstration of the Holy Spirit, by the Word of God and sincere worship in spirit and in truth! The average big denominational church has a packed auditorium on Sunday morning; but if they have services on Sunday night, prayer meeting night, or revival night, there will be only a handful of people in attendance. This is the age of pleasure-loving church members, going through forms and rituals on Sunday, then hanging their religion in the closet along with their Sunday suit until the next Sunday. They have a form of worship—but they deny the power of God, they deny the supernatural, and they deny a living reality in religion.

Paul commands Timothy, *"FROM SUCH TURN AWAY!"* Christians should not encourage liberals, modernists, and formalistic churches that major on form, denying the power of God, the power of the Gospel, the power of the Spirit, and the miracle of true Christian experience. If you are a born again Christian and you are a member of such a church, you should get out of it immediately, because you are supporting the enemies of true Christianity; and even though you may be saved, *you will lose your reward.* (Please read the entire Second Epistle of John.)

Verse 6: "For of this sort are they which creep into houses, and lead captive silly women laden with sins, led away with divers lusts."

These people were described in the previous verses as retaining the theory of godliness, advertising that they believe in God, the Bible, and Jesus—but proving that they do *not* believe by exercising negative power in services that are dead, dry, and lifeless. They practice unscriptural Christianity. (True Christianity is pure religion; pure religion is Christ in you, the hope of glory—and apart from Christ you are dead in sin.) Apart from the blood there is no redemption.

342

Those who practice religions of form without power may parade as the apostles of Jesus and the ministers of God, but inwardly they are ravening wolves and ministers of Satan (II Cor. 11:13–15). Such teachers are cunning, like their father, the devil. They work in the same manner. Satan approached Eve with a seemingly harmless question—but that question planted in her heart a distrust of the Word of God, and it is the *Word of God* which is the *power of God unto salvation* (Rom. 1:16). Christians are born into God's family through the Word (I Pet. 1:23). The faith that makes us sons of God comes through the Word of God (Rom. 10:17). We are made clean spiritually through the Word (John 15:3). If the devil can discredit God's Word in our minds, he has won a tremendous victory.

Here in verse 6 the Apostle has in view a definite type of teachers of form and powerless religion, whose actions are primarily directed toward an influence over women—not born again women, but those who are light-hearted, lightheaded, laden with all kinds of sin and lust. (This does not necessarily refer to sexual lust, but rather to the lust for power, riches, beauty, and position—none of which are to the glory of God.) *"Silly* women"—we must be careful about that word. I think it does not imply lack of brains, but lack of stability. They are not the only ones to be afflicted with this disability, for plenty of men are just as weak; but it happens to be women in this case.

Like Satan, such teachers as Paul has in mind do not openly attack God. They use Bible terms. They speak of the Holy Spirit, redemption, liberty; but they deny the power of the blood, the power of the Gospel, and saving grace apart from man's works. They major on form and program, and deny the power of God's grace and the blood of Jesus to save from sin. They say sin is not sin, that we do not need a "slaughterhouse" salvation, we do not need an old-fashioned mourner's bench with sinners weeping, repenting, and crying out to God for mercy. They tell us we need only to join a fashionable church, shake a preacher's hand, sign a card, be baptized in a beautiful baptistry, give our money to the church, and attend morning services regularly.

They talk of God as a loving, tender Father—a God who would not permit a person to be damned or eternally tormented. They preach the fatherhood of God, the brotherhood of man, and deny the reality of original sin. They maintain that all men are good, none are bad; but *Jesus* said that *all are bad, none are good.* This sort of teaching suits women whose conscience torments them, and yet are unwilling to yield everything to Christ. They live on in fear of death; therefore they are easy prey to these false teachers, who offer an easy religion.

In truth, there are but two classes of people—saved sinners, and lost sinners. Those of us who are saved are what we are because of the grace of God—not through any works of righteousness which we have done. God saved us according to His mercy, by the washing of regeneration and the renewing of the Holy Ghost. We are not saved by joining a church, by being baptized, nor by living a good life—but by the grace of God, the blood of Jesus, and faith in His finished work at Calvary.

Verse 7: "Ever learning, and never able to come to the knowledge of the truth."

In the last days, men will be *"ever learning, and never able to come to the knowledge of the truth."* The church is cursed today with ministers and religious leaders who are educated ignoramuses. The Bible tells us that the fear of the Lord is the beginning of knowledge, and a preacher who fears God will not preach salvation save through the blood of Jesus Christ. Jesus said, "He

344

that entereth not by the door into the sheepfold, but climbeth up some other way, the same is a thief and a robber." A preacher who tells his parishioners that they can get to heaven through church membership, good works, baptism, clean living, or any way except through faith in Jesus Christ, "the same is a thief and a robber"—a spiritual thief.

There are more educated preachers today than this world has ever known—preachers who have attended institutions of higher learning and yet *have never come to the knowledge of THE TRUTH*. What does Paul mean by this? Jesus said, "I am the way, THE TRUTH, and the life: no man cometh unto the Father, but by me" (John 14:6). He said, "Ye shall know THE TRUTH, and the truth shall make you free" (John 8:32). He said, "Sanctify them through thy TRUTH: thy WORD is truth" (John 17:17).

In John 1:1 and 14 we read, "In the beginning was the Word, and the Word was with God, and the Word was God. . . . And the Word was made flesh, and dwelt among us, (and we beheld His glory, the glory as of the only begotten of the Father,) FULL OF GRACE AND TRUTH!" JESUS is truth—and those of whom Paul speaks are masters of religion from the human standpoint, men of extreme wisdom and learning—and yet with all of their schooling, training, study, and learning, they have never come to the knowledge of the truth that except a man be born again, he cannot see the kingdom of God. They have not come to the knowledge of the truth that a man cannot be born again apart from the blood of Jesus Christ. They may preach long and loud—but they never preach the TRUTH. They preach a man-made, bloodless gospel of works, forms, and doctrines formulated by religious bosses and dictators.

Verse 8: "Now as Jannes and Jambres withstood Moses, so do these also resist the truth: men of corrupt minds, reprobate concerning the faith."

Nothing is known of the two men mentioned here. It is believed by some (and I believe) that they were among the magicians in Egypt who counterfeited the miracles of Moses. Exodus 7:10–22 records the story of the appearance of Moses and Aaron before Pharaoh. Aaron cast down his rod, which was changed into a snake—and the magicians did the same thing. On the surface, they seemed to demonstrate the same miracle-working power as Moses and Aaron—but not so. Their counterfeiting had the *appearance*, but not the reality and the power. The rod of the Egyptians *looked* like the rod of Aaron, and under the spell of the sorcerers it seemed to *act* in the same manner; but the counterfeit rod was empowered by the spirit of the devil, whereas Aaron's rod was empowered by God and thereby was victorious in the end.

Paul points out to Timothy that in like manner, these false teachers looked good and sounded good—but inwardly they were powerless ministers of Satan. They used women to advance their cause, because of the deep emotional influence of women. And the devil's program has not changed; it is the same today as it has always been. The enemies of the Gospel resist the TRUTH; they have corrupt minds; they are apostate concerning the faith; they put on a good show and come in sheep's clothing—*but inwardly they are ravening wolves*!

Verse 9: "But they shall proceed no further: for their folly shall be manifest unto all men, as their's also was."

We know what happened in Moses' day—the folly of the magicians was manifest; they failed—and Paul here

346

tells us that the false teachers in the local church and in the community today will meet the same fate. Eventually, their folly will be made manifest unto all men, and they will be cut off; the true Church will be caught out; the false church will be spewed out and judged as it is led by Antichrist.

Jesus is the chief cornerstone of the true Church, against which the gates of hell cannot prevail, and which the floods, tornadoes, and earthquakes of hell cannot shake; but the church of Antichrist is built on sand: it LOOKS good and SOUNDS good—but when the storms come and the rains descend, it will fall . . . *and great will be the fall thereof!*

Verse 10: "But thou hast fully known my doctrine, manner of life, purpose, faith, longsuffering, charity, patience."

The first nine verses of this chapter paint a dark picture—and we are in that picture *now.* These are days of peril, selfishness, formalism, and powerless religion. This is the day of learned preachers who do not preach the truth, who on the surface appear to be genuine, but inwardly they are evil. This is indeed a sad, heartbreaking picture; but *these things will come to pass*, and those of us who believe and study the Scriptures know that things will not get any better but will continually grow worse until Jesus comes and calls His bride to meet Him in the air. That is the blessed hope of the Christian. Even though the picture looks dark for Christians, there is a bright tomorrow. We know that all this darkness only points to His soon return. The Church will not pass through any part of the Tribulation, nor even enter into it. We will be caught out before the revelation of the Antichrist; but we are living today in "the beginning of sorrows," as mentioned in Matthew 24:8.

Beginning with verse 10, Paul returns to his own

347

testimony, declaring that Timothy knew full well what he preached, how he lived, the purpose of his life, the faith he exercised, the longsuffering he demonstrated, the love he proved by his sacrificial living and uncompromising preaching of the Gospel—preaching which cost him his freedom, and in just a few short days would cost him his life! Timothy knew the testimony Paul had lived since the day they met in Timothy's home town.

Paul is not demonstrating a self-righteous spirit nor a "holier-than-thou" attitude. He simply offers this testimony to reassure Timothy and increase his faith in the Christ who saves, keeps, and delivers. When one is aboveboard, when his motives are honest and pure, when self has been crucified and the Holy Spirit has full sway in a life, that person will prove by his daily living that he is what he professes to be—to the glory of God, and not for selfish gain.

Paul here invites Timothy to look back from the present to the day they met . . . back to the time when they joined hands and hearts to spread the Gospel and Timothy became Paul's youthful co-laborer. (Please read Acts 16—all of the chapter.) There had been wonderful experiences they had enjoyed together in preaching the Gospel, wonderful meetings they had held, the enthusiasm of the crowds, people worshipping God in sincerity and truth. There had been opposition by the enemies of the cross; they had suffered assaults, imprisonments, stoning. But in spite of it all, Paul had been faithful—*and patient.*

Verse 11: "Persecutions, afflictions, which came unto me at Antioch, at Iconium, at Lystra; what persecutions I endured: but out of them all the Lord delivered me."

What a testimony! I believe that no one save Christ ever suffered so much bodily agony for the Gospel as did Paul. He faced persecutions, afflictions, shipwrecks, stoning, imprisonments—and yet, the Lord delivered him out of them all! At this point in his life he can say, "The time of my departure is at hand! My fight is over; my work is finished. But Timothy—remember that you have fully known my doctrine, my manner of life, my faith, my longsuffering, my love, and my patience. Henceforth, follow me as I have followed the Lord. Walk in my steps as I have walked in the steps of the Saviour. Be not ashamed of the testimony of God, nor of me, His prisoner. Be a good soldier; fight a good fight—and be patient."

Verse 12: "Yea, and all that will live godly in Christ Jesus shall suffer persecution."

This leaves no doubt about it: *"ALL that will live godly in Christ Jesus SHALL suffer persecution."* There is no way to escape persecution if we live godly lives. The Lord Jesus Christ was persecuted. His enemies said everything ungodly and dirty about Him that could be said. They followed every step He made; and finally they arrested Him, falsely accused Him, tried Him on false charges supported by lying witnesses—*and crucified Him!* If they hated *Him*, they will hate His followers. If they persecuted *Him*, they will persecute us. The only person who escapes persecution is the person who plays ball with the devil. If we refuse to compromise, if we live dedicated, consecrated, Spirit-filled lives, we will suffer persecution—and *God has no pets!* ALL who live godly lives will suffer until Jesus comes, and then our suffering will be over: *"For I reckon that the sufferings of this present time are not worthy to be compared with the glory which shall be revealed in us"* (Rom. 8:18).

Verse 13: "But evil men and seducers shall wax worse and worse, deceiving, and being deceived."

I do not understand how any preacher can read this verse of Scripture and then preach that the church will convert the world and that people are better today than they were a century or half-century ago! There are some who preach that there will be a world-wide revival before the Rapture, but there is not one portion of God's Word that substantiates such teaching. The Scripture is clear: "As it was in the days of Noah"—there were *eight people* saved. All others were destroyed. "As it was in the days of Lot"—only *four people* got outside the city, and even Mrs. Lot turned to a pillar of salt! So as it was in the days of Noah, when eight were saved . . . as it was in the days of Lot, when four were saved—*so shall it be* in the days when the Son of man shall be revealed! Does that sound like revival? Quite the contrary.

"Evil men and seducers shall wax worse and worse." I am not a pessimist nor an alarmist—I am an optimist, but my optimism is in Christ Jesus, not in man. I am looking for Jesus and the Rapture—not for brighter days on earth. We KNOW that evil and ungodly men will become worse and worse. Being deceived, they will deceive others. Religions of deception are growing by leaps and bounds—and today it seems that the masses had rather listen to and support a liar and deceiver than to support a man who tells the truth and practices decency in all phases of his life. Men want to be deceived; they love a lie. After the Rapture when the Antichrist comes, the masses will worship him as God. He is THE LIE. Jesus is THE TRUTH. If you hear a minister preaching that the church will convert the world and bring in the Kingdom, that the Gospel will finally permeate the whole earth, that evil will be eradicated and righteousness will come about through the ministry of the church—*don't you believe it!* Such teaching is unscriptural; it is the doctrine of Antichrist.

Jesus did not put the Church here to convert the world; He commissioned the Church to preach the Gospel and win men to Christ. The believers make up the bride; and when the bride is complete, the Church will be taken out and the world will literally be covered by wickedness. Sin will run rampant, and people will worship the devil. *Then Jesus will come in flaming fire*, taking vengeance on the enemies of God's Christ and the cross!

The Believer's Need of the Word of God

Verse 14: "But continue thou in the things which thou hast learned and hast been assured of, knowing of whom thou hast learned them."

This verse is specifically for Timothy; but all Scripture is for our admonition, instruction, and encouragement. Timothy is to continue in the things he has learned, *knowing of whom he learned them.* His first teaching was from his mother and grandmother, and this teaching was followed by the many years he traveled with Paul and sat under his preaching. In spite of the persecution that would come, in spite of ungodly men, seducers and deceivers, Paul wanted Timothy to *continue* in the pure, positive, powerful, penetrating Gospel that saves, delivers, keeps, and presents believers to God, faultless "in that day." With this in view, Paul reminds him of two precious aids to steadfastness. The one is the remembrance of his teachers, and the other is the recollection of the Holy Book from which they taught him.

Verse 15: "And that from a child thou hast known the holy Scriptures, which are able to make thee wise unto salvation through faith which is in Christ Jesus."

Timothy was just a child when his mother and grandmother taught him the spiritual truths from the precious book of the Law, the prophets, and the Psalms, telling him of the Lord, in whom now all had been fulfilled.

"... *The holy Scriptures, which are able to make*

351

thee wise unto salvation through faith which is in Christ Jesus." Paul was a grace preacher; he preached salvation by grace through faith plus nothing. He clashed with the false teachers in Galatia who were attempting to mix law and grace, works and grace, rituals and grace. He cried aloud, "If ANY come unto you—even an angel—and preach any other Gospel than the Gospel I have preached to you, let him be accursed! Believe no Gospel except that which declares salvation by grace through faith—the Gospel which declares the Incarnation, the shed blood, the resurrection, the ascension, and the coming again of our Lord."

Talk about dogmatic, harsh preachers! *We have none today that can compare with Paul.* He never withheld truth to save the feelings of a false religionist. He was tender, loving, compassionate and longsuffering—but he did not use soft words when he called down condemnation upon those who would destroy the lambs in the flock!

To Timothy he said, "God has appointed you pastor and leader of the people in Ephesus and surrounding areas. You must remember the Gospel which you learned as a child—the holy Scriptures your mother and grandmother taught you. Remember the Word concerning the Lamb of God who was to come to take away the sin of the world— the Lamb who was to be wounded for our transgressions and bruised for our iniquities. The chastisement of our peace was to rest upon Him, and with His stripes we would be healed. Timothy, you learned that prophecy as a child; now preach the Gospel that will bring light to the darkened hearts of sinners, the Gospel that is the power of God to raise sinners from the deadness of sin and make them alive unto God, giving them a living hope and an inheritance incorruptible, undefiled, that cannot and will not fade away (I Pet. 1:3–5)."

Here is salvation: *"For by grace are ye saved through*

faith" (Eph. 2:8). *"Not by works of righteousness which we have done, but according to His mercy He saved us, by the washing of regeneration, and renewing of the Holy Ghost"* (Titus 3:5).

BY GRACE . . . THROUGH FAITH: *"So then faith cometh by hearing, and hearing by the Word of God"* (Rom. 10:17). The very faith through which we receive Jesus is given to us by God through hearing His Word: "For whosoever shall call upon the name of the Lord shall be saved. How then shall they call on Him in whom they have not believed? and how shall they believe in Him of whom they have not heard? and how shall they hear without a preacher? And how shall they preach, except they be sent? as it is written, How beautiful are the feet of them that preach the Gospel of peace, and bring glad tidings of good things! But they have not all obeyed the Gospel. For Esaias saith, Lord, who hath believed our report? *So then faith cometh by hearing, and hearing by the Word of God"* (Rom. 10:13–17).

God's preacher preaches the Word. The poor sinner, his mind blinded by the god of this age, bound in the chains of iniquity, hears the message of the minister who preaches the Gospel; hearing the Gospel brings light to his darkened intelligence, opens his blinded mind. The sinner hears the Gospel, and the Gospel brings saving faith. The unbeliever, seeing the light of the glorious Gospel, believing that Jesus died to save sinners, that He shed His blood on the cross for remission of sin, then exercises faith in the finished work of Jesus; and because of faith in the heart through hearing the Gospel, *the sinner calls—and Jesus saves!* The calling must be prefaced by preaching that is pure Gospel, and by the sinner hearing that Gospel by which he is enlightened and faith is born. That faith is then exercised from the heart—and the lips call:

"That if thou shalt confess with thy mouth the Lord

353

Jesus, and shalt believe in thine heart that God hath raised Him from the dead, thou shalt be saved" (Rom. 10:9).

There it is: *Salvation*—the only message that is able to make sinners wise unto salvation through faith which is in Christ Jesus our Saviour. Through hearing the Gospel, the faith to trust Him becomes ours—and *only* through hearing the Gospel. Man is out of it; *Jesus paid it all!* The only thing man can do is accept the finished work of Jesus Christ by faith. God saves *on the merit of the finished work of Jesus*—the shed blood, the redemption that He bought when He took our sins in His own body and nailed them to His own cross.

"For even hereunto were ye called: because Christ also suffered for us, leaving us an example, that ye should follow His steps: Who did no sin, neither was guile found in His mouth: Who, when He was reviled, reviled not again; when He suffered, He threatened not; but committed Himself to Him that judgeth righteously: Who His own self bare our sins in His own body on the tree, that we, being dead to sins, should live unto righteousness: by whose stripes ye were healed. For ye were as sheep going astray; but are now returned unto the Shepherd and Bishop of your souls" (I Peter 2:21–25).

Verse 16: "All Scripture is given by inspiration of God, and is profitable for doctrine, for reproof, for correction, for instruction in righteousness."

"ALL Scripture . . . ." There are those who say, "I believe part of the Bible, but I do not believe ALL of it." There are ministers who accept portions of the Bible but refuse to accept ALL of it. They say the Bible *"contains"* the Word of God—but Paul said the Bible does *NOT contain* the Word of God . . . *the Bible IS the Word of God*, divinely inspired; and the sixty-six books of our Bible are *all there is* of the Word. The so-called "added"

354

books of the Bible (Maccabees and others) are nothing more than history. They are not inspired of God.

God Almighty is sovereign; and if we are saved through the power of the Gospel; if the Gospel makes us wise unto salvation; if it is not God's will that any man perish but that all come to repentance, we can rest assured that He has preserved and protected His holy Scriptures down through the centuries! The devil cannot annihilate God's Word—nor any part of it. The sixty-six books in our Bible contain all that anyone needs to know about time, eternity, God, the devil, heaven, hell, salvation, damnation, sin, and righteousness. Anything we need to know about our relationship to God and His relationship to us is found in the Bible. We need no *added* books, and *we cannot afford to take any away*. If we add to or take from His Word, God will take away our part out of the book of life. All Scripture is given by inspiration of God. *"Given by inspiration of God,"* according to the Greek dictionary, is one Greek word, meaning *"God-breathed."*

Peter declares the same truth in these words: "Moreover I will endeavour that ye may be able after my decease to have these things always in remembrance. For we have not followed cunningly devised fables, when we made known unto you the power and coming of our Lord Jesus Christ, but were eyewitnesses of His majesty. For He received from God the Father honour and glory, when there came such a voice to Him from the excellent glory, This is my beloved Son, in whom I am well pleased. And this voice which came from heaven we heard, when we were with Him in the holy mount. We have also a more sure word of prophecy; whereunto ye do well that ye take heed, as unto a light that shineth in a dark place, until the day dawn, and the day star arise in your hearts: Knowing this first, that no prophecy of the Scripture is of any private interpretation. For the prophecy came not in old time by the will of man: but holy men of God spake as they were moved by the Holy Ghost" (II Pet. 1:15–21).

Let me emphasize: "Knowing this first, THAT NO PROPHECY OF THE SCRIPTURE IS OF ANY PRIVATE INTERPRETATION. For the prophecy came not in old time by the will of man: BUT HOLY MEN OF GOD SPAKE AS THEY WERE MOVED BY THE HOLY GHOST." Yes, Yes, Yes! *I believe that God Almighty spoke*—and Peter wrote it down. I believe God Almighty spoke and John wrote it down. I believe God Almighty spoke and Paul wrote it down. God spoke, and Isaiah wrote it down. God spoke, and Job wrote it down. Yes, I believe in the *verbal inspiration* of the Bible.

Believers are to study and rightly divide the Word of God. No person has any right to interpret the Bible to fit his or her religious ideas. Scriptures are not to be privately interpreted. The only way to understand the Word of God is to compare spiritual things with spiritual (I Cor. 2:11–13). We cannot make the Bible fit our religion; we must fit our Christianity into the Bible. We are to study and rightly divide the Word. All Scripture is profitable for doctrine, for reproof, for correction, for instruction in righteousness.

Verse 17: "That the man of God may be perfect, throughly furnished unto all good works."

The man of God should use all Scripture in its scriptural setting, taking into consideration the times and seasons, the Jew and Gentile, and the Church of God (I Cor. 10:32). No one has a right to take Scriptures directly spoken to Abraham and Israel, and give those Scriptures to the Church. *The Kingdom and the Church are not one and the same.* God told Noah to build an ark—but He does not want US to build an ark. God told

Abraham to offer Isaac—but He does not want us to offer our sons in like manner. God speaks to specific people at specific times, under certain conditions. The Law was given as a sign between God and Israel—but now, "Christ is the end of the law for righteousness to every one that believeth" (Rom. 10:4). We are not under Law, but under God's grace.

No one has a right to take Scriptures out of their setting in order to prove his religion or his doctrine. We can gather many lessons from the flood, the ark, Sodom, Gomorrah, the Israelites in Egypt—there are many lessons to be learned from God's dealings with the people of Israel; *but we are not to take the promises God made to Abraham and apply them to the Church*! We are to give to the Church the Scriptures that belong to the Church, and we should give to Israel the promises that belong to Abraham and his seed.

The Bible is God-breathed. God spoke by the Holy Ghost, and holy men penned down what He said. Any doctrine that does not fit into the Word of God is false doctrine. Therefore, dear reader, you should check your doctrine against the Word of God. If the minister where you attend church does not preach the doctrine laid down in the Bible, *without addition or subtraction*, you should not support him. If he does not preach "Thus saith the Lord," or if he preaches any other doctrine, do not invite him into your house; do not support him; do not bid him God speed. If you do, you are sinning:

"For many deceivers are entered into the world, who confess not that Jesus Christ is come in the flesh. This is a deceiver and an antichrist. Look to yourselves, that we lose not those things which we have wrought, but that we receive a full reward. Whosoever transgresseth, and abideth not in the doctrine of Christ, hath not God. He that abideth in the doctrine of Christ, he

357

hath both the Father and the Son. *If there come any unto you, and bring not this doctrine, receive him not into your house, neither bid him God speed: For he that biddeth him God speed is partaker of his evil deeds''* (II John 7–11).

Everything we need to know about doctrine is laid down in the Word of God. The Bible furnishes the minister of God with ammunition, power, words for reproof. A good minister does not always preach doctrine—he also reproves and rebukes. The Gospel contains the message of correction—and a good minister of the Gospel preaches Bible doctrine, reproves from the Bible, and corrects error through the Gospel. He does not preach what he thinks; he does not preach through catechisms or a book of doctrine; he preaches the Word of God—THE Book—and laid down in holy Scripture is everything we need for instruction in righteousness. God's preacher does not need to call up Dr. Sounding Brass and Professor Tinkling Cymbal and ask their opinions concerning anything that has to do with right living and Bible doctrine; all the instruction we need is laid down in God's holy Word.

God's Word is a *tool chest* containing every tool we need for preaching—whether it be doctrine, reproof, correction, or instruction. The Word of God is a complete *food center*: In it we find all the spiritual milk, meat, and bread that we need for spiritual growth. The Bible is a complete *clothing store*: It clothes us with salvation, the garments of sanctification, and the robe of righteousness. The Bible is a complete spiritual *hospital*: It contains all necessary medications and instruments for strengthening and building up undernourished, sickly Christians. The Bible contains anything, all things, and everything needed by God's man to do a perfect job of preaching the Word in its entirety, winning sinners, feeding babes in Christ, strengthening the weak, and nourishing the strong and the full grown. Everything God's minister needs is in the Bible.

One of the greatest needs in the pulpit today is for God's preachers to get back to the Bible and stop preaching man-made doctrine, man-made ideas, man's program. We need to get back to *"Thus saith the Lord"* in every phase of Gospel ministry.

II TIMOTHY -- CHAPTER FOUR

A FAITHFUL SERVANT AND HIS FINAL MESSAGE

1. I charge thee therefore before God, and the Lord Jesus Christ, who shall judge the quick and the dead at his appearing and his kingdom;
2. Preach the word; be instant in season, out of season; reprove, rebuke, exhort with all longsuffering and doctrine.
3. For the time will come when they will not endure sound doctrine; but after their own lusts shall they heap to themselves teachers, having itching ears;
4. And they shall turn away their ears from the truth, and shall be turned unto fables.
5. But watch thou in all things, endure afflictions, do the work of an evangelist, make full proof of thy ministry.
6. For I am now ready to be offered, and the time of my departure is at hand.
7. I have fought a good fight, I have finished my course, I have kept the faith:
8. Henceforth there is laid up for me a crown of righteousness, which the Lord, the righteous judge, shall give me at that day: and not to me only, but unto all them also that love his appearing.
9. Do thy diligence to come shortly unto me:
10. For Demas hath forsaken me, having loved this present world, and is departed unto Thessalonica; Crescens to Galatia, Titus unto Dalmatia.
11. Only Luke is with me. Take Mark, and bring him with thee: for he is profitable to me for the ministry.
12. And Tychicus have I sent to Ephesus.
13. The cloke that I left at Troas with Carpus, when thou comest, bring with thee, and the books, but especially the parchments.
14. Alexander the coppersmith did me much evil: the Lord reward him according to his works:
15. Of whom be thou ware also; for he hath greatly withstood our words.
16. At my first answer no man stood with me, but all men forsook me: I pray God that it may not be laid to their charge.
17. Notwithstanding the Lord stood with me, and strengthened me; that by me the preaching might be fully known, and that all the Gentiles might hear: and I was delivered out of the mouth of the lion.

18. And the Lord shall deliver me from every evil work, and will preserve me unto his heavenly kingdom: to whom be glory for ever and ever. Amen.

19. Salute Prisca and Aquila, and the household of Onesiphorus.

20. Erastus abode at Corinth: but Trophimus have I left at Miletum sick.

21. Do thy diligence to come before winter. Eubulus greeteth thee, and Pudens, and Linus, and Claudia, and all the brethren.

22. The Lord Jesus Christ be with thy spirit. Grace be with you. Amen.

Paul's Last Charge

The previous chapter closed with admonition and instruction for Timothy to continue in the things which he had learned, knowing from whom he learned them. He was reminded of how, from a child, he had known the holy Scriptures—the only message on this earth that can make men wise unto salvation through faith. Paul stresses the fact that all Scripture is inspired, dictated to holy men by the Holy Ghost, and is profitable for doctrine, for reproof, for correction, and for instruction in righteousness—that the man of God may be perfectly furnished unto all good works. On the basis of these established truths, Paul places a divine charge upon Timothy:

Verse 1: "I charge thee therefore before God, and the Lord Jesus Christ, who shall judge the quick and the dead at His appearing and His kingdom."

"Timothy, before the God who saved, called, and ordained you, and before the Saviour who died that through His mercy you might be saved, *I charge you* . . . ."

Paul wanted to make sure that Timothy preached the Word without mixture. The Bible is the one and only divinely authorized record of the divine love of God and of what God's love has done (and is doing) for those who will trust in God's Christ. The Bible is the only book that tells us that because of God's love, Christ Jesus met the sin-debt—and through His death purchased redemption, paid the ransom, and took our sins away, bearing them in His own body on the cross (I Pet. 2:24).

The Bible is the only book that tells us that in the beginning, before God made either the earth or man, He planned and perfected our salvation (I Pet. 1:20). It is the only authentic revelation of God and His only begotten Son; it is the only book that tells us that it is not God's will that any should perish, but that all should come to repentance. The Bible declares its inspiration; it is the only book on earth that is a *living* book. The message God wants men to hear is laid down in His Word. God is not concerned about your opinion or mine. He dictated the truth, and the truth makes men free.

Verse 2: "Preach the Word; be instant in season, out of season; reprove, rebuke, exhort with all longsuffering and doctrine."

Paul was deeply burdened. He was facing death; he knew that his departure was imminent, and the urgency of preaching the Gospel weighed heavily upon his heart. He wanted Timothy to announce the second coming of the Lord Jesus, so clearly outlined in I Thessalonians 4:13—18. He wanted Timothy to warn of the judgment to follow—the judgment of everyone for stewardship—and, at the consummation of all things, the judgment of the wicked. (Christians will not be judged after death as to whether they are saved or lost; they will be judged only for stewardship. Please read II Corinthians 5:10 and I Corinthians 3:11—15.)

Paul also had in mind *the kingdom*. There will be a kingdom, and Jesus will be King. Paul wanted Timothy to surrender all of his ability, energy, strength, and resources to the preaching of these tremendous fundamentals of the faith. In patience, love, faith and longsuffering (and in the face of prejudiced opposition by the enemies of the Gospel) he should preach God's message to a dying world.

Timothy was to cry aloud concerning the judgment; he was to announce the coming kingdom. He was to reprove believers when necessary, rebuke the unconcerned, exhort the spiritually minded to higher things—and he was to do this with all longsuffering.

Verse 3: "For the time will come when they will not endure sound doctrine; but after their own lusts shall they heap to themselves teachers, having itching ears."

Paul and Timothy had been blessed with tremendous success in their ministry together. There had been persecutions; but their enemies had been in the minority, compared with the many true believers who heard and followed them. But Paul knew the time was fast approaching when Timothy would find it hard to get people to listen to his message from the pure Word of God. At that time there were many who were willing to listen, willing to obey, willing to accept the message of Christ; but the night was approaching—and those who walk in darkness love darkness because their deeds are evil. Soon Timothy would see his congregations dwindle; and many who had followed him would join another band of preachers, who were not commissioned by Almighty God— men who had invited themselves into the community to set up a newer doctrine filled with mystery, allure, curiosity and adventure—a doctrine having to do with the spirit world. Many would turn from the Gospel of the crucified Christ, His shed blood and salvation by grace, and would flock to listen to myths and fables.

The Apostle warned Timothy of these conditions that would come about, so that he would be ready for the falling away and would not be discouraged. We know through study of the first three chapters of Revelation that the churches in Asia DID dwindle in number, in spirit, and in truth, until only the Philadelphian church stood firm and kept the Word of God (Rev. 3:10). It was concerning these true believers that the Holy Spirit said, ". . . For thou hast a little strength, and hast kept my word, and hast not denied my name. . . . I also will keep thee from the hour of temptation (tribulation), which shall come upon all the world . . ." (Rev. 3:8,10).

The seven churches in Asia actually existed as named in Revelation, but the truth goes much deeper than those local assemblies. The seven churches named are advance portrayals of church history until the Rapture of the true Church and the spewing out of the Laodiceans, and they are very significant in relationship to the entire church age. The false doctrines concerning the spirit-world, holding that people are not bound by matter but can be delivered from the slavery of matter and become part of the spirit-world, found a sure foothold and a strong following—because according to this doctrine of the errorists, one could be religious and yet follow the lust of his own mind and heart in satisfying the desires of the flesh.

The people described in our present verse were never born again. They were religiously inclined, and no doubt some of them had united with the local assembly; but they had never been born of the Spirit nor washed in the blood. Those who are genuinely saved will not succumb to error and turn away from the faith (I Pet. 2:6).

The message of Calvary—the cross and the shed blood—will be neglected and shunned, and the accepted message will be that of the ministers who are *"ever learning, yet never able to come to a knowledge of the truth."* The masses will travel the broad way that leads to destruction.

They will accept doctrine that will stifle the conscience, harden the heart, flatter the mind—but damn the soul.

Paul did not want Timothy to be discouraged or disappointed. He wanted him to be all the more consecrated to preaching the Gospel of the marvelous grace of God, because he knew *there would be some* who would listen to the divine but unfashionable message of the blood— the message that humbles man's heart and does away with foolish pride. Some would accept the Christ-centered message of the cross, the message that Jesus IS coming, that there *will be* a judgment, and that *the kingdom will be set up*.

If God's man preaches that message, *through* the message the Holy Ghost will work miracles in the hearts of men. Many times it seems as if the whole world has gone after the wisdom of men, but we must remain faithful to the Gospel. This was the heart-cry of the old apostle. It was his heart's burden for his young successor, Timothy.

If you will study conditions around you, you will find that many ministers have always followed the line of least resistance. The minority has followed the true Gospel, but the majority has always shunned the message of the cross. Jesus said, "Enter ye in at the strait gate: for wide is the gate, and broad is the way, that leadeth to destruction, and many there be which go in thereat: Because strait is the gate, and narrow is the way, which leadeth unto life, and few there be that find it" (Matt. 7:13,14).

A gospel of myths tickles the ear—but the Gospel of the cross works miracles in the heart. There are millions today who file in and out of fashionable churches; they go there for the specific purpose of having their ears tickled. They listen to a social sermon—possibly fifteen minutes long, every word of it *read*—not preached from the heart as inspired of the Holy Ghost. They hear a social gospel, with no cross, no resurrection—lifeless, bloodless, devoid of miracles and salvation . . . empty words falling from the lips of learned men who have never come to the knowledge of the Truth.

The greatest enemy of the United States and the American way of life is not the Russians and Communism; it is the learned ministers in our pulpits—men turned off the assembly lines of our denominational theological seminaries, having head-religion, not heart-religion, and with a message from the wisdom of men, not from the Word of God. These lying prophets and ministers of Satan are the greatest enemy this country has. Please read carefully Isaiah 56:10–12 and II Corinthians 11:13–15.

Verse 5: "But watch thou in all things, endure afflictions, do the work of an evangelist, make full proof of thy ministry."

In this verse Paul again calls upon Timothy to be watchful . . . *"Watch thou* in ALL THINGS." Paul is keenly aware of the fact that his life will soon be poured out upon the altar of martyrdom as he seals his testimony with his life's blood—and Timothy will be fighting the battle alone, so far as Paul's earthly friendship is concerned. Instead of allowing his death to weaken his testimony or cause him to become less fervent, Paul is urging Timothy at this crucial moment, to arise as he had never done before; to be strong, be sober, accept suffering with all his heart, and to labor in the Gospel to the end. This is good logic—the holy logic Jehovah God Himself used with Joshua so very long before: "Moses my servant is dead; now therefore arise, go over this Jordan, thou, and all this people, unto the land which I do give to them" (Josh. 1:2). God was about to bury His workman; but HE would be present, as ever, to carry on His work.

"Endure afflictions . . . ." Timothy must forget self, forget his own desires and his own ambitions. He must dedicate his body a living sacrifice; his mind must be sanctified, and he must be sober in all phases of life as he ministers in the community where God has placed him. In spite of false teachers who will come, in spite of those who will depart from the faith, in spite of the death of his beloved friend and co-laborer, Paul—he must look to Him who is invisible and endure afflictions for the glory of God:

"While we look not at the things which are seen, but at the things which are not seen: for the things which are seen are temporal; but the things which are not seen are eternal" (II Cor. 4:18). "By faith Moses . . . refused to be called the son of Pharaoh's daughter . . . forsook Egypt, not fearing the wrath of the king: for *he endured, as seeing Him who is invisible*" (Heb. 11:23–27).

Seeing "Him who is invisible," Timothy must live every day yielded to God. He must face hardship, trials, cruel mockings, and perhaps even scourging. As a soldier of the cross he must *endure hardship*. The soldier in the army does not give up the battle when hardships come upon him. He may be cold, tired, wet, hungry—sometimes wounded; but he keeps on fighting, because the enemy must be conquered. As soldiers of the cross, do we dare to be less dedicated to the cause of Christ than soldiers in the service of their country are dedicated to their cause and to their flag? We *must* endure hardness, if we are to accomplish things for God.

The preacher who stands in the pulpit and tells his audience that the Christian life is a gay and carefree walk along a path strewn with roses, is simply advertising Bible ignorance. Jesus said, "Follow me—and I will give you a cross to carry. (And if you do not carry that cross, you are not fit to be my disciple!)" In Luke

17:10 He tells us, ". . . When ye shall have done all those things which are commanded you, say, *We are unprofitable servants: we have done that which was our duty to do.*"

"*Make full proof of thy ministry.*" Paul's thought here is, "Timothy, you are an ambassador of God, bringing men to Christ through the Gospel. You bear the greatest message the world has ever heard! So never let your preaching become a sideline. Keep it first and foremost in your life. Dedicate all of yourself to that ministry, so that when you come to the end of the way you may be able to say as Jesus said, 'I have glorified thee on the earth: I have finished the work which thou gavest me to do' (John 17:4)."

Paul's Last Testimony

Verse 6: "For I am now ready to be offered, and the time of my departure is at hand."

In Philippians 1:21–24 Paul said, "For to me to live is Christ, and *to die is gain.* . . . For I am in a strait betwixt two, having a desire to depart, and to be with Christ; which is far better: Nevertheless to abide in the flesh is more needful for you."

"*TO DIE IS GAIN . . . .*" What mysterious words! Paul was not a quitter; he did not seek to evade the pain, persecution, and heartache of this life. He was not afraid of death, and he looked forward to departing this life to be with Jesus. There are three reasons why he could make such a bold statement:

1. *He obeyed the call of conversion.* (Study Acts 9.)

As Saul of Tarsus, he had persecuted the church in Jerusalem, and was on his way to Damascus to seek out Christians there, "that he might bring them bound unto Jerusalem." But before he reached the city, "suddenly

368

there shined round about him a light from heaven, and he fell to the earth." The light was Shekinah glory from the face of Jesus—and as he fell to the earth he heard a voice calling his name: "Saul, Saul, why persecutest thou me?" Paul asked, "Who art thou, Lord?" and the voice replied, *"I am Jesus, whom thou persecutest."*

Under the power of the voice, prostrate on the ground from the glory that shone down, Paul asked in surrender, "Lord, *what wouldst thou have me do?"*—and he believed what the voice said in reply: *"Arise, and go into the city, and it shall be told thee what thou must do."* There was no need for Paul to say more. He obeyed the voice; and under the hand of Ananias "there fell from his eyes as it had been scales: and he received sight forthwith, and arose, and was baptized. And when he had received meat, he was strengthened. Then was Saul certain days with the disciples which were at Damascus" (Acts 9:18,19).

"And straightway (IMMEDIATELY) he preached Christ in the synagogues, that He is the Son of God" (Acts 9:20). After Paul met the Christ, he started a revival meeting in the synagogue; and his first sermon was on the virgin birth of Jesus! He at once preached the truth he had hitherto denied! He *heard* the Word of God; he *received* the Word—*and he obeyed it.*

2. *He obeyed the call to stewardship.* (Study Acts 26.)

The twenty-sixth chapter of Acts records the magnificent defense of Paul before King Agrippa. In the course of his testimony, he said: "And I punished (Christians) oft in every synagogue, and compelled them to blaspheme; and being exceedingly mad against them, I persecuted them even unto strange cities. Whereupon as I went to Damascus with authority and commission from the chief priests, at midday, O king, I saw in the way a light from heaven, above the brightness of the sun, shining round about me and them which journeyed with me. And when we were all fallen to the earth, I heard a voice speaking unto me, and saying in the Hebrew tongue, Saul, Saul, why persecutest thou me? it is hard for thee to kick against the pricks. And I said, Who art thou, Lord? And He said, I am Jesus whom thou persecutest. But rise, and stand upon thy feet: for I have appeared unto thee for this purpose, to make thee a minister and a witness both of these things which thou hast seen, and of those things in the which I will appear unto thee; delivering thee from the people, and from the Gentiles, unto whom now I send thee, to open their eyes, and to turn them from darkness to light, and from the power of Satan unto God, that they may receive forgiveness of sins, and inheritance among them which are sanctified by faith that is in me. Whereupon, O king Agrippa, *I was not disobedient unto the heavenly vision!*" (Acts 26:11–19).

Paul obeyed the call to service; he became a minister of the Gospel which he had hated and persecuted. Paul was a devout Pharisee—and when he consented to the death of Stephen, he thought he was doing God a favor. But Jesus saved him, and then called him to the ministry to deliver the Gospel message to the Gentiles (known by the Jews as "Gentile dogs"). As Saul of Tarsus he could have said, "Now wait a minute, Lord: I will preach to the Jews; I will gladly give my life in service to my own brethren after the flesh—but please do not ask me to preach to the Gentiles!" But Jesus saved him, and Paul knew it. He became a bondservant of the Lord Jesus, and by his actions and complete surrender said, "I will go where you want me to go—even unto the Gentile dogs. I will say what you want me to say—I will preach Jesus, the Lamb of God. I will be what you want me to be—even a minister to the Gentiles, though I am a son of Abraham!" Saul the persecutor became Paul the preacher—an apostle to the most hated people on the face of the earth in his day. No wonder he could say, "For to me, *to die is gain!*"

3. *The third reason is stated in our next verse:*

Verse 7: "I have fought a good fight, I have finished my course, I have kept the faith."

Listening for the sound of approaching Roman soldiers who would lead him into the courtyard to be executed, this man in the dungeon could say, "I have been a good soldier; *I have fought a good fight.* I have not been a deserter, slacker, nor coward. In the thick of battle and under all conditions I fought a good fight. I am now being promoted to heaven—not to wear a helmet, but a crown! I have finished the work God laid out for me that day on the Damascus road. When the teachers of error stormed Galatia, I kept the faith. When Philetus and Hymenaeus preached falsehood, I preached the truth. Timothy, I have not been disobedient to the heavenly vision!"

Verse 8: "Henceforth there is laid up for me a crown of righteousness, which the Lord, the righteous judge, shall give me at that day: and not to me only, but unto all them also that love His appearing."

Paul obeyed the call of conversion; he believed the words of Jesus and was saved. He obeyed the call of stewardship; he was not disobedient unto the heavenly vision. He was faithful in the service of the Commander-in-Chief of the great Christian army; he fought well and he kept the faith. There was therefore laid up for him a crown of righteousness—and if you and I will do as Paul did, we too will be crowned in that day when the Rapture occurs, when the saints are caught up to sit at the marriage supper of the Lamb in the sky, and receive the reward for deeds done in the body.

"... *And not to me only, but UNTO ALL THEM ALSO THAT LOVE HIS APPEARING.*"

No man knows the day or the hour when Jesus will come; we do not know the day or the hour when we will be called to meet the Lord in death. If this should be the day of the Lord's return, or if this should be the day death comes for me, could I testify as Paul did in the face of death? Have I really fought a good fight? Have I kept the faith? Have I been a good minister, true to the Word and to those to whom I preached? Will I have a crown to cast at the feet of Jesus when we crown Him Lord of all?

According to the last words in this verse, there is a special crown for all who love the appearing of Jesus—those who, like John, can truthfully pray, "Even so, Come, Lord Jesus!" There are five crowns named in Scripture that a believer can earn through faithful stewardship:

1. The *incorruptible crown* — I Corinthians 9:25.
2. The *crown of rejoicing* — I Thessalonians 2:19.
3. The *crown of righteousness* — II Timothy 4:8.
4. The *crown of life* — Revelation 2:10.
5. The *crown of glory* — I Peter 5:4.

The minister who teaches that all saints will enjoy the same eternal reward in heaven just does not know his Bible. Christians will be rewarded for every good deed—even a cup of cold water given in the name of Jesus. Faithful stewardship brings full reward; but if we are lazy and careless, allowing others to serve while we live the life of a spiritual hobo, then those who *serve* will receive the reward.

Those who wake up in hell will be rewarded according to their wickedness, and according to the opportunities

372

rejected when they could have accepted Jesus Christ as Saviour and did not.

Paul's Last Personal Messages

Verse 9: "Do thy diligence to come shortly unto me."

Paul longed to see Timothy just once more before his martyrdom, and apparently he felt that his time of execution was drawing very near. He urges Timothy to come quickly.

Verse 10: "For Demas hath forsaken me, having loved this present world, and is departed unto Thessalonica; Crescens to Galatia, Titus unto Dalmatia."

This verse and those that follow list the names of several individuals. Demas and Luke are also mentioned in Colossians 4:14 and in Philemon 24. We read of Titus in II Corinthians 7:6,13,14; 8:6,16,23; and in Galatians 2:1,3. Crescens is only mentioned here. These men had been with Paul but had all gone their separate ways. Demas, sad to say, had been drawn away by love of the world. He had taken up residence in Thessalonica, a very prominent city in that day from the standpoint of commerce and trade; and probably he had become ambitious for riches and this world's goods. Love of money has ruined the testimony of many good ministers.

The ministry and business simply do not mix. The ministry of the Gospel is a full time job, and in my own experience I have never found time to participate in business since God called me to preach. During my years of preaching, my income has been by faith through the free will offerings of God's people—and as God bears me record, I have never drawn a salary nor set a price on a revival meeting or a service. My living has come through people to whom God spoke, laying it upon their hearts to share the Lord's money to support this ministry.

373

Paul did not say that Demas was lost; he did not consign him to hell. He simply made it plain that Demas had turned his back on him—that as the old apostle stood in the shadows of death, when he really needed friends and the encouragement friends could give, Demas forsook him, "having loved this present world."

Of the reasons why Titus and Crescens left him we know nothing, except that Paul did not suggest that they left him with the wrong spirit, or for any other reason than that they were probably about the Master's business.

Verses 11 and 12: "Only Luke is with me. Take Mark, and bring him with thee: for he is profitable to me for the ministry. And Tychicus have I sent to Ephesus."

We have met Luke previously. In Acts, he does not write down his own name; but in those vivid sections of that book where the writer speaks in the first person, beginning with Acts 16:10, we see him at once as the author and fellow-traveler of the Apostle Paul. He was Paul's personal physician, referred to by the Apostle as "the beloved physician"; and he was with Paul in Rome. Fairweather friends had forsaken him—but Luke was there, on the spot . . . "Luke alone is with me." Luke was not the only true friend left to him in Rome, for he will presently be sending Timothy greetings from other loyal hearts before he closes (verse 21); but apparently he was the only one who stayed at his side in the prison. Luke was a tried and trusted friend, as all Christians should be, ready and willing to help under all circumstances.

Today there are still some Christians like Luke— Christians who stand by God's ministers in their dark hours. Please let me give just a word of personal testimony here. My own faithful friends have stood by me. During one illness, when it was announced that I needed nineteen pints of blood for transfusions, eighty individuals lined up outside the hospital blood bank—and more than three times enough blood was given to meet my need! My friends sent in the funds to pay my hospital bill, which ran into hundreds of dollars. Yes, we all have fairweather friends—those who praise us and support us while we are on top; but thank God for the Lukes who remain with us in all kinds of weather—fair and foul. God will not forget it, and He will certainly reward such faithful stewardship and service.

"Take Mark, and bring him with thee: for he is profitable to me for the ministry." This is "Marcus," mentioned in Colossians 4:10; and Bible scholars agree that he is the same young man mentioned in Acts 12:12 as John Mark. It was Mark's mother who had a cottage prayer meeting in her home the night Peter was released from jail through a miracle (Acts 12:5–17). Mark accompanied Paul and Barnabas on their early missionary journeys (Acts 12:25). He later brought sad disappointment to Paul by turning back from them at Pamphylia (Acts 15:38), which defection led later to the sharp dissension between Paul and Barnabas, causing those two apostles to part company (Acts 15:39); but, without question, Mark had later proved himself as a worthy contender for the faith— for Paul now says, "He is profitable . . . for the ministry."

How easy it would have been for Paul to count Mark out of his life as having put his hand to the plow and looked back, thereby evidencing that he was not qualified to be an apostle of Jesus Christ; but Paul exercised grace, love, patience, and a forgiving spirit. In these last days of his life on earth, he wanted Timothy to bring Mark to see him.

Tychicus is first mentioned in Acts 20:4. He was a native of Asia Minor and was Paul's assistant on his third missionary journey. When Paul was first imprisoned in Rome, Tychicus was with him (Eph. 6:21). In this present prison experience, Paul sent Tychicus on a mission to Ephesus.

Verse 13: "The cloke that I left at Troas with Carpus, when thou comest, bring with thee, and the books, but especially the parchments."

Some critics have asked, "Is such a statement inspired? Does God's Word have room for a personal request for a cloke?" Some of the greatest scholars the world has ever known declare this to be the most moving sentence in all of Paul's epistles, written under inspiration. It shows us that God has time to be concerned about the most insignificant thing that has to do with our comfort and well-being in the human side of our living. The request in this verse shows us how the strongest spiritual leader responds to a pathetic bodily need such as Paul was experiencing at that time. He knew that he was living in his last days, and that the steps of his executioner would soon be heard in the corridor outside his cell. But in spite of this knowledge, he still wanted the books that he loved, and his cloke as protection against the approaching winter and the equinoctial storms that soon would be coming. Paul had evidently left a warm cloke at Troas at the home of Carpus, his beloved friend. (Bible scholars suggest that possibly the house where Paul left his cloke was the same house where he preached the night a young man fell from the window and broke his neck—Acts 20:9.)

One cannot help but ask, Did Paul really need the coat? Was his life spared until winter? Did the dear old saint ever see his beloved books and the parchments? He may have been spared until winter; he may have bowed his head in thanksgiving as he wrapped the warm cloke around his body and in the cold gloom of the dungeon—perhaps by the light of a flickering candle—labored over his books a few moments each day. Whatever the outcome of his request may have been, these words have touched hearts and caused tears to flow down the cheeks of saints.

These words should shame those of us who think we have suffered for the sake of the Gospel. We should bow our heads and ask God to forgive us for grumbling or feeling like we are not appreciated. Regardless of what we may be called upon to suffer, or how much we may be mistreated and ignored, *"the sufferings of this present time are not worthy to be compared with the glory which shall be revealed in us"* (Rom. 8:18).

". . . Especially the parchments." It is possible that the parchments referred to were holy Scripture, the Word of God, Paul's joy and delight. Possibly they contained some of his own writings, now preserved for us in the Word of God.

Verse 14: "Alexander the coppersmith did me much evil: the Lord reward him according to his works."

Again Paul names one of his enemies: *"Alexander the coppersmith."* Outside of this passage we know nothing about this man. Bible scholars do not agree that he is the same Alexander mentioned in I Timothy 1:20, and this is probably the reason Paul identifies him as *"the coppersmith."* We know that he was an enemy to the Gospel, that he did "much evil" to Paul—and the language used here in the Greek suggests that he disputed with Paul openly, standing up in meetings and disputing or attempting to argue with him. Others suggest that this Alexander was a wolf in sheep's clothing, pretending to be a disciple, using pretention to play traitor to the true Church and ensnare Paul, thus finally leading him to imprisonment and execution. Regardless of what Alexander did and how he did it, Paul testified that he did much evil to him, and predicted that the Lord would reward him according to his works. Paul warned Timothy to be on guard against him, because he knew that whatever Alexander had done in opposition to *him*, he would do the same against Timothy.

The King James version reads, "The Lord reward him according to his works"; but Greek authorities say it should read, "*The Lord SHALL reward him.*" Paul was not requesting the Lord to destroy Alexander, nor was he praying down judgment upon him; but he knew that the Lord rewards according to one's labor—whether it be good or evil. He committed Alexander entirely to the Lord to be dealt with, but he wanted Timothy to be careful lest *he* be a victim of this enemy of the Gospel.

Verse 15: "Of whom be thou ware also; for he hath greatly withstood our words."

As I suggested earlier, it seems that Alexander the coppersmith took issue with Paul while he was preaching the Word of God. Notice the words, "*Be thou ware.*" This man was one of those to whom Jesus referred in His Sermon on the Mount when He clearly said, "*Give not that which is holy unto the dogs, neither cast ye your pearls before swine, lest they trample them under their feet, and turn again and rend you*" (Matt. 7:6).

Timothy was not told to go to see this fellow and witness to him—oh, no! On the contrary, he was warned to beware of him as an enemy of the Gospel. There are dear Christians who waste precious time "casting pearls before swine." There is not one verse of Scripture that commands the Christian to witness to one who deliberately denies the Word of God and the plain truth of the Gospel, or who advertises that he is an agnostic or an atheist. Christians are not instructed to witness to such a person or attempt to win him through the Scriptures.

378

We are to spread the Gospel to sinners (Jesus came to seek and to save that which was lost)—but an atheist or an agnostic has no need of a Saviour . . . he does not believe there is anything to be saved *from* nor saved *to*. We are not to argue with individuals who deny the fundamentals of the faith and reject the pure Gospel of God's grace.

Verse 16: "At my first answer no man stood with me, but all men forsook me: I pray God that it may not be laid to their charge."

This verse seems to be a continuation of the same thought: *"At my first answer . . . ."* In other words, Paul is saying, "The first time I encountered opposition from Alexander the coppersmith, I answered him with the Word of God—but *no man stood with me*; all men forsook me and left me standing alone. *I pray God that it may not be laid to their charge.*" This is the same spirit and attitude in which Jesus prayed, "Father, forgive them, for they know not what they do." Stephen prayed as his enemies stoned him to death, "Lord, lay not this sin to their charge" (Acts 7:60).

Many times God's men prayed that judgment might befall their enemies. Frequently in the Psalms (and on several occasions in Jeremiah) we read prayers for judgment concerning the enemies of God. In Revelation 6:10 the martyrs asked, *"How long* before judgment is poured out upon our enemies?"* In Galatians 5:12 Paul prayed, "I would that they were cut off (dead) which trouble you!" But here, he asks God NOT to lay this sin to the charge of his fellow Christians who left him to stand alone in the face of a subtle, deadly attack on the Gospel—the same Gospel which they had received unto salvation. Alexander was a ruthless foe to the Gospel of the grace of God, but his crime will be punished by the Righteous Judge. God will mete out to him his just reward.

379

Verse 17: "Notwithstanding the Lord stood with me, and strengthened me; that by me the preaching might be fully known, and that all the Gentiles might hear: and I was delivered out of the mouth of the lion."

"The Lord stood with me!" When even our dearest friends turn us down, God will be faithful. Though we may be unfaithful, He must prove true. ". . . He hath said, I will never leave thee, nor forsake thee. So that we may boldly say, The Lord is my helper, and I will not fear what man shall do unto me" (Heb. 13:5,6). Timothy was to have faith in God and not look at circumstances or people around him. Everyone may let him down, but *God* will never fail him nor disappoint him; and when he needs strength, God will strengthen him. When Jesus fell beneath the burden of the sins of the world, His perspiration became as great drops of blood—and there was no one to come to His rescue. Even the favored disciples slept through His agony. *But God sent an angel* to strengthen Him (Luke 22:43). "And being in an agony He prayed more earnestly: and His sweat was as it were great drops of blood falling down to the ground. And when He rose up from prayer, and was come to His disciples, He found them sleeping for sorrow, and said unto them, Why sleep ye? rise and pray, lest ye enter into temptation" (Luke 22:44–46).

Paul said, "In spite of the fact that all of my earthly friends failed me and no one stood with me, the Lord stood with me and gave me strength, *that by me the preaching might be fully known, and that all the Gentiles might hear*: and I was delivered out of the mouth of the lion." He is here using the words spoken in Psalm 22:21: "Save me from the lion's mouth." The devil can take the form of a roaring lion as well as that of an angel of light, if it suits his purpose for the job he is attempting (I Pet. 5:8; II Cor. 11:13–15). The most effective way to handle

380

the devil is to feed him the Word of God as Jesus did on the Mount of Temptation. He can handle anything you or I may say, but he cannot digest God's holy Word. Paul refers to the enemies of the Gospel as "the lion."

For believers, verse 17 paints one of the greatest pictures of the Bible—a picture well known to most Christians. It does not hang in the great art gallery of Scriptures such as John 3:16, Acts 16:31 and Ephesians 2:8, but in a remote corner—the closing paragraph of Paul's last letter. Many believers are well acquainted with this verse and read it often. It is among the jewels in their treasure chest of Scriptures.

The aged apostle to the Gentiles, worn from many labors, much suffering, and sorrows too numerous to mention, cries out: "At my first answer, no man stood with me! Every man forsook me: BUT THE LORD STOOD BY ME!" Whatever may darken our way and blind the spiritual eye, even though we may not be able to see Him in person, the Lord stands by the saint. Mysteriously, not visible to the human eye, He gives power and grace sufficient for trials, temptation, and heartaches.

As Paul sat in the dungeon, the same Jesus whom he met on the Damascus road, whom he had accepted and served with faithfulness, stood by his side—and he was unafraid. God took care of Paul, and He will take care of His preachers and His saints today. The devil cannot destroy a believer without God's permission—and even then he can only destroy the body; *he cannot touch the soul*. Nothing can happen to God's saint or His minister without HIS permission. Trusting God, a believer who lives right, unspotted from the world, is indestructible until God has finished with him here upon this earth.

Verse 18: "And the Lord shall deliver me from every evil work, and will preserve me unto His heavenly kingdom:

to whom be glory for ever and ever. Amen."

On many occasions Paul was delivered "out of the mouth of the lion" (the very jaws of death). In this verse he says, *"The Lord shall deliver me from every evil work, and will preserve me unto His heavenly kingdom."* I believe Paul preached every sermon God intended him to preach, said every word God intended him to say, and made every missionary journey God intended him to make. All hell could not stop him, because he was dedicated unreservedly to God, counting all things loss, that he might gain Christ. He said, "I became as all men are, that I might win some. . . . God forbid that I glory, save in the cross." Every facet of his life was dedicated to the cause of Christ and to the preaching of the Gospel.

"To whom be glory for ever and ever! Amen!" Paul was a bondservant who wanted his Lord to receive all the honor, all the glory, praise, and worship for everything he had ever said or done to advance the cause of Christ. He met Jesus on the road to Damascus—and from that day until he closed his eyes in death, he was a bondslave to the Christ. He lived to preach the Gospel; he made tents in order that he might preach the Gospel without being chargeable to any man—supplying his own physical need, to prevent any criticism or a false impression that he was preaching for money. He preached to the glory of God. He said, *"Woe is me if I preach not the Gospel!"* He wanted a lost world to know the Jesus he had met on the Damascus road. Sitting in a dungeon, chained to an iron ring in a rock wall as he awaited the day of his execution, he could say, "I have fought a good fight, I have finished my course, I have kept the faith. Henceforth a crown awaits me—a crown awaits ALL who love His appearing."

Verses 19 and 20: "Salute Prisca and Aquila, and the household of Onesiphorus. Erastus abode at Corinth:

but Trophimus have I left at Miletum sick."

These are almost the last words of the last letter Paul ever wrote. As always in his letters, he dictated the names of a few personal friends whom he wished to greet personally. Two dear friends of many years, Priscilla and Aquila, were at Ephesus at the time, and Paul wanted Timothy to visit them with his greetings. From Romans 16:3 we know that these dear saints had helped Paul in his ministry, perhaps at the cost of great sacrifice.

Onesiphorus, whose household had also been of great help and comfort to the Apostle, was also to be warmly greeted. Earlier in the letter, Paul prayed that God would have mercy on this household—and now he sends them his personal good wishes, wanting them to know that he loves them and still counts them among his friends.

Next he thinks of Erastus, a friend who lived at Corinth, who is also mentioned in Romans 16:23 and Acts 19:22: "So (Paul) sent into Macedonia two of them that ministered unto him, Timotheus and Erastus; but he himself stayed in Asia for a season" (Acts 19:22). "Gaius mine host, and of the whole church, saluteth you. *Erastus the chamberlain of the city* saluteth you, and Quartus a brother" (Rom. 16:23). According to this Scripture, Erastus was the city treasurer of Corinth, and evidently a Christian.

Paul next mentions his dear friend Trophimus, whom he had left at Miletum, sick. Undoubtedly this dear friend would have traveled to Rome with Paul had he been physically able to do so. He was an Asian Christian, and is mentioned in Acts 20:4 and 21:29: "And there accompanied him into Asia Sopater of Berea; and of the Thessalonians, Aristarchus and Secundus; and Gaius of Derbe, and Timotheus; and of Asia, Tychicus and Trophimus . . . (for they had seen before with him in the city Trophimus an Ephesian, whom they supposed that Paul had brought into the temple.)"

Paul had the gift of healing in his early ministry . . . he even raised the dead; yet he left Trophimus at Miletum, *sick*. Did he lose his *faith*? No! Did he lose the *gift*? No! What happened? As the transition period transpired, many of the gifts, signs and wonders (such as drinking deadly poison, handling poisonous serpents, healing with the touch of the hands, and raising the dead) ceased, when the perfect law of liberty came and all of the Bible was put into writing.

Paul said to the Corinthians, "When that which is perfect is come, then that which is in part shall be done away" (I Cor. 13:10). We do not need to see signs and wonders today in order to believe God: *We believe Him simply because He has spoken*. All Scripture is God's inspired Word, profitable for doctrine, correction, instruction; and through it the man of God is perfectly furnished with all that he needs to preach the Gospel and win souls in this day of grace. *"The just shall live by faith"*—not by signs nor by miracles, not by might nor by power.

Jesus said, "Go ye into all the world, and preach the Gospel to every creature. He that believeth and is baptized shall be saved; but he that believeth not shall be damned. *And these signs shall follow them that believe*; In my name shall they cast out devils; they shall speak with new tongues; they shall take up serpents; and if they drink any deadly thing, it shall not hurt them; they shall lay hands on the sick, and they shall recover" (Mark 16:15–18).

Such gifts belonged to the apostles, and they used them: "Therefore we ought to give the more earnest heed to the things which we have heard, lest at any time we should let them slip. For if the word spoken by angels was stedfast, and every transgression and disobedience received a just recompence of reward; How shall we escape, if we neglect so great salvation; which at the first began to be spoken by the Lord, and was confirmed unto us by them that heard Him; *God also bearing them witness, both with signs and wonders, and with divers miracles, and gifts of the Holy Ghost, according to His own will*?" (Heb. 2:1–4).

There were many signs and wonders during the transition period before the Word of God was written down. These signs and wonders proved that Jesus was the Son of God, Saviour of sinners—but we do not need that proof today: *We have the written Word of God.* So my precious shut-in friends, you who suffer on beds of affliction and long to be well, do not let anyone tell you that the reason you cannot be healed is because you do not have the faith! Just thank God for your salvation—and when Jesus comes you will have a body that is perfect, without disease or handicap.

Verse 21: "Do thy diligence to come before winter. Eubulus greeteth thee, and Pudens, and Linus, and Claudia, and all the brethren."

Paul could have written this second letter to Timothy during the warm days of late summer. In the dungeon it was damp and cold, and Paul was an old man. He needed his cloke, and also wanted to see his dearly beloved son in the Lord; so he urged Timothy to do all in his power to reach the prison in Rome before winter. Paul here spoke from the human standpoint, and from the heart: "*Do thy diligence to come before winter.*" Such a pathetic, soul-rending request from an old saint facing a martyr's death for his faith!

"*Eubulus greeteth thee, and Pudens, and Linus, and Claudia, and all the brethren.*" These are believers who send greetings to Timothy. As has been pointed out, it seems that Dr. Luke is the only one who stayed with Paul day in and day out—but it could be that this little circle of friends were allowed to visit Paul with very special permission.

Verse 22: "The Lord Jesus Christ be with thy spirit. Grace be with you. Amen."

The last message of this dear old apostle closes. "The Lord Jesus Christ be with thy spirit (Timothy). Grace be with you (*all*)." All of the believers in the church at Ephesus and also the other churches where Timothy would visit, were included in this closing. Timothy would make known to them the greetings and prayers of the beloved old saint.

Paul prays that Jesus will be very near and dear to this young preacher, His Spirit abiding closely; and he invokes the eternal power and grace of God to follow Timothy, that he may conduct his ministry to the glory of God for the sake of Christ. He commends his son in the ministry to the Lord Jesus Christ and the grace of God. Thus the farewell of the Apostle Paul, minister to the Gentiles, a man committed to God as possibly no other human was committed. He was dedicated to the spreading of the Gospel without fear or favor, and without mixture. The message Paul had preached was pure grace—minus works, minus law, minus man's wisdom: "For by grace are ye saved through faith; and that not of yourselves: it is the gift of God: Not of works, lest any man should boast" (Eph. 2:8,9).

"Not by works of righteousness which we have done, but according to His mercy He saved us, by the washing of regeneration, and renewing of the Holy Ghost" (Titus 3:5).

I close this book with the sincere prayer that if you who read these lines are not recipients of God's grace, if you are trusting in "religion," church membership, baptism, good works, good living, that you will accept the grace of God this moment.

To those of you who are born again, I close in the words of the Apostle Paul: *"The Lord Jesus Christ be with thy spirit. Grace be with you. Amen!"*

The Epistle of Paul the Apostle
to Titus

THE EPISTLE OF PAUL THE APOSTLE
TO TITUS

INTRODUCTION

Concerning the young man Titus, nothing more is known than what we find in the epistles of Paul. Titus is not mentioned in the Acts of the Apostles, nor does his name appear anywhere in the New Testament except in the writings of Paul.

Through the inspired pen of the Apostle to the Gentiles, we learn that by birth Titus was a Gentile. In Galatians 2:3 he is called a Greek: "But neither Titus, who was with me, *being a Greek*, was compelled to be circumcised." From this verse we learn that up to that time Titus had not been circumcised. Probably up to the time of his conversion he had lived as did other Gentiles and had not been converted to the Jewish faith. The father and mother of Titus were undoubtedly both Greeks—and thus he was distinguished from Timothy, whose mother was a Jewess, although his father was a Greek: "Him (Timothy) would Paul have to go forth with him; and took and circumcised him because of the Jews which were in those quarters: for they knew all that his father was a Greek" (Acts 16:3).

If Titus had been converted to the Jewish faith, it is to be presumed that he would have been commanded to be circumcised according to the Law. Titus 1:4 makes it clear that he was converted to Christianity by the Apostle Paul: "To Titus, *mine own son after the common faith*: Grace, mercy, and peace, from God the Father and the Lord Jesus Christ our Saviour." However, where Titus lived and when he was converted to Christianity are unknown. We have no record of his home nor of the date of his conversion.

391

We do know that he was converted before the fourteenth year of Paul's Christian life, because at that time Titus, a Christian, was with Paul at Jerusalem: "Then fourteen years after I went up again to Jerusalem with Barnabas, and took Titus with me also" (Gal. 2:1). It seems reasonable that Titus lived somewhere in Asia Minor. The Greeks lived there in great numbers; and Paul labored much among them, with many converts to the Christian faith through his preaching to the Greeks. However, it cannot be proven where Titus lived.

Titus went with the Apostle Paul to Jerusalem when Paul, along with Barnabas, was sent there by the church at Antioch to answer certain questions before the apostles and the elders in the church—questions concerning converts among the Gentiles. (Study Acts chapter 15, and compare Galatians 2:1.) It is not known why Paul took Titus with him on that particular journey. It is possible that he was taken to Jerusalem because he was an example through which Paul could illustrate that God had saved Gentiles as well as Jews. Referring to that visit, Paul said, "Neither was Titus compelled to be circumcised." From this statement it seems that Paul pointed out that Titus was a Gentile who had been converted to Christianity and was indeed an example of the believer.

It would seem that the case of Titus was discussed in the meeting at Jerusalem, and some insisted that he be circumcised: "And that because of false brethren unawares brought in, who came in privily to spy out our liberty which we have in Christ Jesus, that they might bring us into bondage" (Gal. 2:4).

Paul and Barnabas, through the help of the Holy Spirit, caused the Jewish brethren (the apostles and the elders in Jerusalem) to agree that it was not necessary that the Gentile converts (known as "heathen") be circumcised: "Wherefore my sentence is, that we trouble not them, which from among the Gentiles are turned to God: But that we write unto them, that they abstain from pollutions of idols, and from fornication, and from things strangled, and from blood" (Acts 15:19,20).

After the council at Jerusalem, Titus probably returned with Paul and Barnabas. Silas and Judas surnamed Barsabas were also in the group: "Then pleased it the apostles and elders with the whole church, to send chosen men of their own company to Antioch with Paul and Barnabas; namely, Judas surnamed Barsabas, and Silas, chief men among the brethren" (Acts 15:22). We believe that later Titus traveled with Paul and labored with him much of the time, because of II Corinthians 8:23: "Whether any do enquire of Titus, he is my partner and fellowhelper concerning you: or our brethren be enquired of, they are the messengers of the churches, and the glory of Christ." Certainly from this statement it would seem that Titus had been with Paul—and even at that time was not well known among the Jewish Christians, some of whom had no doubt asked questions about this young man, desiring to know who he was, and, being a Gentile, what office he held.

There are other verses that seem to assure us that Titus was Paul's companion, and that Paul felt him to be quite essential to his comfort and labor in the Lord: "Nevertheless God, that comforteth those that are cast down, comforted us by the coming of Titus" (II Cor. 7:6). "I had no rest in my spirit, because I found not Titus my brother . . ." (II Cor. 2:13). "Therefore we were comforted in your comfort: yea, and exceedingly the more joyed we for the joy of Titus, because his spirit was refreshed by you all" (II Cor. 7:13). "For Demas hath forsaken me, having loved this present world, and is departed unto Thessalonica; Crescens to Galatia, Titus unto Dalmatia" (II Tim. 4:10). "I desired Titus, and with

393

him I sent a brother. Did Titus make a gain of you? Walked we not in the same spirit? Walked we not in the same steps?" (II Cor. 12:18).

There is reason to believe that Titus spent some time with Paul in Ephesus. The first epistle to the Corinthian church was written at Ephesus and undoubtedly sent to Corinth by Titus. It also seems that Paul, on such an occasion, would certainly send someone in whom he had perfect confidence and who had been traveling with him long enough to be familiar with the doctrine Paul preached. Titus, on this occasion, was sent not only to deliver the epistle to the church in Corinth, but also to endeavor to heal the divisions in the church. He was to complete a collection for the poor saints in the church in Jerusalem—a collection that had already been started, but it had never been completed and delivered to the needy believers in Jerusalem. "Insomuch that we desired Titus, that as he had begun, so he would also finish in you the same grace also" (II Cor. 8:6).

After this, Titus met the Apostle Paul in Macedonia; but whether he was with him when he went with the collection to Jerusalem, and during his imprisonment in Caesarea, or on his voyage to Rome, we have no information, and we do not know. "For, when we were come into Macedonia, our flesh had no rest, but we were troubled on every side; without were fightings, within were fears. Nevertheless God, that comforteth those that are cast down, comforted us by the coming of Titus" (II Cor. 7:5,6).

We next hear of Titus when Paul left him in the island of Crete, that he might "set in order the things that are wanting, and ordain elders in every city . . ." (Titus 1:5). Bible scholars agree that this occurred probably in the year 62 A. D., after Paul's first imprisonment in Rome. It is implied that Paul had undertaken to accomplish some important work there; but something—we know not what—had prevented him from completing the project, and he therefore left Titus to complete the ministry. The arrangements for Titus to stay at Crete were temporary. In Titus 3:12 it is clear that Paul did not intend for him to be a permanent bishop at Crete: "When I shall send Artemas unto thee, or Tychicus, be diligent to come unto me to Nicopolis: for I have determined there to winter."

Titus was with Paul in Rome during his second imprisonment there, although he did not remain with Paul until his trial took place, but left him and went into Dalmatia (II Tim. 4:10). What became of Titus after that, we are not told in the Scriptures. Therefore we will not speculate, even though tradition makes certain suggestions about his ministry and his death. All we *know* is what Paul tells us in his epistles.

Why Paul departed from Crete without completing the work in the church there—and especially without ordaining elders—is not certain. There is a striking resemblance between circumstances here and those which caused Paul to leave Timothy at Ephesus (I Tim. 1:3,4). He left Timothy at Ephesus to complete an important work, and it seems that the same circumstances led him to leave Titus at Crete. We know that Paul was driven out of Ephesus before he had finished the work in the local church there. (Study Acts 19 and 20—the entire chapters.) It could be that some of the same disturbances took place in Crete, and when Paul was forced to leave, he committed the ministry to Titus, instructed him to finish it as soon as possible, and then come to him at Nicopolis (Titus 3:12).

Paul probably wrote the epistle to Titus at Nicopolis. If so, it was probably written after Paul's first imprisonment at Rome, about the year 63 or 64 A. D. Bible scholars do not agree on this, but it is not important that we determine the exact date. We know that Paul wrote the epistle, we have the message, and that is what counts.

The occasion of the Epistle to Titus is specified by Paul, in clear understandable language. He left Titus at Crete to "set in order the things that are wanting, and ordain elders in every city" (Titus 1:5). It seems that Paul left suddenly, and it was extremely important that Titus have more complete instructions concerning the church at Crete than Paul had been able to give him before leaving there. Therefore, the Epistle to Titus is occupied mainly with advice appropriate to a minister of the Gospel, engaged in the duties which Titus was to perform in the local church at Crete. The principal difficulties Titus would meet as he labored there would come primarily from two sources: First, the character of the Cretians, and second, the strong influence of teachers of Judaism. These two things would give Titus more trouble than all other attacks by Satan.

The character of the Cretians themselves was of such a nature that Titus must be alert and vigilant at all times. These people were characterized by insincerity, falsehood, and gross living: "One of themselves, even a prophet of their own, said, *The Cretians are always liars, evil beasts, slow bellies*" (Tit. 1:12). Therefore, there would be great danger that their religion would be shallow and insincere, and Titus must be alert to warn and caution the people lest they be corrupted and led away from the simplicity and purity required in the Gospel message to believers: "This witness is true. Wherefore rebuke them sharply, that they may be sound in the faith" (Tit. 1:13).

Titus must also be alert and diligent concerning the influence of the Judaizing teachers; he must guard against them. It is clear that Jews lived at Crete: ". . . And strangers of Rome, Jews and proselytes, Cretes and Arabians, we do hear them speak in our tongues the wonderful works of God" (Acts 2:10,11). It is probable that through those who had gone from that island to Jerusalem to attend the feast of Pentecost and who had been converted on that occasion, the Gospel of the grace of God was first preached on the island of Crete.

We learn in the Epistle to Titus that one of the great dangers to piety in the churches of Crete arose from the diligent efforts of the teachers of Judaism. They taught a mixture of law and grace—the same argument they had set forth in Ephesus and in the churches of Galatia. (Study carefully Titus 1:10,14–16; 3:9.) In order to keep the believers from succumbing to the arguments of these Judaizers, it was necessary to have true ministers of grace preaching the Gospel in all of its simplicity in every place where the Judaizers were at work. Paul left Titus to appoint men to occupy positions in the different churches where they could keep their eyes and ears open, so that, if Judaizers did begin to teach "another gospel," mixing law and grace, the men appointed by Titus could earnestly contend for the faith and prevent much hurt to the babes in Christ.

There is a very striking resemblance between this epistle and the first epistle to Timothy. Both letters were addressed to young ministers, sons of Paul in the Gospel, left by him to preside in their respective churches during Paul's absence. Both letters are principally occupied in describing the qualifications required for those who are appointed to offices in the local church. Both Timothy and Titus are cautioned concerning the same prevailing corruptions, and in particular against the same misdirection of error that was sure to appear—through the teachers who attempted to mix law and grace.

The minister to the Gentiles (the Apostle Paul), now an old man, attempts to lay heavily upon the hearts of Timothy and Titus the great responsibility that rests upon their shoulders as having to do with their office of authority in the local church. It is a grand and glorious privilege to be a leader in the local church, but it is also a very grave and weighty responsibility. Woe unto the shepherd who allows the wolves to get into the flock, devour the lambs, and scatter the sheep!

THE EPISTLE OF PAUL THE APOSTLE
TO TITUS

CHAPTER ONE

THE DIVINE ORDER FOR LOCAL CHURCHES

1. Paul, a servant of God, and an apostle of Jesus Christ, according to the faith of God's elect, and the acknowledging of the truth which is after godliness;

2. In hope of eternal life, which God, that cannot lie, promised before the world began;

3. But hath in due times manifested his word through preaching, which is committed unto me according to the commandment of God our Saviour;

4. To Titus, mine own son after the common faith: Grace, mercy, and peace, from God the Father and the Lord Jesus Christ our Saviour.

5. For this cause left I thee in Crete, that thou shouldest set in order the things that are wanting, and ordain elders in every city, as I had appointed thee:

6. If any be blameless, the husband of one wife, having faithful children not accused of riot or unruly.

7. For a bishop must be blameless, as the steward of God; not self-willed, not soon angry, not given to wine, no striker, not given to filthy lucre;

8. But a lover of hospitality, a lover of good men, sober, just, holy, temperate;

9. Holding fast the faithful word as he hath been taught, that he may be able by sound doctrine both to exhort and to convince the gainsayers.

10. For there are many unruly and vain talkers and deceivers, specially they of the circumcision:

11. Whose mouths must be stopped, who subvert whole houses, teaching things which they ought not, for filthy lucre's sake.

12. One of themselves, even a prophet of their own, said, The Cretians are alway liars, evil beasts, slow bellies.

13. This witness is true. Wherefore rebuke them sharply, that they may be sound in the faith;

14. Not giving heed to Jewish fables, and commandments of men, that turn from the truth.

15. Unto the pure all things are pure: but unto them that are defiled and unbelieving is nothing pure; but even their mind and conscience is defiled.

16. They profess that they know God; but in works they deny him, being abominable, and disobedient, and unto every good work reprobate.

The Apostle's Salutation

Verse 1: "Paul, a servant of God, and an apostle of Jesus Christ, according to the faith of God's elect, and the acknowledging of the truth which is after godliness."

I Timothy opens: "Paul, an apostle of Jesus Christ by the commandment of God our Saviour, and the Lord Jesus Christ, which is our hope."

II Timothy opens: "Paul, an apostle of Jesus Christ by the will of God, according to the promise of life which is in Christ Jesus."

Titus opens: "Paul, a *servant* of God, AND an apostle of Jesus Christ, ACCORDING TO THE FAITH OF GOD'S ELECT."

The Greek word here translated "according to" means "with reference to." That is, Paul was appointed by Almighty God to be an apostle, as having to do with the faith of those whom God had chosen in Christ to make up the New Testament Church—*as a body*, chosen in Christ by God the Father before the foundation of the world. Paul was chosen by God in order that they might be led to believe the pure Gospel—the Gospel of the grace of God—minus legalism, Judaism, or any other "ism." The Church as a body was chosen by God in the beginning, but the individual becomes a member of the Church of the living God through faith in the finished work of Jesus Christ. The Church as a body was foreordained of God, chosen of God, and known by God; but individuals choose to become members of the New Testament Church by

400

hearing the Gospel and believing the record that God has given of His dear Son (I John 5:10—14).

Paul clearly sets forth at the beginning of each of his epistles the fact that he is *God's* apostle . . . not *of* man, nor *by* man, nor *through the power* of man—but *by the living God.* Paul was chosen and ordained of God to preach the Gospel and make known the good news that Jesus died to provide salvation for all. It is God's good pleasure to save sinners, but the sinner must hear the Word of God and become a believer *by hearing* the Word. Therefore, God sends men—called of God, appointed and anointed by the Holy Ghost—to preach the Word. (Study carefully Romans 10:9—17 and John 5:24.)

Paul, God's servant, an apostle of Jesus, as having to do with the faith of God's elect—the faith once delivered unto the saints (Jude 3)—and the *"acknowledging of the truth."* Paul was ordained of God to preach the truth. Jesus said, "Ye shall know the truth, and the truth shall make you free" (John 8:32). Again, "Sanctify them through thy truth: thy word is truth" (John 17:17). In answer to Thomas when he asked, "We know not whither thou goest; and how can we know the way?" Jesus replied, "I am the way, the truth, and the life: NO MAN COMETH UNTO THE FATHER, BUT BY ME" (John 14:5,6). Only *truth* will set men free from sin. Truth mixed with error will never set sinners free. It must be pure truth—*grace* minus man's tradition, dogma, or doctrine. Paul was a preacher of truth—and he declared that if an angel from heaven, or any other creature (or even Paul himself), should preach any other Gospel than the Gospel of grace, that messenger should be accursed (Gal. 1:8).

Paul was called and ordained to preach the Gospel in order that unbelievers might hear and know the truth. The primary concern of any preacher is to preach the truth among men without fear, favor, or apology, pointing always to the Lord Jesus, the Saviour—the ONLY Saviour, *"for there is none other name under heaven given among men, whereby we must be saved"* (Acts 4:12).

This verse closes with the phrase, *". . . which is after godliness."* That is, *truth received* brings godliness, piety, righteousness. If we walk in the truth, we will become more like Him with whom we walk and fellowship.

God did not call Paul to give book reports or sermonettes on current events. He was not appointed to give out scientific data, historical facts, or political truths. He was called of God to preach the truth as having to do with salvation—truth which, *received*, leads men into salvation. Truth received guides men into holy living and prepares them for a holy heaven. Heaven is a prepared place for a people who prepare to go there at the end of life's journey. Only people *who are prepared* will enter that celestial city—and the only way for anyone to make that preparation is to hear the Word of God and receive "the engrafted Word, which is able to save the soul" (James 1:21).

Verse 2: "In hope of eternal life, which God, that cannot lie, promised before the world began."

"In hope of eternal life" is not speaking of the fact that Paul cherished the hope of eternal life, but that the "faith of the elect," which he aimed to secure, was in order that men might have the hope of eternal life. In the sense used here, it is not Paul's *personal* hope, but that *others* might have hope through the truth that God had given to him to give to the Gentiles. The truth Paul was appointed to preach was designed to secure to man a well-founded hope of true salvation.

In II Timothy 1:8—11 Paul admonished Timothy, "Be not thou therefore ashamed of the testimony of our Lord, nor of me His prisoner: but be thou partaker of the afflictions of the Gospel according to the power of God; *who hath saved us*, and called us with an holy calling, not according to our works, but according to His own PURPOSE and grace, which was given us in Christ Jesus before the world began, but is now made manifest by the appearing of our Saviour Jesus Christ, who hath abolished death, and hath brought life and immortality to light through the Gospel: Whereunto I am appointed a preacher, and an apostle, and a teacher of the Gentiles."

In other words, Paul wanted Timothy to know for sure that he was dedicated, preaching the truth, and making known the hope which poor sinners can possess *if they will embrace Christianity by faith in the finished work of Jesus.* Paul was appointed to preach the truth, that men might know Christ and have the hope of salvation—the hope that *he* possessed in his own bosom because he obeyed the words of Jesus on the road to Damascus.

"*. . .WHICH GOD, THAT CANNOT LIE, PROMISED.*" In Hebrews 6:18 Paul declares a second time that God cannot lie: "That by two immutable things, in which *it was impossible for God to lie*, we might have a strong consolation, who have fled for refuge to lay hold upon the hope set before us." God cannot lie. His nature always speaks the truth. No circumstance can arise which will cause God to depart from the truth. *This fact is the foundation* of all our hopes concerning salvation and eternal peace with God.

Man—even the most dedicated, consecrated person— can lie. I would not knowingly lie to you, dear reader, for all the money in the world; but it is not *impossible* for me to lie. The very fact that God is GOD makes it impossible for HIM to lie. God is holy; He is righteous; He is truth—and truth cannot become a lie. If truth is stated, it can never be anything BUT truth—and *God is truth!*

"In the beginning was the Word, and the Word was with God, and the Word was God. . . . And the Word was made flesh, and dwelt among us, (and we beheld His glory, the glory as of the only begotten of the Father,) full of grace and TRUTH" (John 1:1,14). It is not impossible that between the covers of any book on earth (besides the Bible) there could be a lie—or many lies; but the holy Word of God is truth: "Sanctify them through thy truth: thy Word is truth" (John 17:17); and according to Jesus, God will judge according to His Word:

"He that rejecteth me, and receiveth not my words, hath one that judgeth him: *the Word that I have spoken, the same shall judge him in the last day*" (John 12:48).

"*. . . Promised . . . .*" The only hope of salvation is in the promise of God. Regardless of whether or not you understand what you read in the Bible, IT IS TRUTH! The God who cannot lie promised salvation to all who will hear His Word and believe on His Son; but He also promises that all who refuse to believe His Word and trust in His Son must be damned: "Verily, verily, I say unto you, He that heareth my Word, and believeth on Him that sent me, hath everlasting life, and shall not come into condemnation; but is passed from death unto life" (John 5:24).

HEAR THIS: "He that believeth on the Son of God hath the witness in himself: he that believeth not God hath made Him a liar; because he believeth not the record that God gave of His Son" (I John 5:10). If we refuse to believe the record of God we thereby brand Him a liar— but what IS the record God has given?

"And this is the record, that God hath given to us eternal life, and this life is in His Son. He that hath the Son hath life; and he that hath not the Son of God hath not life. These things have I written unto you that believe on the name of the Son of God; that ye may know that ye have eternal life, and that ye may believe on the name of the Son of God" (I John 5:11—13).

The record God has given is simply this: God the Father gives to us eternal life, and the life that He gives us is His Son. If we have the Son of God, we have everlasting life; if we have *not* the Son of God, we do not have life. The way we possess the Son of God is to believe in His finished work and receive Him by faith according to the record God has given. When we believe on the Lord Jesus Christ, the Holy Spirit comes into our hearts to assure us, to lead us, and to seal us (Rom. 8:9,14—16; Eph. 4:30). It is a serious thing to hear the Word of God, to know that God so loved the world that He gave Jesus to die for sinners—and then refuse to accept the Lord Jesus. Such action on the part of an unbeliever is sin enough to damn that soul to the lowest hell.

The only hope of salvation is in the promise of God. If we do not find salvation in God's promise, then there IS no salvation! Salvation is for "whosoever will." Christ died for the sins of the whole world (I John 2:2; John 3:16).

For all who desire to know the truth minus dogma and tradition, one verse will suffice: "The Lord is not slack concerning His *promise*, as some men count slackness; but is longsuffering to us-ward, NOT WILLING THAT ANY SHOULD PERISH, BUT THAT ALL SHOULD COME TO REPENTANCE" (II Pet. 3:9). This verse needs no explanation.

God has made a general promise that they who repent and believe shall be saved. Anyone hearing the Word of God, believing that Christ died for the ungodly; anyone who will trust in the Lord Jesus Christ, believing that He was crucified, buried, and that He rose again; anyone who will receive the Lord Jesus on the terms

405

of the Gospel—*God will save.*

To the jailer in Philippi who asked, "Sirs, what must I do to be saved?" Paul and Silas said, "Believe on the Lord Jesus Christ, and thou shalt be saved, and thy house. *And they spake unto him the Word of the Lord*, and to all that were in his house. And he took them the same hour of the night, and washed their stripes; and was baptized, he and all his, straightway . . . and rejoiced, believing in God with all his house" (Acts 16:31 ff). The jailer was saved by hearing the Word of God. (Faith comes by hearing, and hearing by the Word.) We are saved by grace through faith—"and that not of ourselves: it is the gift of God." All persons who have entered (or who *will* enter) the rest of God, have entered (or will enter) because of hearing and believing the Word of Him who cannot lie, the Word of Him who promised.

You, dear reader, are invited to believe on the Lord Jesus Christ—*"and thou shalt be saved."* God, who cannot lie, made this promise *"before the world began."* What the Holy Spirit is saying here, through the inspired pen of Paul, is that the *purpose* was formed before God formed the universe. Before God created this earth or anything therein, God the Father, God the Son, and God the Holy Ghost planned, perfected, and finished salvation (I Peter 1:18—25).

I believe in the sovereignty of God. God knows the end, and has known it from the beginning. God HAD no beginning (Psalm 90:1,2). In the beginning, *God was.* I do not understand it, but I believe it—and I am happy that I do *not* understand the sovereignty of God. If I did, I would be sovereign; I would be equal with God— and I am glad that my God is greater than I! The sovereignty of God has nothing to do with the free will of man. God provided salvation for "whosoever," but whosoever is saved must *as an individual* have faith in God.

Verse 3: "But hath in due times manifested His Word through preaching, which is committed unto me according to the commandment of God our Saviour."

"But hath in due times"—that is, at the appointed time, at the proper time, the time which God intended—the BEST time. In Genesis 3:15 God promised the seed of the woman. In Galatians 4:4 Paul tells us that in the fulness of time, Jesus came—born of a woman. God has a plan; God has a program—and His plan will be worked out in every minute detail. All hell cannot stop Him, regardless of how fervently sin and sinners attempt to frustrate His plan. He who is sovereign and all-powerful will reign supreme in the end, and throughout the endless ages.

In due times God has *"manifested His Word through preaching."* The meaning here is simply that God has made known His eternal purpose through the preaching of the Gospel—the good news that the spotless Lamb has been slain, the blood has been shed, and God accepted the perfect, righteous, sinless sacrifice of His only begotten Son Jesus. This is good news to the sinner, whom God could and should damn in the lake of fire forever. But since Jesus took our place and overcame in all details—physical, mental, spiritual, earthly, or whatsoever; since He conquered the world, the flesh, the devil, death, hell, and the grave, and has the keys of hell and the grave, *He is now seated at the right hand of God the Father, exalted.* In Him the Father is well pleased, and Jesus now mediates between God and man. This is the good news of the Gospel. God has made known His eternal purpose through the preaching of the Gospel.

God committed this message to Paul—and not only to him, but to others. Paul wanted Titus to know for sure that the message he delivered was God's inspired Word, given to him by God and not obtained from man. But he

407

goes further, to explain, ". . . *according to the commandment of God our Saviour.*"

Paul points out again and again that he was divinely commissioned, and that he was engaged in the work of preaching the Gospel by the authority of Almighty God. Please study Galatians 1:1,11,12; I Corinthians 1:1; Romans 1:1–5. In all these Scriptures Paul clearly points out the fact that God called him, ordained him, sent him forth—*and provided the message he was to preach*! That message was the Gospel—"the power of God unto salvation to every one that believeth; to the Jew first, and also to the Greek" (Rom. 1:16). In that Gospel is revealed the righteousness of God, and that the just shall live by faith (Rom. 1:17).

In this verse of our present chapter, Paul refers to *"God our Saviour."* In our testimonies we often thank the Lord Jesus for saving us—and that is as it should be; but we should also "joy in God," because it is God who so loved us that He turned His head while His only Son paid our sin-debt. Never forget that God saves us "FOR JESUS' SAKE" (Eph. 4:32). Had it not been for the love of the Lord Jesus and His willingness to take our place on the cross and die the death that we *should* have died, you and I would be destined to be damned. Jesus bore our sins in His own body on the cross—and did it willingly. He endured the cross, despising its shame, for the joy that was set before Him—the Church without spot or wrinkle, the Church for which He died (Eph. 5:25–30; Heb. 12:1,2; Eph. 2:4–7).

Verse 4: "To Titus, mine own son after the common faith: Grace, mercy, and peace, from God the Father and the Lord Jesus Christ our Saviour."

"To Titus, *mine own son after the common faith.*" This definitely tells us that Paul led this young man into

408

salvation. He was Paul's son in the faith, as was Timothy (I Tim. 1:2). *"After the common faith"* does not mean that saving faith is ordinary or common in the sense that it is of low origin, or cheap. *"Common"* denotes *"belonging to all,"* in contrast to "one's own"—or as distinct from what is peculiar to a few. This verse refers to the faith of all believers; and what Paul is saying here is simply, "Titus, my son in the Gospel." Paul had begotten Titus, and he was born into the family of God through the Gospel—". . . the engrafted Word, which is able to save your souls" (James 1:21).

". . . *Grace, mercy, and peace* . . . ." Grace precedes mercy; apart from grace there IS no mercy. God could send each of us to hell—and rightly so. God is holy . . . He is righteous; we have sinned, and "the wages of sin is death." But by grace we can be saved; God can be just and yet justify the ungodly. Apart from grace there is no mercy, and apart from grace there is no *peace*. But, "being justified by faith, we have peace with God through our Lord Jesus Christ" (Rom. 5:1). Grace, mercy, and peace come *"from God the Father and the Lord Jesus Christ our Saviour."*

Jude refers to the *common salvation*: "Beloved, when I gave all diligence to write unto you of the common salvation, it was needful for me to write unto you, and exhort you that ye should earnestly contend for the faith which was once delivered unto the saints" (Jude 3). The "common salvation" has the same meaning as "common" in Titus 1:4 . . . it is ONE salvation—all men, regardless of race, creed, or whatsoever, are saved alike. *"Common faith"* is ONE faith—for there is only one: Faith in the Lord Jesus Christ. The question is not the *amount* of faith nor the *kind* of faith you have, but IN WHOM DO YOU HAVE YOUR FAITH? *"What think ye of Christ? Whose Son is He?"* (Matt. 22:42). If you believe that

Jesus is the Christ, the Son of God, then you are born of God (I John 5:1). The sin-question is settled; it was settled when Jesus said, "It is finished!" It is the *Son*-question, now.

Jesus asked His disciples, "Whom do men say that I the Son of man am? And they said, Some say that thou art John the Baptist: some, Elias; and others, Jeremias, or one of the prophets." Jesus then asked, "But whom say YE that I am? And Simon Peter answered and said, *Thou art the Christ, the Son of the living God*" (Matt. 16:13-16). In John 6:53 Jesus said, ". . . Except ye eat my flesh and drink my blood, ye have no life in you." And when He said this, ". . . many of His disciples went back, and walked no more with Him. Then said Jesus unto the twelve, Will ye also go away? Then Simon Peter answered Him, LORD, TO WHOM SHALL WE GO? *Thou hast the words of eternal life*" (John 6:53-68).

Today we hear much about "church unity . . . co-existence . . . one-world church"—and all denominations joining together to write a common Bible. But such teaching is foreign to the Word of God! We have THE Bible, the Word of God; and regardless of what modernists may say or do, *all men are saved alike.* The faith that saves is "common faith"; the salvation it brings is "common salvation." Jesus is not *A* door . . . *a* way . . . *a* good shepherd . . . *a* life. He is THE Way, THE Door, THE Good Shepherd, THE Life. He is THE Bread, THE Light, THE Water—*He is our life!* In John 14:6 He said, *"No man cometh unto the Father, but by me."*

Instructions Concerning Bishops

Verse 5: "For this cause left I thee in Crete, that thou shouldest set in order the things that are wanting, and ordain elders in every city, as I had appointed thee."

"For this cause left I thee in Crete." Paul had

departed from the island of Crete—perhaps hurriedly—and had instructed Titus to set in order the things that were "wanting"—the things that were *left undone*. No doubt Paul refers to some arrangements which he had begun but found it impossible to complete (for reasons not discussed in this epistle). Whether he was driven from the Isle because of persecution, or called away on other duties demanding his attention in other assemblies, we do not know.

The Greek word for "set in order" occurs nowhere else in all of the New Testament. It means "properly . . . to make straight upon . . . to put further to rights." It is used "in the sense of setting right again what was defective, a commission to Titus, not to add to what the Apostle himself had done, but to restore what had fallen in disorder since the Apostle had laboured in Crete; this is suggested by the *epi*" (by W. E. Vine, in the Greek Lexicon). There were many things left unfinished, which Titus was to set in order, make straight, and arrange in the absence of Paul—perhaps the most outstanding one being to appoint elders in the cities where the Gospel had been preached and local assemblies had been founded. Titus was to *"ordain elders in every city."* The word "ordain," as having to do with elders, deacons, or ministers, means "to invest with a ministerial function or power; to introduce, establish, and settle in the pastoral office, with the customary forms and solemnities" (Webster).

Titus was to appoint and set men over the churches—but with what ceremony we do not know, because it is not stated here. There is no reason to suppose that he did this except as a result of the choice of the people. He did not set himself up as a "lord over God's heritage" nor as a spiritual dictator. Elders (or as the Greek would have it, "presbyters") were also called bishops—for Paul, in describing their qualifications (verses 6–9), calls them

411

bishops (also compare I Timothy 3:1). ". . . Ordain elders in every city . . . if any be blameless . . . FOR a *bishop* must be blameless . . . ." If elders and bishops in the days of the apostles were of different ranks, this instruction given to Titus would be wholly without meaning—and certainly Paul did not put words in these epistles just to fill up space. According to W. E. Vine in his Expository Dictionary of New Testament Words, the terms are identical in meaning:

"*EPISKOPOS*—literally an overseer (*epi*, over, *skopeo*, to look or watch), whence Eng. 'bishop,' which has precisely the same meaning, is found in Acts 20:28; Phil. 1:1; I Tim. 3:2; Tit. 1:7; I Pet. 2:25. *Presbuteros*, an elder, is another term for the same person as bishop or overseer. See Acts 20:17 with verse 28. The term 'elder' indicates the mature spiritual experience and understanding of those so described; the term 'bishop,' or overseer,' indicates the character of the work undertaken. According to the Divine will and appointment, as in the New Testament, there were to be bishops in every local church, Acts 14:23; 20:17; Phil. 1:1; Tit. 1:5; Jas. 5:14. Where the singular is used, the passage is describing what a bishop should be, I Tim. 3:1; Tit. 1:7. Christ Himself is spoken of as 'the . . . Bishop of our souls,' I Pet. 2:25."

The qualifications which Paul gives concerning bishops are not those which pertain to church prelates, or bishops of a diocese, as we know them in the church today. On the contrary, here it has to do with an overseer such as a pastor of a church, or an evangelist. It is clearly set forth in verse 7 that the men whom Titus was to appoint were bishops, and yet it is certainly absurd to suppose that Paul meant bishops such as we know them in some of the religions and denominations today.

"*In every city* . . . ." According to the modern idea

of a bishop, ONE would have been sufficient for Crete; but Titus was commanded to appoint bishops in *every* city.

There were many cities on the island of Crete. Some historians suggest that there were between ninety and one hundred cities on the island, and it may therefore be presumed that some of them were towns with but a few inhabitants. It certainly would not seem probable that each of these cities—or villages, as the case may have been—would have been large enough for a bishop as we think of bishops in the local church today. I am sure Paul hoped that as Titus visited the various cities to appoint bishops there, local assemblies would be founded in the towns where none had yet been organized. Thus new churches would be brought into existence through the preaching of the Gospel by this young man whom Paul called "mine own son after the common faith."

". . . *As I had appointed thee.*" The Greek here means, "As I commanded thee . . . or, gave thee direction." This is a different word than the one used in the former part of the verse and rendered "ordain." Paul did not instruct Titus to ordain elders in the same manner that Paul had ordained him. But Titus was to appoint men to be over the local church in the different cities, and to do it as he had been *directed* by the Apostle Paul. No doubt Paul had given oral instructions to Titus before he left, and laid down exactly how it was to be done. Titus was to follow Paul's instructions because those instructions came from the Lord.

Verse 6: "If any be blameless, the husband of one wife, having faithful children not accused of riot or unruly."

There were men in the churches in Crete who met these qualifications for an elder, but they had not yet been appointed. Paul instructed Titus to make such

413

appointments, and he then lays down the qualifications so that no mistake will be made on the part of Titus in appointing the right persons to fill these responsible positions.

Elder and bishop designate the same office. Read Acts 10:17 and 28. You will note that the word is always plural, never singular. There is no account of just one elder in a local church. The duties and functions of elders are to rule in the local assembly (I Tim. 3:4,5; 5:17). They are to guard the body of revealed truth, forbidding error to enter in, which perverts the truth as revealed to the Apostle Paul (Titus 1:9). Elders "oversee" the local church in the same fashion as a shepherd oversees his flock (Acts 20:28; John 21:16; Heb. 13:17; I Pet. 5:2). Elders are "set" in the churches by the Holy Spirit (Acts 20:28), and great stress is laid upon their due appointment (Acts 14:23; Tit. 1:5).

In the early days of the New Testament church, elders were *ordained*--the Greek word means "to elect . . . to designate with the hand." In Acts 14:23 the elders were elected or appointed by the laying on of the hands of the apostles. In Timothy and Titus the qualifications for an elder become a definite part of the Scriptures laid down for the guidance of the local churches in appointing elders (I Tim. 3:1–7).

"If any be blameless, the husband of one wife . . . ." In I Timothy 3:2 we explained this fully, and all that need be said here is that a bishop must be a one-wife man. There is no place in the church for a bishop or an elder with two living wives. Because of the important office he holds, a bishop must be *blameless* in all things. It is possible for a believer to live a blameless life if fully surrendered and wholly dedicated to the will of God and led by the Spirit of God. The first qualification a bishop must meet is that he be "blameless, the

414

husband of one wife."

". . . *Having faithful children.*" (Notice also I Timothy 3:4,5.) What Paul is saying here is that an elder or bishop must have a well-governed family, a family which fully respects him, a family well trained in spiritual matters. If the family of a bishop were insubordinate and opposed to spiritual matters, or if members of the family were unbelievers or scoffers, that man could not be entrusted with the government of the church of the living God.

It is clearly set forth here that an elder or bishop must be a family man, with a wife and children who respect him to the fullest degree. His family must be spiritually minded; they must love the church and the things of God and cooperate with the head of the family in all things. If a man cannot rule his own house and lead his own family concerning spiritual matters, how could he direct the church? If he were a man who did not have the respect of his family, he could not hope to have the respect of the church.

Verse 7: "For a bishop must be blameless, as the steward of God; not self-willed, not soon angry, not given to wine, no striker, not given to filthy lucre."

Paul is here stressing that in order to perform the duties of a bishop, a man should be blameless—one against whom no accusation could be brought. A bishop must not be self-willed (note II Peter 2:10). The Greek word used here does not occur anywhere else in the New Testament. It means "self-complacent, assuming, arrogant, imperious." One who is self-complacent is not fit for the office of a bishop. A person who is dogmatic, impatient, unyielding, haughty, is not fit for the office of bishop. A bishop is not to compromise with error or evil; neither is he to be self-willed and selfish. Self-centered people cannot represent the Lord Jesus, the most unselfish One who ever lived upon the face of this earth.

Paul said, "I become as all men are, that I might win some." Certainly HE was no compromiser when it had to do with preaching the pure grace of God and the pure Gospel, without fear, favor, or apology!

"Not soon angry." It is the divine duty and very special responsibility of leaders in the church to be an example of the believer in every phase of life, regardless of whether that leader be minister, deacon, Sunday school teacher, or evangelist. Paul referred to the Christians as "living epistles, read of men." In all that we do and say, we should exemplify Christ. We should walk so close to Jesus and be so completely yielded to the Holy Spirit that others would see Jesus in our lives.

Therefore, a bishop must not be one who becomes angry at the least little thing that may come his way, with which he does not agree or which he does not appreciate. He cannot "fly off the handle" or give people "a piece of his mind." If he is to represent the Lord Jesus Christ, he must exercise love, compassion, humility, and sacrifice as did his Lord in all that He did while here on earth.

"Not given to wine." Greek authorities tell us that the literal translation here should read, "Not ready to quarrel and offer wrong, as one in wine." This Greek word occurs only twice in the New Testament—here in verse 7, and in I Timothy 3:3. By way of comparison, Paul is saying, "A bishop should not act or speak like those who are speaking over wine, as in revelry." We might illustrate in this way:

Persons who sit over wine and continue to drink will become boisterous and loud. In many instances, arguments arise and sometimes lead to bodily injury. A

416

bishop—or any leader in the church—simply must not show that kind of spirit. He must be a peaceable man, not quarrelsome. Wine usually produces a spirit of contention and strife that a bishop must never show.

In Ephesians 5:18 Paul said, "Be not drunk with wine, wherein is excess; but be filled with the Spirit." A bishop should be filled with the Spirit, thus bearing the *fruit* of the Spirit, which is "love, joy, peace, long-suffering, gentleness, goodness, faith, meekness, temperance: against such there is no law" (Gal. 5:22,23).

"Not given to filthy lucre." A bishop must not be desirous of base gain financially. For leaders in the church to be desirous of "filthy lucre" is strongly condemned everywhere in the New Testament, but especially with regard to a minister of the Gospel. A preacher has a right to a livelihood, and the church should support him (study I Corinthians chapter 9); but nothing will hinder the usefulness of a minister of the Gospel so quickly and completely as will the love of money.

Paul warned Timothy, ". . . The *love of money* is the root of all evil" (I Tim. 6:10a). It is extremely important that ministers of the Gospel and leaders in the local assembly be examples of what men should be in their daily walk . . . in business, in the community, and in relationship with their fellowman. No true minister of the Gospel preaches for money. Certainly "the labourer is worthy of his hire" (Luke 10:7; I Tim. 5:18); but Paul tells us, ". . . My God shall supply all your need according to His riches in glory by Christ Jesus" (Phil. 4:19). If God calls a man to preach the Word, God is also able to supply his every need if that minister is willing to trust God and lean not to his own understanding.

Verse 8: "But a lover of hospitality, a lover of good men, sober, just, holy, temperate."

417

"... *Lover of hospitality*"—(see the discussion on I Timothy 3:2).

"*A lover of good*" ... *anything* that is good, pure, righteous, upright. It may refer to good men—men of honest report, men who have a good testimony. It may refer to a good cause which benefits suffering humanity—the right kind of charity, carried on in the name of the Lord Jesus, the greatest Giver of all. A bishop must be filled and permeated by love; he must be hospitable in all things. One who holds this office in the local church should love every good thing in the community and be ready to promote everything that is good and upright, everything that will glorify God. He should love every good man—whether they belong to the same church, or not. He should not make enemies by splitting hairs over denominational points.

The bishop must be "*sober*"—not only with reference to abstinence from liquors, but also concerning other things. The word means "sober-minded," or self-controlled, temperate, or discreet. A bishop is to be temperate and sober in all walks of life and behaviour; he is not to become drunk on pride, temper—nor any other way.

Not only should he be sober—he must also be "*just.*" He must be honest, upright, open and aboveboard in all of his dealings with his fellowman. He must be a "*holy*" man. The world watches the lives of all believers, especially the lives of the leaders in the local assembly. It is of utmost importance that a bishop be careful to live above reproach. Any leader in the church can do little good if he is not holy in his living, faithfully dedicated to God in all his duties, holding his passions and appetites under absolute control. Read Acts 24:25; I Corinthians 7:9; 9:25; and Galatians 5:23.

A bishop of God must be "*calm minded.*" He must not be self-willed; he must not "fly off the handle" and

418

say ugly words. He must not be one who occasionally drinks wine or who is greedy after money. If he is not a sober, just, holy man, temperate in all things, better had he never been born than to profess to be a leader in the things of God and yet, by his daily living, hinder the cause of Christ and bring reproach upon the testimony of the church in the community!

Verse 9: "Holding fast the faithful word as he hath been taught, that he may be able by sound doctrine both to exhort and to convince the gainsayers."

"*Holding fast the faithful word*" refers to the true doctrines of the Gospel. A bishop is to hold fast to pure doctrine and oppose anyone who would bring in error or teach false doctrine in the community or in the local assembly. He is to definitely oppose all systems of false philosophy. He must be a man who is firm in doctrine, in his belief concerning the faith once delivered unto the saints. He must be a man who can be relied upon and trusted concerning spiritual matters and depended upon to maintain and defend the pure Gospel of the grace of God which Paul had so fervently and uncompromisingly preached, and by which hundreds had been converted to Christianity and local assemblies had been established. A bishop must be a man of strong character as well as of clean heart and blameless life.

"*As he hath been taught.*" This statement makes it quite clear that a bishop should be one who has been taught—not a novice, a learner, nor a babe in Christ. He is to be a man well established in the Word of God, according to the teaching which was preached by Paul— the apostle to whom God revealed the truth of the Gospel of the marvelous grace of God.

This does not mean *as he individually* had been taught, but that he was to hold fast the pure doctrine of faith as it had been delivered by men whom God had appointed to make known the good news of the Gospel to mankind. *"The faithful word"* (doctrine or teaching) denotes the Gospel which had been communicated to mankind by the Holy Ghost as God spoke to men appointed of God—holy men—and gave to them the message they were to give to the world . . . not a message of human reason, but a message by divine teaching—yea, as the Holy Ghost spoke to holy men, they penned down and taught the doctrine.

". . . That he may be able by sound doctrine both to exhort and to convince the gainsayers." The bishop or minister, by sound doctrine and Bible teaching, was not only to denounce the gainsayers, but through the pure Gospel he was to seek to *convince* them. He was not to compromise with them, but neither was he to be a dictator who might drive them away instead of seeking to convince them that the truth of God makes men free. The bishop was to "exhort *and* convince." He was to persuade them, if at all possible, to turn from error and embrace the truth, thereby becoming believers and children of the living God rather than servants of dead idols, after the manner of the believers in Thessalonica: "For they themselves shew of us what manner of entering in we had unto you, *and how ye turned to God from idols to serve the living and true God*; and to wait for His Son from heaven, whom he raised from the dead, even Jesus, which delivered us from the wrath to come" (I Thess. 1:9,10).

A good minister of the Gospel uses both exhortation and argument. Those who know the truth (but need encouragement to follow it) need to be exhorted and admonished *concerning* the truth; while those who are ignorant and unlearned (never having been exposed to the truth) and those who are *opposed* to the truth need both

420

exhortation AND argument. We should *exhort* them to turn to Christ—and then give them a sound argument as to why they *should* turn to Christ. We should "be ready always to give an answer to every man that asketh . . . a reason of the hope that is in (us) with meekness and fear" (I Pet. 3:15). We should be able to present a sound argument for being a believer and following Christ.

". . . *The gainsayers.*" These were simply opposers of the Gospel. The Greek reads, "Those who speak against" the Gospel. The gainsayers were definitely opposed to the truth of the death, burial, and resurrection of the Lord Jesus according to the Scriptures: "But to Israel He saith, All day long have I stretched forth my hands unto a disobedient and gainsaying people" (Rom. 10:21).

Warnings Against False Teachers

Verse 10: "For there are many unruly and vain talkers and deceivers, specially they of the circumcision."

In this verse we learn that there were many people in Crete who were definitely opposed to Christianity. Some were Gentiles, and some were "of the circumcision" (Jews). Many were indisposed to submit to authority and hear the dogmatic preaching of Paul and his co-laborers. Many were vain talkers, *professing* with their lips but *denying* in their hearts and by their daily living. These vain talkers *talked religion*—but lived lives which did not coincide with their oral testimony. They operated under the guise of religion, but were given more to *talk* than to the duties of practical Christianity. Jesus called them "wolves in sheep's clothing," and said, "By their fruits ye shall know them." Such people make a great show of piety, but inwardly they are filthy vessels—clean only on the outside.

421

"Specially they of the circumcision" points out the Jews who urged the Gentile Christians to be circumcised, and demanded that they follow this custom of the Law in order to be saved. The fifteenth chapter of Acts records that a special council was held in Jerusalem concerning this matter. (Read the entire chapter.) This statement also assures us that there were many Jews in the island of Crete. Paul knew Titus would meet with much opposition from the legalizers and Judaizers, and therefore gave this warning.

Verse 11: "Whose mouths must be stopped, who subvert whole houses, teaching things which they ought not, for filthy lucre's sake."

We are told that the Greek word used here for *"stopped"* is not found anywhere else in the New Testament. This is its singular occurrence, and it means "to check, to curb, as with a bridle; to restrain or bridle in, to put to silence." What Paul is saying to Titus is simply this: "They must be checked. This error must be stopped. We cannot permit these teachers to continue sowing their seed of error."

Paul was not suggesting that civil power be brought in to put down these oppressors of the Gospel; he meant that they must be stopped in a Christian way. The Word of God *will* silence teachers of error, and the only agency to be used in such cases is exhortation and presentation of the truth. These are proper means of silencing false teachers.

I have said many times in my meetings that a minister who allows a crooked board of deacons to run him out of town, SHOULD be run out of town! "For the Word of God is quick, and powerful, and sharper than any two-edged sword, piercing even to the dividing asunder of soul and spirit, and of the joints and marrow, and is a discerner of the thoughts and intents of the heart" (Heb. 4:12). The Word of God is "like as a fire . . . *and like a hammer that breaketh the rock in pieces*" (Jer. 23:29).

If a minister preaches the Word in all of its purity and power, he has a message that *cuts*—going and coming. He has a message which, like a hammer, crushes and drives in truth, driving out error. The minister of the Gospel has the dynamite and the power to drive out wrong and implant truth. False teachers cannot stay long where the truth is fervently, uncompromisingly, and consistently preached from the pulpit! Ministers need no message other than the message of God: "I will instruct thee and teach thee in the way which thou shalt go: I will guide thee with mine eye. Be ye not as the horse, or as the mule, which have no understanding: whose mouth must be held in with bit and bridle, lest they come near unto thee" (Psalm 32:8,9).

These gainsayers ". . . *subvert whole houses.*" They were turning whole families away from the truth. (Read also Matthew 23:14 and II Timothy 3:6.) They were *"teaching things which they ought not, for filthy lucre's sake."* For gain, they taught doctrines that made them popular, drawing people to them, causing their followers to have confidence in them and contribute money *to them* instead of to the local assembly.

It is possible that they were telling the people that they needed offerings for the relief of the poor; or perhaps they would suggest that they help Christians in other localities where the church was being persecuted. It is not unlikely that these false teachers and gainsayers asked for money for *themselves*, suggesting that they were destitute, hungry, and very poor.

Religion has the strongest appeal for funds of any enterprise on earth. Lying prophets have caused innocent people to give their life's savings to what they thought was a worthy cause, when actually the money went into the coffers of some false teacher who was greedy for filthy lucre with which to "feather his own nest" and live like a king—while, through lies and hypocrisy, he caused trusting people to give their money to him.

In all ages since the church began there have been religious imposters and racketeers who have taken advantage of the power of religion, to obtain money from their deluded followers. Christians cannot be too careful about their giving. It is the duty of every believer to contribute to the support of the Gospel. It is a duty (as well as a glorious privilege) to promote every good cause, and spread the good news of salvation to the ends of the earth; *but it is no less the duty of every Christian to carefully examine every cause he or she supports!*

We will be held responsible for every dollar we give. It matters not how sincerely we give it, if it is used in the wrong way we will be held responsible, along with the one who misuses God's funds. We should never give to any person nor to any cause until we know for sure that our gift is going to promote that for which we give it.

During my years as a minister of the Gospel I have learned some things concerning money matters that I wish I had not learned. I have discovered that there are many religious racketeers. I shall never cease to thank God for the seasoned ministers and legal advisers who helped me in the early days of my ministry, in setting up a financial system which is above reproach from the standpoint of state and civil authority, as well as from the standpoint of being a good steward of God's money. I thank God that I can face the world, I can face every individual, and I can face God in eternity with every dollar that has been placed in my hands since I began preaching the Gospel.

There are counterfeit evangelists, counterfeit Bible teachers, counterfeit pastors—but we cannot condemn all evangelists, Bible teachers, and pastors just because of those who are insincere. There may be a few rotten apples in a barrel, but we do not discard the entire barrel of apples because of the few that are spoiled. Jesus chose twelve disciples, and one of them was a devil; but in that same disciple band were eleven other men who followed Jesus because they loved Him. Judas will always be with us in spirit and in practice, but so will John the Beloved be with us in like manner. It is sad that there are religious racketeers, but we do have them— and as the end approaches there will be more and more such men. We must therefore be extremely cautious about our giving.

Verse 12: "One of themselves, even a prophet of their own, said, The Cretians are alway liars, evil beasts, slow bellies."

"One of themselves" . . . (one of the Cretians). Probably the reason Paul emphasizes this is that he wants the believers to be cautious concerning their own people, as well as being on guard against the Jewish teachers of error. Cretians as well as Judaizers were teaching error and were guilty of seeking after "filthy lucre."

". . . *Even a prophet* . . . ." The word used for "prophet" in this verse was, in Paul's day, often applied also to a *poet*. The Greeks looked upon their poets as inspired men, believing that they wrote under inspiration of the gods. Thus, the prophet referred to in this verse could have been a poet. The Dictionary of New Testament Words goes so far as to name the poet Epimenides, in reference to this verse.

425

"The Cretians are alway liars, evil beasts, slow bellies." It was very important that Titus be careful in selecting persons for leadership in the churches on the island of Crete, for the people there—both Jews and Cretians—were well known for their unwholesome character. The Cretians were known as being "always liars." Quoting from the writer Wetstin: "To be a Cretian became synonymous with being a liar, in the same way as to be a Corinthian became synonymous with living a licentious life." Thus the scholiast says, *"To act the Cretian is a proverb for 'To lie.'"*

The reason for this characteristic is unknown, although Bishop Warburton suggests that the Cretians acquired this label because they claimed to have among them the tomb of Jupiter. They also claimed that such gods as Jupiter were only mortals who had been raised to divine honors—and because of this, the Greeks maintained that the Cretians always proclaimed a falsehood by asserting this opinion concerning the gods. Whatever the reason for it, the Cretians were referred to as "always liars."

Their prophet referred to them as *"evil beasts."* In character they demonstrated the character of a beast or a brute, which implies that they were not fully civilized; they were not refined. They succumbed to unrestrained indulgence of wild passions and practices of life. They lived more like animals than like civilized human beings.

They were referred to as *"slow bellies."* They were gormandizers. There were two vices among the Cretians: sloth and gluttony. You may rest assured that an industrious man will not be a gormandizer; and by the same token, a gormandizer will not be an industrious man. They were described as an indolent, worthless people. They were a race of gluttons—a people whose main concern had to do with their stomachs: "Whose end is destruction,

426

whose God is their belly, and whose glory is in their shame, who mind earthly things" (Phil. 3:19).

If we seek first the kingdom of God, all other things will be provided in abundance. We are to put God and spiritual things first—and when one's god is his stomach he certainly serves a very poor god. There have been few races of people on the face of this earth described in the terms used in referring to the people who lived on the island of Crete in Paul's day. The Cretians were uncivilized, animalistic, wild, liars, lazy, gluttonous. Few people have ever demonstrated all of these bad habits and qualities; but in spite of their almost total depravity, God loved them, Christ died for them, and *"the iniquity of us all"* was laid upon Jesus.

Verse 13: "This witness is true. Wherefore rebuke them sharply, that they may be sound in the faith."

"This witness is true" is testimony to the fact that these people were everything the poet had said they were; and the fact that this was the general character of the Cretians was reason extraordinary that Titus should be on guard in a very special way in appointing leaders in the churches in Crete.

Since they were animalistic in their practices of life—liars and gluttons—Titus was to *"rebuke them sharply."* The word "sharply" here means "cuttingly, severely," and comes from the word *"to cut off."* Titus was to use words easily understood, words of severity and reproof that would strike home, making them understand that their character was wicked and ungodly beyond description. He was not to soft-pedal his message, nor be mealy-mouthed. He was to call sin by its right name; he was to spare neither their thoughts nor feelings. The Cretians knew they were sinful; they knew they were doing wrong; therefore, they needed to be rebuked sharply.

427

"... *That they may be sound in the faith.*" That is, that they may not allow the prevailing vices and lust to corrupt their views of religion. Paul wanted the Cretians who embraced Christianity to have a good, sound, solid experience, and to build on the sure foundation, Jesus Christ being the chief cornerstone. He knew that these people must be rebuked, and advised in terms they understood, that lust and vice do not mix with righteousness. Christianity is pure religion. Religion, *as such*, will mix with anything; but *Christianity is pure religion* and cannot be mixed with legalism, worldliness, dogmas, or tradition. Paul wanted pure Gospel, solid conversions, and men appointed over the local churches who would lead the people without wavering, regardless of what might arise.

Verse 14: "Not giving heed to Jewish fables, and commandments of men, that turn from the truth."

Paul advises here, as he did in I Timothy 1:4, that attention and time should not be bestowed upon fables. Such trifles should not be regarded as important. The fables referred to were probably the idle superstitions and conceits of the Jewish rabbis. The Greek word here rendered "fable" primarily signifies "speech, conversation." The people were not to pay attention to a discourse of fiction or mystic ideas. We know that in that day, such things did abound—among the Greeks as well as among the Jews. The fables to which Paul refers were composed of frivolous, unfounded tales and stories which were regarded with high esteem and as of much importance; and some of the leaders desired to incorporate them into the doctrines of Christianity. Paul, having been reared among these superstitions, knew the fallacy of them and how they would eventually draw the mind of the believer from truth, and would corrupt true religion.

One of the most successful schemes of the devil in

damning souls has been to mingle fable with fact. There are many religions that preach some truth; and, to many people, because they preach *a portion of the Gospel*, they seem good. All religions may have some good points; but there is only one *good* religion, *pure* religion—and that is *Christianity*. The truth of God will not mix with anything else. Jesus said, "Ye shall know the truth, and the truth shall make you free" (John 8:32). God is not the author of confusion. Fables and fiction confuse the mind, but the truth of God makes sure the heart and mind and sets the sinner free.

The devil does not care how religious we are nor how dedicated to religion we may be, just so long as that religion detours around the deity of Christ, the blood of His cross, and the bodily resurrection. The devil cares not how long nor how loud we preach, so long as we do not incorporate into our message the blood, the deity, and the resurrection "according to the Scriptures." Satan can handle any fable or fiction, any message that is man-made; but the truth of God puts him to flight!

Verse 15: "Unto the pure all things are pure: but unto them that are defiled and unbelieving is nothing pure; but even their mind and conscience is defiled."

"Unto the pure all things are pure" does not mean that dope and alcoholic beverages which will dull the mind and destroy the body, are pure. There is probably a direct teaching here concerning ceremonial meats and drinks among the Jews. (In this connection, study the entire fourteenth chapter of Romans.) Some foods were regarded as clean and could be eaten, while others were considered unclean and were therefore forbidden. What Paul is saying is that those distinctions ceased when Christ died and rose again: "Christ is the end of the law for righteousness to every one that believeth" (Rom. 10:4).

In this Christian era, it is not what we eat or drink that saves us or damns us; it is *"What think ye of Christ? Whose Son is He?"* "As many as received Him, to THEM gave He power to become the sons of God, even to them that believe on His name: which were born . . . *born of God"* (John 1:12,13).

In Paul's day, under the Law of Moses, a Jew dare not eat pork nor drink certain drinks; but in this day, meats and drinks neither save nor damn—although a child of God, led by the Spirit of God, will not eat or drink those things that will destroy the body. God puts His law in our hearts and leads us by His Spirit (Rom. 8:14), and if we are led by the Spirit we will not fulfill the lust of the flesh. Truth makes free; and when we KNOW and obey the truth, we eat and drink those things that are wholesome, good, and profitable to body and soul.

A person who is a true child of God will not use this passage to attempt to prove that all things are right and lawful for the Christian. There are those who say that if you *think* something is not sin, then to you it is *not* sin; but such reasoning is not to be found in the Word of God. The Bible clearly teaches that we are to "have no fellowship with the unfruitful works of darkness, but rather reprove them" (Eph. 5:11). "Love not the world, neither the things that are in the world. If any man love the world, the love of the Father is not in him" (I John 2:15). "Abstain from all appearance of evil" (I Thess. 5:22). "Prove all things; hold fast that which is good" (I Thess. 5:21). "Whether therefore ye eat, or drink, or whatsoever ye do, do all to the glory of God" (I Cor. 10:31).

The principle here involved is a pure, truly pious mind; and if we have such a mind we will not eat or drink those things that will destroy our testimony. The believing heart does not major on the distinction of food and drink, festivals, ceremonies, rites, holy days, holidays. These things have nothing to do with purity of heart and spirit, and the conscience of the believer is not to be burdened with nor enslaved by them. The heart of a believer is to be controlled by the Holy Spirit of God and by the laws of God laid down in the New Testament. We are not under the Law of Moses. We live by faith, not by sight. We live as the Holy Spirit leads us into paths of righteousness.

"But unto them that are defiled and unbelieving is nothing pure." This statement is very clear: The unbeliever is lost, totally depraved, without strength, hopeless, helpless, without God and eternally damned unless he embraces Christianity by faith in the finished work of Christ. To the sinner, NOTHING is pure. Proverbs 21:4 tells us, ". . . The plowing of the wicked is sin." James 4:17 says, ". . . To him that knoweth to do good, and doeth it not, *to him it is sin!*"

To hear the Gospel and reject it is enough sin to damn any poor sinner. It is not eating, drinking, nor participating in ungodly lust that damns the sinner; but "He that believeth NOT is condemned already, *because he hath not believed in the name of the only begotten Son of God*" (John 3:18b). John 3:36 tells us, "He that believeth on the Son hath everlasting life: and he that believeth NOT the Son shall not see life; *but the wrath of God abideth on him!*"

To the unbeliever, everything is made the means of increasing his depravity, his unrighteousness and his ungodliness. It makes no difference what ordinances of religion unbelievers may observe and practice; it matters not what distinctions they may make concerning meats, drinks, days, ceremonies or religious events; such observances will not change their state of depravity. Making distinctions in foods, drinks, and clothing only fosters

431

pride and produces self-righteousness. Those who do these things are attempting to justify themselves through their own goodness and labors, following the commandments of men instead of submitting to the love of God. They push aside the mercies of God and satisfy their own lusts. They are corrupt at heart, and observance of ordinances, ceremonies, abstinence from food and drink makes them no better; it simply leads to deeper depravity and greater damnation.

"But even their mind and conscience is defiled." This defilement goes much deeper than outward defilement of the body. The mind and conscience—the very *inner man*—is defiled, polluted, and rotten. Every action leads to greater corruption, and the inner man becomes more and more despicable in the sight of a righteous God. An unbeliever does not remain the same; day by day he becomes worse—and regardless of how much good he may seem to be doing, the Scripture tells us that "we are all as an unclean thing, *and all our righteousnesses are as filthy rags*" (Isa. 64:6). In our present epistle we learn that it is "not by works of righteousness which we have done, but according to His mercy He saved us, by the washing of regeneration, and renewing of the Holy Ghost" (Titus 3:5).

Verse 16: "They profess that they know God; but in works they deny Him, being abominable, and disobedient, and unto every good work reprobate."

"They" refers primarily to the Jewish teachers of verse 14. These Jewish professors in religion claimed that they had a singular knowledge concerning God. They were the chosen of God, the elect of God, the seed of Abraham. In John 8:32 Jesus said, "Ye shall know the truth, and the truth shall make you free." The Pharisees answered, "We be Abraham's seed, and were never in bondage to any man: how sayest thou, Ye shall be made

432

free?" Jesus replied, "If ye were Abraham's children, ye would do the works of Abraham. . . . Ye are of your father the devil, and the lusts of your father ye will do!" (John 8:32–44 in part).

Like the Pharisees, these teachers professed with their lips—"*but in works they deny Him.*" Their daily practice of life proved that they did not know God. They were "*abominable*" in their conduct. The Greek word used here for "abominable" does not appear again in the New Testament. It is an adjective and is used to describe those who profess to know God but deny Him in their works. The meaning is "detestable, to be held in abhorrence." In our language, "a debased, despicable, deplorable, disgusting person."

"*And disobedient, and unto every good work reprobate.*" The word "reprobate" signifies "not standing the test, rejected of God. Here in Titus 1:16 it is used of the defiled, who if they are put to the test in regard to any good work (in contrast to their profession), they can only be rejected" (Vine). These men were "void of judgment." In reference to all that was wholesome, pure and good, the conduct of these people was such that it could not be approved, and deserved to be rejected. It was because of the claims of such teachers who were attempting to enforce their teachings of the Mosaic Law, together with fables and other error, that Titus was warned to exercise extreme caution and care in placing men in places of authority in the local churches.

Someone may ask, "Does this spirit among religious leaders still exist, or did it die out with the Cretians? Are there those today who profess that they know God, but by their works deny Him? Are there those whose conduct is such that it should be hated, despised, and abhorred by spiritually-minded church leaders? Do we have those who are disobedient to the faith once delivered unto the saints, and disobedient to the commands of God in the New Testament as having to do with righteousness and Bible holiness? Do we still have those whose character is like that of the Cretians in regard to true piety and Bible holiness?"

Yes, these Cretians are dead—but their descendants live on in local assemblies today. In my years of travel, working with churches and ministers in many denominations, I have seen some of God's dear pastors bring heartache and tragedy upon themselves by using little precaution in selecting leaders in the church—especially deacons, stewards, elders, and trustees! A church would be better off with no deacons at all—or with only two or three—than with men appointed to the board when they do not qualify for that office.

Better had the pastor teach the entire Sunday school, than to appoint teachers who sow seeds of error and live lives that are not spiritual. Yes, there are those today who stand in the way of sinners and sit in the seat of the scornful. "Religion" has done a good job of confusing people. God is *not* the author of confusion, but of usshakeable assurance. "Religion" confuses; but *truth makes men free*! The straight and narrow way to heaven is blocked many times to many poor sinners by spiritually dead "professors" of religion, who announce long and loud with the mouth—but by their works and daily life in the community, deny that they have ever met God. Jesus said, "By their works ye shall know them!"

TITUS — CHAPTER TWO

THE WORK OF A TRUE, GOD-ORDAINED MINISTER

1. But speak thou the things which become sound doctrine:

2. That the aged men be sober, grave, temperate, sound in faith, in charity, in patience.

3. The aged women likewise, that they be in behaviour as becometh holiness, not false accusers, not given to much wine, teachers of good things;

4. That they may teach the young women to be sober, to love their husbands, to love their children,

5. To be discreet, chaste, keepers at home, good, obedient to their own husbands, that the word of God be not blasphemed.

6. Young men likewise exhort to be sober minded.

7. In all things shewing thyself a pattern of good works: in doctrine shewing uncorruptness, gravity, sincerity,

8. Sound speech, that cannot be condemned; that he that is of the contrary part may be ashamed, having no evil thing to say of you.

9. Exhort servants to be obedient unto their own masters, and to please them well in all things; not answering again;

10. Not purloining, but shewing all good fidelity; that they may adorn the doctrine of God our Saviour in all things.

11. For the grace of God that bringeth salvation hath appeared to all men,

12. Teaching us that, denying ungodliness and worldly lusts, we should live soberly, righteously, and godly, in this present world;

13. Looking for that blessed hope, and the glorious appearing of the great God and our Saviour Jesus Christ;

14. Who gave himself for us, that he might redeem us from all iniquity, and purify unto himself a peculiar people, zealous of good works.

15. These things speak, and exhort, and rebuke with all authority. Let no man despise thee.

Things Which Become Sound Doctrine

In chapter one, Paul instructed Titus concerning the organization of local churches in the various cities of the island of Crete, and warned him to be extremely cautious in selecting bishops, elders, ministers, teachers, and leaders in the local assembly.

In chapter two, he gives Titus instructions regarding his own responsibility to the believers in the local assemblies, and the method he is to employ in teaching the pure Gospel. He sets forth the kind of doctrine Titus should teach and the kind of instruction that he as God's faithful minister should give to the various classes of hearers and believers in Crete:

Verse 1: "But speak thou the things which become sound doctrine."

In other words, "Titus, do not incorporate your own ideas or opinions into your message when you preach. Teach the things that are doctrinally sound. Do not add anything to the Gospel you have heard, and do not take away from it."

In this day and hour, many times the Right Reverend, Most Noble, Esteemed Doctor steps behind the sacred desk on Sunday morning and reads his little essay. He opens by saying, "In my humble opinion, the way I see it, it could have been thus, by chance, we are not at all sure . . . ." Thus he goes for perhaps fifteen minutes, while the congregation listens with empty hearts—and when he has finished his discourse, they *leave* with empty hearts.

God is not concerned about your opinion or mine. He is not concerned about the way we see things. *He has spoken*, and His Word is forever settled in heaven (Psalm 119:89). Regardless of what Dr. Sounding Brass or Professor Tinkling Cymbal think or say about it, their opinions are not worth a plugged nickel! God said it, it stands, and we must believe it or roast in hell. (And it makes no difference what you have heard about hell—*the fire is there*, and if you do not believe it this side of the grave, you WILL believe it on the other side.)

"... *Things which become sound doctrine*" simply means that Titus is to preach nothing that is opposed to the Word of God nor anything that deviates from it. He is to preach "Thus saith the Lord"; and he is not to incorporate tradition, fables, dogma, or the commandments of men into his message. He is to preach pure Gospel—minus man's ideas or suppositions.

Paul's own message was the death, burial, and resurrection of Jesus Christ "according to the Scriptures" (I Cor. 15:1–5). His message was singular—*the cross, the blood, the crucifixion*: "For I determined not to know any thing among you, save Jesus Christ, and Him crucified" (I Cor. 2:2). "... Without shedding of blood is no remission" (Heb. 9:22). "That if thou shalt confess with thy mouth the Lord Jesus, and shalt believe in thine heart that God hath raised Him from the dead, thou shalt be saved" (Rom. 10:9). The cross is the heart, soul, and essence of the Gospel. A gospel without a cross is empty, dead, and hopeless. A Christ without a cross can never save; a cross without a Christ can never save—and a religion without blood is vain.

Verse 2: "That the aged men be sober, grave, temperate, sound in faith, in charity, in patience."

"... *The aged men*." There is no reason to think that Paul here refers primarily to the aged men who occupy an *office* in the church. He refers to ALL aged men in the church.

"... *Be sober, grave, temperate, sound in faith, in charity, in patience*." Titus was to preach to the aged men, as well as to the younger ones, that believers are to be sober, grave, temperate, sound in faith, sound in charity and in patience. God does not have one moral standard for a young person and another standard for those who are aged—and insofar as practical Bible holiness is

437

concerned, God does not have one standard for the minister and another for laymen. Whatsoever is sin for the minister is sin for the layman—and vice versa.

However, Paul desired Titus to direct his instructions to the different *classes* of his hearers. There is *one standard* of Christianity for all classes and ages; but aged believers need special instructions that the young would not understand, and the young need special instructions that the aged do not need. Paul points out that the aged men are to be sober (temperate, sober minded) and grave (serious). The word is one in which the sense of gravity and dignity are combined. The dictionary describes it as "denoting that which inspires reverence and awe." The aged men are not to enter their "second childhood" and act like a child again from the standpoint of frivolous thinking and foolish practices of life. They must act their age in all things.

They must be *temperate* in all things. Just because they are nearing the end of life's journey does not give them a license to be intemperate in anything—eating, drinking, or any other phase of daily living. They are to be *sound in faith*, and be careful that the enemy does not plant seeds of unfaithfulness, causing them to go off on a tangent or head down a blind alley religiously. It is easy for the devil to play tricks on the mind if we do not keep our minds entirely centered in the Word of God and in the faith once delivered to the saints.

The aged believer must be sound *"in love (charity)."* He should love all—and especially those who are good and godly in the church. By this time in life he should have overcome all the fiery, impetuous, envious, wrathful passions of his earlier years. By the time he is aged he should be "preserved" in the Lord. The older preserves are, the sweeter they are; and if kept long enough, preserves will become sugar. So the longer we live for

Jesus, the sweeter we should become in the Lord. We should be able to truthfully sing, "Every day with Jesus is sweeter than the day before"!

I know that many old people are not appreciated. They are abused, and are not loved. There is nothing that hurts me more deeply than to see an aged person abused or unwanted. I have high regard and great respect for gray hair, stooped shoulders, and a wrinkled face. I believe I am alive today because of the prayers of the white-haired saints across this nation. Twice in five years I have stepped to the very valley of death, and prayer brought me back. I feel in my heart that the prayers of the aged saints (not forgetting the prayers of the younger believers) surely brought me back from the valley of the shadow into which I stepped. But there are times when the aged become unhappy; they grumble, and they become unlovely. My aged brothers and sisters in Christ, I beg you, do not allow the devil to mar your beautiful Christian testimony by becoming a "grouch" or a grumbler! Rejoice—because it will not be long until you will lay down this old body of pain—a body that has become slow to think and slow to move—and you will rest with Jesus in Paradise. Then when the Rapture occurs, in the first resurrection you will have a body that will never age, never tire, never be diseased, never corrupt— a body like the glorified body of Jesus (I John 3:1–3).

". . . *In patience.*" Patience is certainly a grace that only God can give to a believer. I recognize the fact that old age brings infirmities, trials, heartaches and heartbreaks. Friends pass on, and many times old people seem alone—*and lonely*. But instead of becoming irritable, they should realize that God has allowed them to become old, and they should pray for Him to give extra patience with each and every passing day. Aged believers should submit to the trials, the heartaches, and the disappointments of their advanced years, knowing that Jesus said, "I will never leave thee nor forsake thee" (Heb. 13:5). Paul said, "If *God* be for us, who can be *against* us?" Therefore, regardless of what may or may not come to pass, we know "that all things work together for good to them that love God, to them who are the called according to His purpose" (Rom. 8:28).

My aged brothers and sisters in Christ, *look up!* Be sweet! Look to Jesus, not at circumstances around you. Keep in mind that *this may be the day* when the trumpet will sound! But if the Lord should delay His coming, it will not be long until you will renew your youth before the throne of God, in the presence of Jesus and the angels. Therefore, "Rejoice evermore!"

Verse 3: "The aged women likewise, that they be in behaviour as becometh holiness, not false accusers, not given to much wine, teachers of good things."

The aged women are also admonished to display behaviour as becometh holiness. Their conduct should be such as the Gospel requires. They are to be holy. *"The aged women"* may refer to the wives of aged deacons or leaders in the church. In their daily walk and talk and habits of life they are to follow holiness and set the example for younger women who are believers.

"Not false accusers." In I Timothy 3:11 the same word is used and is there translated "slanderers." The aged women are to be careful how they use their tongues in the community; they are not to be false in their conversation concerning fellow church members—nor even concerning unbelievers. They are to tell the truth at all times, and be silent if they cannot speak those things which become holiness and which would contribute to holy living—both to themselves and those with whom they come in contact.

440

"Not given to much wine." Paul means the same thing here that he meant in Titus 1:7 when he referred to a steward of God as being "blameless . . . not selfwilled, not soon angry, not given to wine." The Greek suggests that it means that these women are not to talk and act like women who linger over wine. Wine causes one to talk who may ordinarily be silent, and wine will cause one to make statements that are false or exaggerated. Therefore, the aged believing women are not to act like women who sit long at wine. This does not condone drinking even *a little* wine—certainly not the kind we have in liquor stores and wineries today. There is no excuse for any spiritually minded person being confused over total abstinence from alcoholic beverages.

These aged women are to be *"teachers of good things."* They are to instruct the younger women in the church. Seasoned believers among the female sex should be admonished to be holy, upright, quiet, truthful; not acting like women who drink wine, but teaching "good things" to the younger women and girls in the assembly.

Verse 4: "That they may teach the young women to be sober, to love their husbands, to love their children."

"They" refers to the aged believing women in the local assembly. The Greek word translated "sober" could have been translated *"wise."* It is the same word translated "temperate" in verse two, and it is the same word used in I Timothy 3:2, there translated "sober." The meaning of the Greek word is that the aged women should instruct the younger women to have their desires and passions well under control and regulated in the fear of God, as becometh a Christian or as becometh holiness.

The aged women are to teach the younger believing women *"to love their husbands."* In Ephesians 5:25 the Apostle Paul commands husbands to love their own wives,

441

and in verse 33 of the same chapter he commands the wife to reverence her husband. Here in our present verse, Paul simply points out that the young woman should be sober-minded and love her husband, which is her first duty to him. All true happiness in marriage is based on mutual love—the husband loves the wife with all of his heart, and the wife loves the husband in like manner. When this type of love departs, happiness takes flight. It matters not how wealthy the couple may be—they may live in a mansion; but wealth and a magnificent home cannot bring happiness where there is not love, or where love has cooled on the part of either husband or wife. Regardless of how humble the home may be—whether in the city or remote countryside—if mutual love exists between husband and wife, that home is a suburb of heaven. The house may be a mansion, the furniture of the finest; the couple may fare sumptiously every day and dress "in purple and fine linen." The sweetest music musicians can afford may be heard throughout the house—but if two hearts are not knit together in love, that mansion is a hell on earth.

No husband knows real love for his wife and family if he is not saved. He may think he loves his family with all of his heart, and that may be true as far as it is possible with an unbelieving heart; but real, true love is known only by born again believers. The same is true with the woman. Man and woman do not know real, pure love—*perfect love*—apart from the love of God in their hearts.

". . . *To love their children.*" The last part of this verse seems unnecessary—and yet it is very important. Most animals will fight and die to protect their young, but some men and women are so totally depraved that they lose all respect and love for their own flesh and blood—their children. The aged saints are to teach the

442

younger women to love their children. Any precious mother with a baby in the home has a full time job twenty-four hours a day, seven days a week. No other person will ever love your child as *you* love it if you are a true mother. No other person can train and discipline that child as you will if you are a true mother. *No person can take the place of a mother*; therefore, mothers should love their children above fame, fortune, beauty, houses, or social prestige. Children should come first in the heart of a mother; and she should forsake all except her husband to give her love, time, and attention to her children. The best friend any child will ever have on the face of this earth is a godly, consecrated mother who loves him.

The description given of a guilty world in the eyes of God in Romans 1:18-32 is very enlightening. Study it.* Paul tells us that in the end of the age, there will be those "without understanding, covenant breakers, without *natural affection*, implacable, unmerciful" (Rom. 1:31). "*Without natural affection*" simply means that they will love the unnatural. It is natural for a mother to love her children—but some mothers love the night club, the wine bottle, the arms of another man more than they love their own flesh and blood. There are thousands of poodles and cats that receive the attention and caresses that a baby should be receiving.

Lest I be misunderstood, let me say that I am not against pets; but they should be kept in their place and should never take the place of a child in the home. For some reason unknown to man, God did not see fit to allow children in all homes—and there are many wives who would give all they possess if there *could be* a precious baby in their home. But there are thousands of homes where children are not wanted and thousands of married women

* Order the author's verse-by-verse study on Romans.

who refuse to permit children to come into the home because a baby would interfere with their career and with social activities. These women substitute a poodle dog, a pussy cat, or a parakeet! God have mercy on such a wife when she stands before Him!

This is even true in the lives of some believing women, as well as among the unsaved. Some Christian wives refuse to permit a family. They are dedicated to their job, their social activities, their career—and sometimes (believe it or not), to their pets! Strange but true, some wives DO need to be taught to love their babies.

Verse 5: "To be discreet, chaste, keepers at home, good, obedient to their own husbands, that the Word of God be not blasphemed."

The Greek word used here for "*discreet*" is the same word translated "temperate" in verse two, and "sober" in verse four. The young women are to be "*chaste*," simply meaning they are to be pure in heart and in every detail of life.

These young wives are to be taught by the aged women that they are to be "*keepers at home.*" This does not mean that the wife is never to go out of the home, never to take part in any outside interests; but she is not to neglect the duties of the home in order to participate in things outside the home. In other words, she is not to be better known outside the home than *in* the home, by her own husband and family. She is to be diligent at home— not lazy or slothful, not unconcerned about the home and the things pertaining thereto—but to give her best to the home, seeing that things are in order and that the home is kept as becomes a Christian. Young wives are not to omit their own duties and become "busybodies" in others' affairs.

Earlier in this series I made the statement that

Christianity puts the right kind of pride in the heart—and a woman who is a believer should take pride in her home, which is her castle. She should keep that home clean, neat, and presentable. A young married woman with a baby and a home, if she does her duty, has a full time job.

Dear ladies should never forget that God made woman to make this world a sweeter, brighter, happier place in which to live. Adam was lonely; his life was empty. He found not a helpmate as he named the animals. Therefore, God removed a rib from Adam's side and made Eve, and gave her to Adam to be his helpmate. God did not give Eve to Adam for his slave. Wives are not to be chattels or slaves. They are to love and esteem their husband, their children, love their home and be diligent in that field. A young woman who is not willing to make a home for her husband and her family should stay single.

Husbands are commanded to love their wives as Christ loved the Church and gave Himself for it; and in like manner, wives are commanded to be in subjection to their own husbands, because the husband is the head of the wife even as Jesus is the head of the Church (Eph. 5:25 ff). Therefore, Christianity is the patron of domestic virtues and regards the appropriate duties in a family as those most intimately connected with its own progress in the world. There can never be a great local church without great Christian families; and there will never be a great Christian family without Christian fathers and mothers—not only Christian in word, but in deed and in truth. Great homes make great churches; great homes and great churches make great nations. A Christian home is a place of contentment—a place of peace; and when domestic duties are neglected, the home suffers severely. Regardless of how much a mother may do outside the home, whatever self-denial and zeal she may contribute to outside interests, and regardless of how much good she may accomplish outside the home, if she neglects her home she has brought reproach upon Christianity. The duty of a Christian mother is first to her home, and these other interests must be secondary.

Notice the next characteristic of a Christian wife and mother: She must be "*good.*" In all respects and in all relations, the wife and mother, the sister, must be good. There can be no greater compliment paid to a woman, no higher characteristic ascribed to her, than to say, "She is *good!*"

The sweetest creation on the face of this earth is a sweet woman. The most precious thing this side of heaven is a godly mother or wife. But the meanest creature this side of hell is a *mean* woman! Why do I say the sweetest thing this side of heaven is a sweet woman, and the meanest thing this side of hell is a mean woman? The answer is simple:

God created everything, and then removed a rib from Adam's side and made Eve. Why? Adam was not complete. He was lonely; God saw the loneliness of Adam, and He made woman. God made woman to make this world a sweeter place in which to live—a brighter, happier place. But some poor women do not contribute sweetness, happiness, or joy. They make a hell on earth out of the home in which they abide. A woman has a greater capacity to love than does a man. She has a greater capacity to hate than does a man. She has a greater capacity to be good and do good than a man does, and she also has a greater capacity to be ungodly and plain mean! A woman is a special creation of Almighty God; but when she leaves God out of her life she becomes a tool of the devil.

Someone has said, "There has never been a great man who did not have a great woman in his life"; and I think it can also be said that there has never been an ungodly man to whose wretchedness a woman did not contribute!

"... *Obedient to their own husbands.*" I refer again to Ephesians 5:22–33, where Paul, inspired of God, uses husband and wife as examples of the Church and Jesus. God created Adam and gave him dominion over everything. Man is the head of the woman, and the wife is to be obedient to her own husband in all things. Study carefully Ephesians 5:22–33 and Colossians 3:18.*

Without hesitation, I say that the woman has her place in God's economy. God created woman for a specific purpose—but He did not create her to rule man! Any home, any church, or any nation that is ruled by a woman is headed for destruction. Do not misunderstand me. Womanhood has made a gigantic contribution to Christianity, education—yes, even politics and business; but when a church does not have enough men to carry on the affairs of that church from the standpoint of business—such as pastoring and other offices of importance—then that church is just about out of business, whether they recognize that fact or not.

However, if it were not for the dear women in some churches, many times the Sunday school would be almost bereft of teachers—and, of course, it is perfectly all right for a godly woman to teach, so long as she does not "usurp authority over the man." Like it or not, God put man at the head of the creation, from the standpoint of the human family.

"*That the Word of God be not blasphemed.*" That is, that the outside world (unbelievers) may have no occasion to speak hurtfully or injuriously of the Gospel of the grace of God. Believers—ALL believers (although here Paul is dealing primarily with mothers and wives)—should live

* Commentaries on Ephesians and Colossians by the author are available from The Gospel Hour, Inc.

consistently pure, holy lives. God forbid that inconsistent living on the part of professing mothers and wives bring reproach upon the Gospel, upon the church, and upon the family that is supposed to be a Christian family. The thing that Paul is attempting to drive home to Titus (and in turn Titus is to drive the same truth home to the hearts of the people in the churches in Crete) is that Christianity ought to produce the virtues laid down here; and when these virtues are not demonstrated by professing mothers and wives, then they bring reproach and disgrace upon the church and upon the Gospel. Such ought not to be!

It is a grand and glorious privilege to be a mother. God honored woman by allowing her to conceive and bring forth His only begotten Son. Man had no part in the birth of Jesus; the virgin Mary gave Him His flesh, and God gave Him His blood (Acts 20:28). But as grand and glorious as is the privilege of being a wife and mother, so grave, great, and weighty is the responsibility! Woe be unto the woman who professes to be a godly mother, but in her home activity she denies that she is in her heart what she professes with her lips. Never entertain the idea that you—man or woman—can profess one thing and live another—and get by with it! It is utterly impossible.

Verse 6: "Young men likewise exhort to be sober minded."

The Greek word used here for "sober minded" can also be translated "discreet." That is, young men who profess to be followers of Jesus Christ should be intreated at all times to be prudent, serious in deportment, discreet in all things. They should by all means surrender soul, spirit, and body unreservedly unto God; and they should master their appetites and passions, thereby being good examples of the believer, not bringing reproach upon the church and upon the Saviour. Since they are Christians, they should set up self-government in their own hearts and lives. They should set standards for themselves that would bring glory to God—and then trust God for strength, grace, and power to live up to those standards.

Christianity should give to the young believer strength and courage to have a well-governed mind, which in the hour of temptation will keep him from indulging in passions to which the young are tempted and prone to succumb. Young men who name the name of Jesus should be steady in their behaviour, solid in their belief, superior to sensual temptations, constant in the exercise of self-government.

The reason: Young men who profess to be Christians are representatives of Jesus on this earth. Unbelievers watch their every move. The young men are the hope of the church in the future, and a young man who cannot govern himself and control his passions and appetites certainly could not be a leader in God's house. If young men succumb to the lusts of the flesh and the temptations thereof, sooner or later these lusts will destroy the body, which is the tabernacle of God. Paul's desire concerning the young converts in the churches in Crete was, "I pray God your whole spirit and soul and body be preserved blameless unto the coming of our Lord Jesus Christ" (I Thess. 5:23).

Verse 7: "In all things shewing thyself a pattern of good works; in doctrine shewing uncorruptness, gravity, sincerity."

In this verse Paul turns his attention to Titus. He is not only to teach others with *words*, but to show them *by example* how they should live: *"In all things shewing thyself a pattern of good works."* "Titus, you set the example; and admonish others to follow you as you follow Jesus." (On the word rendered "pattern" see Hebrews 8:5; I Corinthians 10:6; Philippians 3:17.)

". . . *In doctrine.*" Paul instructed Titus to teach pure, sound doctrine, not deviating from pure grace. He was extremely jealous for the cross, the blood, the grace of God—and he preached Jesus Christ, crucified, buried, risen "according to the Scriptures." He preached pure grace, and declared if any other preach anything else, "let him be accursed" (Gal. 1:8). It is not unusual that Paul point out to Titus that he must be true to Bible doctrine, not deviating from pure doctrine to please any man or to satisfy his own desires. Notice I Timothy 4:16.

". . . *Shewing uncorruptness.*" The word here could have been translated, "purity." It has the same meaning. Titus is not to allow any erroneous doctrine to be preached or taught in the assemblies in Crete. Only pure doctrine, free from all error, can be allowed. Titus was to preach the Gospel that would make men pure, better men—and sound doctrine does just that. The Word is a lamp to our feet, a light to our pathway, bread to strengthen, water to satisfy, and the power of God to keep us.

Titus is to be an example in "*gravity.*" The same Greek word is also translated "gravity" in I Timothy 3:4, but in I Timothy 2:2 it is translated "honesty." The *deeper* meaning of the word is "*venerableness.*" What Paul is saying to the young preacher is simply that he is to be honest, upright, above reproach in his teaching, preaching, and living. He is to be an example in any and all things that will insure respect from the church, and from unbelievers as well.

The meaning here is that the manner in which God's preacher delivers the message God has given to him should be a manner to command the respect of the listeners. His message should evidence good sense, undoubted piety, and should demonstrate that he is acquainted with the subject, proving that he has spent much time in study and prayer. The message should be serious, simple, and delivered with all earnestness. It is a great and grave responsibility for God's preacher to stand in the pulpit and deliver God's Word to men and women who are eternity-bound!

Titus was to be an example in *"sincerity."* The word used here in the Greek is translated "immortality" in Romans 2:7 and in II Timothy 1:10. In I Corinthians 15:42, 50, 53, and 54 it is translated "incorruption." It is translated "sincerity" in Ephesians 6:24 and here in our present verse. The word is not found in any other place in the New Testament. It means incorruption, incapacity of decay—and therefore, as used here, would be synonymous with purity. To sum up this verse, Titus is to be a pattern and example in pure works, pure doctrine, pure gravity and pure sincerity. Titus is to be PURE!

Verse 8: "Sound speech, that cannot be condemned; that he that is of the contrary part may be ashamed, having no evil thing to say of you."

The word "sound" is commonly applied to the body—meaning "that which is healthy or whole." It is used metaphorically of "sound speech." Titus was to teach, preach, and use language that would be helpful—and healthy—from a spiritual standpoint . . . true, pure, uncorrupted. The Word of God is milk to babes in Christ; it is bread and meat to the stronger believers, and it is living water to the thirsty souls of *all* believers. Paul wanted Titus to speak only *sound* words that would edify, strengthen and build up the believers, and keep them healthy and clean spiritually.

Titus was to speak sound words *"that cannot be condemned."* He was to preach a Gospel that is the power of God unto salvation—not weak or anemic, not unsound; but pure in every detail—a Gospel with which no one could find fault. He was to speak pure words, serious

451

words; his message was to demonstrate solidity in doctrine, in spiritual argument, and in the faith once delivered unto the saints—the truth which makes men free (John 8:32).

". . . *That he that is of the contrary part may be ashamed, having no evil thing to say of you.*" This part of the verse simply states a fact which will be true if Titus preaches the Gospel as laid down by the Apostle Paul. The enemy will be ashamed that he opposed such a message, because the Word of God will not return void; it will accomplish that whereunto it is sent. Any minister who defends the faith and preaches the pure Gospel of the marvelous grace of God will never be forced to apologize for the message he has delivered, because it will always bring forth fruit. Paul wanted Titus to be a fruitful minister; he wanted those to whom Titus preached to be healthy, strong believers.

Verse 9: "Exhort servants to be obedient unto their own masters, and to please them well in all things; not answering again."

In his letter to the believers at Ephesus and also in I Timothy 6:1–4, Paul exhorts the believers to be obedient to their masters, to please them in service. In Paul's day there were still many slaves and slavemasters. Some of the masters had been saved, while others had not. Hundreds of slaves had been born again, and Paul knew that if the Christian slaves did not render the right kind of obedience and service to their masters, they would be poor testimonies for the grace of God. Therefore, he wanted the servants who were believers to be obedient to their masters, to serve them well, to please them in all things, and not to be disputing or arguing with them— because such a servant would never influence his master to become a believer. Paul knew that the believing servants could win their masters if they would prove to them

452

that Christianity saves, satisfies, and brings peace that passeth all understanding—peace that position and money cannot attain.

"To please them well in all things" does not mean that the servant is to dishonor God in order to please his master, but only insofar as pleasing his earthly master does not contradict his belief in the heavenly Master. The Christian servant was not to do anything morally or spiritually wrong to please his master; but neither was he to do anything to antagonize his master, because of his faith in God. He was to do all in his power to win his master by daily demonstrating the peace of God in his heart, the testimony of God from his lips, and in service rendered to his master. He was not to be a disobedient servant, contradicting his master, nor rendering half-hearted, slovenly service. He was to do what his master required so long as it did not interfere with a godly conscience. He was not to put forth his own opinion and argue any matter with the master, recognizing the fact that he was a servant and that he was to obey—not to reason and instruct. To sum it all up, the servant is to obey his master in everything that is not contrary to the will of God. He is to do this without contradicting or disputing with the master.

Verse 10: "Not purloining, but shewing all good fidelity; that they may adorn the doctrine of God our Saviour in all things."

"Not purloining . . . ." The word "purloin" means to take or carry away another's property for one's own use, and would be applied to anything belonging to the employer, which a servant might take for himself. The servant was not to appropriate to his own use anything that belonged to his master—and, of course, this sin has been prevalent among servants (especially slaves) down through the years. Many times a servant feels that he

does not receive what is due him, and therefore he takes it. Paul is here instructing Titus to preach against this vice which is, in plain words, nothing less than stealing; and it is a sin to steal.

"*But shewing all good fidelity*." In laboring and in taking care of the property or whatever the master intrusts to the servant or slave, a believing servant should care for and protect his master's property as carefully as though it were his own.

"*That they may adorn the doctrine of God our Saviour in all things*." That is, that the servant may show the fair influence of Christianity on him in all respects. He should show that Christianity makes him more industrious, more honest, and more obedient. Christian servants were not to be hateful and argumentative, but kind and considerate, showing that they were better fitted to perform their duties, regardless of how humble those duties might be.

These believing servants were to show that the Christian religion definitely changed every detail of their life and that they were better servants because of their Christian belief. By their labors and attitude toward their masters, they were to prove what they believed in their hearts; and by this conduct they might hope to win their masters to Christianity and cause them to see that the Gospel *does* make a change in the life of one who believes.

Regardless of how insignificant you may feel, dear believer, one in the most humble walk of life may so live as to be an ornament to Christianity, a signboard that advertises well the profit in being a Christian. Those in humble positions may be used of God just as greatly as those who may be favored with many more advantages from many standpoints. Paul is here teaching that servants may do tremendous good by living daily in such a way that their lives will be epistles read of men. They should be living sermons in their actions and attitudes toward their slavemaster, or toward the person to whom they are in service.

The Grace of God and Its Work

Verse 11: "For the grace of God that bringeth salvation hath appeared to all men."

To me, verses 11 through 15 comprise one of the greatest passages in the Bible. In verse 11 we learn that *the grace of God brings salvation*—and apart from grace there IS no salvation. We are saved by God's grace. Saving grace becomes ours by faith (Eph. 2:8; Rom. 10:17). Therefore, every person who is saved, *is saved by grace.* Then notice: Grace BRINGS salvation. Salvation does not become ours through sincere living, giving, praying, begging, or abstaining. The *grace of God* brings salvation to the heart of the believer.

"*The grace of God that bringeth salvation HATH APPEARED TO ALL MEN.*" Thus, we learn that there is no such thing as "limited atonement" (known to some as "hyper-Calvinism," extreme predestination, or fatalism). There are many outstanding religionists who teach and preach that some are elected to be saved, while others are NOT elected to be saved—and therefore of necessity they are to be damned. According to these teachers and preachers, if you are not "elected" you cannot be saved; there is no need to try. These ministers do not believe in revival campaigns nor in inviting—yea, in beseeching—people to be saved. They teach and preach that if you are elected, you will be saved, and if you are not elected you cannot be saved. But our present verse tells us that the grace of God that brings salvation "*hath appeared to all men*"! Therefore, any and all who will hear the Word of God and believe on the Lord Jesus Christ, can be saved—regardless of race, color, or whatsoever.

Jesus came "to seek and to save that which was lost" (Luke 19:10); and if a person will admit that he is lost, *he is eligible for salvation.* Jesus came to call—not the righteous, but sinners—to repentance. "They that are whole need not a physician; but they that are sick" (Luke 5:31). He came to save "whosoever will."

Verse 12: "Teaching us that, denying ungodliness and worldly lusts, we should live soberly, righteously, and godly, in this present world."

In our present verse we learn that the grace of God not only brings salvation, but *the grace that saves us* immediately sets up a classroom in our hearts, and *becomes the teacher.* The grace of God teaches us—first, *to deny ungodliness.*

Just what IS ungodliness? The answer is clear to all who are willing to be taught of the Holy Spirit: *Anything that is not godly is UNgodly.* Anything that does not bring praise, adoration, and honor to God certainly brings disgrace and dishonor upon His name. Therefore, anything that is not godly and to God's glory, whatsoever it may be, can be classified under "UNgodliness." There is no neutrality, no middle ground with God. It is either righteous, or UNrighteous. It is holy, or UNholy; pure, or IMpure; godly, or UNgodly. The grace of God teaches us to deny ungodliness.

Grace, the divine teacher which salvation brings to our hearts, goes further; it also teaches us to *"deny worldly lusts."* What IS worldly lust? We are commanded: "Love not the world, neither the things that are in the world. If any man love the world, the love of the Father is not in him. For all that is in the world, the lust of the flesh, and the lust of the eyes, and the pride of life, is not of the Father, but is of the world. And the world passeth away, and the lust thereof: but he that doeth

456

the will of God abideth for ever" (I John 2:15–17).

In this enlightening passage we learn that anything the eyes gaze upon which would draw us away from God is "the lust of the world"; and when the flesh craves that which is unholy and unrighteous, that is *worldly lust.* When the mind thinks and plans unholy activity, that is the lust of the world. These lusts (plural) will pass away with the world, but if we do the will of God we will abide forever. God's grace teaches us to deny worldly lusts. Notice that the negative (in a Christian's life) precedes the positive here. We must *deny* these things in order to live the kind of life we should live and practice the things described in the last part of verse 12.

"Ungodliness" here means all that would be included under the word *"impiety."* That is, all failure on the part of the believer in the performance of proper duties and practices by the believer toward God. *"Worldly lusts"* here refers to any and all things that are improper having to do with desires, habits, and appetites of this life—the desire for wealth, pleasure, honor, sensual indulgence; and (as having to do with the believer) it refers to such passions as the men of this world are prone to go after, follow, and indulge in. It includes all those things in which one should not indulge if he has been truly born again, if he has had a change of heart by the grace of God through the miracle of the new birth as described by Jesus in John 3:1–7.

Let me emphasize the Bible fact that we are not saved by denying ungodliness and worldly lusts. The positive precedes the negative as having to do with redemption; but as having to do with holy living, the negative precedes the positive. That is, if we are to live sober, righteous, godly lives in this present world, we must of necessity deny anything that is ungodly, and we must deny all worldly lusts.

457

Having denied worldly lusts and ungodliness, we are to *"live soberly."* This means that we should exercise due restraint on our passions and practices of daily living. We should be sober—not only in abstinence from alcohol, but in our appetites, passions, and anything that would draw us away from godliness and right living. The believer is to be a living epistle read of men. We are to live lives that will enable us to invite others to follow us as WE follow Jesus. We should be able to invite them to walk in our steps as we walk in HIS steps.

Paul taught the Ephesians, "Be not drunk with wine, wherein is excess; but be filled with the Spirit" (Eph. 5:18). Many preachers preach that it is a dreadful sin to get drunk on wine—but they never mention the sin of not being filled with the Spirit. If it is a sin to get drunk on wine, then it must of necessity be a sin for the believer not to allow the Holy Spirit to fill his life.

We are to live *"righteously,"* or "justly," referring to the proper performance of our duties *as having to do with our fellowman.* It means that in our daily living Christianity teaches us to perform all duties in relation to others with fidelity. We must discharge our duty to our fellowcitizens and neighbors, to the poor, the needy, the oppressed, or to any who are providentially placed in our way, as honest, upright Christians.

The grace of God teaches us to live *"GODLY."* That is, "piously"—not self-righteously. We are to live piously in the faithful performance of *our duties to God,* who so loved us that He gave Jesus to die for us. We are to deny all that is ungodly, and we are to practice godly living in all that we do. Thus, we have here an outline of what Christianity requires:

1. *Our duty to ourselves*—we are to live soberly; and sober living requires control over passions, appetites,

458

and practices of life.

2. We see *our duty to our fellowmen* in all the relations we sustain in life.

3. We see *our duty to God*. We are to live a pious life. We are to walk aright and, in the words of Paul, *"abstain from all appearance of evil."* The believer who does these things meets all the responsibilities of his condition and relations as having to do with New Testament Christianity.

If we are sober in our thinking and in our practices of life; if we treat our fellowmen justly and right; if we live a pious life, dedicated to righteousness—then we are what we should be for Jesus *"in this present world."*

Yes, we are saved *now*. In this *present world*, we are NOW the sons of God (I John 3:1–3). And it is altogether possible for a believer to deny ungodliness and worldly lusts. It is possible—and for the believer it is *normal*—to live soberly, righteously, justly and godly right here in this present world. In Romans 8:35–39 we learn that "we are more than conquerors through Him." Hell has nothing to hurl at us that can overcome us if we depend on Jesus. In I Corinthians 10:13 we learn that the devil has no temptation with which to tempt us through which he can cause us to fall, because *God is faithful*—and the God who loved us, gave Jesus to die for us, and provided grace to save us, will give us the victory over any and all temptations. Whosoever is born of God overcometh the world, "and this is the victory that overcometh the world, *even our faith"* (I John 5:1–5). We are IN the world—but we are not OF the world. Jesus lived here before He asked you and me to live *for* Him here. He conquered the world, the flesh, and the devil; therefore, we are more than conquerors through Him. But the grace of God teaches more:

Verse 13: "Looking for that blessed hope, and the glorious appearing of the great God and our Saviour Jesus Christ."

The grace that saves us—apart from which there is no salvation—teaches us not only to deny ungodliness and worldly lusts, and to live soberly, righteously, and godly in this present world, but it also teaches us to look "FOR THAT BLESSED HOPE!" I do not hesitate to make the next statement: *All believers* believe in the second coming of Jesus Christ! We may not all agree on every detail of prophecy *concerning* His second coming—but if we are born again, we are recipients of God's grace; and if we are recipients of God's grace, then grace teaches us to look for the blessed hope, for "the glorious appearing of the great God and our Saviour Jesus Christ," who willingly bore our sins in His own body on His cross, that we might be saved from the *penalty* of sin, saved from the *power* of sin—and when He comes in the Rapture, we will be saved *from the very presence* of sin.

If you want to know for sure whether your decision was genuine or counterfeit, whether your religion is Christianity or man-made, you can certainly know by comparing your decision and your experience with these verses we are now studying. Shall we put your decision to the test?

When you decided to join the church, when you went forward and gave your hand to the preacher, or when you walked down the aisle with others to make a decision, *what happened?* Did any of your ungodly habits fall away? You did not quit anything in order to BE saved, but did any of your old habits automatically become ugly and distasteful to you? If you loved strong drink, or the poker game and the dance hall, did any of those worldly lusts become ugly and distasteful, and did you put them out of your life? Since you made your decision, have you been sober in your thinking, in your daily practices of life?

460

Are you still drunk on pride, or perhaps obsessed by the desire to be rich? Are you drunk on the desire to be attractive and popular in the world of society? What about your daily living? Do you live right, or do you live wrong? Do you treat your fellowmen right in business and in the community? Do you deal justly and honestly with them? How do you feel toward God? Do you love Him, and daily give Him thanks for your health, food, and raiment, for your job, your family, your automobile? Do you live a godly life? And *do you look for Jesus*?

I do not mean do you stand in the yard and look toward the heavens—but are you expecting Him *at any time; would you love to see Jesus return to this earth today*? Among the last words in Revelation are the words of Jesus: "He which testifieth these things saith, Surely I come quickly!" And John answered, "Even so, come, Lord Jesus!" Could you pray, "Even so, come quickly, Lord Jesus"? Or does it frighten you to think of His coming?

In Hebrews 9:28 we read, "So Christ was once offered to bear the sins of many; *AND UNTO THEM THAT LOOK FOR HIM SHALL HE APPEAR THE SECOND TIME* without sin unto salvation." According to this verse, Jesus is coming for those who look for Him—and *the grace of God TEACHES us* to look for that blessed event! If you do not believe in the second coming of Jesus Christ and if you are not looking for His return, it all adds up to the clear fact that you are not saved. God's grace that brings salvation teaches us to look for Jesus.

The second coming of Jesus Christ is, to the believer, *"that blessed hope."* It is not a frightening doctrine, but a *blessed* doctrine. Study carefully I Thessalonians 4: 13—18, where Paul closes this great portion of Scripture on the Rapture with this admonition: *"Wherefore comfort one another with these words."* The second coming of

461

Jesus Christ is a comforting hope, an assuring hope. It is blessed and most precious to the believer.

In I John 3:1–3 we are assured that we are the sons of God NOW; but when Jesus appears we will be like Him, and John declares that "every man that hath this hope in him purifieth himself, even as He is pure." The second coming of Jesus is not only a blessed, happy, joyous hope, but it is a purified hope that causes believers to live godly, pure, and righteously, knowing that the Lord Jesus, our Saviour, may come at any second of any day.

". . . *And the glorious appearing . . . .*" It will be a glorious day for the believer. The bodies of believers who have died will be raised incorruptible. Those of us who are living when Jesus comes in the Rapture will be changed "in a moment, in the twinkling of an eye." These mortal bodies will put on immortality, and we will have a body just like the body of Jesus (I Thess. 4:13–18; I Cor. 15:51–55; I John 3:1–3).

That will be a glorious event for believers, because we will see Jesus face to face. We will sit down at the marriage supper in the sky. We will be rewarded for our stewardship (II Cor. 5:10; I Cor. 3:11–15); and we will return to this earth to reign with Him for one thousand glorious years (I John 3:1–3; Rev. 20:5,6).

The hope of the Church is the glorious appearing of the great God and our Saviour, Jesus Christ. The Church is in the world, but not OF it. Our citizenship is in heaven, our Head (Jesus) is in heaven, our Foundation is in heaven. We are members of His body, bone of His bone, flesh of His flesh. We are pilgrims in this world; we are looking for a city whose builder and maker is God! But we will never occupy that city until Jesus comes and we are caught up to meet Him in the air. We will then receive our glorified bodies and our reward.

The Church will never be at home as long as it is in this world. We are here to make disciples of all nations, baptizing them in the name of the Father, Son, and Holy Ghost, teaching them to observe all things that Jesus has commanded; and when the Church is complete, we will be caught up to meet Jesus in the clouds in the air—and that will be glory!

"The great God" does not mean that Jehovah God is coming. There is no place in the Bible that teaches that Almighty God (Jehovah) will return to this earth. Jesus is the wonderful "Counsellor, The MIGHTY GOD, The everlasting Father, The Prince of Peace" (Isa. 9:6). So the statement here, *"the great God,"* simply means *Jesus*—who, of course, was God in flesh. He is our Saviour, and He is coming back to receive His own.

There have been those who tried to cause men to believe that Jehovah God would appear *along with Jesus the Son*; but fundamental Christianity has always taught and preached that "the great God and our Saviour" refers to Jesus Christ, who bore our sins in His body on the cross that we might be saved.

Verse 14: "Who gave Himself for us, that He might redeem us from all iniquity, and purify unto Himself a peculiar people, zealous of good works."

The opening statement of this verse, *"who gave Himself for us,"* certainly points to Jesus. It was God the Father who so loved us, God the Son who died on the cross for us; and God the Holy Spirit is in the world today calling out a bride for the Son. *The Bride* is the New Testament Church, made up of all believers. We are looking for that blessed hope and the glorious appearing of our Saviour. We love Him because He first loved us. We love Him and we are looking for Him because

He gave Himself for us. We want to see Him because we have loved Him—some of us—for many years; and we long for the day when we can look into His precious face, fall at His feet, and thank Him for His love and His saving grace!

"Who gave Himself for us, *that He might redeem us from all iniquity.*" There is redemption in no other. The blood of Jesus Christ, God's Son, cleanseth us from all sin. It is in Jesus that we have redemption. Without shedding of blood is no remission. We are not redeemed with things that corrupt—as silver and gold—BUT WITH THE PRECIOUS BLOOD OF JESUS, as of a lamb without spot or blemish:

"Forasmuch as ye know that ye were not redeemed with corruptible things, as silver and gold, from your vain conversation received by tradition from your fathers; but with the precious blood of Christ, as of a lamb without blemish and without spot: Who verily was foreordained before the foundation of the world, but was manifest in these last times for you" (I Pet. 1:18—20).

"And, having made peace through the blood of His cross, by Him to reconcile all things unto Himself; by Him, I say, whether they be things in earth, or things in heaven" (Col. 1:20).

"In whom we have redemption through His blood, the forgiveness of sins, according to the riches of His grace" (Eph. 1:7).

Notice—"*who gave Himself.*" He was not forced or driven; He willingly laid His life down: "Therefore doth my Father love me, because I lay down my life, that I might take it again. No man taketh it from me, but I lay it down of myself. I have power to lay it down, and I have power to take it again. This commandment have I received of my Father" (John 10:17,18). He gave Himself that HE might redeem us. HE does the redeeming when WE do the believing. He redeems "from all iniquity." A holy God demands holiness: Without holiness no man shall see God (Heb. 12:14). Nothing shall enter that city that defileth; only the pure and the spotless shall enter there. Such purity, such holiness, could be provided only by a holy God; therefore, God gave Jesus, *Jesus* gave *Himself*, to redeem us from all iniquity and make us pure and spotless through the covering of His precious blood.

Notice the words, ". . . and purify *unto Himself* a peculiar people." God saves us for Christ's sake (Eph. 4:32). Jesus redeems us unto Himself, and we who make up the true Church are His peculiar treasure. Jesus loved the Church and gave Himself for it (Eph. 5:25—30). In the ages of ages—the eternity ahead of us—God will display the exceeding riches of His grace through the Church on display in the Pearly White City, suspended between heaven and earth, illuminating all of God's creation (Eph. 2:7; Rev. 21).

Believers are a *"peculiar people"* . . . not queer, but *peculiar.* The word means "one's own possession" (Vine's Lexicon)—and here means they were to be regarded as *belonging* to the Lord Jesus. It is described in Deuteronomy 7:6: "For thou art an holy people unto the Lord thy God: the Lord thy God hath chosen thee to be *a special people unto Himself*, above all people that are upon the face of the earth."

In I Peter 2:9 we read, "But ye are a chosen generation, a royal priesthood, an holy nation, *a peculiar people*; that ye should show forth the praises of Him who hath called you out of darkness into His marvellous light."

It is true that believers are peculiar in that they do not love the things of the world nor practice them; they do not see or feel as does the world; and they *are* peculiar

465

in the respect that they are unlike others—but this goes much deeper: The redeemed are a peculiar *treasure*, a precious, unusual possession to the Lord Jesus Christ. We are His people, His possession. He purchased us; He bought us back at the tremendous expense of His own blood. We are *His peculiar people.*

". . . *Zealous of good works.*" In Ephesians 2:10 we read, "For we are His workmanship, created in Christ Jesus unto good works, which God hath before ordained that we should walk in them." We are saved to serve. God never saved any person to sit down and do nothing. He saves to serve; saving faith is living faith, and living faith is working faith: "For as the body without the spirit is dead, so faith without works is dead also" (James 2:26).

True faith produces works. We are not SAVED by works, but we work when we ARE saved! God does not expect all believers to be full time ministers, missionaries, Bible teachers nor evangelists; but all believers are *full time Christians*, and all Christians are full time witnesses. We are to work—and we WILL work, we will be anxious to work, if we are saved. Certainly that puts some religionists and church members in difficult circumstances, because many of them claim to have been saved for many years, yet they never work for the Lord. They have never proved their salvation by their works. Works do not save us, but works prove that we ARE saved; and the grace of God teaches us to be anxious, ready, and alert to do good works.

Verse 15: "These things speak, and exhort, and rebuke with all authority. Let no man despise thee."

Titus was to preach "these things" without compromise, without keeping anything back. He was to preach them—not simply as advice or counsel from a

466

minister, but as the command of God. He was to preach "these things" without fear or favor, and to do it with *all authority*.

God's minister does not need to apologize for preaching grace, pure grace, and ONLY grace for salvation. God's minister need not apologize for preaching against ungodliness and worldly lusts, naming these sins to those to whom he preaches. God's minister steps in the pulpit to preach sober, righteous, godly living—right here in this present world; and he does it with authority and without apology. The minister of Jesus Christ preaches the return of the Lord according to the Scriptures—and he teaches his people to look daily, momentarily, with expectancy, knowing that He who said, "I go, I come again" will surely keep His word! This same Jesus will come in like manner as He departed into heaven while the disciples looked on. God's preacher does not need to soft-pedal or apologize for preaching the personal, imminent return of Jesus Christ. We need not apologize when we preach that Jesus gave Himself, gave His blood—His life—that we might be redeemed from all iniquity and made pure, holy, and righteous for His sake and for His glory . . . a peculiar treasure—not just an ordinary people, but a precious pearl of great price. We are to teach the people that grace produces works, faith without works is dead, and *dead faith does not save.* These things speak, exhort, and rebuke *with all authority.* Do not apologize! Do it in the name of God, to the glory of God—and because of the command of God.

"Let no man despise thee." "Titus, conduct yourself in such a way, walk moment by moment in such a way, that everyone will be forced to respect and esteem you as God's minister. Do nothing and go nowhere that will bring reproach upon the name of Jesus, upon the church, and upon *you*, God's minister. Live what you

preach; preach without apology; preach with all authority; preach with all sincerity and fervency. Exhort the people to look for Jesus, to live clean, pure, holy lives; but rebuke them when they fail to come up to the standards of Christianity. Titus, you are God's representative on earth; you are God's undershepherd in the church. Be faithful, live above reproach—*and let no man despise thee*!"

THE WORK OF A TRUE, GOD-ORDAINED MINISTER (continued)

1. Put them in mind to be subject to principalities and powers, to obey magistrates, to be ready to every good work,

2. To speak evil of no man, to be no brawlers, but gentle, shewing all meekness unto all men.

3. For we ourselves also were sometimes foolish, disobedient, deceived, serving divers lusts and pleasures, living in malice and envy, hateful, and hating one another.

4. But after that the kindness and love of God our Saviour toward man appeared,

5. Not by works of righteousness which we have done, but according to his mercy he saved us, by the washing of regeneration, and renewing of the Holy Ghost;

6. Which he shed on us abundantly through Jesus Christ our Saviour;

7. That being justified by his grace, we should be made heirs according to the hope of eternal life.

8. This is a faithful saying, and these things I will that thou affirm constantly, that they which have believed in God might be careful to maintain good works. These things are good and profitable unto men.

9. But avoid foolish questions, and genealogies, and contentions, and strivings about the law; for they are unprofitable and vain.

10. A man that is an heretick after the first and second admonition reject;

11. Knowing that he that is such is subverted, and sinneth, being condemned of himself.

12. When I shall send Artemas unto thee, or Tychicus, be diligent to come unto me to Nicopolis: for I have determined there to winter.

13. Bring Zenas the lawyer and Apollos on their journey diligently, that nothing be wanting unto them.

14. And let our's also learn to maintain good works for necessary uses, that they be not unfruitful.

15. All that are with me salute thee. Greet them that love us in the faith. Grace be with you all. Amen.

Verse 1: "Put them in mind to be subject to principalities and powers, to obey magistrates, to be ready to every good work."

"Put them in mind to be subject to principalities and powers, to obey magistrates . . . ." Titus was to instruct the believers in the churches to be subject to lawful authority. Christians are to be subject to principalities and powers so long as those powers do not require them to denounce God, disobey Him, or knowingly go against His will. God does not expect us to obey any atheistic ruler who commands us to do things that we know are sinful and contrary to God's Word. He would not require us to commit sin in obedience to the command of the president, the governor, nor anyone else in authority. We are to obey the Lord in all things, and we are to be subject to magistrates and rulers so long as they do not cause us to denounce God or knowingly sin against Him in what we do or say.

". . . To be ready to every good work." The believer should be ready at all times to help out with every good work, whether in the church or out of the church. There are many good things in which we can participate and to which we can lend our influence, our finances, and our support, which are not directly connected with the church. The church has a task to perform that no other organization on earth can do, but there are other good civic organizations which perform duties that are good and needful; and we should be willing to help any cause that will help those in need, help our country or our fellowman in the things that are right and honest and decent.

Verse 2: "To speak evil of no man, to be no brawlers, but gentle, shewing all meekness unto all men."

"To speak evil of no man." The idea is that we are

470

not to slander, revile, or defame anyone. We are not to say anything about another for the express purpose of doing him an injury. If it is necessary to comment about a person, even though it is the truth, we should never do this for the purpose of revenge or to find pleasure in it. In telling the truth we should be very careful to state only what we know and not color our statements with evil insinuations.

Believers should be especially careful not to speak evil of the leaders in the church. We may not *agree* with them—but to speak evil of them, condemning and criticizing them in the presence of unbelievers, is a bad testimony and will certainly not help either the rulers or the church. We can do much more good by praying, beseeching God in their behalf, than we can by criticizing them and what they are doing. Believers should demonstrate the Spirit of Christ in all that we do and say; and in so doing we will do much more to advance the cause of Christ and win others to Christianity than we will by displaying the spirit of evil in what we say and do.

We know that many of our secular and national leaders are not born again. Therefore, we need to pray, first and foremost, that those who are not Christians will accept Christ as Saviour. God's Word says, *"The natural man receiveth not the things of the Spirit of God, for they are spiritually discerned and he cannot know them."* We need to pray that God will open the eyes of our leaders and give them wisdom to walk as He leads, because God ordains all power. He puts up whom He will and puts down whom He will. If rulers and leaders do not know this, we should pray for them, that their blinded eyes may be opened. Speaking evil of them and criticizing them in public will not help them, nor us, nor our city, community, state, or nation.

". . . No brawlers, but gentle, shewing all meekness

unto all men." A brawler is a man who is contentious or easy to pick a quarrel. Paul is saying to Titus, "Put them in mind that they are not to be quarrelsome, taking offence on every issue. They are not to be always going about with 'a chip on the shoulder,' daring someone to knock it off." Instead of being contentious, the believers in the churches were to demonstrate humility, gentleness, meekness, at all times and toward all classes of people—those who were in authority, or those who were poor and of very humble class. Believers are not to show distinction.

Verse 3: "For we ourselves also were sometimes foolish, disobedient, deceived, serving divers lusts and pleasures, living in malice and envy, hateful, and hating one another."

I sometimes use this verse as a text, and deliver a sermon on the subject, *"The Photo of Sinners."* We who are Christians now, once conformed to this picture of wickedness. (The "we" also includes Paul and Titus.) The verse does not necessarily mean that every believer has been guilty of all the things pointed out here. Some things are mentioned that no doubt Paul was not guilty of before his conversion; but he is simply pointing out to Titus that he should preach to the people in the churches over which he is appointed bishop or God's undershepherd, that they should live holy lives, and especially manifest a spirit of humility, order, peace, kindness, and due subordination to local authorities. Titus should point out to the believers that they were formerly disorderly, wicked, sensual—sinners by nature; but having heard the Gospel, through the power of the Gospel they had been saved from these things by the grace of God, and now they were new creations in Christ Jesus and by their daily practices should prove to unbelievers that they have had a change of heart.

The minister of the Gospel is never to be proud or

arrogant. He is to point unbelievers to *Christ*—not to his own righteousness or ability to live above the world. The minister is to remember that before his conversion he was in the same condition as the unbeliever to whom he now preaches. The minister is not to forget that he is not superior to others because of HIS ability, but because of the grace of God and the power of God. The minister is to exhort the wicked to repent. Remembering his own life of sin and wickedness will help him to fervently preach the grace of God which worked a miracle in his own heart; and having had a miracle of grace performed in his own heart, he knows what the grace of God can do for all who will receive it.

Paul always gave credit to whom credit was due; he said, "I am what I am by the grace of God." And again, "The life I now live in the flesh, I live by the faith of the Son of God, who loved me, and gave Himself for me." Therefore, Titus was to demonstrate humility in his preaching, remembering that before his conversion, he, too, was *"foolish."* The Greek word used here for "foolish" is translated "fools" in Luke 24:25. In Romans 1:14 it is translated "unwise," and in Galatians 3:1,3 and I Timothy 6:9 it is translated "foolish."

This word is sometimes a term of reproach, denoting ungodliness and wickedness; and in this sense we are forbidden to call our fellowman a fool (Matt. 5:22). In Matthew the word implies contempt or extreme wickedness, but the one employed in our present Scripture denotes "weakness or dullness."

In Luke 24:25 Jesus rebukes the disciples for not seeing what had been prophesied by the prophets and what He Himself had so clearly taught them during His public ministry: "Then He said unto them, O fools, and slow of heart to believe all that the prophets have spoken." The Greek word used here and also in Titus 3:3,

473

Romans 1:14, and Galatians 3:1,3 signifies senseless, unworthy lack of understanding, and sometimes carries a moral reproach and describes one who does not govern his lusts. Paul is saying to Titus, "You and I were sometimes foolish—we were thoughtless, we were dull as having to do with our spiritual life and the eternity that faces us."

Dear reader, I think you will agree that it is foolish for any person to go on serving the devil and sin, knowing that from the standpoint of common sense, man did not just happen upon this earth, and surely the God who created man must and WILL mete out justice to every man. The Word of God has stood the test of time; and the Word of God stands today in spite of all hell has hurled at it! The Bible teaches, "the wages of sin is death . . . be sure your sins will find you out . . . sin brings corruption." As we look around us and see the *results* of sin, surely we are foolish if we go on in sin, having been exposed to the light of the Gospel and the evidence that is presented daily in the lives of unbelievers!

All sinners are foolish to serve sin. God is the giver of every good and perfect gift (James 1:17). Sin brings momentary pleasure, but sin has no future. The wages of sin is singular—DEATH; but the gift of God is eternal life, joy unspeakable and full of glory, and every need supplied. True Christians are living proof of the Bible. Unbelievers and the results of sin are proof that sin pays wages as spelled out in the Word of God.

Dear reader, if you are not a born again child of God you are following a foolish route; you are living a foolish life. May God help you today to wake up and realize that the wages of sin is death, and then by faith accept the gift of God—which is eternal life in Jesus Christ, our wonderful Lord.

"We ourselves were . . . *disobedient.*" The same
Greek word occurs in Luke 1:17; Romans 1:30; II Timothy
3:2 and Titus 1:16, and signifies "unwilling to be persuaded, spurning belief, obstinate rejection of the will
of God."

Unbelievers are disobedient to the law, to their parents, to civil authority—and most of all, they are disobedient to God. The whole duty of man is to fear God and
keep His commandments (Eccl. 12:13). In answer to the
lawyer's question, "Which is the great commandment in
the law?" Jesus replied, "Thou shalt love the Lord thy
God with all thy heart, and with all thy soul, and with
all thy mind. This is the first and great commandment.
And the second is like unto it, Thou shalt love thy neighbour as thyself" (Matt. 22:36–39).

It is natural for man to be disobedient; parents well
know this. We do not need to teach our children to be
disobedient, because disobedience is born in the hearts
of all who come into this world. It is natural for the
natural man to disobey God, parents, civil authority, the
laws of nature—and everything else with which he comes
in contact—until that natural man is born again and becomes a new man with a new heart and a new spirit. If
you would like a picture of the unregenerate heart, the
best place to find it is in the Bible. In Mark 7:21–23 God
gives us a perfect photograph of the unbeliever's heart:

"For from within, out of the heart of men, proceed
evil thoughts, adulteries, fornications, murders, thefts,
covetousness, wickedness, deceit, lasciviousness, an evil
eye, blasphemy, pride, foolishness: All these evil things
come from within, and defile the man."

I wonder if there is one person reading these lines
just now who is not a believer? If so, my dear unbeliever,
can you truthfully say that you have never felt in your

heart that you should be converted and serve God? Have you never felt the need to become a Christian? If you have had that impression and did not yield to God, then you are disobedient to Him—and all you need do to open your eyes in hell is to disobey the call of the Holy Spirit! "How shall we escape, if we neglect so great salvation; which at the first began to be spoken by the Lord, and was confirmed unto us by them that heard Him; God also bearing them witness, both with signs and wonders, and with divers miracles, and gifts of the Holy Ghost, according to His own will?" (Heb. 2:3,4). To His own people, the Jews, Jesus said, ". . . And ye will not come to me, that ye might have life" (John 5:40).

"We ourselves also were sometimes . . . *deceived*"— (led astray into error, seduced to wander, to be out of the way, deceiving one's self). All unbelievers are deceived. The devil is the master deceiver; he has had six thousand years' experience in his art, and he knows HOW to deceive. A definite characteristic of the natural man is that he sees nothing in its true light; he walks amidst constant, changing (though beautiful) illusions; he is deceived. Read Matthew 24:4,5 and 11; II Timothy 3:13; I Peter 2:25; and Revelation 18:23, where the same word occurs. In Revelation 12:9; 20:3,8 and 10 the word is applied to the devil, the great deceiver who has led the whole world astray!

But when the natural man becomes a born again believer, he *sees* through the eyes of the Spirit, he *feels* through the hands of the Spirit, he *hears* through the ears of the Spirit: *he is a new creature in Christ Jesus!*

The devil deceives unbelievers by telling them that if they become Christians, there will be no joy in life for them. He deceives them by telling them that they must give up all that is worth living for, that there will be no pleasure left in life for them if they become children of God. Psalm 16:11 tells us, ". . . At (God's) right hand there are pleasures for evermore!" In I Peter 1:8 we read, ". . . Yet believing, ye rejoice with joy unspeakable and full of glory!" The devil has nothing but momentary pleasure to offer—pleasure that brings heartache, disappointment, and (in the end) everlasting destruction in the lake of fire!

"We ourselves also were sometimes . . . *serving divers lusts and pleasures.*" That is, "Titus, before we were born again, you and I were guilty of indulging in passions, lusts, pleasures; but now we have a new heart, a new spirit, new desires. Before we were converted we were under the influence of different kinds of lusts and all species of worldly sins and pleasures. We obeyed the call of lust; we were slaves to lust and pleasure. But now, the Holy Spirit leads us, and we walk in paths of righteousness for His name's sake—yet we have nothing to boast of nor brag about. I am what I am by the grace of God; and the life I now live in the flesh I live by the faith of the Son of God, who loved me and gave Himself for me."

"We ourselves also were sometimes . . . *living in malice and envy.*" The Greek word here translated "malice" means badness in quality, the vicious character generally, wickedness—and could have been translated "living in evil"—all kinds and species of evil, lust, pleasure and ungodliness. Read Romans 1:18–32, noting especially these words in verses 29–31: ". . . Being filled with all unrighteousness, fornication, wickedness, covetousness, maliciousness; full of envy, murder, debate, deceit, malignity; whisperers, backbiters, haters of God, despiteful, proud, boasters, inventors of evil things, disobedient to parents, without understanding, covenantbreakers, without natural affection, implacable, unmerciful."

"Living in . . . *envy*" means that unbelievers live in

displeasure at the happiness and prosperity of their neighbors and fellowmen. Unbelievers have hearts filled with covetousness, desiring what others have, never satisfied with what they themselves have; therefore, they do not have peace of mind or happiness. They live in envy, seeing what their fellowmen have, and lamenting the fact that *they* do not have it.

"We ourselves were sometimes . . . *hateful.*" The Greek word here translated "hateful" does not occur anywhere else in the New Testament. The meaning is, "the conduct of the unbeliever is such as to be worthy of the hatred of others." The true nature and spirit of an unbeliever is hateful in the eyes of believers. I think most of us who are born again will admit that before our conversion we were hateful in many, many ways—and very unlovable. I have said many times that no one but God Almighty could love human beings. Now I say "Amen!" to that statement. I am glad God loved me while I was so unlovely; He has saved me for the sake of His lovely Son—the Lord Jesus Christ. Were it not for the love of God I would burn in hell.

"We ourselves also were sometimes . . . *hating one another.*" There is but little brotherly love among unbelievers. The unbeliever loves himself. There are exceptions—but generally one who does not know God lives for self and for this world, laying up treasures on earth, satisfying the lust of his own heart, caring very little for others. Paul is instructing Titus to remember all this, and declares that this is reason enough why Christians should not allow themselves to be proud and haughty, but should be gentle, mild, kind, and considerate even toward those who are evil, knowing that they are deceived and blinded, in bondage to sin and slaves to the devil. They need a friend, and the only person on earth who has the answer to their need is the believer. We have the

Gospel that will liberate unbelievers and set them free. Jesus said, "Ye shall know the truth, and the truth shall make you free" (John 8:32). We who know Jesus have the truth—and we can preach that truth to unbelievers, thereby helping them to see the folly and foolishness of serving the devil. We who are born again have nothing to brag about or boast about except the grace of God that saved us.

Verse 4: "But after that the kindness and love of God our Saviour toward man appeared."

In verse 3, Paul describes the natural man (himself and Titus included) *before* the love of God came into their hearts. The meaning in verses 4 and 5 is, "WHEN the love of God was manifested in the plan of salvation, He saved us from this state by our being washed and purified." The idea is not that the love of God appeared *after* we had sinned in this way, but that *WHEN* His mercy was thus displayed we were converted.

God's love was in the beginning, and it was in the beginning that God loved you and me. Before God ever made this earth or anything therein, it was already settled that one day Jesus would pay the sin-debt. Read I Peter 1:18—20. God's love was manifested in Jesus, who wrapped up the love of God in flesh and brought it down to man. Thus the love of God was displayed on the cross as Jesus willingly took our place and laid His life down for sinners—strengthless, hopeless, enemies of God. Jesus in His kindness, goodness, tender mercy and love laid His life down that WE might be saved!

The act of redemption was one of great kindness, great goodness—and no one but God Almighty could have *thought* or *wrought* redemption. The plan of salvation as laid down in the New Testament—(the ONLY plan whereby man can be redeemed from iniquity)—was born in the heart of God, and God is love. The plan of salvation was founded on love, by God to man, and was the highest expression of God's love. Jesus on the cross was a display of God's best for man's worst. The God of all grace and mercy made Jesus to be sin for us, that we in Jesus might be made the righteousness of God:

"For He hath made Him to be sin for us, who knew no sin; that we might be made the righteousness of God in Him" (II Cor. 5:21). When the kindness of God our Saviour to man was manifested, He saved us from those sins of which we had before been guilty. The Word of God clearly sets forth the fact that we are all sinners by nature: "All we like sheep have gone astray; we have turned every one to his own way; and the Lord hath laid on Him the iniquity of us all" (Isa. 53:6).

Verse 5: "Not by works of righteousness which we have done, but according to His mercy He saved us, by the washing of regeneration, and renewing of the Holy Ghost."

"Not by works of righteousness . . . ." Paul was very careful to make known the eternal fact that man cannot become righteous by works. The plan of salvation is not based on what man can do, nor upon man's ability to live righteously: "But we are all as an unclean thing, and all our righteousnesses are as filthy rags . . . ." (Isaiah 64:6).

If man could have saved himself by his own good works, there would have been no need of salvation through the Lord Jesus Christ. If our own good works were the basis for eternal life, the work of Christ would be unnecessary and vain. If man by his own good works or ability could save himself, then the greatest tragedy of all eternity would be the cross of the Lord Jesus Christ. But the cross was NOT a tragedy; it was a divine imperative. Jesus said, "And I, if I be lifted up from the earth, will draw all men unto me" (John 12:32). To Nicodemus He said, ". . . As Moses lifted up the serpent in the wilderness, even so must the Son of man be lifted up" (John 3:14). A "must" with God is a MUST!

". . . *But according to His mercy He saved us.*" Salvation has its origin in mercy; and because of God's great mercy we are saved—not by justice, for if we had our just rewards we would all be damned. Salvation was born in the heart of God, displayed in the body of Christ on the cross, and becomes ours by our receiving the finished work of the Lord Jesus Christ. When we come to receive salvation, no other element enters but mercy. God does the saving; man cannot save himself, nor can he *help* God save him. We are saved entirely apart from our own efforts. We simply exercise faith in the finished work of Jesus Christ—and *for Christ's sake, according to God's mercy, HE SAVES US.*

We are saved "*by the washing of regeneration, and renewing of the Holy Ghost.*" The washing of regeneration comes through hearing the Word of God: "Now ye are clean through the Word which I have spoken unto you" (John 15:3). "Husbands, love your wives, even as Christ also loved the church, and gave Himself for it; that He might sanctify and cleanse it with the washing of water by the Word" (Eph. 5:25,26).

The Word of God is the living water that washes, regenerates, "reborns," revives, redeems, and makes ready for heaven. The incorruptible, engrafted Word is able to save us; the Word is light—and upon the entrance of that Word, we have light. When we receive the Word of God, the Holy Ghost takes up His abode in our bosom (Rom. 8:9, 14, 16; Eph. 4:30).

"*Renew*" means *to make new*; and in Titus 3:5 the

481

"renewing of the Holy Spirit" is not *a fresh bestowment* of the Spirit; but it means *that which the Holy Spirit produces*, recognizing the Bible fact that the Holy Spirit is the author of the New Birth. It is applied to that change which the Holy Spirit makes in a man: "Therefore if any man be in Christ, he is a new creature: old things are passed away; behold, all things are become new" (II Cor. 5:17). *The new creation* (or new man) has different desires, hopes, and plans than those of the unregenerated man.

Works have nothing to do with redemption. Faithful stewardship has everything to do with *rewards*, but we are *redeemed* by *the blood*. We are saved by faith; true faith produces works, and *we prove our faith by righteous works*: "For we are His workmanship, created in Christ Jesus unto good works, which God hath before ordained that we should walk in them" (Eph. 2:10).

Verse 6: "Which He shed on us abundantly through Jesus Christ our Saviour."

Greek authorities tell us that "which He shed on us" literally reads, *"which He poured out upon us."* (See Acts 2:17, where the same word is used in speaking of Pentecost.) There is no particular allusion here to the Day of Pentecost; but the sense is that the Holy Spirit has been imparted richly *to all* who were converted, at any time or place. What the Apostle says here is true of all who become Christian in any age or land.

We cannot do anything to merit the Holy Spirit. The Holy Spirit is poured out upon us, abundantly, richly, by the Lord God Almighty. The meaning is that the Holy Spirit had been poured out in an abundant measure in order to convert men from their wickedness.

Notice verse 4: "But after that the kindness and love of God our Saviour toward man appeared" . . . and then in verse 6, "which He (God) shed on us abundantly through Jesus Christ our Saviour." Therefore God the Father, God the Son, and God the Holy Ghost are *one* in providing salvation; you cannot separate them. *God* loved us and gave Jesus. *Jesus* loved us, left the Father's bosom to come into the world, took a body and died for sin. He then returned to the Father; and on the Day of Pentecost *the Holy Ghost* came—and is in the world now, calling out a people, a bride, the New Testament Church.

Jesus Christ is the hub of salvation, and all the spokes are connected to the hub. Whatever redemption provides, it provides because of Jesus. The fullness of salvation originates in Jesus and proceeds from Him.

Verse 7: "That being justified by His grace, we should be made heirs according to the hope of eternal life."

"Being justified by His grace." Paul again points out that salvation is not by works; works never saved anyone, and never will. "Therefore being justified by faith, we have peace with God through our Lord Jesus Christ" (Rom. 5:1). The grace of God makes us just, but grace becomes ours through faith; and when we exercise faith in the finished work of Jesus, God's grace becomes ours and we are justified in the sight of God. That means that in God the Father's sight, we are just as though we had never sinned. We are just as just as Jesus is just, because He is our Saviour and we abide in Him and He in us (Col. 1:27; 3:3; Rom. 8:1).

When God the Father looks at believers, He sees the blood—and in His sight we are just as pure, righteous, and holy as the blood that covers us. Since we are justified by God's grace, we are sons of God; being sons of God, we are heirs of God and joint heirs with Jesus Christ our Lord (I John 3:2; Rom. 8:17). God has received us as His children. He allows us to hope, knowing that we shall live with Him forever, having the assurance that we are saved by His grace, covered by His blood, possessors of divine nature and *sealed until the day of redemption* (Eph. 4:30). We belong to the family of God, and He has made us heirs.

In the New Testament, *justification and righteousness* are inseparable. The Greek word *"dikaios"* is translated *"righteous,"* and the Greek word *"dikaioo"* is translated *"to justify."* The believing sinner is justified because Christ, having borne his sins on the cross, shedding His blood for the remission of sin, has been "made unto him righteousness" (I Cor. 1:30). Justification has its beginning in grace (Rom. 3:24; Titus 3:4,5). Justification is through the redemptive work of Christ. Christ has vindicated the Law: He fulfilled every jot and tittle of it (Rom. 3:28–30; 4:5; 5:1; Gal. 2:16). We can define justification thus: "Justification is the judicial act of God, whereby God simply declares righteous one who believes on Jesus Christ as Saviour." The justified believer, relying entirely upon the finished work of Christ, has been in court—*God's court*—only to learn that nothing is laid to his charge (Rom. 8:1,33,34). Jesus, through His redemptive work, paid the sin-debt in full—and when the unbeliever trusts in the Lord Jesus as Saviour, the blood covers all sin: ". . . If we walk in the light, as He is in the light, we have fellowship one with another, *and the blood of Jesus Christ His Son cleanseth us from all sin*" (I John 1:7).

"We should be made heirs." An heir is one who succeeds to another's property upon the other's death. We who are heirs of God shall be partakers of that inheritance which God confers upon those who accept Jesus Christ as Saviour. That inheritance is eternal life—here and hereafter. Romans 8:17 tells us that we are joint

heirs with Christ—and Christ is *THE Son of God*. As such, He is heir to the full honor and glory of heaven. Christians are united *TO Christ*, and they are thus positionally destined to partake *with Him* of His glory and all the glories of heaven. Christians are the sons of God in a different sense from the Sonship of Jesus. HE is the *"only begotten* Son of God," while believers are sons *by a spiritual birth* (John 3:5).

The connection between Christ and Christians is often referred to in the New Testament. The fact that they are united here is often given as an assurance that they will be united hereafter. John 14:19: ". . . Because I live, ye shall live also." II Timothy 2:11,12: ". . . For if we be dead with Him, we shall also live with Him: If we suffer, we shall also reign with Him . . . ."

Verse 8: "This is a faithful saying, and these things I will that thou affirm constantly, that they which have believed in God might be careful to maintain good works. These things are good and profitable unto men."

"This is a faithful saying . . . ." The reference here is to the doctrine declared in the preceding verses. That is, the doctrine just stated as to how we are saved and justified—the doctrine of salvation by grace through faith in the finished work of Jesus—is of the highest degree of importance in all the Word of God. There is no doctrine more important than that of salvation by grace. Therefore, this IS a faithful saying, and these things should be constantly declared, affirmed, and preached without apology. The primary message of the Bible is *salvation*. Reaching unbelievers and saving sinners is the nearest, dearest thing to the heart of God. Thus, Jesus said, "Go ye therefore, and teach all nations, baptizing them in the name of the Father, and of the Son, and of the Holy Ghost: Teaching them to observe all things whatsoever I have commanded you: and, lo, I am

with you alway, even unto the end of the world" (Matt. 28:19,20).

It is impossible to teach an unbeliever the things of God: one must believe and be born again before he can receive them, because "the natural man receiveth not the things of the Spirit of God: for they are foolishness unto him: neither can he know them, because they are spiritually discerned" (I Cor. 2:14). The divine truth revealed in Titus 3:3—5 should be the subject of all preaching. There should be no occasion when God's minister does not incorporate into his message the plan of salvation *"according to the Scriptures."*

". . . That they which have believed in God might be careful to maintain good works." This sets forth Paul's belief that the doctrines of the Gospel would lead men to holy living. "Good works" here refers not only to acts of benevolence and charity, but also has to do with all that is upright, good, honest, and holy. "We are HIS workmanship, created in Christ Jesus," and therefore we should follow His steps.

"These things are good and profitable unto men." The Bible doctrines here stated are not mere matters of speculation; but they are ordained of God and were given to promote human happiness, peace, and spiritual prosperity. These doctrines should be consistently preached and taught in all churches by God's ministers.

Warnings

Verse 9: "But avoid foolish questions, and genealogies, and contentions, and strivings about the law; for they are unprofitable and vain."

Titus was to shun *"foolish questions"* (which lead to contentions rather than to godly edification), *"and genealogies."* This refers to the Jewish teachings. The

Hebrews kept careful genealogical records, so that in the course of time they might, without much exaggeration, be called *endless.* The Jews attached great importance to these records and were very careful to preserve them.

You remember in John 8 the Jews were very angry with Jesus, and in the course of their conversation they proudly threw in His face the assertion that they were of Abraham's seed, and did not need to be set free from sin: "They answered Him, We be Abraham's seed, and were never in bondage to any man: how sayest thou, Ye shall be made free?" (John 8:33).

But now that the Saviour has come, the middle wall has been broken down between the Jews and Gentiles: "But now in Christ Jesus ye who sometimes were far off are made nigh by the blood of Christ. For He is our peace, who hath made both one, *and hath broken down the middle wall of partition between us*" (Eph. 2:13,14). The distinction of tribes is now useless, and there is no reason for these endless genealogies to be regarded by Christians. The whole Jewish system served to keep up great pride of blood and birth, which was definitely opposed to Christianity.

"*. . . And strivings about the law.*" Titus was to warn the people not only against foolish questions, genealogies, and contentions, but also against strivings about the Law. The Jews took great joy and pride in advertising their knowledge and authority on the Law of Moses. They followed Jesus continually with the one desire to trap Him, asking Him questions concerning the Sabbath, washing of hands, tithing, and various subjects having to do with the Law. Jesus assured them that He had not come to destroy the Law, but to fulfill it—every jot and tittle. The Jews loved to discuss the Law as having to do with meat, drinks, holy days and holidays; but we are reminded that Christianity is not meats, drinks, and days, but "CHRIST IN YOU, the hope of glory." Christianity is a *Person*, not a system.

Paul declares that such strivings and discussions are *"unprofitable and vain."* I am sure that most of God's ministers (myself included) have wasted precious time in talking about frivolities and arguing points of doctrine, when we should have been lifting up the Lord Jesus Christ. Any person, if he is saved and surrendered to the Lord God Almighty, will automatically fall into line with Bible doctrine. A spiritually minded person will read the Bible and accept the Word of God, refusing tradition, dogma, fables, and doctrines of men.

To argue foolish questions and strive about meat, drinks, etc., only leads to hard feelings, bitterness, and a bad spirit in the church. Oftentimes, these discussions are very difficult to settle, and lead into a serious spiritual condition in the local assembly. There is much disputing today, pro and con; but Jesus instructed His ministers, "Go ye into all the world, and *preach the Gospel* to every creature . . ." (Mark 16:15).

Religions and denominations have manufactured their own terms, and they take great pride in using them; but we would save ourselves much heartache, dissension, and bitterness if we would stick to Bible terms and preach the Word in Bible language, instead of in the language of churchmen and denominational bosses! If the devil cannot make a liberal or modernist of a preacher, he does not give up: He attempts to silence the effectiveness of his ministry by detouring him around the heart of the Gospel (which is the cross, the blood, the finished work of Jesus), and seeks to steer him down a blind alley of disputation, tradition, dogma, man-made doctrine, or fables.

Verse 10: "A man that is an heretick after the first and second admonition reject."

The word "heretic" is today applied to anyone who holds some fundamental error of doctrine. Webster defines a heretic as "one who holds and teaches opinions repugnant to the established faith, or that which is made the standard of orthodoxy."

The Greek word as it is used here does not appear elsewhere in the New Testament. The true meaning of "heretic" as used here is "one who is a promoter of a sect or party, religiously." The term might be applied to those who make divisions in the local church, instead of striving to promote unity and peace. Such a person may form his own sect or group, teaching what he chooses on some point of doctrine, independently of the church. Thus in disagreement, he sets up his own little sect or religion. According to the Scriptures, such a man is a heretic.

The same truth is set forth here that Paul declares in Romans 16:17: "Now I beseech you, brethren, mark them which cause divisions and offences contrary to the doctrine which ye have learned; and avoid them." We might say a heretic, in Bible language, is one who creates dissensions, introduces error, and is a factious person.

The heretic is to be approached by the pastor and the deacons (or leaders in the church) on at least two occasions . . . "after the *first* and *second* admonition." (Read Matthew 18:15–17.) That is, the pastor and the people are not to be hasty or rash in dealing with the heretic. Give him an opportunity to explain himself and state his reason for acting as he does . . . give him an opportunity to repent and abandon his heresy. Jesus came not into the world to condemn the world, but to save sinners. It is not the will of God that any perish, but that all repent. Therefore, all men under all circumstances should be given an opportunity to repent; and then after the first and second admonition, if the heretic refuses to repent, he is to be turned out of the church.

Paul does not tell us in what way the admonition is to be given, whether in private or in public meetings. The method no doubt is to be adapted to the circumstances of the case. But if, after the first and second admonition, the heretic refuses to repent, the church is to *"reject"* *him*. The word in the Greek means "reject or excuse." The same word is used in Luke 14:18. In Acts 25:11 it is translated "refuse"; in II Timothy 2:23 it is translated "avoid," and in Hebrews 12:19 it is translated "intreated."

Especially should the admonition be observed in regard to appointing one to an office in the church. Titus was to reject those who were not in perfect accord with fundamental Bible doctrine, because to appoint them to office would be to invite division in the local church. He was to see to it that a person who caused dissensions, one who was a factious person, should not be allowed to hold office in the local church. The language here goes so far as to suggest that such a person should not even be *admitted to membership* in the church. Note Matthew 18:17: "And if he shall neglect to hear them, tell it unto the church: but if he neglect to hear the church, *let him be unto thee as an heathen man and a publican*"!

The truth set forth here by Paul is that a factious person, one who causes division or aims to form sects or parties in the church, is to be given two opportunities to repent; and if such a person does NOT repent after two visits by the pastor and leaders in the church, then he is to be excused from the church. However, he is not to be mistreated or harmed—in body, soul, property, or reputation—for if by action we demonstrate to such a person that we dislike or hate him, how could we ever hope to lead him into right doctrine and salvation? Our desire should be to lead all men to Jesus, but heresy is not to be tolerated in the local assembly.

Verse 11: "Knowing that he that is such is subverted, and sinneth, being condemned of himself."

The meaning here is, that the man who is a heretic has turned from the right way; he has turned from the truth of the faith once delivered to the saints. Literally, he is turned out (or changed for the worse). Such a one should be rejected, and believers should withdraw fellowship from him.

The conscience of a heretic condemns him. A person who is truly a heretic knows he is wrong; he knows he is sinning; he knows he should be rejected by the church, because God has placed in the bosom of every man a conscience that will not allow him to do wrong and not be reminded of the wrong he is doing. A person who claims to be religious and yet advocates error or teaches doctrine that is poison, is the worst enemy the church has. It is sad enough to go to hell, but it is worse to be religious— and lost! The heretic who attempts to divide the church and cause a schism in the church knows that he is doing wrong in attempting such, and he knows that he should be separated from the believers. His own conscience will lash, whip, and torment him—and that will be punishment enough in this life.

A spiritually-minded pastor will not put up with heresy in the local assembly. If the pastor is spiritually minded he will detect such. He is God's representative in the local flock; he is the Lord's under shepherd, and it is up to him to see to it that the wolves do not come in in sheep's clothing. Therefore, any person who attempts to divide the church or cause strife among brethren, should be separated *from* the church and not allowed to fellowship with those who believe in and hold to the faith.

Final Directions and Greetings

Verse 12: "When I shall send Artemas unto thee, or Tychicus, be diligent to come unto me to Nicopolis:

for I have determined there to winter."

Artemas is not mentioned anywhere else in the New Testament. We know nothing about him, but undoubtedly he was a true believer, possibly converted under Paul's ministry.

Tychicus is mentioned in Acts 20:4, Ephesians 6:21, Colossians 4:7 and in II Timothy 4:12. This man was certainly a believer and stood high in the confidence and affection of the Apostle Paul. In Ephesians 6:21 and 22 Paul describes him as "a beloved brother and faithful minister in the Lord."

"Be diligent to come unto me to Nicopolis." Paul is reminding Titus to be alert and make sure that he arrives at Nicopolis by winter, because Paul was *"determined there to winter."* Just why Paul wanted to make sure Titus would visit him there, we do not know. There is no record that Paul organized a church there. We are sure that he preached the Gospel, and most assuredly there were converts; however, it could be that to Paul the field seemed to be extremely promising and that was the reason he requested Titus to leave his important post of duty on the island of Crete and come to visit him at Nicopolis.

Verse 13: "Bring Zenas the lawyer and Apollos on their journey diligently, that nothing be wanting unto them."

Zenas the lawyer is not mentioned anywhere else in the New Testament. We know nothing about him, but we are sure he was a born again believer. No doubt he belonged to the class of persons often referred to in the New Testament as lawyers, who dealt primarily with expounding the Jewish law. It does not necessarily mean that they practiced law as we know lawyers today. It could be that there were many Jews in Nicopolis, and Paul felt that this converted lawyer might be able to win some of the Jews to Christianity by coming to visit him.

Apollos is mentioned in Acts 18:24; 19:1; and in several places in I Corinthians. He was also well skilled in the Law of Moses and in Jewish law, and was "mighty in the Scriptures" (Acts 18:24). Evidently Zenas and Apollos traveled together, perhaps having already been on a journey, probably preaching the Gospel. Paul knew of their ministry, and supposing that they would be in Crete he therefore instructed Titus to bring them with him.

". . . *Diligently.*" (Note II Timothy 4:9.) The Greek means "speedily." That is, "Hurry up their journey, lose no time in getting started, come as quickly as possible."

"That nothing be wanting unto them." These words mean that everything necessary for the journey should be supplied by the believers in Crete. Paul wanted these brethren to have hospitable treatment that would afford them the necessities of life to make the trip comfortable. The laborer is worthy of his hire, and they that preach the Gospel shall live by the Gospel. Paul did not want these ministers embarrassed by the want of that which was needful for their journey and which would make them comfortable in their travels. Some Bible scholars think that it is most probable that they were sent by the Apostle Paul to visit the churches in Crete, and now he is instructing Titus to bring them to Nicopolis to visit him.

Verse 14: "And let our's also learn to maintain good works for necessary uses, that they be not unfruitful."

"And let our's" . . . That is, our friends, fellow-believers, brothers and sisters in Christ. Paul had just instructed Titus to aid Zenas and Apollos, and here he adds that he desires the same as pertaining to all the believers in Crete. That is, all the believers should give to these traveling ministers, that their needs might be met.

". . . *To maintain good works.*" The Greek reads, "Profess honest praise." The meaning is that all believers should be distinguished for good works—including benevolent deeds, acts of charity, honest labor, and whatever would enter into the conception of an upright life. "We are His workmanship, created in Christ Jesus unto good works," and *faith without works is dead.* We should be diligent to work, and by so doing, glorify God and help our brothers and sisters who are believers.

". . . *For necessary uses . . . .*" That is, such as are required by their duty to their families and their demands of charity as having to do with other families who may be in need, or friends, or strangers who may need food or shelter. Believers should be charitable and diligent in good works.

". . . *That they be not unfruitful.*" That is, that all may see that their religion is not barren, vain, or worthless, but that it produces a happy, busy, fruitful life—a life of charity toward not only the church, but society as a whole. Read John 15:16 and Ephesians 4:28. We prove to the world that our Christianity is genuine by what we *do*, not by what we say. We can talk long and loud—but if our actions do not back up what we say, then the world will watch what we DO and will not listen to what we SAY. Someone has said, "I had rather *see* a sermon than to *hear* one, any day!"

Verse 15: "All that are with me salute thee. Greet them that love us in the faith. Grace be with you all. Amen."

In most of Paul's epistles, he closes by naming those who send love and salutation; but in this closing it is implied that Titus himself had been traveling with Paul and that he knew those who were with him. Paul evidently refers—not to those who were residing in the place where he was—but to those who had gone with him from Crete as his believing companions and fellow-helpers.

"Greet them that love us in the faith." That is, in the faith of the Gospel, the faith once delivered unto the saints (Jude 3). No names are here mentioned, but compare this passage with I Thessalonians 5:26 and Colossians 4:15.

"GRACE BE WITH YOU ALL." Paul begins his letters to the churches in grace, and he closes in grace. He was extremely jealous for the preaching of the grace of God—pure grace, without mixture. Again let me remind you of the burning, blistering words in Galatians 1:6–9: "I marvel that ye are so soon removed from Him that called you into the grace of Christ unto another gospel: Which is not another; but there be some that trouble you, and would pervert the Gospel of Christ. But though we, or an angel from heaven, preach any other gospel unto you than that which we have preached unto you, let him be accursed. As we said before, so say I now again, If any man preach any other gospel unto you than that ye have received, *let him be accursed*"!

Paul puts himself first: "Though WE . . . ." That is, "If I or any of my co-laborers preach any other gospel than the grace of God . . . If a shining angel from heaven should preach anything except pure grace without mixture . . . If *anyone* preach anything except the Gospel of the death, burial, and resurrection of Jesus according to the Scriptures . . . If any preach anything except the shed blood for the remission of sin and salvation by grace through faith without works, *let him bé accursed*! Let him be cut off and drop into hell fire!"

The Apostle Paul was converted on the road to Damascus. He was traveling to Damascus (Acts 9), and just before he reached the city gates, a light shone down

495

from heaven. Saul fell to the ground. He heard a voice, and the voice said to him, "Why persecutest thou me?" Saul answered, "Who art thou, Lord?" And the voice answered, "I am Jesus whom thou persecutest." And then Saul said, "What wilt thou have me do?" and Jesus replied, "Go into the city and you will be told what you must do." Paul arose from the ground. He could not see. Those who were with him led him into the city. God instructed Ananias to go to the house where Paul was. Ananias obeyed; he went to Saul and instructed him in the way of salvation. Saul was converted; he was baptized; and when he had received meat, immediately he preached in the Jewish synagogues—and his subject was, "CHRIST . . . IS THE SON OF GOD!" (Acts 9:20). From that day until his head fell into Nero's basket and he sealed his testimony with his life's blood, Paul had a singular subject: He preached Jesus Christ, the Son of God, crucified, buried, risen, and coming again—"*according to the Scriptures!*"

If these messages have blessed you in the least, to God be the glory. If you have been converted while studying these messages, a line from you would greatly encourage my heart; but if you have been saved through reading these messages, be sure to pass this book on to an unsaved friend—and pray with me that God will speak to hearts through these printed pages. May God richly bless you.

The grace of our Lord Jesus Christ be with you. Amen!